GW00992968

WATERFRONTS

WATERFRONTS
Cities Reclaim
Their Edge

Ann Breen and Dick Rigby
The Waterfront Center

**Maps by Diane Charyk Norris
and Charles Norris**

McGraw-Hill, Inc.

New York   San Francisco   Washington, D.C.   Auckland   Bogotá
Caracas   Lisbon   London   Madrid   Mexico City   Milan
Montreal   New Delhi   San Juan   Singapore
Sydney   Tokyo   Toronto

Library of Congress Cataloging-in-Publication Data

Breen, Ann.
    Waterfronts: cities reclaim their edge / by Ann Breen and Dick Rigby.
        p.   cm.
    Includes index.
    ISBN 0-07-068458-8
    1. Waterfronts—United States—Case Studies.   2. Waterfronts—Design
and construction—Case Studies.   3. City planning—United States—Case
studies.
    I. Title.
    HT167.B679
    307.3'4—dc20   93-10764
                                                                    CIP

1 2 3 4 5 6 7 8 9 0   KHL/KHL   9 9 8 7 6 5 4 3

ISBN 0-07-068458-8

*The sponsoring editor for this book was Joel E. Stein, the editing supervisor was
Caroline Levine, and the production supervisor was Pamela A. Pelton. It was set in
Goudy on a Macintosh system.*

Book format design: Susan Maksuta.

Printed and bound by Kim Hupp Lee.

for Ilona Deak-Ebner Ellinger, my mentor,
and John, Sara, David, and Catherine,
my children
A.B.

for Chris Rigby, Nan Rigby, and Betsy Rigby
D.R.

There's no telling what the power of the people and the river can do.

PETE SEEGER, 1982

CONTENTS

Chapter 6. The Recreational Waterfront   163

ACKNOWLEDGMENTS

For us to acknowledge by name all who have assisted in putting this book together would be a formidable undertaking, for *Waterfronts: Cities Reclaim Their Edge* is the product of an awards program organized by the Waterfront Center, a nonprofit corporation that we began in 1981. Since its formation, we have enjoyed participation and support from thousands—members, some of whom have been with us since day one; speakers and panelists at our annual conferences, who would themselves number 400 or so over the 10 such meetings we've run; a faithful group of correspondents for our magazine, *Waterfront World,* a community of 60 or so who have over the years, faithfully and voluntarily clipped newspaper and periodical stories about waterfronts for us; a board of advisors, which likewise has over the years numbered 60 or more souls of all persuasions and differing parts of the globe, who have lent us their names, and more important, their counsel in helping the center find its way.

A representative sample of this basic support group is listed in Appendix A. These are the Friends of the Waterfront Center—people and organizations responding to a fund-raising appeal in 1991 to assist us in preparing this book. The group, numbering 115, quite literally helped make the pages here happen with their backing. The Friends of the Waterfront Center share with us an abiding interest in urban waterfronts. Their support for the book was timely, helpful, and sincerely appreciated.

Waterfronts: Cities Reclaim Their Edge presents 75 case examples of waterfront work. These were selected in an annual juried competition called Excellence on the Waterfront, begun by the Waterfront Center in 1987, with a grant from the National Endowment for the Arts/Design Arts Program, Washington, D.C., to identify and publicize quality urban waterfront planning development. We also received assistance for three years from the National Marine Manufacturers Association, Chicago, thanks to George Rounds there.

Making the selections from over 500 submittals in the first five years of the program was a distinguished group of jurors, whose critical role in this process we salute here. The names of these interdisciplinary juries, 1987 through 1991, appear in Appendix B. It was this group who, by their presence, helped give the Excellence on the Waterfront program stature in the design and development communities.

The Excellence on the Waterfront juries had very good projects to pick from. We thank the 500 entrants who, over the years covered by this book, made it all possible. The truth is that many worthy projects were, for one reason or another, passed over in the difficult task of selecting the 15 percent of entrants whose work is discussed in these pages. We salute all who took the time and trouble to put together submissions in the center's Excellence on the Waterfront program, which includes some of the top design, planning, and development talent in North America, and overseas.

Lastly, we come to individuals and organizations who stand out particularly as having played especially significant roles in the development of this book. We're indebted to them all, and hope this recognition repays them in some small way for their support and encouragement.

- Dorn McGrath, professor of urban planning at George Washington University and director, Institute for Urban Development Research. Before there was a Waterfront Center there was Ann's thesis on the subject, done for the Department of Urban and Regional Planning at GWU that Dorn led in its most productive years, and whose active support since 1976 has been instrumental.

- A generous grant from the Graham Foundation for Advanced Studies in the Fine Arts, Chicago, was the first direct financial backing for our work. We are grateful to Carter Manny of this esteemed organization.

- The College of Fellows Fund of the American Architectural Foundation at the

American Institute of Architects, which group also came forward with timely assistance. Thanks to R. Lynn Carroll of the Foundation.

- Individuals Ann Buttenwieser, Phyllis Lambert, and Harriet Saperstein, each of whom has been especially generous to us in backing this work.

- Paul Willen, architect and waterfront aficionado, who came forward with encouragement for us to undertake an awards program at just the right moment.

- David Wallace, Stuart Dawson, Charles Davis, Ken Greenberg, and Grant Jones, our able jury chairmen, who made the awards program even stronger, and Allen Eskew and Jane Thompson for carrying forward.

- For inestimable assistance in helping with project files, Meg Loftus, a young architect of talent. And thanks also to Cindy Swank, a volunteer assistant from Trinity College in Washington. To Prof. Roy Merrens of York University for taking vacation time to look over part of the manuscript. To Joe Moseley of Texas for a site investigation.

- For Charles and Diane Norris, architects of Cambridge, Massachusetts, whose handiwork is seen on these pages in the finely detailed locational and sites maps. And, boon companions on numerous waterfront investigations.

- To Barry Hersh and Mike Krieger, who cochair the center's finance committee, a daunting task.

- To Joel Stein, senior editor for architecture, McGraw-Hill, for seeing merit in our initial proposal, and the entire publishing and production staff.

- Our staff, Ginny Murphy and Susan Kirk, for invaluable contributions to the workings of the center as well as to predecessors Martha Evelyn and Mary Beth Grimaldi.

Ann Breen and Dick Rigby

WATERFRONTS

Introduction

URBAN VALUES: A NEW APPRECIATION

A city is made by the social congregation of people, for business and pleasure and cere-mony, different from shop or office or private affairs at home. A person is a citizen in the street. A city street is not, as Le Corbusier thinks, a machine for traffic to pass through but a square for people to remain within.

PAUL AND PERCIVAL GOODMAN
Communitas

Oregonians have made it clear that they do not want to pave Oregon. They don't want their downtowns to die, and their farmlands to disappear.

GOV. BARBARA ROBERTS
in Center City Report, newsletter of the International Downtown Association

The colorful central waterfront in downtown Seattle is a magnet for people.(*Breen/Rigby*)

This is a book about the dynamic area of cities and towns where land and water meet—the urban waterfront.

We're partial to the subject, to be sure, but we do feel there is ample evidence that the waterfront, broadly defined, is, and has been for years, the most fertile area of planning and development in our communities. In these pages we offer some documentation and examples of what we mean.

While waterfront development is a major phenomenon in its own right, as we trust this book attests, what's happened on urban waterfronts in the last 30 years has not occurred in a vacuum.

Waterfronts: Cities Reclaim Their Edge is, therefore, also about redeveloping cities and their traditional downtowns. And it is also in part about a still larger context, where we see taking shape a new appreciation for what we'll call "urban values," in a countertrend to the general denigration of such values in our culture, and development trends focused outside cities.

In this Introduction we will try to describe the context of the urban waterfront phenomenon, before setting out in Chapter 1 a brief history of this complex and multifaceted transformation. The heart of the book, Chapters 2 to 9, describes and analyzes prototypical examples of the wide variety of current urban waterfront transformations.

Waterfronts as Part of City/Downtown Revivals

We acknowledge openly that we are unabashed city lovers. While others look at cities and see only crime, more crime, dirt, drugs, poverty, the homeless, the underclass, and racial discord, we observe these, but at the same time see vitality, beauty, cultural stimulus, diversity, and a sense of community.

We perceive the transformation of urban waterfronts in North America over the last 30 years contributing to, and often playing the major role in, ongoing efforts to restore the centers of our cities and towns to economic and social health.

Efforts to restore cities go seriously underreported, in our opinion. Most indices of our time emphasize the considerable problems. It is not that we are blind to the problems, but rather it is as much as because of our desire to balance the discussion and perceptions of cities that we point to some positives. We're joined in this by the authors of *Downtown, Inc.*:

> By the 1980's the long-awaited revitalization of downtown was a reality in many cities and under way in others. The professionals who wrote about cities overlooked this turn-around; their books and articles were overwhelmingly critical and negative throughout the 30-year-period.[1]

The determination to develop healthy core areas in our communities—not to let the center city die—applies with as much vigor to small towns as to the classic big-city examples. For every Boston and Pittsburgh, there are hundreds of smaller cities and towns pursuing regeneration. As Mayor Jerry Abramson of Louisville said, concluding the lead article on "Reinventing the City" in the June 1992 issue of *Landscape Architecture*: "The second-tier cities of America is where the action is." (p. 43) We'd add that this is also true for third-tier cities as well.

The basic "pride of community" force is a powerful motivation and seems little appreciated in the general planning, architectural and economic development literature. It's what moves people of all backgrounds to work against the odds to restore, revive, or sometimes just hold on to their downtown area, of whatever dimension, using a waterfront to advantage if they have one to work with. The general city/downtown revival effort combines a fascinating mixture of self-interest and altruism. At it's most basic, it's the desire not to live in a place people make fun of.

What's most impressive is the effort itself. In Des Moines, Davenport, and Beaumont, in Beaufort, North Carolina, and Beaufort, South Carolina, in Portland, Maine, and Portland, Oregon, in Fall River, Missoula, and Winnipeg, and in all points between, citizens, businesspeople, local politicians, bureaucrats, artists, or some combination, are struggling to make their cities better, working especially to keep their downtowns intact. Many observers focus on the results and find them of poor design or otherwise ill-conceived. While this is often, discouragingly, true, it misses the enduring power—the pride of community—behind the effort in the first place.

Downtowns Alive

Downtowns, given up for dead years ago, have persistently refused to die. According to one study, in fact, the 1980s saw a robust, if not alarming, boom in downtowns. Between 1960 and 1984, our 30 largest cities built 1325 office buildings with 550 million square feet of space. Downtowns managed to keep or exceed their 20 percent of the total new office construction of this period. Hotel and retail space likewise expanded dramatically.[2] One criticism has been that this development ignores social problems. An answer is that a first step in addressing city problems is to bring the center back to life.

Central cities have *not* been losing population, contrary to most impressions. In fact, the 1990 U.S. Census documented that central cities *grew* between 1980 and 1990 as a percentage of a growing population. In a three-part population classification, central cities have in fact held their percentage of the total since 1930. In that year, central cities contained 30.8 percent, and the suburbs 13.8 percent, of the population. By 1950, the central cities were still at 32.8 percent, while the suburbs grew to 23.3 percent. And by 1990, the totals were: central cities, 31.3 percent; suburbs, 46.2 percent.

While Census data are used to prove many points, it seems clear that (1) the United States is overwhelmingly metropolitan when you put together cities and suburbs; (2) most suburbs still revolve around the core city; and (3) many of these center cities—large, medium-sized, and small—continue to attract people, whatever the differences in social class from earlier days.

One result of the riots in Los Angeles in 1992 was to focus attention on cities and downtowns. Stories appeared like one in *The Washington Post*: "The Urban Boom—Who Benefits?" The gist was that downtown Los Angeles, and cities everywhere, burst with development in the 1980s, boosted by favorable changes in tax laws.[3] This finding seemed to be a surprise.

To cite just a few random downtown investments, many of which involve waterfronts:

- St. Paul, Minnesota, opened a stunning new concert hall in 1985.

- A new, traditional baseball stadium opened to rave reviews in April 1992 in downtown Baltimore. The stadium is likely to be a trendsetter, much like the adjoining Inner Harbor is (see Chapter 5).

- "The District" has been created in Rock Island, Illinois, where restaurants and nightspots prosper in an area that was moribund as late as 1985.

- In Halifax, Nova Scotia, a cluster of waterfront structures has been restored as Historic Properties in an effort dating to the early 1970s.

- Milwaukee is at work on a Riverwalk through the center city to help spark activity there.

- Newark will be the site of the New Jersey Performing Arts Center, part of a "cultural district"; there's a Renaissance Newark organization at work.

- Fort Lauderdale has built a riverwalk along the New River, opened a performing arts center there, and has spruced up the walkways along its beachfront.

- In Cleveland there are major new investments and dynamism, including The Flats nightlife district along the Cuyahoga River.

- San Francisco said that it had seen enough of the downtown boom, and in 1986 voted a lid on development.

- A Harbor Center is envisioned in Buffalo, with a major aquarium to draw over a million people a year.

- Honolulu published a downtown waterfront master plan in January 1990.

Even in the dreariest downtowns—and there are many—there are stirrings: people with plans, a determined minority pushing for action, or perhaps just an individual with a vision. Meanwhile, the dominant impression continues to be that, except for a few bright spots like San Francisco, downtowns have had it.

Everyone has heard of the urban devastation in the South Bronx. For many years its vivid images symbolized the American city. Few would believe that, even at its lowest point, there were signs of vitality in the South Bronx (read also: Camden, Detroit, Oakland, etc.), including the Bronx River Restoration, a citizens' group, and the Kelly Street neighborhood effort documented by Roberta Brandes Gratz in *The Living City*.[4]

Against this backdrop, and often playing a determining role, occurs the urban waterfront phenomenon. Downtown and general city revitalization projects are reflected in most of the case studies in this book, dramatically so in many examples—Baltimore, Racine, and Galveston come quickly to mind.

Of the 75 individual projects discussed in this book, only a handful are not directly in, or adjacent to, the core of their communities. Two of the cases—Harbour Town on Hilton Head Island, South Carolina, and Seaside in Florida—created their own town centers. Our sample, albeit small, is generally reflective of urban waterfront work as a whole.

There are many headlines in our files that read something like "Chattanooga, Attempting to Reinvent Itself, Looks to Its River."[5] To belabor a point made earlier, downtown-waterfront revivals are not just a big-city phenomenon.

In Moncton, New Brunswick, a remodeled Main

Street was sparked by a group called Resurgo, Inc., which is now taking on waterfront redevelopment there. In Owensboro, Kentucky, Mayor David Adkisson is planning additional riverfront investment to build on a new, $9 million RiverPark Center arts complex and adjoining park. In Yorktown, Virginia, population about 460, there are new waterfront condominiums fitting into an overall waterfront master plan, which plan was announced in public ceremony in April 1992. In St. Joseph, Missouri, despite a major highway barrier to its riverfront, new investment, cleanup, and civic celebration has taken place within a few short years along the Missouri River, starting from a virtual blank slate. In Columbus, Georgia, despite a sagging downtown retail scene, leaders hope to capitalize on public/private investment in a handsome riverfront convention center/hotel complex and nearby warehouse conversions with restaurants and other initiatives.

We've seen this determination first hand in the above cities and in scores of other waterfront communities—from Ketchikan, Alaska, to Conway, South Carolina, to San Carlos Island, Florida, to Kalamazoo, Michigan, to mention a few, disparate

examples. These are typical of the urban stories that are not being generally reported. That they represent a powerful force is suggested by the following examples:

- How does one explain the feat of raising $280,000 in a depressed economy to light up a highway bridge over the Mississippi, linking Davenport, Iowa, and Rock Island, Illinois?

- Why do investors pay thousands of dollars a month to keep afloat a cherished downtown hotel, as they have done for more than seven years, knowing when they started that the restoration would not pay? (From an impeccable source, city not named to protect the privacy of the investors.)

- Why did citizens in Toronto revolt at what they perceived to be the overdevelopment and stylelessness of condominiums, and absence of sufficient open space, on their downtown waterfront?

- Why would volunteers turn out for a mayor's task force to plan river improvements when previous efforts had run aground, as in Knoxville?

The lighting of Centennial Bridge linking Davenport, Iowa, with Rock Island, Illinois, typifies grassroots determination to revive traditional core cities. (*Larry Fisher*, Quad City Times)

- Why would citizens come out in a snow shower to attend a workshop in Kingston, Ontario, to debate the future of a single downtown waterfront block that had been argued over for 10 years?

- Why would 150 people attend a meeting to discuss the location of tree plantings on a waterfront park in Burlington, Vermont?

- Why would volunteers not only pay for, but install themselves, a sidewalk on San Carlos Island, Fort Myers, Florida?

- Why, as will be cited in Chapter 1, would two activists in New Orleans take on the entire downtown establishment and a leading national development guru over a riverfront expressway when the waterfront was walled off by warehouses and invisible to the public?

Why indeed?

These and similar actions reflect pride of community. People care about their urban waterfront resource and their center city, even when they live away from them.

Growing Appreciation for Urban Values

We see the amount and extent of downtown urban waterfront undertakings as one of the more visible manifestations of a growing appreciation for urban values in North America. This appreciation has its roots in certain social, environmental, and cultural factors that have come to the fore in recent years, including environmental concerns, interest in historic preservation, and related community activism and changing social values.

The following physical qualities summarize what we mean by the phrase "urban values":

- Concentrated versus dispersed physical development

- Integration of a wide range of activities and land uses, including cultural attractions, versus segregated uses with limited cultural assets

- A diverse versus a homogeneous population

- Mixed architecture, including older and/or historic structures, versus architectural sterility

- Walkability versus car domination (and neglect or outright hostility to the pedestrian)

- A portion of the public using public transportation versus little or no public transit

- A strong sense of place versus anonymity of place

In its broadest sense, these urban values reflect an instinct among people everywhere, in all cultures, to socialize. We concur with urban observer William Whyte: "What attracts people most, in sum, is other people."[6]

Humans as social animals is hardly a new thought. In other cultures (think of Paris, Rio de Janeiro, Tokyo), you scarcely need to make the point. In North America, with our decided antiurban tendencies and seeming preference for isolated, individualized modes of living and travel, we tend to forget this fundamental urge to congregate, to see and be seen, that exists within us all. This urge to socialize persists today even amid an impersonal, alienating pattern of settlement.

It underlies the growing appreciation of urban values that we detect. Some critics tout the dispersed pattern in many American cities as the new standard; they see traditional urban values as passé and advocates such as ourselves as having been to too many Italian hill towns or other, traditional European cities.

But the basic desire of people to socialize is very American. It's in large part why car-loving Texans flock to San Antonio's River Walk (Texans comprise the largest single source of visitors there). It's part of the reason for the crowds at San Francisco's Fisherman's Wharf and Boston's Faneuil Hall/Quincy Market. It's at least a partial explanation also of the Disneyland phenomenon, where people are made to feel safe, the place is clean—and they flock to mingle among each other.

Environmental Concerns and Urban Values

Growth Control and Concentration

People are beginning to rethink wasteful, sprawl development that continues to consume land and natural resources at an alarming rate. Examples:

- Oregon enacted legislation in 1973 that has designated an "urban growth boundary" around its cities and towns.

- Maryland has adopted a "critical areas program."

- New Jersey adopted in 1992 a growth management plan that the State Planning Commission estimates will save billions of dollars.[7]

- In San Francisco, a Greenbelt Alliance is developing support for a San Francisco Bay trail network that now stands at 767,000 acres of park, open space, or under conservation easement.[8]

- Mayor (now Governor) Pete Wilson of San Diego supported Horton Plaza downtown development to help slow "Los Angelization" of San Diego. So successful is downtown Horton Plaza that it has been joined by The Paladion, a three-story mall with exclusive shops that is said to rival Rodeo Drive in Los Angeles.

- The Puget Sound Council of Governments Vision 2020 Project cuts in half the square miles to be used in urban growth from existing zoning. The plan, adopted in October 1990, channels growth into five cities plus subregional centers and towns in a conscious effort at concentrating development, curbing sprawl and saving open space.[9]

Waterfronts function as community gathering places for festivals and events—typically they are on neutral turf where everyone feels welcome. (*Alabama Gulf Coast Chamber of Commerce*)

Environmental groups have come to realize that sprawl underlies many pollution problems. A fledgling "growth management" movement promotes the redevelopment and expansion of center cities. *Developments* is the newsletter of the National Growth Management Leadership Project, based with the 1000 Friends of Oregon.

Prince George's County, Maryland, outside Washington, DC, plans to concentrate development in older suburban centers to slow sprawl, changing zoning codes and providing tax incentives. Likewise, planners are working to develop pedestrianization and humanization of Rosslyn, Virginia.[10]

Highway planners in New York, New Jersey, and Connecticut have come to realize that it's futile to continue adding new roads—it just encourages further sprawl and congestion. Conclusion: Fix what is there, don't build new.[11]

Retrofitting Suburbs

Not incidentally, there's growing disenchantment with existing suburbs and a serious rethinking of their prevailing development patterns, further bolstering our sense that things are beginning to change to reflect urban values. We put forward the following phenomena:

Suburbs are no longer utopian retreats for middle- and upper-middle-class families. A number of contemporary reports document this phenomenon from different perspectives, for example, *Bourgeois Utopias, The Rise and Fall of Suburbia*,[12] and *Edge City: Life on the New Frontier*.[13] They chronicle that the prototypical bedroom suburb of the 1950s has been overtaken by the spread of offices, malls, conference centers, and the like.

The results are, in part, congestion, less affordable housing, increases in crime—in short, the urbanization of the suburb. These new-style suburbs can be, and are, called "new cities." They can also be taken as an inevitable trend to concentrate development, to build places for socialization, to place work somewhere near residences—in short, to reinvent the city, only physically outside it and without its negatives, for the moment. To us the trend is a backhanded affirmation of the universality of urban values, and why cities were invented in the first place.

Confirming this, "neotraditional" town planning is moving from the pages of architectural magazines to become the hottest thing in suburban developments (see Seaside, Florida, in Chapter 7). It reflects the basic reworking of the standard subdivision and has made appearances in such diverse locations as Gaithersburg, Maryland, well outside Washington, DC, Orlando, Florida, and Epsom, New Hampshire. The trend, popularized by architects Andres Duany and Elizabeth Plater-Zyberk of Miami, is becoming so orthodox that it made it to the program of the 1990 annual conference of the National Association of Home Builders.

Echoing this trend on the West Coast, suburban developer Phil Angelides, having determined that his projects were dysfunctional, hired Peter Calthorpe

Associates of San Francisco in 1989 to prepare a design for a traditional small town. The change in plans for Laguna West cost him $4 million.[14]

Increasingly, existing suburban communities are building a "town center," places with an attempted lively mixture of activities, sometimes because of pressure from residents said to miss the traditional downtown. Miami Lakes, Florida, and Buffalo Grove, Illinois, are among communities involved.

Tyson's Corner, Virginia, Irvine, California, and Parkway Center, Dallas, Texas, prototypes of the satellite suburb, now are undergoing planning studies to make them more workable and more livable—like real cities, in short.[15]

Historic Preservation/Contextualism and Urban Values

There has been a marked and continued growth of the historic preservation movement in the United States, which has been accelerating since the 1960s. It goes without saying that most concentrations of historical, architecturally interesting buildings are found in cities and towns. Cultural tourism, which has made cities such as Charleston, South Carolina, popular, revolves around celebration of a community's heritage. We see concern for historic structures at the core of a broader interest in community character. In order to retain or recall the character of a place, more emphasis is placed today in building in context or, to use another name commonly given,

the vernacular approach. Among the signs:

From the well-publicized flap over Prince Charles and his well-articulated plea for neighborhood values, to recent American Institute of Architects (AIA) awards, architectural contextualism is in. The 1992 AIA "Firm of the Year" is Polshek and Partners, New York, known for sensitive new architecture in older neighborhoods. The citation noted the firm's "sophisticated contextual response" in its designs.[16] Recent "Architect of the Year" medal recipients were Joseph Esherick (1989), E. Fay Jones (1990), Charles W. Moore (1991), and Benjamin Thompson (1992)— all of whom design buildings appreciated by the general public. Thompson, for instance, wrote:

In practice, we must stop designing for ourselves and the critics and instead begin to identify with the joys and terrors of the man who will spend his life in what we build. That means we must design for people.[17]

These awards confirm a dramatic swing away from modernist architecture and the impersonal, antiurban projects it spawned. Many projects built in center cities during the last 30 years were the antithesis of people-friendly or contextual design. Some look like impenetrable fortresses; others have no activity on the street level to appeal to the pedestrian.

In the fall of 1986, in a major upheaval, Rod Hackney was elected president of the Royal Institute of British Architects (RIBA). Hackney, an advisor

At its best, the public realm in American cities is welcoming, attractive, enjoyable and safe, as in historic Boston Commons, a well-used mid-city gathering place. (*Breen/Rigby*)

to Prince Charles, was the quintessential outsider who challenged modern architecture's approach to cities, and the RIBA's policies in particular. His upset of the establishment candidate, Raymond Andrews, was a shocker.[18]

Cities or developers are taking steps to correct antiurban structures of the 1960s. In London, the South Bank Arts Centre, known for its fortresslike concrete massiveness, is on its way to being humanized. A $300 million scheme of architect Terry Farrell calls for tearing down some structures and introducing new galleries, shops, cafes, and movie theaters.[19]

Likewise, retrofits of the massive Prudential Center, Boston, and Renaissance Center, Detroit—two downtown suburban-style megaprojects—are being undertaken to humanize them. Even Los Angeles, the quintessential spread city, has developed a visible center, albeit mostly offices.

The conscious integration of pace-setting downtown projects such as Faneuil Hall and Horton Plaza into their city contexts is another reflection of respect for city character. Both projects have had a major impact on the development community, which is an imitative group. They stand in contrast to the trend—regrettably, still extant—to erect self-contained, inward-looking, mixed-use centers in traditional downtowns.

Conclusion

We put forward appreciation of cities and traditional urban cultural values as a countertrend to predominant impressions today.

After all, aren't center cities obsolete, as *Newsweek* magazine all but declared? Didn't "preeminent urban-planning specialist" Daniel Mandelker, Washington University, tell the magazine: "A handful of cities are redefining their roles. But the rest are losing their place in society. We don't need them anymore."[20]

On the other hand, our observations confirm reports in, among other studies, *Downtown, Inc.*, from an academic perspective, *Living City*, by a veteran reporter of urban affairs, and *City: Rediscovering the Center*, by a seasoned observer, that downtowns and city centers have hope.

In its broadest sense, the urban waterfront phenomenon is an important part of a growing counter to our predominant suburban pattern of development. It is a leading indicator reflecting an affirmation of the value of the core city, which we sense—mixed with hope—will become stronger during the 1990s.

There is a ferment going on in the development and architectural communities today. It's largely unappreciated in the general press, but it could be potent.

The May 1992 riots in Los Angeles will have the effect of confirming to some that cities are passé. To others, however, the event called attention to the massive amount of development that had taken place downtown (and the issue of whether it helped minorities), the wastefulness of our inattention to cities, and the need to rebuild.

We believe that America will gradually become more urban, in the sense of concentrating future development in traditional downtowns, in older towns and in remade suburbs, where investments in infrastructure have already been made.

Land development patterns will surely change in the years ahead if taxpayers make the connection between sprawl and deterioration of air, water, land, and landscape esthetics.

Notes

1. Bernard J. Frieden and Lynne B. Segalyn, *Downtown, Inc.: How America Rebuilds Cities*, MIT Press, Cambridge, MA, 1989, p. xi.

2. Ibid., p. 268.

3. Michael Abramowitz, "The Urban Boom: Who Benefits?" *The Washington Post*, May 10, 1992, p. H1.

4. Roberta Brandes Gratz, *The Living City*, Simon & Schuster, Inc., New York, 1989, p. 414.

5. John Burgess in an article in *The Washington Post*.

6. William H. Whyte, *City: Rediscovering the Center*, Doubleday, New York, 1988, p. 10.

7. Iver Peterson, "Study Backs New Jersey's Growth Plan," *The New York Times*, Mar. 7, 1992, p. 31.

8. Kevin Kasowski, "Sprawl: Can It Be Stopped?" *Developments*, Summer 1991, p. 13.

9. Jonathan Barnett, "Accidental Cities: The Deadly Grip of Outmoded Zoning," *Architectural Record*, February 1992, p. 96.

10. Liz Spayd, "Counties Try Breathing New Life Into Area's Older Suburbs," *The Washington Post*, Feb. 16, 1992, p. 1.

11. Iver Peterson, "New York Region Concludes: Don't Expand Transit; Fix It," *The New York Times*, Mar. 13, 1992, p. 1.

12. Robert Fishman, *Bourgeois Utopias: The Rise and Fall of Suburbia*, Basic Books, New York, 1987.

13. Joel Garreau, *Edge City: Life on the New Frontier*, Doubleday, New York, 1991.

14. Daniel Akst, "Developer Learns How Costly It Can Be To Build a Better Suburb," *Los Angeles Times*, p. 1.

15. Jonathan Barnett, "Accidental Cities," *Architectural Record*, February 1992, p. 96.

16. "Polshek and Partners Named Firm of the Year," *Architecture*, February 1992, p. 23.

17. "Benjamin Thompson Wins Gold Medal," *Architecture*, January 1992, p. 17.

18. Rod Hackney, *The Good, The Bad & The Ugly: Cities in Crisis*, Frederick Muller, London, 1990.

19. "Farrell and Krier Plan A Kinder, Gentler England," *Architectural Record*, January 1992, p. 21.

20. "Are Cities Obsolete?" *Newsweek*, Sept. 9, 1991, pp. 42–43.

THE URBAN WATERFRONT PHENOMENON

If there is magic on this planet, it is contained in water.

LOREN EISELEY
The Immense Journey

But, for one Savannah there are a hundred squalid, pointless turnings-away from the American rivers. The hatred is almost pathological—the standard pattern of neglected banks, railroad yards, fag-ends of town pulling away their skirts from the too-too nasty mess. A whole book could be written on American river banks alone, for they form the biggest single waste of opportunity in the whole environment.. And not only rivers—some places, fishing and tourist places, even actually manage to turn their backs on the sea. Just how disintegrated can urban life get?

IAN NAIRN
The American Landscape

A derelict shoreline typical of many urban waterfronts. This area on the Cape Fear River in Wilmington, North Carolina, shown here in 1980, was subsequently transformed with a handsome riverwalk (*Breen/Rigby*).

Introduction and Definition

Our starting point is that most magical of properties, water. At once calm and dynamic, profoundly symbolic in religion and literature, water evokes primeval emotions in all of us. The lure of water is powerful and universal. This fact, best expressed by our writers and artists, underlies everything that follows.

The urban waterfront redevelopment phenomenon of our time began in earnest in the 1960s, bloomed in the 1970s, accelerated in the 1980s, and will continue unabated for the foreseeable future, recessions included. Viewed historically, urban waterfronts have undergone cycles of change over the decades; ours is but the latest in the pattern, converting major areas of industrial, shipping, and transportation uses to more public endeavors.

By "urban waterfront" we mean the water's edge in cities and towns of all sizes. The water body may be a river, lake, ocean, bay, creek, or canal. By a waterfront "project" we include everything from a wildlife sanctuary to a container port, and the full spectrum of uses in between. The "project" may be planned as a unified undertaking, or it may be a haphazard development occurring over time, with multiple owners and participants.

For our purposes a waterfront project may include buildings that are not directly on the water but are tied to it visually or historically, or are linked to it as part of a larger scheme. Thus, Pike Place Market in Seattle and the Brooklyn Esplanade in New York are, to our minds, part of the waterfront scene in those cities even if they are not directly on the water.

To measure the urban shoreline within a given city of any size—say, Chicago, with both its lakefront and riverfronts, or Seattle, with its bay, lakes, and channels—gives an indication of how much territory is potentially involved. The sheer amount of urban shoreline, coupled with the great diversity of waterfront undertakings, makes it impossible to quantify the full extent of current redevelopment: New York City alone has 578 miles of shoreline; the San Francisco area has 276 miles of bayfront.

Urban waterfront redevelopment as we know it today embodies the historic alteration of land and water uses along the edge of thousands of cities, large and small, throughout the world. Complex and multifaceted, current waterfront redevelopment is attributable to a number of factors, notably:

- Technological changes post-World War II, which led to abandonment and/or deterioration of thousands of acres of industrial land along shorelines

- The historic preservation movement

- Heightened environmental awareness and water cleanup

- Consistent pressure to redevelop central city areas

- Federal urban-renewal and related assistance

These and other forces combined to bring about dramatic changes in the last 30 years that have altered the face of urban shorelines for present and future generations. The recent shift from predominantly industrial use of the urban waterfront is as profound as the initial eighteenth- and nineteenth-century development of harbors and shores for industry, and its use in earlier times for shipping, storage, and shipbuilding.

Urban waterfront planning and redevelopment is currently a civic interest that is pervasive and powerful. Some of the most notable and highly acclaimed developments in the world, such as Battery Park City in New York, Darling Harbour in Sydney, Australia, Granville Island in Vancouver, Rowe's Wharf in Boston, and Seaside in Florida, are waterfront projects. One of the most notable bankruptcies of all time, at Canary Wharf in London, was also a waterfront undertaking.

This chapter will summarize the history of waterfront redevelopment generally since the 1960s, assess what it means, outline important issues raised, and take a look at what's ahead. Our focus will be on North America.

A Pervasive Phenomenon

Most cities are located on or near a water body of some type. Of the 75 largest cities in the United States, only six are not located on a significant body of water: Atlanta (even here you can find Peachtree Creek if you look hard enough); Tucson (which does have the Santa Cruz riverbed); Charlotte, North Carolina (it has Sugar Creek); Anaheim and Santa Ana, California (which do have Santa Ana River remnants); and Lexington, Kentucky. Two marginal calls are Fresno, California, and Birmingham, Alabama, which have minor rivers or canals.

According to the Census, there are approximately 10,000 municipalities in the United States with populations of 2500 or more. Let's assume that one-half to two-thirds of these cities have a waterfront project of some kind: We then have 5000 to 6000 communities involved in a waterfront undertaking of some sort. This is a crude measure, but suggests the extent of what we are talking about.

Contemporary urban waterfront redevelopment is now an international undertaking. While North America is generally thought to be in the lead (in part because the United States was first in shifting to cargo containerization, thereby abandoning older port facilities), London's south bank redevelopment (Royal Festival Hall and the National Film Theater date to 1951) and St. Katherine Dock (1960s) on the Thames, and Liverpool's docks projects, are contemporaneous with the first U.S. stirrings.

The spread of the waterfront phenomenon is suggested by the following. Cities outside North America with current, major urban waterfront projects/plans include Amsterdam, Barcelona, Belfast, Bristol, Buenos Aires, Cape Town, Djakarta, Dublin, Gloucester (UK), Kobe, Leningrad, London, Manila, Nagoya, Osaka, Rotterdam, Shanghai, Seoul, Tokyo, Valencia, and Yokohama—to mention just a few examples.

In Britain, a survey in 1978 by the Urban and Economic Development Group found a "general picture of inactivity" in 21 port cities. By 1989, however, the same group discovered over 90 redevelopment schemes under way in cities along the country's rivers, canals, and coasts; 70 percent of the projects involved 10 acres or more.[1]

The award-winning projects described in this book are representative of the range and diversity of the waterfront phenomenon. They demonstrate that "waterfront redevelopment" has always been extensive, involving far more than a few well-publicized marketplaces. The projects and plans come from all sections of the continent—indeed, the world. There are projects in our sample from 23 states, three Canadian provinces, and four other countries. City sizes range from Allegan, Michigan, with a population of 4564, to New York City, with a population of 7,322,564.

The investment in the 75 projects described is an estimated $12,376,630,000, both public and private money, which represents just a tiny fraction of the overall public and private investment made in waterfronts in the last 30 years.

A Recognized Field of Interest

As the 1990s begin, waterfront planning and development is something of a field in its own right, not unlike historic preservation. "Waterfront development" is one area of specialization for members of the American Planning Association. *Process: Architecture* published a special issue on the "waterfront" in 1984. In 1990 the jury on urban design of *Progressive Architecture* found that most entries were waterfront projects. *Landscape Architecture* devoted its February 1991 issue to "new urban waterfronts." Many design and engineering firms list "waterfront planning" as a field of specialization in their promotional materials.

The Waterfront Center has published its bimonthly magazine, *Waterfront World*, since 1982, and has held 18 conferences and workshops on the topic since 1983. Numerous other waterfront convocations have been held around the world in the last decade. In 1991 there were three urban waterfront conferences in Europe alone. As the Bibliography attests, the literature in the field has been growing, especially in the last 10 years. Specialty courses on urban waterfronts are held at a number of universities, including the Harvard Graduate School of Design and New York University's Graduate School of Public Service.

Background

The City Beautiful Movement

The focus of this book is on the waterfront phenomenon as it has occurred in the last quarter of the twentieth century. It would be remiss, however, not to recognize the "City Beautiful" era that occurred at the turn of the century and acknowledge its special impact on certain city waterfronts. It has to be said that the "City Beautiful" effort occurred in a select number of cities concurrent with emphasis in most waterfronts of the time on industry and transport.

Handsome shoreline parks, plazas, walkways, bridges, and riverside drives—beautiful public spaces—remain today as testimony to the work of such leaders in the field as Daniel Burnham, Frederick Law Olmsted, and John C. Olmsted. Burnham, Olmsted, and others traveled extensively in Europe and employed the best ideas learned there in their work. For example, Edward H. Bennett and Andrew Wright Crawford, in their *1917 Plan of Minneapolis*, cited and illustrated numerous European models. In that plan they noted: "American cities have neglected the opportunities of their water-fronts with a regularity equalled only by that with which European cities have accepted theirs."

Proponents of the movement were deeply concerned with urban beautification. They had idealistic notions about civic well-being and the social benefits of public landscapes and parks. Local improvement societies blossomed throughout the country. From Brooklyn to San Diego, major beautification schemes were set in motion. Four waterfront gems from this era stand out: the Chicago Lakefront, the banks of the Charles River in Boston, Detroit's Belle Isle, and Philadelphia's Fairmount Park along the Schuylkill River.

Grand civic visions appeared at this time in Canada as well. For example, the *1912 Waterfront Plan for the City of Toronto* (see Chapter 8) was far-sighted. It served as the blueprint for much harbor development that has followed, including a considerable amount of the public parks, beaches, and open space that grace the shoreline of Lake Ontario today, as a means of gaining public support for the major industrialization contemplated. Equally visionary was the Vancouver City Council, which in 1889 dedicated as permanent parkland a 1000-acre promontory of forest lands almost completely surrounded by water. Stanley Park is one of the great urban waterfront preserves in the world, with a 6-mile trail along the water's edge, next to downtown.

The WPA

Any discussion of antecedents to the present waterfront movement should also include one of the nation's largest public works projects. The Works Progress (later called Projects) Administration was established in 1935 as a job-creation program to help the country out of the Depression. Until its demise in 1943, some 116,000 buildings, 78,000 bridges, and 651,000 miles of roadway were constructed, in addition to many parks, playgrounds, and bathing beaches. While they may not have been as grandiose as many projects of the "City Beautiful" era, the WPA's effort was more widespread and had a lasting impact on many waterfronts.[2]

San Antonio's Paseo del Rio, one of the most inspirational waterfront projects, stands out as the premier example. Carrying out the design of archi-

The open edge, here from a 1930s WPA project in San Francisco. The National Maritime Museum occupies the nautically inspired structure in the rear. (*Breen/Rigby*)

tect Robert Hugman, 1000 WPA workers, including stonemasons, artisans, and craftspeople, built one of the most interesting and romantic riverwalks anywhere. The total cost of the project was $430,000 (the city's share was $75,000). The project included 21 blocks, 8500 feet of riverbank, and 17,000 feet of river and sidewalks. A total of 21 bridges—each different—and 31 stairways were constructed by 1940.[3]

Another WPA project is Aquatic Park near Fisherman's Wharf in downtown San Francisco, with a boat-shaped, Art Deco-style bathhouse built in 1939 (now a maritime museum). Still another example is in South Bend, Indiana, where carefully crafted walls, benches, tables, and an amphitheater on the St. Joseph River are now being restored as part of the city's riverwalk expansion.

Technological Change after World War II

After World War II, a number of factors came together to affect the urban waterfront and lay the groundwork for the waterfront redevelopment phenomenon of our era.

A series of technological changes in American ports and industry were responsible for a widespread increase in abandoned and underused territory and facilities along water bodies. This territory became ripe for redevelopment beginning in the late 1950s and early 1960s.

The United States led the world in shifting to containerization of cargo, spelling the end of the predominance of traditional "break bulk" dock facilities. Container ports require large, new spaces, plus more acreage for back-up space, deeper and wider channels for the ships, and access to good transportation. Truck and interstate systems supplemented the railroads as the primary transportation link for cargo. Cruise ship terminals and piers were abandoned as airplane travel increased. The commuter ferry likewise was abandoned as more bridges and roadways were built and the private automobile became dominant.

At approximately the same time, many outmoded industrial plants and their rail networks, located on water bodies, were replaced. If abandoned ports were relatively few in the national picture, obsolete industry and transportation facilities on water bodies could be found everywhere, along inland rivers as well as on the coasts.

Also, America's entire pattern of settlement began to shift in earnest in the 1950s, away from central cities in favor of suburban sites.

Vast amounts of urban waterfront land thus became available, relatively cheaply and without dislocating current users. One first use for these abandoned shoreline areas was for the burgeoning interstate highway system. Location along the waterfront involved little displacement of residents or businesses.

Unfortunately, these roadways resulted in numerous cities being severed from their water bodies. Philadelphia, Hartford, Louisville, Seattle, and Cincinnati come to mind as cities where barriers of between 6 and 14 lanes of traffic come between the downtown core and the waterfront. The highways built at this time reflected an antiurban attitude as well as gross insensitivity to rivers and other water bodies. Boston in the mid-1950s built the Fitzgerald Expressway between downtown and the waterfront. Today it is rectifying this blunder by putting the roadway underground.

Pollution of the nation's waterways further exacerbated the image of the waterfront at the time as derelict, abandoned territory. Writer Wesley Marx summed it up:

> The common urban waterfront is hardly approachable, much less swimmable, encrusted with wharves, switching yards, sewage outfalls and other industrial barnacles. It is the true civic outcast, the ghetto of ghettos, familiar only to longshoremen, sanitary engineers and carp.[4]

In his book, *The American Landscape*, critic Ian Nairn observed:

> A whole book could be written on American river banks alone, for they form the biggest single waste of opportunity in the whole environment.[5]

The public's perception of urban waterfronts at this time, the late 1950s, was of a dangerous, violent, and forbidding territory. The film, *On the Waterfront*, shot in 1954 in Hoboken, New Jersey, confirmed the public's worst suspicions.

The container revolution contributed to opening up the urban waterfront. Here the Port of Vancouver, Canada, provides areas for the public to view its operations. (*Breen/Rigby*)

Factors That Led to Change

A number of different factors led cities to begin to discover and seize the opportunity presented by dilapidated, overlooked waterfront tracts.

Environmental Cleanup

The beginning of the environmental movement is usually dated as 1970, when the Environmental Protection Agency (EPA) and the National Oceanic and Atmospheric Administration (NOAA) were created in Washington and Earth Day took place. This represented a fundamental shift in values. Americans had become disturbed at the deteriorating quality of the air, water, and landscape. Major federal initiatives were launched to address the first two problems, namely, the National Environmental Policy Act of 1969 (Public Law 91-90, January 1, 1970) and the air and water pollution control laws (the Clean Air Act Amendments of 1970, Public Law 91-604, December 31, 1970; the Water Quality Improvement Act of 1970, Public Law 91-224)

Federal water cleanup spending, begun in earnest in the 1970s, constitutes one of the largest public works programs ever undertaken. Some $50 billion in federal grants was spent between 1972 and 1992 to construct new and higher-quality water treatment facilities. This sum was matched by an additional $26 billion in local and state monies. By the 1980s there were reports of species of fish returning to rivers and lakes where they had not been seen for years, just one index to the public that waterways were in fact being cleaned up.

Of great importance for the urban waterfront was that what had been a negative—filthy water—was now on its way to becoming a positive. The inherent interest on the part of people everywhere in getting into or near water bodies was suddenly more plausible.

The Cuyahoga River in Cleveland, so polluted in the later 1950s that it was flammable, is now healthier. In but one example of what the cleanup program has contributed, the Flats area alongside the Cuyahoga is now a popular entertainment district, with restaurants, clubs, and outdoor cafes crowded along its banks near Lake Erie. Water taxis ferry nightclub customers across the river from one spot to the next. There's a Flats Oxbow Association, a nonprofit organization for the area that monitors and promotes the businesses there.

At the grass-roots level, 1970 witnessed the first Earth Day. Organizations such as the Sierra Club, The Audubon Society, The Nature Conservancy, and others grew in numbers and power. The Sierra Club, founded in 1892 by John Muir, doubled its membership from 324,000 in 1982 to 637,000 in 1992. Likewise, the National Audubon Society, founded in 1905, expanded from 350,000 members in 1985 to 600,000 today. Many other organizations date their founding to the early 1970s, including

Grassroots determination to revive inner cities is a powerful force. Here Ruth Anderberg, a founder of the Bronx River Restoration citizen's group, at work cleaning up the Bronx River in New York City in an early urban waterfront reclamation. (*Bronx River Restoration*)

Clean Water Action (1971), the Natural Resources Defense Council (1970), the Trust for Public Land (1972), and American Rivers (1973).[6]

Preservation Ethic and Downtown Comeback

For a variety of reasons there occurred, beginning in the 1960s, a growing appreciation for historic preservation. In part a revolt against continued degradation of the landscape, in part a reaction against the mindless destruction of beloved structures, and in part a reaction to the relatively bland and soulless style of modern architecture, Americans began to appreciate older buildings, older neighborhoods, and conservation values.

Together with the environmental movement, the emphasis on historic preservation marked a basic shift in mainstream values in the United States. The urban waterfront fit well into the new value systems.

In 1966 the National Historic Preservation Act was passed, establishing a major federal role; the National Trust for Historic Preservation was chartered in 1949, but the 1966 legislation provided funding for state programs. In 1954, the trust had a membership of 1250. By 1992, membership had reached 235,000, including a doubling in size in the preceding 10 years.

Preservation was boosted in 1976 by the passage of legislation providing a major tax credit, under strict guidelines, for the rehabilitation of commercial buildings. The tax credit immediately altered the business equation for developers, and no longer made it automatically more economical to destroy buildings and build new ones.[7] The credit has since been watered down, however, and its use has been reduced.

All of this helped foster an appreciation for cities in general and contributed to a renewed interest in historic waterfront structures and sites in particular. Urban pioneers began reclaiming handsome old homes and commercial structures, many available at bargain levels at first. In numbers this group was small, but it was vocal and highly visible. Many preservation projects undertaken in the late 1960s and early 1970s were in the vanguard of what today are vital and interesting neighborhoods, and not coincidentally, major tourist attractions.

In but one example of the preservation movement at work on a waterfront, there was established in the early 1960s in New Bedford, Massachusetts, an organization called Waterfront Historic Area League (WHALE). New Bedford was once home to a thriving whaling industry and subsequently to textile manufacturing. The waterfront district had fallen on hard times, however, and by the 1960s urban renewal was poised to raze the old buildings that remained.

A group of citizens formed the nonprofit WHALE to protect the historic character of the waterfront, and with it, their city. The group was a spin-off of the Old Dartmouth Historical Society.

In 1963 the group financed a building survey, and within three years a 14-block area had been placed on the National Register. In 1970, WHALE began purchasing property using a revolving fund. The buildings were then resold and restored by new owners. The league was instrumental in saving many old structures from the wrecking ball, some through relocation within the city. The group also received help from the National Trust to help develop a design plan for street and sidewalk improvements. In 1975 the city used Federal Community Development Block Grant funds to further its work.

WHALE also fought hard to retain the fishing industry on the waterfront, convincing the local Teamsters Union to stay. A 1931 building that houses union offices was restored. In 1976 a craft fair attracted 20,000 people, helping to reacquaint people with the historic waterfront and the changes that were taking place. An early leader of WHALE, John Bullard, was elected mayor in 1985.

With similar motivations to preserve community character, shops and offices were established in the Old Port Exchange in downtown Portland, Maine; commercial buildings were restored in the historic center of Fernandina Beach, Florida; an old cotton exchange became a cluster of shops in Wilmington, North Carolina; warehouses were reborn as offices, condominiums, restaurants, and shops in seventeenth- and eighteenth-century port and mill buildings in the Georgetown section of Washington, DC; and nearby, a former torpedo factory became home to artists' studios and shops amid restored Colonial homes in Old Town, Alexandria, Virginia; new mixed uses helped revive small, historic sections such as The Strand in Galveston, Texas, LeClede's Landing in St. Louis, Larimer Square in Denver, and Pioneer Square in Seattle, to cite a few examples, many associated with their waterfronts.

During the 1960s and 1970s, cities invested in their downtowns to try to stem the exodus of retail stores, offices, and housing to the suburbs. (See the Introduction for a brief discussion.) To counter the outflow, a first reaction from the planning and design communities was to suggest mimicry of the competing suburban shopping malls. "Pedestrian malls" sprang up in downtowns all over the country, from Kalamazoo, Michigan, to St. Charles, Missouri, to Poughkeepsie, New York, to Cape May, New Jersey, to Pasadena, California; some succeeded, most didn't. But the instinct not to let downtowns die was affirmed.

More constructively, the National Main Street Center program was launched in 1977 to help smaller center cities compete, based on pilot city projects in Madison, Indiana, Galesburg, Illinois, and Hot Springs, South Dakota. Its success led to its adoption as an official program of the National Trust for Historic Preservation to assist communities nationally in downtown revival efforts. The goal is to stimulate downtown economic comebacks within the context of historic preservation. About 600 communities are involved today.

For many cities, downtown restoration and waterfront redevelopment were one and the same. In others, one effort preceded the other (in Boston, downtown urban renewal of Scolloy Square came first; in Oakland, waterfront redevelopment was the leader).

Federal Assistance

The availability of federal urban renewal funds and other assistance programs had a significant impact in Oakland, Baltimore, Seattle, and Newport, Rhode Island, among other cities, in the early days of waterfront redevelopment, before they became well-known success stories.

Many cities funded by the predecessor of the Department of Housing and Urban Development (HUD) channeled money into old waterfront areas. For instance, more than 80 cities were identified in 1971 as being involved in some sort of waterfront project by architect Arthur Cotton Moore in his insightful study, *Bright Breathing Edges of City Life*. Newport, Louisville, Oakland, Boston, and Baltimore are among his examples.

After urban renewal, which shut down in 1974, HUD funds continued to flow in significant amounts to waterfronts through the Community Development Block Grant Programs and, later, Urban Development Action Grants.

Many major waterfront parks received significant funding through the Department of the Interior's Land and Water Conservation Fund, such as Henry C. Chambers Waterfront Park in Beaufort, South Carolina; International Park, Toledo, Ohio; Kemper Center, Kenosha, Wisconsin; River Parks, Tulsa, Oklahoma; Riverside Park, Jackson, Mississippi; Roberto Clemente Park, Pittsburgh, Pennsylvania; and Town Lake, Austin, Texas, among many.

The National Park Service was also an important player in the formative days of waterfront redevelopment. Its presence on urban waterfronts is significant: Golden Gate National Park in San Francisco, Ellis Island and Gateway National Park in New York City, the Chesapeake & Ohio Canal in Maryland, the Illinois & Michigan Canal Heritage Corridor in the Chicago area, and Lowell Heritage Park in Massachusetts are examples.

During the 1960s and 1970s, the Corps of Engineers, the Department of Transportation, and the Economic Development Administration invested considerable sums in infrastructure, shoreline protection, bridge, and commercial/industrial projects. The multifaceted federal investment in cities during these years led to some early successes that inspired and stimulated others. Problematic developments also occurred, it is acknowledged. The momentum developed is such that waterfront redevelopment continues apace, even in the absence today of much federal "pump priming."

Among smaller federal efforts, in the early 1970s more than 15 city waterfronts were being studied through the "City Edges" program funded by the National Endowment for the Arts (NEA). The Design Arts Program of the NEA has continued to fund scores of waterfront planning and research projects throughout the country. The Office of Ocean and Coastal Resource Management in the Department of Commerce funnels funds to state agencies, some of which pass along waterfront planning assistance to localities. New York's coastal program is run by the Division of Coastal Resources and Waterfront Revitalization.

Recreation/Fitness

Thousands of joggers, bikers, and walkers took to the outdoors during the 1970s as interest in healthy pursuits became widespread, creating a demand for more trails, pathways, and open spaces. Two pioneering initiatives taken in response to this phenomenon were the Platte River Greenway in Denver (see Chapter 6), and the Willamette River Greenway in Portland, Oregon, launched by the late Governor Tom McCall of Oregon, which has resulted in an extensive trail system.

The 1967 and 1973 Oregon legislatures established the Willamette River Greenway Program, which extends 255 miles from St. Helens to Cottage Grove. The goal of the program was "to protect, conserve, enhance and maintain the natural, scenic, historical, agricultural, economic and recreational qualities of lands along the Willamette River."[8] The state works with local governments to achieve the goals. Portland, for example, with its own plan and guidelines, has a network of trails both downtown and amid outlying open spaces (see Sellwood Riverfront Park in Chapter 3).

In the late 1970s, a proposal for linked riverfront parks was put forward by the recreation department in Detroit, Michigan, with the goal of creating continuous pedestrian/bicycle paths connecting a series of parks and open spaces along 10 miles of the Detroit River. The project is largely in place today, with Chene and Mt. Aubin parks joining Hart Plaza and Belle Isle as major public spaces on the river.[9]

Based no doubt on successes like these and others around the country, the fledgling "greenway" movement in the United States was born in the 1980s and has identified river corridors as providing prime opportunities to expand trail networks.[10] As of the early 1990s there were more than 200 greenways in the United States, from the Illinois and Michigan Canal Heritage Corridor to the Yakima Greenway in Washington State. The Rails-to-Trails Conservancy identified 450 trails involving 4925 miles that have been converted from industrial to recreational use.[11] Changes in federal highway funding priorities hold the promise of a new, large source of funding for extensions and additions to the system.

An increased boating and fishing population has grown to problem proportions in many jurisdictions. Extreme shortages of boating slips were reported in the late 1980s in some parts of the country, and rental prices skyrocketed. There were 10,996,253 registered boaters in 1991. The estimated total of recreational boats owned in 1991 was 16,248,000 (including canoes and kayaks), compared with 8.8 million in 1971.[12]

Recreational fishing in and near cities is also increasingly popular. A U.S Fish and Wildlife Service survey in the early 1990s found that over 18 million of a total of 60 million anglers live in metropolitan areas of 1 million or more—an increase of over 10 percent from 1980. Also, over 100 major metropolitan areas were found to have urban fishing programs.

Recreational fishing piers are unsung installations that create a kind of instant community among the participants, on their own or as components of a waterfront park (see Charleston Waterfront Park in Chapter 6). They play an educational role beyond catching fish—namely, building understanding and respect for the environment in which fish live.

Tourism

North Americans are mobile; extended families live in all parts of the continent. With favorable exchange rates, more foreigners are discovering the United States and Canada. In 1990 Americans took 1.27 billion person trips, defined by the Travel Industry Association of America as one person on one trip 100+ miles from home. They traveled most often for pleasure or to visit friends and relatives (76 percent), using cars, trucks, or RVs (79 percent). On the average trip they ventured more than 800 miles and stayed in commercial lodging 44 percent of the time.

In the United States in 1989, the travel industry produced $632.4 billion in expenditures and output, $186.5 billion in wages and earnings, and 10.7 million jobs. In the same year tourism generated a payroll of $79.4 billion and over $41 billion in tax revenue for federal, state, and local governments.[13]

It is thus small wonder that another background factor in the rejuvenation of waterfronts has been expansion of tourism. For better or worse, many if not most cities have been scrambling to capture tourist dollars by creating more "destinations." Baltimore lays claim to as many visitors coming to the Inner Harbor as go to Disney World.

Meanwhile, cities such as San Francisco, Newport, Rhode Island, Annapolis, Maryland, and Charleston, South Carolina, cope with the problem of managing overcrowding on their waterfronts. For these and other communities, a major issue is how to keep visitation from becoming excessive, thus threatening the attraction itself. Another question for many cities today is whether or not to build facilities expressly for tourists, or to accommodate local area residents first and let visitors follow. Granville Island in Vancouver (see Chapter 5) is an example of the latter approach.

A related factor is the new-found attraction of city locales for suburbanites. The intrinsic lure of some downtown areas, including many on waterfronts, is a very real form of tourism. The streets of Georgetown, D.C., Austin, Texas, The Flats in Cleveland, and LeClede's Landing in St. Louis are weekend magnets for young people.

Pioneering Citizens

During the 1960s, separate actions in different sections of the country, ostensibly unconnected, sig-

naled a strong, latent public interest in the intrinsic value of urban waterfronts, and foretold the widespread grass-roots involvement to come.

■ The San Antonio River Walk story owes its very existence to three sets of dedicated and farsighted individuals. The first was a group of women, led by Emily Edwards, who objected in the 1920s to a city plan to pave over the small San Antonio River downtown as a flood-control measure. They argued, successfully, for any alternative approach that would leave the river open.

Architect Robert Hugman came forward in the late 1920s with a vision—a walkway lined with shops along the small, curving river, to create an intimate, friendly space one story below the city's hot streets.

The River Walk itself was built as a Works Progress Administration project in the late 1930s. As there were no shops or activities at first, the walkway, isolated from the city above, became dangerous and was declared off limits to military personnel in the 1950s.

Two businessmen, David Straus and Cyrus Wagner, picked up Hugman's original vision and launched a virtual crusade among downtown businesses to get them to see the opportunity at their back doors. Beginning in the early 1960s, restaurants and shops opened behind and one level down from existing stores on the street. The entrepreneurs capitalized on the beautifully detailed walkway. The rest is history—the attractiveness of lively shops and restaurants combined with active water use was affirmed.[14]

■ A citizen uproar in the early 1960s halted extension of the Embarcadero Freeway along the waterfront in San Francisco. The overhead roadway, one of a number thrust along abandoned waterfront territory in various cities, was conceived as a high-speed link between the Bay Bridge (to Oakland) and the Golden Gate Bridge.

The route was along the central and northern waterfront, directly over Fisherman's Wharf and in front of some of the city's most prestigious housing on Russian and Telegraph Hills and Pacific Heights. A section was built downtown, away from any residential views, but severing the Ferry Building from downtown. It is this portion that came down after suffering damage in the 1989 earthquake.

Similar opposition to a proposed condominium project that would have replaced the Ghirardelli chocolate factory, and blocked views from Pacific Heights, also occurred in the 1960s. This led to adaptive reuse of the buildings into a marketplace consisting of dozens of specialty shops plus cafes, public plazas, and restaurants overlooking San Francisco Bay. The complex retains the

Ghirardelli name in lights, said to be a factor in persuading the family to reject a condominium developer's offer. When put together in the mid-1960s, however, the idea of a shopping complex without department store "anchors" was radical. It is the direct forerunner of the Faneuil Hall/Quincy Market complex that, 10 years later, was discovered by the press.

The two actions—halting the Embarcadero overhead expressway and restoring the Ghirardelli complex—saved the popular Fisherman's Wharf area. In its earlier days, going back into the 1920s, the area was where fresh fish were sold to customers directly from a fleet based here. Later came inexpensive and good Italian restaurants overlooking the fleet, popular with locals and then tourists. Tourists still flock to the area, now the site of a proliferation of shops, vendors, tour boats, restaurants, and motels.

Citizens likewise became upset at the condition of San Francisco Bay itself, formed the Save the Bay Association, and forced a ballot initiative that led to making permanent in 1969 the San Francisco Bay Conservation and Development Commission. This body's main charges were to halt filling of the bay and to secure recreational public access. It has largely succeeded, and remains today a pacesetter for regional permit authorities, albeit not without major controversies.

■ Citizen revolt over a Mississippi River expressway proposed by New York's masterbuilder Robert Moses, and backed by the business and political leadership of New Orleans, also occurred in the early 1960s. The surprising expressway defeat in 1969 made possible a later replacement of a wharf structure with a short linear park, the Moonwalk, the first public opening to the Mississippi River downtown. The riverfront expressway defeat likewise helped save the historic French Quarter that adjoins the river, one of the world's favorite visitor destinations.

The expressway fight, led by two determined activists, Richard Baumbach and William Borah, caused a bit of a shock wave, coming as it did during a time of unquestioned approval of more and larger highways.

It shared with San Francisco a gut rebellion against a walling off of the city from the downtown river—the more remarkable in New Orleans because there was nothing akin to Fisherman's Wharf or Pacific Heights views to protect, only shipping warehouses that sealed off the public. Still, the inherent instinct to protect the river for the public was manifest years before there was a recognized waterfront phenomenon anywhere, let alone in New Orleans.

These unrelated but parallel actions demonstrated the power of people's basic interest in urban waterfronts and the lure of water bodies as small as the San Antonio River or as large as San Francisco Bay.

West Coast Leadership

Baltimore's Inner Harbor, Boston's central waterfront, and Toronto's Harbourfront are most often offered up as the pioneers in today's waterfront phenomenon. There's little point, however, in putting one city or another "first." The fact is that the first stirrings occurred in the 1950s in a number of places, paving the way for the more widespread actions of the 1960s. We begin with major city examples on the West Coast because the actions here are less well known.

For instance, In 1951, in honor of the City of Oakland's centennial, Jack London Square on the Oakland Estuary was formally dedicated, reflecting an effort to reach back to the historical roots of the area. By the early 1960s several restaurants at the square were popular attractions. A banquet hall/convention center and TV studios were constructed by the Port of Oakland to fill out the complex.

Over the next 10 years, a mixture of offices, marina, yacht club, and shops were added, as well as a pedestrian walkway along the water's edge. It was observed that the success of the businesses at Jack London Square proved the potential of a waterfront location for such activities, and other cities around

The modern-day waterfront phenomenon may have begun here—at Ghirardelli Square marketplace, overlooking San Francisco Bay. (*Breen/Rigby*)

The opening to the Mississippi River in New Orleans, featuring the well-used Moonwalk. Steps allow visitors to get close to the river. (*Breen/Rigby*)

the Bay were soon following suit. Later the area fell on hard times; the Port of Oakland is currently in its third round of planning for the site.

Across San Francisco Bay, three old warehouses along the San Francisco waterfront were restored, recycled, and opened to the public during the 1960s: Ghirardelli Square (1964, Wurster, Bernardi & Emmons, Inc., architects; Lawrence Halprin & Associates, landscape architects); The Cannery (1967, Joseph Esherick & Associates); and Wharfside (late 1960s, Joseph Esherick & Associates).

In another pioneering West Coast city, Seattle, the grande dame of authentic American markets—the Pike Place Market—was placed on the National Register of Historic Places in 1971, after citizen action prevented its destruction. In 1974 the city began a major renewal of the structure, which, when completed, returned to the citizens of Seattle a respectfully restored, lively market offering magnificent views of Elliott Bay and the central waterfront.

Also in the early 1970s, the city purchased waterfront property from Piers 57 to 61. One of the major attractions constructed during this decade was the $5.5 million Seattle Aquarium, occupying Piers 59

and 60, a forerunner of another popular type of waterfront installation. The aquarium sits next to Central Waterfront Park, constructed between 1973 and 1975, which provides a point of public access in this key location. Farther north along the waterfront is Pier 79, which was converted into an entertainment shopping facility in the 1970s.

In Oakland, San Francisco, and Seattle by the year 1975 there were in place the forerunners of what would soon be discovered to be a major phenomenon—waterfront redevelopment in center cities.

The reclamation and redevelopment in these cities, by public and private entities—marketplaces, residences, parks, restaurants, offices, aquariums, and open spaces—reflected the range of land uses, and the accompanying controversies, that constitute waterfront redevelopment in North America and elsewhere.

The Tall Ships of 1976

The dramatic Tall Ships celebrations of the 1976 Bicentennial brought thousands of people to urban waterfronts. Such visits were a first for most, and the event is seen as the occasion on which waterfronts were discovered by the general public in East Coast cities such as Baltimore, Boston, New York, and Norfolk.

The surge of people to abandoned and derelict waterfront areas to see historic sailing vessels, captured dramatically on television, had a profound impact. The media attention reinforced the public's growing perception of the special opportunities that waterfronts represent. This public included citizen visionaries as well as the professional planning, design, and development communities.

In Norfolk, Virginia, at the time of the Tall Ship visit, there was an Omni Hotel on the waterfront, plus vacant land (later to be the site of the Waterside festival marketplace). In New York, scene of a dramatic "parade of sail" up the Hudson River, there was a 92-acre blank landfill along the waterfront in lower Manhattan, now Battery Park City. Also in New York, on the East River, the South Street Seaport Museum in 1976 was struggling to save ships and historic buildings; it since has become primarily a marketplace and offices.

In Boston at the time of the Bicentennial, old waterfront warehouses were being reclaimed and the North End neighborhood saved from urban renewal. The restored Faneuil Hall/Quincy Market and Waterfront Park opened in 1976, gaining major media attention. Meanwhile, in Baltimore, another pioneering waterfront city, in 1976 there was a promenade and a world trade center under construction.

The stage was set for waterfront projects to take off.

Baltimore, Boston, and Toronto

The three cities recognized by the media and academics as the leaders of the waterfront redevelopment movement are Baltimore, Boston, and Toronto. These are the most publicized, and the most studied by scholars and practitioners in search of waterfront wisdom.

It may be the strength of leadership, the presence of a formal plan, the size, scope, and concentrated focus of the redevelopment efforts in these three cities, that made their waterfront turnarounds more pronounced than their West Coast counterparts. Or, more likely, that they are located nearer major media centers.

In these three cases, as was equally true in scores of other, less publicized waterfront revitalizations, the early vision came and the planning process began in the late 1950s and early 1960s.

Baltimore

The remarkable resuscitation of downtown Baltimore, and especially the Inner Harbor, is one of the greatest urban success stories extant and is justly celebrated. It has served as a model for cities throughout North America and, indeed, the world.

Business leaders took action in the mid-1950s to halt downtown's downward spiral, the first initiative being the hiring in 1957 of a planning firm (Wallace McHarg Roberts & Todd of Philadelphia) to prepare a downtown master plan. The resulting first project, the Charles Center mixed-use development on 33 acres, was a single bold and dramatic undertaking designed to symbolize change and a halt to deterioration.

In 1963, with Charles Center on its way to reality, the move to the harbor began in earnest, building on an earlier cleanup of deteriorated piers and sheds (begun, in fact, in 1950). An Inner Harbor plan was produced in 1964, again by the Wallace firm, calling for linking a "living, 24-hour-a-day city into intimate, vivacious contact with the harbor whence it sprang." With the tearing down of what was left here, Baltimore began with a clean slate at Inner Harbor.

A combination of city bond funds and federal grants began the transformation of the 240 acres of land around the small central harbor, beginning with a new bulkhead, followed by a wide brick promenade, and installation in 1972 of the first public attraction, the *U.S.S Constellation*. Festivals and events of all kinds were sponsored at the Inner Harbor as a way to bring attention to the slowly redeveloping waterfront. The 1976 Bicentennial Tall Ships event drew thousands to the harbor. A science center (1976, Edward Durrell Stone) was opened, and a World Trade Center tower went up (1977, I. M. Pei). See the Baltimore Inner Harbor Shoreline, Chapter 5, for continuation of the story with additional details and a timetable.

Baltimore has also experienced flops, such as a poorly conceived "urban amusement park" in an old power house, and inappropriate development, such as the over-large Scarlett House condominium, both on the Inner Harbor.

Boston

By the late 1950s, the Boston central waterfront was a picture of urban decline—typical of many older cities—consisting of ailing sewage and electrical facilities, rundown streets, and architecturally interesting but little-used warehouses and other structures.

After his election in 1959, Mayor John Collins launched a major urban renewal program that included the waterfront as an important component. He hired Ed Logue as head of the Boston Redevelopment Authority (BRA). He challenged the Chamber of Commerce's Waterfront Redevelopment Division to undertake preliminary planning. In 1962, a *Report on the Downtown Waterfront* was issued and a separate nonprofit organization, the Waterfront Development Corporation, was established to work in tandem with the BRA to come up with an urban renewal plan.

Preceding this, individual pioneers had perceived the quality inherent in the old warehouses left behind on the harbor's piers. Conversions into apartments and offices had begun quietly and largely out

The Inner Harbor in Baltimore, in 1967, before its complete makeover. At the center is a park and roadway, built on reclaimed land, that preceded the redevelopment of the 1970s and 1980s. Structures at the left, or southern, side of the Inner Harbor were torn down. (M. E.. *Warren*)

of sight; the waterfront was severed from the city by an expressway.

A key difference between Baltimore and Boston is the presence of a stock of fine stone buildings in Boston, and Baltimore's leveling of its dilapidated harbor remnants. Boston was relatively early in drawing pioneering downtown waterfront residents. Baltimore's waterfront residents were in historic neighborhoods such as Fells Point, until new condominiums were built at the Inner Harbor.

In 1969 Boston made a $5 million investment in the New England Aquarium (Cambridge Seven Associates, Inc.), one of the first new structures on the central waterfront. New 40-story apartment towers (1971, I. M. Pei), a $2.1 million Waterfront Park (1976, Sasaki Associates, Inc.) (see Chapter 6), and several wharf warehouse conversions to retail and housing rounded out the picture during this time.

In 1976, amid the Tall Ships Bicentennial observance, the Faneuil Hall/Quincy Marketplace opened with great fanfare near the waterfront and captured major national attention. The highly popular market area has become a symbol for reviving Boston. The credits here go at least to Benjamin and Jane Thompson, Cambridge designers, and James Rouse, whose Columbia, Maryland, firm had been a major developer of suburban shopping centers. So unorthodox was the proposition to create a downtown shopping district without major department store "anchors," which conventional wisdom required, that no Boston bank would fund the venture at first.

(Obviously, nobody had visited Ghirardelli Square!)

The publicity about Quincy Market's great popularity also cemented in the public's mind a link between festival marketplaces and waterfront redevelopment. Waterfront redevelopment in Boston actually involves over 100 acres and includes housing, parks, the aquarium, marinas, offices, and light industry, among many other uses.

Along the downtown waterfront during the 1980s, a Long Wharf hotel (1982, Cossutta and Associates), partial restoration of the wharf itself (1989, Sasaki Associates, Inc.) (see Long Wharf, Chapter 4), and the Rowes Wharf mixed-use project (1987, Skidmore, Owings and Merrill) (see Chapter 5) were completed. The success has spread to other parts of the harbor, and waterfront redevelopment is now taking place at Charlestown Navy Yard, Columbia Point, and in the nearby towns of Lynn, Quincy, Hingham, and Salem, among others.

Toronto

The well-publicized Harbourfront project, occupying 100 acres on the central waterfront, is to Toronto what the downtown waterfront is to Boston and the Inner Harbor is to Baltimore. Like these cities, the Harbourfront project is multifaceted and has evolved gradually since the early 1970s. Also likewise, it is but a small portion of the whole, which in this case is a total of 2100 acres of city lakefront. While Baltimore and Boston enjoyed general public acceptance, Toronto, after initial support, experienced major controversy and derailment in the late 1980s.

Harbourfront is largely a residential project, whatever its original intent may have been. It also has major mixed-use complexes, the largest of which, the Queens Quay Terminal adaptive reuse, contains offices, shops, condominiums, and a theater (see Chapter 4). Major public events programming takes place here, and has since the earliest days of the undertaking, numbering as many as 4000 annual events. (See Programming Facilities, Chapter 2.)

Harbourfront is effectively an entire new neighborhood on Lake Ontario where before there had been industry, warehouses, and rail facilities. It has been accompanied by major controversy about gentrification, open space or the lack of it, and charges about "walling off" the waterfront. By the late 1980s, the public upset reached Ottawa (Harbourfront Corp. was a federal government entity) and a cabinet minister, David Crombie, one-time mayor of Toronto, resigned to take over a new commission set up to chart the course at Harbourfront and elsewhere on the waterfront in the 1990s.

The story begins in 1972 when the government of Canada purchased some of the central waterfront acreage. The shoreline here is separated from the central business district by the Gardiner Expressway and major railroad lines. Four years later, Harbourfront Corp. was established as a Crown Corporation charged with planning, executing, and selling a mixed-use project. In the very earliest announcements, spokespersons referred to the aim of building a public park on the lakefront. This was to come back to haunt the project.

In 1980 a "Development Framework" plan was adopted and the federal government approved a $27 million payment that was to induce private investment over the next seven years. The theory was that these investments, in condominiums among other things, would underwrite the considerable public events programming that Harbourfront sponsored to attract the public to use the space, and which use in turn would convince investors of the viability of the undertaking. After 1987 Harbourfront was to be self-supporting.

In one particularly telling turn of events, plans called for a 13-story condominium on one site. By the time bidding was solicited, the Canadian real estate market was in the doldrums. As a result, only one bid was received, calling for three condominium/apartment towers, two of 30 stories.

So hard-pressed was Harbourfront Corp., facing its crucial deadline for self-sufficiency, that it approved the developer's plans. The buildings went up, were put on the market at fairly moderate prices, were sold and leased right away. The public, meanwhile, looked at the height, the boxy style, and erupted. These particular buildings attracted more notoriety than any other project in Canada in recent years, according to the former director of architecture and urban design in Toronto, Kenneth Greenberg.[15] Another point of contention was plans by Harbourfront for more condominiums near the

water's edge, beside Queen's Quay Terminal.

The controversy that followed, including charges of bad faith on the part of the government and Harbourfront in selling the land meant for park space for private housing, halted all development in 1987 and led to the Royal Commission on the Future of the Toronto Waterfront. Eventually, in 1991, Harbourfront Corp. was effectively disbanded, its planning and development functions placed elsewhere. It was reconstituted as Harbourfront Centre, which still offers myriad events for the citizens of Toronto.

The Festival Marketplace Fad

Both in the media and in many academic presentations about urban waterfronts, there is an equating of the waterfront phenomenon to festival marketplaces. These marketplaces broke into public consciousness with a splash in the mid-1970s—they were something new, and positive, happening in cities, and many were on the water. They were taken by many to be essentially what was happening on redeveloping shorelines.

Thoughtful observers noted that the festival marketplace phenomenon passed quickly, as failures cropped up in Toledo (see Portside Festival Market in Chapter 5), New Orleans (see Jackson Brewery, Chapter 4), Minneapolis, Flint, and Richmond. A careful analysis appeared in the *National Journal* on Sept. 17, 1988, entitled "Faltering Festivals." Others less closely tuned to what's going on write about it today as if festival marketplaces were still in vogue and the essence of what waterfront redevelopment is about.

We have in *Newsweek* magazine, Mar. 27, 1989, a headline, "Rough Sailing on the Waterfront," a story almost entirely about festival marketplaces, including mention of one in Richmond that is not on the river.

The facts on the festival marketplace seem to be these: By one estimate, there were a total of 22 such installations as of 1986;[16] by another definition, there are 53 "festival centers," of which 23 are on water.[17]

By whatever definition, the number of such marketplaces is miniscule compared to the extent of general urban waterfront redevelopment in thousands of communities—trails and walkways, parks, cultural facilities, condominiums, offices, restaurants, industrial and working waterfront facilities, ports, ferry docks, and the myriad uses to which waterfronts are put today. As this book illustrates in Chapters 2 and 6, the amount, extent, and quality of the public realm being carved out along water bodies everywhere is astonishing. It has gone largely unreported nationally.

Festival markets, and by mistaken extension, redeveloping waterfronts, are a tempting target for critics who see them as overly commercial, overly privatized shoreline.

Calvin Trillin, in a delightfully written piece in the *New Yorker*, set the tone:[18]

There are some who look on the process as "revitalization." There are some, like Andrew Kopkind, who look on it as a group of middleclass sophisticates taking territory away from working people....

...others have described Quincy Market as basically a suburban shopping mall done up in the instant charm of ye ole exposed brick—the new kitsch of advanced capitalism. Its detractors see it as a Disneyland model of a market. Even critics who have praised Quincy Market highly—Ada Louis Huxtable of The (New York) Times, for instance—write about it with some uneasiness.[19]

Others seem to have taken their cue from Trillin. Critic Ellen Posner wrote in Atlantic, for example:

Waterfronts everywhere are being covered with large, upscale residential and commercial structures, with ironically named, extremely boring "festival marketplaces," and, more and more, with huge aquariums.

It is one thing to decry "cookie-cutter" design, standardization of retail stores, and the sanitization of colorful waterfronts. It's another, mistaken, thing to trivialize waterfront redevelopment effort as consisting essentially of lookalike marketplaces and aquariums.

The impact and meaning of the Faneuil Hall/Quincy Market reopening in 1976, with its companion Waterfront Park (see Chapter 6), is lost on critics who somehow can't see beyond the fern plants. Basically it was a place in the center city where people felt safe. After that, they enjoyed themselves. While the project was on its way to legendary status in the municipal/development communities, Suzanne Stephens wrote in Progressive Architecture:

Both of the inner-city shopping mall types—recycled buildings or new enclosed skylight galleries—reflect a strong element of escapism. The culture of consumption has always focused on this motif. But the tendency toward ersatz nostalgia on the one hand, and controlled, filtered worlds on the other, pushes escapism over the edge of banality.[20]

How is restoring a marketplace to be a marketplace "ersatz"? What is wrong with urban plazas, street performers, benches and bars, where diverse people gather to enjoy themselves and each other? Aren't cities in good part about commerce ("consumerism" in the pejorative)? Didn't the ancient Greeks and Romans have marketplaces (the agora and the forum)?

A more telling assessment of the impact of the Faneuil Hall/Quincy Market/Waterfront Park complex comes from the authors of Downtown Inc.:

By the mid-1970s urban specialists had been working nearly 40 years without producing a truly popular, nationally recognized achievement. Urban renewal, model cities, and new towns in-town were all dead, and public housing was barely alive....City experts and the urban press were aching for at least one success, and Faneuil Hall Marketplace finally gave it to them. It had a series of themes just right for the times (food, historic buildings, piazza feeling).[21]

By the end of the 1970s and early 1980s, the well-publicized stories of Boston, Baltimore, and Toronto, coupled with increasing awareness of downtown waterfront changes that had taken place in cities such as Newport, Rhode Island, Savannah, Georgia, St. Louis, Missouri, Sacramento, California, Cincinnati, Ohio, Portsmouth, New Hampshire, and Norfolk, Virginia, among many, contributed to a rapid spread of interest.

Challenges

It is important to remember, as more communities join in, that each waterfront story varies according to the particularities of geography, heritage, timing, politics, business leadership, and chance. This means that the rote copying of other's successes can end in economic failure, or projects that are unsympathetic to their context.

Different political setups influence how a waterfront undertaking proceeds from early vision to completion, a process that can easily take 25 years. Leadership in these cases will pass from one hand to another.

Strong mayors are sometimes able to move communities, as in Baltimore, Biloxi, or St. Paul. Or the impetus can come from the private business community (San Antonio, Boston, New Orleans), independent citizen's organizations (Cleveland, Davenport), or a concerned, persistent individual (Toledo). A port authority led the way in Oakland.

With the success of the waterfront redevelopment movement have come a variety of challenges. Some are simply manifestations of general urban and societal issues, others are more unique to water bodies. It should be noted that there have been conspicuous failures—Canary Wharf in the Docklands of London in 1992 was the most spectacular bankruptcy, but there were also closings or bankruptcies in Minneapolis, Jersey City, Flint, and New Orleans.

Location and Timing

Geography is an underlying determinant. Baltimore's Inner Harbor is small, intimate, and next to the central business district. This is a major key to the success there, yet it is often overlooked by many who seek to emulate it, who see only a formula of a mix of uses and a marketplace.

Within a city, projects vary over time. Cities, especially as they begin waterfront redevelopment and have no proven success in these often-deserted areas, are so anxious to secure investment that they tend to give too much away. City bureaucrats are often not skilled at bargaining. There is a tendency to take the first legitimate offer, for fear that no oth-

ers will come along and they will be accused of drop-
ping the ball.

Elected officials frequently have short-range vision,
keyed to their terms of office, which is generally two
or four years. This leads to bad planning decisions,
access compromises, or "quick-fix" solutions that
backfire. For instance, Newport, Rhode Island, in the
early days of urban renewal, in its eagerness to attract
investment, forfeited public access in front of a hotel
along the waterfront. Portland, Maine, recently lost a
major opportunity for public access on one of its key
central waterfront parcels at a new condominium project. Davenport, Iowa, installed an old Army dredge
along its riverfront without a plan for follow-up
investment. With the later arrival of gambling boats,
the dredge moved elsewhere.

Redevelopment occurs in phases. Boston, in the
city's early days of reinvestment on the waterfront, was
so eager for downtown developers that it compromised
excessively. As the city became a more attractive
investment market, it grew more demanding. This is
particularly true with respect to public access. Boston
in the 1980s was much more aggressive in insisting
that public walkways be provided and view corridors
be protected, among other things (see Rowe's Wharf,
Chapter 5). Now, with the market downturn of the
early 1990s, there may be unfortunate compromises at
Fort Point Channel and Fan Pier, where views may be
blocked and the quality of public access diminished by
new buildings being planned.

Public Accessibility

It's axiomatic that people love water and want to
reach it and touch it. Beyond this fundamental
desire, the public's right to shoreline access has a
legal basis in the public trust doctrine, whose roots
for most of the United States go back to Roman
times, when free access to navigable waters and the
foreshore was the right of every citizen. Spanish legal
traditions are even stronger in affirming the public's
right to the water (the "right of thirst").

Massive public investment in recent years further
bolsters the sense that a fully accessible waterfront
(except where safety is involved) should be the goal
in all waterfront undertakings. This means physical
access to and along the water body, visual access
down view corridors, sensitive siting and design in
terms of height and bulk, and a barrier-free setting. It
also means that public areas should be psychologically welcoming. The tradition of sidewalks along city
streets should be analogous to walkways along public
water bodies.

There is unfortunately a tendency to block off.
with walls and gates the public's access to and along
water bodies in many cities. This is especially true of
condominium and housing projects in pioneering
market areas, as many former industrial waterfronts
are (examples are Jersey City, Toledo, and Detroit).
In appealing to a basically suburban market to take
up city living, it is felt necessary to promote security
and safety. Fear of crime is perhaps the major deterrent to urban activity of all kinds.

Liability

Also working against efforts to install open waterfront walkways and parks, especially without railings,
is a fear of liability. The reality is that juries are sus-
ceptible to making large awards in suits over drown-
ings, for instance, and this creates fear on the part of
municipalities, developers, and designers alike. This
is despite the fact that thousands of miles of shorelines are unfenced, even in highly populated urban
park areas. Also, fear mitigates against efforts to get
private property owners to provide access easements
without iron-clad guarantees that they won't be held
responsible.

The Tidal Basin in Washington, D.C., promenades in Baltimore and Norfolk, and the Fisherman's
Wharf area in San Francisco are a few among hundreds of examples where generally no fencing or railings exist at the water's edge. Water can be seen as
an inherent danger obviating the need for barriers,
much as paths on coastal cliffs have no fences and
beaches spill uninterrupted into the ocean.

Environmental Issues

Urban waterfronts present a host of environmental
challenges. Many former industrial sites contain
toxic substances that must be removed or capped. It
took time for people to discover the unfortunate
residue of earlier industrial practices.

As a result, Seattle's acclaimed reclamation of Gas
Works Park on Lake Union ran into trouble some
years after it was completed as black sediment, containing polynuclear hydrocarbons (PNAs), bubbled to
the surface. Similarly, the grass in a waterfront park in
Detroit one day turned up blue in spots. An enormous
riverfront park in Kansas City is sealed off and posted
as dangerous to the public health. Today, borings and
tests are routinely done on former industrial sites, and
expensive cleanups are undertaken. Cleaning up an
Allied Chemical Co. property on Baltimore's Inner
Harbor East is to cost $60 million, in but one example
of the investment needed to make some waterfront
property developable.

Natural disasters such as flooding, hurricanes, and
severe tides require special design solutions. The
design and development community has to take into
account these factors and build sufficient safeguards.
Not all those working with shorelines and water bodies have the requisite experience.

So compelling is people's desire to be close to
water that they will continue to take chances and
build in hazardous areas—witness the flurry of
rebuilding along the Carolina coast after the 1990
hurricanes. A regulatory attempt to restrict the
rebuilding on beaches in South Carolina reached the
Supreme Court as an unwarranted "taking" of private property; an inconclusive decision remanded
the case to the state in July 1992.

Sometimes an environmental problem can turn
into an unparalleled opportunity to turn around a
waterfront. Disasters very often are followed by large
sums of federal and state assistance. This occurred in

Walkways can co-exist with industry, as here on the Seattle shoreline. (*Robert Kaye*)

Conway, South Carolina, where hurricane relief funds helped accelerate and facilitate the planning and redevelopment of the riverfront there.

This is also the case in Grand Junction, a city of 28,000 in western Colorado located at the confluence of the Colorado and Gunnison riverfronts. While the riverfront was identified by the city as an area of opportunity in the mid-1980s, as late as 1988 the river banks in Grand Junction were dominated by the tailings left over from uranium mining, and with massive automobile junk yards.

Funds from the federal government for the cleanup of the mining residue became an important catalyst that moved Grand Junction to act to clear the auto wrecks. The riverfront action did not occur in isolation, but rather can be seen as building on an earlier, central business district improvement program.

A Grand Junction/Mesa County Riverfront Commission was established in 1987, and in the next year, a design team funded by the National Endowment for the Arts was brought into the city to generate ideas. The team included representatives from Jones & Jones Architects and Landscape Architects, Seattle; The Townscape Institute, Cambridge, Massachusetts; Urban Edges Inc., Denver; and the Waterfront Center.

With a combination of funds from public, private, and philanthropic sources, the city has as of 1991 moved ahead with purchase of key riverfront sites and has launched cleanup programs. Land and ease-ment donations have also been secured. The prospect is that a green, open space will result along the riverbank, adjacent and accessible to the central business district, forming a major new entry point into Grand Junction. Other uses will be added later under the city's plans.

Working Waterfront

For years the urban waterfront was the exclusive realm of ports, fishing fleets, shipbuilding and boat repair yards, warehouses for all types of products, tug yards, mills and manufacturing plants, grain silos, concrete terminals, coal and salt piles, waste-water treatment plants, tank farms, and similar activities, many regarded as noxious or unattractive. Changing technology made many of these installations obsolete and was the impetus for the redevelopment that endangers the remaining industrial uses.

Rising land prices that have accompanied water-front redevelopment threaten to displace traditional occupants—particularly small, often marginal marine enterprises—many of which contribute to a local economy and add to a city's character. These vulnerable waterfront denizens survived in the past in part because they occupied cheap land.

The Seattle fishing fleet, although it is not small when taken in the aggregate, is such an example, one of four cases discussed in the Waterfront Center's 1985 report, *Caution: Working Waterfront*. The industry banded together in the early 1980s when it saw city decisions favoring replacement of marine businesses with higher-paying uses on Lake Union, traditionally its home base. The industry lost its first test case, but raised its political visibility to such an extent that it felt it had won its point.

Efforts to legislate or control the impact of the marketplace on waterfronts with zoning are awkward, and raise nettlesome issues as difficult as the original problem. For instance, the idea of limiting waterfronts to "water-dependent" uses is the antithesis of good, city-specific urban planning. What's "water-dependent" can't be defined. (Is a seafood restaurant, sailing magazine editorial office, or boat-building factory "water-dependent"—when all three can, and do, exist apart from water bodies?)

Such regulations will lead inevitably to arbitrary, bureaucratic decisions that are not necessarily sensitive to what makes an eclectic, interesting waterfront. In an example of what can and will happen under such regulations, a restaurant that served as a social center for the Portland, Maine, fishing fleet based downtown was forced to relocate by a "water-dependent" zone put in place to save the fishing industry.

A three-part series in the *Portland Press-Herald* on that city's effort to restrict its waterfront uses began:

Portland's waterfront is in trouble.

Five years after voters chose to reserve the waterfront for marine industries only, the area suffers from neglect, empty space and lack of investment. The marine-only zoning has hurt the very businesses it was intended to help.[22]

Waterfront Character/Use Mixes

"Character" is an elusive quality that makes one person or place unique. Very often, the more unique or characterful, the more interesting a place is, especially in a time of homogeneity.

There is a lack of understanding of the nature of many waterfronts, and that part of their attraction is their funkiness. The 1950s coffee shop, the ramshackle roadhouse, the weather-beaten watering hole, the fish shack, the bait shop, plus the helter-skelter ropes and rust that accompany the industrial waterfront, are viewed by many as just plain messiness. To others, however, these types of places and atmosphere are genuine and a source of waterfront charm. These areas also provide an opportunity to make contact with an earlier time. A lack of appreciation for some waterfronts leads to overzealous cleanup and replacement programs. What appears to be messy and disorderly may be a viable marine industry (such as a boat-repair yard or other small family business).

There is also a lesson here about the mistake in prescriptive zoning to preclude mixing uses, especially in cities. The lesson would seem that it is better to decide each case on its merits for a specific site, at a given time, and if it appears to work, to proceed.

The working waterfront, as here in Sausalito, California, is threatened in many places by new development.(Breen/Rigby)

Many of the most interesting waterfront areas mix incongruous or seemingly incompatible activities—a restaurant amid ship-repair dry docks (San Francisco), condominiums beside a commercial fishing industry (Portland, Maine), a library with a retail marketplace (Dartmouth, Nova Scotia), an art school next to a concrete plant (Granville Island, Vancouver), a park within a port (Oakland, California), a farmer's market next to a sewage treatment plant (Ithaca, New York), and condominiums beside an active port (Charleston, South Carolina).

These interesting urban mixes offer a welcome contrast to many of today's bland environments. Waterfronts likewise possess a grittiness and no-nonsense quality that is an attractive contrast to many of today's sleek developments.

Granville Island, a project in downtown Vancouver, British Columbia, has become a model development of a former industrial site where new, commercial uses have been introduced and the original industrial character maintained; in fact, some industrial uses continue amid shops and arts and crafts studios. See Chapter 5.

Design Issues

The individual locale, the existing buildings, the idiosyncratic nature of waterfronts, and most especially, the presence of a water body, call for careful design. There's hardly a waterfront without a past. A particularly troubling tendency by some architects and developers is to repeat standard building forms when working in these areas. And so we have waterfront designs executed with no respect for context, or even for water views.

The story is told that architects of a national hotel chain designed an installation near the San Antonio River without ever having been there. In another example, a Hyatt Hotel on the Savannah Riverwalk reflects the atrium concept popular in hotel design and is focused inward, taking precious little advantage of its river views. Also, it intrudes rudely over a graceful Riverwalk. Similarly, the Kellogg Foundation office building in Battle Creek, Michigan, puts a large, blank wall along the river and has fenced off and made discontinuous a beautifully executed linear walkway (see Chapter 6).

Important opportunities to reuse historic structures, and thus retain some of our industrial, maritime, and cultural heritage, are present. Pittsburgh is an example both of wholesale removal of old structures on its "Golden Triangle" and of its riverfront steel plants—and of the careful restoration of downtown rail facilities at what is now known as the Station Square complex on the Monongahela River. In South Norwalk, Connecticut, the Maritime Center—an otherwise handsome adaptive reuse of an old industrial building—presents as its most prominent feature an off-putting blank brick wall next to the water, with restricted public access. Halifax, Nova Scotia, has a stunning example of a new hotel being sensitively fitted into the old historic waterfront. Right next to it, however, is Purdy's Wharf—a self-contained complex of sleek, modern, white highrises that look as if they belong in Houston. Chapter 4 includes examples of successful conversions.

Education/Interpretation

Public areas along waterfronts—and some private areas as well—offer an unusual opportunity to educate people of all ages about the social, maritime, cultural, and environmental heritage of an area. Urban waterfronts usually have historic connections, very often including the founding place of a city or its reason for being. This means that urban waterfront sites inevitably possess an opportunity to interpret, portray, and personify an area's history, both to itself and to the visiting public. Urban waterfronts can thus create a sense of civic pride.

Cincinnati's Bicentennial Park along the Ohio River (see Chapter 6) contains outstanding examples of historic interpretation in its sculptured entranceway, historic plaques, paving tiles, and illustrations of natural phenomena.

Another area of opportunity lies in environmental education. Besides water itself, there is shoreline ecology and surrounding flora and fauna to discover. Most cities have small patches of urban wild, and some are blessed with fairly large acreages of wetland or other natural areas surprisingly close to the central business district. Toronto's Leslie Street Spit,

Washington's Roosevelt Island, New York's Jamaica Bay, Boston's Harbor Islands, Buffalo's Tift Farm, and London's Camley Street Park are examples. A model small-city effort is located in Corpus Christi, Texas (see Hans Suter Wildlife Area, Chapter 3). School programs, civic groups, and park districts can and do use these waterfront areas to teach city dwellers a bit about the nearby natural world.

Waterfronts are also logical, and dramatic, sites for public educational facilities, including museums—maritime, art, science, and other—as well as halls of fame and aquariums, the latter a particularly striking phenomenon with a great potential to involve citizens of all ages directly with their environment. Amphitheaters, outdoor auditoriums, major concert facilities, and other cultural venues, such as an art museum in Milwaukee, enjoy waterfront locales.

One of the common failings of many of the 75 projects detailed in this book is a lack of interpretation of both natural and historic features of the sites and regions. Included, however, are a number of outstanding examples in this area, which can well serve as models.

Public Spaces

Many waterfronts are choice sites for spectacular public gathering spaces. This includes grand plazas and parks, some with amphitheaters and bandshells.

Detroit's Hart Plaza doubles as a permanent festival ground complete with sunken skating rink/amphitheater. Nearby Chene Park houses an enormous performing arts venue. Norfolk's downtown waterfront park and the public open space around the Waterside festival market are the sites of ambitious public programming and festivals.

One of the major attributes for public waterfront projects is that they become ideal, neutral territory for festivals and other community gatherings. In fact, the 1980s saw a proliferation of waterfront festival events of all kinds. In city after city there are stories about the great interest that is shown when a Tall Ship, a Navy vessel, or sometimes just a sailing boat, appears at a city dock.

There are 27 parks, walkways, and other public open space facilities described in this book, plus 5 cultural and educational facilities, nearly half of the 75 projects and plans described. This is reflective of waterfront redevelopment generally rather than some sort of aberration of the selection process.

Prospects

Waterfront projects of all kinds will continue, feeding on the continued successes that far outweigh the failures. Some will be extensions of past work, some will be makeovers, while others are starting new.

Housing will continue to be one of the major new uses to which urban waterfront territory is put, representing the most fundamental shift of all from previous industrial occupancy. With it comes a tendency in many jurisdictions to either seal off the public, or make that public feel unwelcome. This issue will be a flash point of controversy throughout the 1990s.

General debate will grow as appreciation for the waterfront's value increases. Waterfronts engender passionate disputes, some to the point of irrationality. Many a community has stalled waterfront projects, both public and private in sponsorship, because there is sufficient opposition to thwart them.

Most people feel that they have some stake in a waterfront, which in point of fact they do, the water body itself being basically in public ownership. Few city areas provoke as much debate and controversy now that waterfronts have been "discovered." Thus in Hoboken, New Jersey, two recent referendums on whether to approve a development plan favored by the city administration and the Port Authority of New York & New Jersey have been defeated by narrow margins, most recently in March 1992.

The awareness of the strength and importance of cultural attractions on waterfronts is growing, that more than shops are required to make an interesting experience and encourage repeat visitation. People appreciate lively sections of cities and especially areas with a bit of their heritage preserved.

There is already growth in such water uses as ferry systems and excursion vessels, trends that are likely to continue. Commuters use ferries not only in major markets such as San Francisco, New York, and Boston; a ferry service across Lake Michigan, connecting Manitowoc, Wisconsin, with Ludlington, Michigan, was reopened in 1992 by a private entrepreneur. The service now carries passengers as well as cars.

Gambling boats are a major new feature of waterfronts in Iowa, Illinois, Mississippi, and soon, Louisiana and likely other states as well. Initial attendance exceeded expectations, but with increased competition, the future is uncertain. Two boats left Iowa for Mississippi after one year, said to be the result of betting limits in Iowa, while new boats are readied elsewhere.

Another trend that will accelerate is the addition of aquariums in particular, and cultural features in general, to urban waterfronts. Aquariums have demonstrated their pulling power over time. To objections that they are too "trendy" or imitative, backers note that the Japanese, for instance, have approximately 80 aquariums and are building more. The ability of aquariums to educate a fascinated public about the aquatic environment is unparalleled.

Urban waterfronts are and will continue to be a most important and dynamic area of urban planning and development for years. Giant waterfront projects are under way or in prospect in New York, Chicago, and San Francisco, for example, as well as in hundreds of other cities large and small in North America, as well as overseas.

Water will continue its magical lure as a key to continued efforts to rebuild healthy urban centers. Our current, historic phase of urban waterfront redevelopment will stay in the forefront of urban planning and development for decades to come.

Notes

1. Nicholas Falk, "Quay to Success," *Leisure Management*, February 1991, p. 31.

2. William H. Harris and Judith S. Levey, eds., *The New Columbia Encyclopedia*, Columbia University Press, New York, 1975, p. 3006.

3. Vernon G. Zunker, *A Dream Come True: Robert Hugman and San Antonio's River Walk*, Vernon G. Zunker, San Antonio, TX, 1983.

4. Wesley Marx, *The Frail Ocean*, Ballantine Books, New York, 1969, p. 143.

5. Ian Nairn, *The American Landscape*, Random House, New York, 1965, p. 66.

6. National Wildlife Federation, *1991 Conservation Directory*, Washington, DC, 1991; Claire D. Hughes, "Taking Action," *Sky Magazine*, March 1992, p. 29.

7. Urban Land Institute, *Adaptive Use, Development Economics, Process and Profiles*, Urban Land Institute, Washington, DC, 1978.

8. Bureau of Planning, Portland, Oregon, *Willamette Greenway Plan*, adopted by the City Council November 5, 1987.

9. Detroit Recreation Department, *Linked Riverfront Parks Project*, Schervish Vogel Merz, October 1979.

10. Kristin Merriman, "Greenways: A New Face," *Outdoor America*, Summer 1989, p 22; Charles E. Little, *Greenways for America*, Johns Hopkins University Press, Baltimore, 1990.

11. Rails-to-Trails Conservancy, news release, Mar. 11, 1992.

12. National Marine Manufacturers Association, *Boating 1991*, Chicago, 1992.

13. Travel Industry Association of America, 1990 Travel Activity report.

14. Ann Breen and Dick Rigby, "Sons of River Walk. How a Masterpiece of Design has Inspired Communities across the Nation," *Planning*, March 1988.

15. Kenneth Greenberg, *Urban Waterfronts: Accent on Access*, The Waterfront Press, Washington, D.C., 1989, p. 10.

16. International Council of Shopping Centers, *Shopping Centers Today*, New York, May 1991.

17. *Centers, Upscale Specialty, Urban Mixed-Use and Festival*, JOMURPA Publishing, Inc., Spring Valley, N.Y., p. 369.

18. Calvin Trillin, "Thoughts Brought on by Prolonged Exposure to Exposed Brick," *New Yorker*, Mar. 22, 1977,.

19. Ellen Posner, "A City That Likes Itself," *Atlantic*, p. 97.

20. Suzanne Stephens, "Introversion and the Urban Context," *Progressive Architecture*, December 1978, p. 53.

21. Op. cit, p. 174.

22. Clarke Canfield, "Waterfront: From Frenzy to Neglect," *Portland* (Maine) *Press-Herald*, Mar. 30, 1992, p. 1.

Selecting the Cases: Background

The 75 projects and plans described and analyzed in Chapters 2 through 9 were selected from about 500 entries in annual juried competitions sponsored by the Waterfront Center, 1987 to 1991.

The center began its "Excellence on the Waterfront" awards program to identify and publicize some of the best waterfront projects, for others to learn about and be inspired by. The competition continues.

The Waterfront Center, a nonprofit educational corporation based in Washington, DC, reflects a balanced viewpoint among the varied, sometimes competing, interests in the urban waterfront. Its conferences, publications, and awards program all reflect an objective, even-handed approach among private and public development interests, citizens' organizations, environmental concerns, the full range of design professionals involved, historic preservation, boating and other recreational pursuits, plus public art, festivals, and cultural venues. The center was incorporated in 1981 by Ann Breen and Dick Rigby.

Selecting the projects, and later, plans, that are featured in *Waterfronts: Cities Reclaim Their Edge,* were five varied juries. The jurors, listed in the Appendix, represent architectural, landscape architectural, and planning disciplines; private and quasi-public economic development organizations; local government; public art; state environmental programs; public-interest groups; design criticism; and academia.

The awards program was divided into categories reflecting the broad scope of current urban waterfront undertakings. These categories constitute the chapter groupings that follow. In some cases we have reassigned cases to subject areas we feel are more fitting than the category in which they received an award.

Each chapter contains for each project/plan a description, one or more illustrations, a site map, a list of credits, and an appraisal.

The chapters are organized as follows (with the awards category description and an example for each):

- Chapter 2—The Cultural Waterfront (artistic, cultural, educational installations, including public art, aquariums, fountains)—Dodge Memorial Fountain, Detroit

- Chapter 3—The Environmental Waterfront (shore stabilization, wetland preservation)—Harmon Meadow Wetland Restoration, Hackensack, New Jersey

- Chapter 4—The Historic Waterfront (including maritime preservation, adaptive reuse, lighthouse and ferry preservation, and warehouse conversions)—the ELISSA restoration, Galveston, Texas

- Chapter 5—The Mixed-Use Waterfront (includes projects with some combination of housing, retail, office, restaurant, market, and/or cultural spaces)—RiverPlace, Portland, Oregon

- Chapter 6—The Recreational Waterfront (includes parks, walkways, and boating facilities)—Santa Monica Pier Carousel Park, Santa Monica, California

- Chapter 7—The Residential Waterfront (includes resorts)—Charlestown Navy Yard Rowhouses, Charlestown, Massachusetts

- Chapter 8—Waterfront Plans—Chicago River Urban Design Guidelines

- Chapter 9—The Working Waterfront (commercial fishing, boat repair, heavy industry, and port uses)—Fisherman's Terminal, Seattle, Washington.

The cases included here are 75 very good examples of waterfront project planning and execution, occurring in all parts of North America and, increasingly, overseas. Four of the projects included are, in fact, from outside North America. While the international sample is small, in part because in its first years the center's awards program was restricted to North America, these cases reflect the growing interest in all parts of the globe in waterfront transformations, and for generally the same reasons as in North America.

These cases are *not* the 75 best urban waterfront projects of the time. That's a virtual impossibility to select.

While the awards program has always been open to older, historic work, these entries are harder to compile. Thus, some of the truly pioneering urban waterfront projects—San Antonio's original River Walk, Ghirardelli Square and the Cannery in San Francisco, Station Square in Pittsburgh, or Boston's Emerald Necklace of parks, to cite five special waterfront installations—are not included. They or others like them are, however, part of Chapter 1's discussion of the history of the waterfront phenomenon.

These 75 projects and plans received awards because the jurors felt that they, in varied ways, embody the center's judging criteria. These are:

- Sensitivity of the design to the waterfront and the water body

- Quality of the design and its harmony with the surroundings

- Civic contribution

- Environmental values reflected

- The educational role embodied

Not every project reflects all the criteria in equal measure; rather they embody those appropriate to the project type.

In the pages that follow, each case includes information on size, cost, and participants in the work. This information was, generally speaking, supplied by one or more of the participants and verified to the best of our ability. Names, addresses, and phone numbers are current as of mid-1992, when this information was compiled.

A word on the terminology used in the list of credits at the end of each project/plan description. We use the term "sponsor" for the agency responsible for the undertaking, be it a private developer, a public agency, or a quasi-public entity. We use the term "designer" for the lead design firm, encompassing architectural, urban design, planning, landscape architecture, and/or project management functions. We have attempted to identify engineering specialties and to specify landscape architecture when that alone was supplied. We have used professional designations in architecture and landscape architecture when known, but not titles in firms. We list sponsors and design firms in order, from the general to the specific. If in doubt we've used the term "consultant." When we received conflicting versions of which firm should be listed first, we have used the firm that entered the project in the Waterfront Center awards program, or the alphabet, to determine order.

Each case is accompanied by a two-part map. One gives general location within a community, the other shows the site and the immediate surrounding territory. The maps underscore the importance the authors and the center's juries give to the context in which urban waterfront work takes place. They will help the reader locate the project/plan within a region, and in a community. The maps were prepared by Charles and Diane Charyk Norris, architects of Cambridge, Massachusetts.

One, usually both, of the authors has visited all but five of the 75 cases. The descriptions reflect our personal assessment of the projects and plans, the literature available on each, and the award entry data. In two of the five cases we were not able to investigate personally, surrogates provided first-hand reports.

The information used here generally reflects the status of a project as it was submitted, in 1987 to 1991, to the center's jury, and contains the basis on which it was selected. More up-to-date information is included for many projects, especially where a dramatic change in circumstance has occurred, including bankruptcies, major additions, or changes in ownership and management. Within each chapter, cases are presented in alphabetical order by the city in which the project or plan is located.

We have taken the award submittal and the jury comments as our starting point. The assessments here are ours and may, or may not, reflect the opinions of the jury members choosing them. Any mistakes are our responsibility entirely.

≈2≈

THE CULTURAL
WATERFRONT

Our bodies and spirits need the fresh breezes that blow from the water. We need both its calm and its stimulus. We need the sense of community, the opportunities for festivity, for artistic expression, recreation and commercial bustle that urban waterfront offers. We need what August Heckscher has called "the public happiness."
In these often desperate times of anxiety and confusion, we need all this desperately.

WOLF VON ECKARDT,
address at Urban Waterfronts '83, Washington, D.C. *

*Ann Breen and Dick Rigby, *Urban Waterfronts '83: Balancing Public/Private Interest*, The Waterfront Press, Washington, D.C., 1984

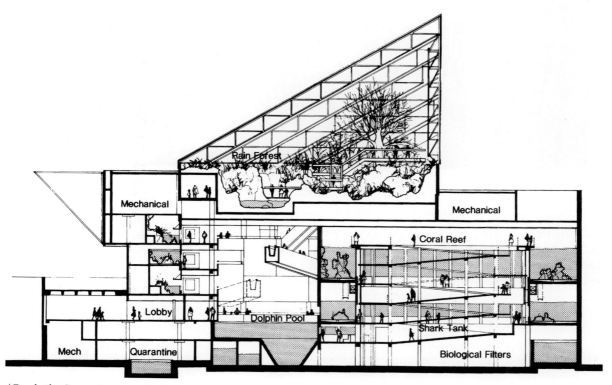

(*Cambridge Seven Associates, Inc.*)

National Aquarium in Baltimore
Pier 3, 501 East Pratt Street
Baltimore, Maryland

Summary

A pioneer among modern aquariums; a standout in design, popularity, and civic self-image.

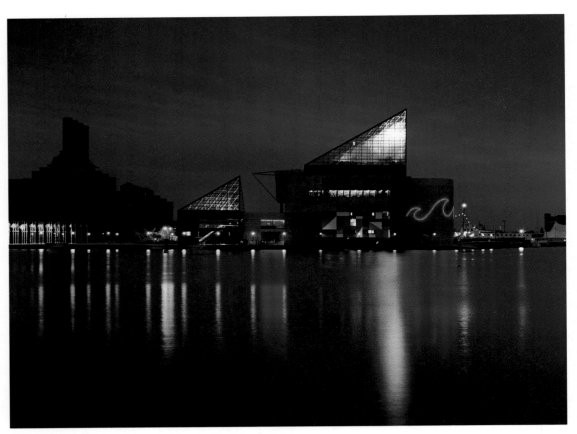

(*Steve Rosenthal*)

Description. The National Aquarium in Baltimore occupies a prominent spot in the Inner Harbor. Its bold, sculptural design at the end of Pier 3 juts dramatically into the harbor of America's showcase waterfront redevelopment.

Inside the 115,000 square feet in the original building (since added to) are a variety of experiences along a carefully orchestrated walkway. The average tour takes approximately two hours.

The midway point on the tour, five stories up, is a lush Amazon rain forest housed in a glass pyramid. Beyond the fascinating display here, which includes free-flying birds, reptiles, amphibians, and mammals, are excellent views of both Baltimore and its outer harbor, stretching to Chesapeake Bay.

Although it was modeled on Boston's successful aquarium, which opened in 1970, Baltimore's aquarium was a bit of a gamble when it was conceived. The original building cost $21.3 million of city budget. It opened to enthusiastic crowds, however, and attendance has been strong ever since. Its success enabled the addition in 1990 of a marine mammal pavilion, costing $35 million of city and state funds, grants, and revenues.

Attendance was at the 1.5-million level before the addition of the mammal pavilion, making the aquarium Maryland's top tourist attraction in 1985.[1]

The aquarium's dimensions are impressive. Within its seven stories are 1 million gallons of water. It houses about 5000 specimens, including 400 species of birds, fish, reptiles, plants, marine mammals, invertebrates, and amphibians. In the rain forest on the top visitor level are 400 types of plants, 100 species of birds, and a variety of fish.

A marine mammal pool in the original building can be viewed from underwater. An Atlantic coral reef exhibit in a 13-foot-deep tank features vivid tropical fish. A shark tank in a 220,000-gallon pool contains several samples of this species on view at different levels.

An additional feature are Maryland habitats with indigenous species, embodying a trend that is expected to receive greater emphasis in future aquariums. There are four exhibits on Maryland, including a mountain pond, a tidal marsh, Atlantic beach, and a simulation of the continental shelf offshore.

Throughout the aquarium are large color photographs of different species. Visitors are surrounded by the sounds of marine life.

Beyond the physical plant, the aquarium has

integrated itself in a major way into the community. School children by the thousands are brought here for what cannot help but be a stimulating experience, one in which a conservation message is forcefully put forward.

The National Aquarium, so named by congressional action pushed by the Maryland delegation while Washington's tiny, basement "National Aquarium" suffered in silence, has mounted a major community outreach effort. Hundreds of volunteers act as exhibit guides, divers, shop clerks, office assistants, and the like. The facility is also engaged in research, teaming up with such nearby institutions as Johns Hopkins University, the University of Maryland, and others.

The aquarium membership program, which reached 50,000 in just five years, has grown to become one of the largest of any zoo or aquarium. An example of Baltimore's innovative approaches was its "adoption" program, where a donor receives a certificate of adoption of a selected fish, mammal, or bird (there were a few who took the adoption program literally and expected a creature to be handed over). Group tours with reduced rates are another source of attendance and revenue.

A breakdown of the 1984–1985 year showed general admissions of 990,749, group sales of 112,034, school groups with 96,496, members at 42,232, and group events numbering 26,363, totaling 1,267,874.

This kind of early success, which has been sustained with continued marketing and promotion plus changing exhibits, produced income of nearly $7 million in 1984–1985, a sample year. It allowed the aquarium to set aside over $1 million for "capital and program projects," part of the funds that underwrote the 1990 expansion.

So popular was the aquarium in its first years for private, evening receptions that the administration had to curtail these occasions out of concern for the creatures.

Design Features. The National Aquarium is distinguished by its soaring glass pyramid roof, atop a decidedly modern concrete base. The glass pyramid is repeated over the entrance. The sail-shaped building faces the Inner Harbor promenade over a small inlet and makes a strong visual connection for thousands of visitors.

The concrete wall on the western exposure is relieved by bright, multicolored tiles and, at night, by signature curved neon tubes. Pier 3, on which the aquarium sits, has a completely open apron. A variety of boats use the pier edge, integrating the facility into the busy Inner Harbor scene.

The National Aquarium, building on the experience of its design firm, Cambridge Seven Associates, Inc., of Cambridge, Massachusetts, at the New England Aquarium in Boston a decade earlier, is organized around the controlled pathway principle. The visitor is directed along a designated path through the exhibits. The interior galleries open from time to time to allow glimpses of the exhibits ahead.

Appraisal. The National Aquarium in

(Steve Rosenthal)

Baltimore is an eloquent statement of the power of modern architecture—that the distinctive, pure building form works when it is well done, especially in settings that call for boldness. The seven-story-tall pyramid atop the aquarium can be seen down many a downtown Baltimore street. It is a fitting symbol for a city that has made a dramatic comeback since the desperate days of the 1960s.

Beyond that, the aquarium is a powerful educational instrument, reaching young and old with a message about their environment that is unequaled in its impact. Its weakest design feature was a somewhat barren entrance area, but that has since been modified.

The National Aquarium in Baltimore represents one of the major milestones in the evolution of public aquariums, embodying an advance over the Boston facility, its linear predecessor. It has justifiably taken a place in the roster of significant public facilities.

Aquariums have proliferated since the National Aquarium opened in August 1981, because of the great success there as well as in Boston (1970) and in Monterey (1984). Large aquariums have recently opened, or are in active planning, in Camden, New Jersey; Chattanooga, Tennessee; Charleston, South Carolina; Cleveland, Ohio; New Orleans; and elsewhere. Chicago's pioneer Shedd Aquarium on Lake Michigan recently added a major "oceanarium" exhibit.

In planning its expansion to house marine mammals, the aquarium ran into opposition from animal rights advocates. There's a feeling that this facility may be the last of its kind for the foreseeable future because of the growing opposition to displaying these creatures even when they are born in captivity.

The Baltimore aquarium has encountered operational problems, as might be expected in such a complicated facility. One was that equipment housed under the marine mammal tank was too noisy, until the problem was corrected in a renovation in the mid-1980s. The new pavilion mammal tank has smaller tanks where the animals can rest, plus another that allows medical procedures to be done without having to drain the main facility—a feature said to be missing from the original design.[2] In the fall of 1993, the central tank was scheduled to be closed for a $10.3 million renovation.[3]

National Aquarium in Baltimore
Cost. $21.3 million
Source. 100 percent public financing
Dimensions. 115,000 square feet
Completion date. August 8, 1981
Notes. Major addition, 1990

Sponsor. Capt. Nicholas Brown, U.S. Navy, ret.
National Aquarium in Baltimore

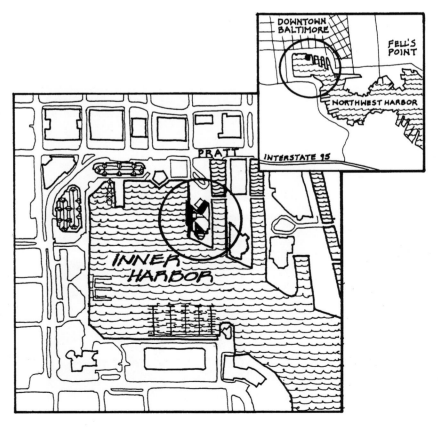

50 E. Pratt St./ Pier 3
Baltimore, MD 21202
(410) 576-3821

Sponsor. Honora Freeman
Baltimore Development Corporation
36 S. Charles St.
Baltimore, MD 21201
(410) 837-9305

Sponsor. Commissioner's Office
Department of Housing & Community
Development
417 E. Fayette St.
Baltimore, MD 21202
(410) 396-3232

Designer. Peter Chermayeff, FAIA
Cambridge Seven Associates, Inc.
1050 Massachusetts Ave.

Cambridge, MA 02138
(617) 492-7000

Exhibit Design. Frank Zaremba
Lyons/Zaremba, Inc.
153 Milk St.
Boston, MA 02109
(617) 330-9144

Structural Engineer. LeMessurier Consultants
1033 Massachusetts Ave.
Cambridge, MA 02138
(617) 868-1200

Lighting. H.M. Brandston & Partners, Inc.
1421 West 24th St.
New York, NY
(212) 924-4050

(*Balthazar Korab, Ltd.*)

Horace E. Dodge & Son Memorial Fountain
Hart Plaza
Detroit, Michigan
Top Honor Award 1988

Summary

A bold, powerful sculpture anchors riverfront plaza, symbolizes city.

Description. Rising 25 feet above the granite expanse of Hart Plaza, the stainless steel Dodge Fountain, designed by the late sculptor Isamu Noguchi together with Shoji Sadao, is a dramatic presence on the Detroit River.

The fountain is a civic contribution of Anna Thompson Dodge, who bequeathed $2 million for the project. The site, stipulated in her will, is located at the foot of the city's principal thoroughfare, Woodward Avenue.

A major feature of the sculpture is the imaginative use of water. Guided by a computer, the fountain runs through a sequence of 31 different combinations of water sprays and lighting arrangements. Noguchi described the fountain as "an engine for water." The water spray functions as a popular cooling-off spot in the summer. When it is lit at night, the bold, arched structure takes on an even more dramatic form, suggestive of the industrial power of Detroit and its machines.

The fountain, which cost $2.75 million to build in 1977, was renovated in 1988 for $800,000, financed by the City of Detroit and private and foundation contributions. The complexity of the original design caused early mechanical problems. The repairs included a thorough cleaning, pump repairs, valve replacements, new fountain lights, and a new control system.

The City of Detroit sponsors numerous festivals and events all year at the center-city plaza, from large summer ethnic festivals to winter skating. Its public role has helped fix the fountain in the city's mind as a fitting symbol for Detroit. In fact, it was used by the city's Bicentennial Commission in 1976 for this purpose.

The fountain and surrounding plaza are part of the first attempts at reviving Detroit's riverfront. Other projects include the adjoining Renaissance Center complex (also opened in 1977), along with Cobo Hall and Ford Auditorium, a bike trail, and nearby apartment towers. Despite criticism, especially of Renaissance Center for its fortresslike design, the projects connote an unwillingness to give up on downtown.

Up the Detroit River today there are now several investments, including public parks, private offices and housing, a planned marina, plus warehouse conversions—positive signs in a city where recurring bouts of unemployment have been coupled with major social problems. The Detroit riverfront, anchored by the Dodge Fountain, constitutes one of the bright spots in the beleaguered city.

Design Features. The description of the Dodge Fountain attests to its boldness and dramatic size. The twin legs of the sculpture are 5 feet in diameter, and have a stride, or width between them, of 78 feet. Serving the fountain's sprays is

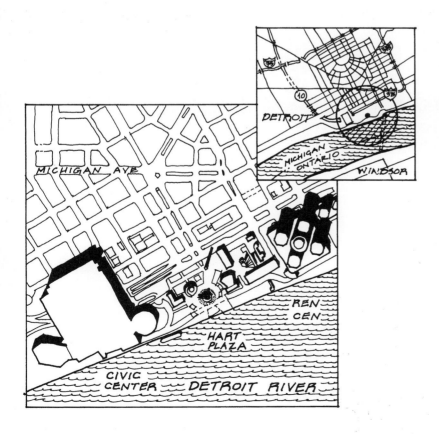

a reservoir below the plaza that holds 55,000 gallons of water. Pumps are capable of delivering 17,000 gallons per minute.

The ring section of the fountain measures 24 feet in diameter. There are 24 bays in the middle section, or torus, each with 14 holes for nozzles and lights. Nozzles in the fountain's center send a stream of water 35 feet in the air.

The skin and space frame comprising the sculpture weight a total of 30 tons.

Appraisal.   The design is simple and bold. The water sprays, especially when illuminated at night, are spectacular.

In addition to its artistic strength, the fountain serves as a water play area in warm summer weather, helping to animate the surrounding plaza.

Hart Plaza, also designed by Noguchi, is an example of a hard-edge design more in favor in the 1970s than at present. To many it is off-putting in its wide, open spacing without benefit of many trees or much in the way of seating. The Waterfront Center jury award in 1988 was to the Noguchi fountain sculpture only.

Horace E. Dodge & Son Memorial Fountain
Cost. Original fountain, $2.75 million; renovation, $800,000

Source. $2 million from Dodge family, remainder from City of Detroit
Dimensions. 11,500 square feet
Completion date. 1977

Sponsor. Mayor Coleman Young
    City of Detroit
    1126 City-County Building
    Detroit, MI 48226
    (313) 224-3400

Sponsor. Daniel H. Krichbaum
    Recreation Department, Water Board Building
    735 Randolph St.
    Detroit, MI 48226
    (313) 224-1100

Sculptor. Isamu Noguchi (deceased)
    Fuller & Sadao, PC Architects
    32-37 Vernon Blvd.
    Long Island City, NY 11106
    (718) 278-1954

Fountain consultant. Richard Chaix
    P.O. Box 3565
    Carmel, CA 93921
    (408) 624-8824

Structural engineer. Weidlinger Associates
    333 7th Ave.
    New York, NY 10001
    (212) 563-5200

(George Heinrich)

Lake Harriet Bandshell
Lake Harriet and
West 42nd Street
Minneapolis, Minnesota

Summary

An exquisite lakeside public concert shell that sings entirely on its own.

Description. Minneapolis is blessed with a major chain of lakes within the city limits that are a significant feature of its park system. The Lake Harriet Bandshell, completed in 1986, sits on the northwest shore of Lake Harriet, one of the largest of these connected lakes.

On a typical summer weekend, Lake Harriet and the park are very busy. A divided walkway around the lake is heavily used by hikers, runners, bikers, bladers, and families with strollers. Weekend concerts at the bandshell draw large crowds that quickly fill up the formal bench seating provided for performances. Picnickers sprawl over a nearby hillside with grand views of the bandshell and the lake.

The bandshell and adjoining refectory is a landmark within an old-fashioned park full of green space, picnic benches, trees, and boating, fishing, and swimming areas. The present bandshell carries on a tradition of music facilities in the park. First was a Grand Pavilion of 1888, followed by a Pagoda Pavilion in 1891, a Classic in 1904, and a 1927 Bandstand.

The major feature of the 2850-square-foot structure is the large glass-paned window that serves as a backdrop for the performers and affords a view of the lake. Immediately behind the lake is a dock for a tour boat and other vessels. The building, a project of the parks department, cost $495,000 plus $205,000 for site work and landscaping.

The adjacent refectory complex echoes the bandshell in design and houses food concessions, storage, receiving areas, public toilets, and a central pavilion that is used as a warming hut by winter skaters.

Attractive landscaping enhances both the bandshell and the refectory.

Design Features. Taking its cue from 1891 park structures, some of which still remain on site (albeit neglected), the design of this bandshell is both strong and romantic. This is no small, delicate pavilion for a few performers, but rather a major concert stage capable of housing an orchestra.

Simple gray shingles and white trim work beautifully in the park setting. Four tall turrets at each corner of the stage area are topped with white pennants and lend a very festive air. White lattice work adds a decorative touch throughout. Even the stage area is finely done; especially beautiful is its ceiling. The huge window on the lakeside is a brilliant stroke.

Appraisal. This beautiful and romantic bandshell provides the citizens of Minneapolis who frequent this park with a building that will forever conjure up memories of happy summertimes. The Lake Harriet Bandshell is a model

(*Breen/Rigby*)

for other park departments as a distinctive example of doing something not only well, but exceptionally well.

Lake Harriet Bandshell
Cost. Building, $495,000; site work and landscaping, $205,000
Dimensions. 10 acres, building 2850 square feet
Completion date. 1986

Sponsor. Gary H. Criter
Minneapolis Parks and Recreation Board
310 Fourth Ave. South
Minneapolis, MN 55402
(612) 348-2142

Designer. Milo H. Thompson
Bentz/Thompson/Rietow, Inc.
2600 Foshay Tower, No. 2600
Minneapolis, MN 55402
(612) 332-1234

Structural/electrical engineer. Bakke Kopp Ballou & McFarlin
219 North Second St.
Minneapolis, MN 55401
(612) 333-7101

Acoustical engineer. Kirkegaard & Associates, Inc.
4910 Main St.
Downers Grove, IL 60515
(708) 810-5980

Designer. Martin & Pitz Associates, Inc.
1409 Willow St.
Minneapolis, MN 55403
(612) 871-0568

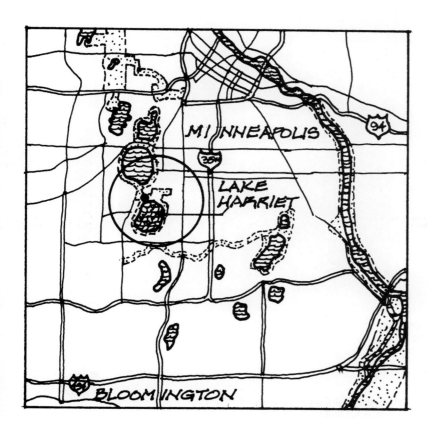

Understated entrance to Monterey Bay Aquarium echoes the feel of the sardine factories that once thrived here. (*Monterey Bay Aquarium*)

Monterey Bay Aquarium
886 Cannery Row
Monterey, California
Top Honor Award 1987

Summary

An educational bellwether and singularly handsome architectural tribute to historic Cannery Row and Monterey Bay.

Aquarium opens to and engages the bay that is the focus of its exhibits. (*Monterey Bay Aquarium*)

Description. Rising on the 2.2-acre site of the old Hovden cannery, built in 1916 and in operation until 1972, is this 216,000-square-foot aquarium. The cannery was one of the last to go, after the sardines disappeared.

The aquarium opened in October 1984, and attracted 2.3 million people in its first year of operation. Since then crowds have averaged 1.8 million visitors annually.

The aquarium's stated mission is to "stimulate interest, increase knowledge and promote stewardship of Monterey Bay and the world's ocean environment through innovative exhibits, public education and scientific research." By concentrating on and emphasizing the local Monterey Bay ecosystem in its exhibits, the aquarium broke new ground in the aquarium field. Traditionally, aquariums featured exotic species from throughout the world. Unlike many aquariums, the visitor is not programmed here on a single path, but rather is free to roam the facility according to his or her interests.

The popular centerpiece of the Monterey aquarium is the Giant Kelp Tank, which holds 335,000 gallons of water, rises two stories, and is open to the sky. Seven-inch-thick, clear acrylic walls, weighing well over 2 tons and manufactured by Mitsubishi Rayon Company in Japan, house this exhibit. Schooling anchovies in the kelp tank are fed daily by a diver, to the delight of the audience. A two-story, 55,000-gallon sea

otter exhibit is another major attraction. The aquarium, as part of its conservation mission, conducts a sea otter research, rescue, and care program.

More than 6500 specimens, representing 525 species of animals, plants, and birds, fill 23 gallery spaces. The open-air aviary contains the world of shore birds, and a tide pool vividly displays wave action. Touch tanks overseen by volunteers allow a special learning experience. The educational staff recruits, trains, and supports more than 600 volunteers, who donate more than 60,000 hours annually. About 125 new guides are trained each year during a 48-hour, college-level course.

By the close of 1991, close to 500,000 students had visited the aquarium for free tours and classes. A series of teacher institutes, supported by a $500,000 National Science Foundation grant, is offered to science teachers of all grade levels.

Several historical artifacts and interpretive displays incorporate the unique cultural setting of the aquarium. A special Cannery Row exhibit area tells the story of the days when the seafood industry was king and Monterey was the "Sardine Capital of the World."

Complementing the exhibit areas are a 183-seat ocean-view restaurant, a 273-seat auditorium, a gift and bookshop, plus research and office spaces.

Three original smokestacks from the Hovden Cannery have been reconstructed. Restored boilers are on view, while the remainder of the aquarium is new construction.

The aquarium project—the brainchild of four biologists from the neighboring Hopkins Marine Station—was initially backed by funds from the Packard Family (namely, a $50 million gift). The philanthropists' daughter, Dr. Nancy Burnett, was one of the four biologists who brought the idea to her father. Her sister, Julie Packard, also a marine biologist, is the director of the aquarium today. The institution is self-supporting.

A new wing is scheduled to open in 1996, designed by Esherick Homsey Dodge and Davis of San Francisco, architects of the original building. It will be in "Cannery Row style," and will be devoted to regional offshore and deep submarine canyon environments. Its centerpiece will be a 1-million-gallon exhibit to showcase these outer Monterey Bay waters. Also planned is a permanent gallery of delicate jellyfish. Total project cost is $50 million, to come from operating revenues and contributions.

Design Features.   Perched on the curving shoreline of Monterey Bay, the physical setting is dramatically beautiful. Rather than facing inward, the architecture—with ample overwater decks, outdoor perches, and huge windows—takes full advantage of the waterfront, affording fabulous views and direct contact with the sounds and smell of the sea.

The Monterey Aquarium is spectacular and unassuming at the same time. From the street, the facade is quintessentially vernacular. It fits in so comfortably, it is hard to believe you are approaching a new, multimillion-dollar aquarium.

One critic summarized the building well:

> It is almost non-architecture: a forthright, no-nonsense, concrete, glass, and wooden edifice with gently sloping "factory" roofs and expansive windows that blend in with the rest of Cannery Row....Throughout the facility, there's an unabashed use of industrial fittings. Air ducts and water pipes hang undisguised from the ceilings.
>
> Yet despite all this purposefulness, there is nothing plain about the interior. The displays resound with the aquarium's ecological message, giving the

Monterey Bay Aquarium trademark kelp tank with diver, on twice-daily feeding. (*Monterey Bay Aquarium*)

(Jane Lidz)

entire complex a deeply affecting sense of spiritual celebration.[4]

A minor flaw is a lack of quality public access to the waterfront around the aquarium. At the current facility, unless you enter the aquarium itself, and pay, daytime access to the water's edge is provided only at the end of a service driveway. This no doubt complies with California permitting requirements, but it misses the intent. It should be noted that the new wing promises to offer "free public access to the waterfront."[5]

Appraisal. Steinbeck's novel, *Cannery Row*, celebrated the honest, gritty nature of the industrial waterfront and the work of dedicated marine biologist Ed ("Doc") Ricketts. The design of the Monterey Bay Aquarium and its ongoing work respect this legacy.

The Monterey Bay Aquarium broke new ground in the field by celebrating the local environment and ecology.

Probably more than any other public aquarium now in existence, the Monterey Bay Aquarium represents the "state of the art." The designers were not subject to elected officials and the city coffers. They had plenty of capital and a long lead time. They were able to study other aquariums, identify their problems, and learn from their mistakes.[6]

While it should be recognized that the private nature of the aquarium's funding had some definite advantages, these conditions don't automatically spell success, so credit goes to the multitalented design team.

This extraordinary aquarium accomplished its educational and esthetic goals, and also has had major economic impact on this once-derelict waterfront.

Monterey Bay Aquarium
  Cost. $50 million
  Source. Private donation
  Dimensions. 216,000 square feet
  Completion date. 1984

Sponsor. Julie Packard, Executive Director
  Monterey Bay Aquarium
  886 Cannery Row
  Monterey, CA 93940
  (408) 648-4800

Project manager. Linda Rhodes
  Rhodes/Dahl
  867 Wave St.
  Monterey, CA 93940
  (408) 647-1122

Designer. Charles M. Davis
  Esherick Homsey, Dodge and Davis
  2789 25th St.
  San Francisco, CA 94110
  (415) 285-9193

Structural/civil/marine engineer. Hal Davis
    Rutherford & Chekene
    303 Second St., Suite 800N
    San Francisco, CA 94107
    (415) 495-4222

Mechanical/electrical engineer. Syska and Hennessey
    120 Montgomery St.
    San Francisco, CA 94104
    (415) 788-6000

Exhibits design. Ace Design
    301 Industrial Center Bldg.
    Sausalito, CA 94965
    (415) 332-9390

Exhibits design. Bios
    84 University, Suite 800 North
    Seattle, WA 98101
    (206) 587-2451

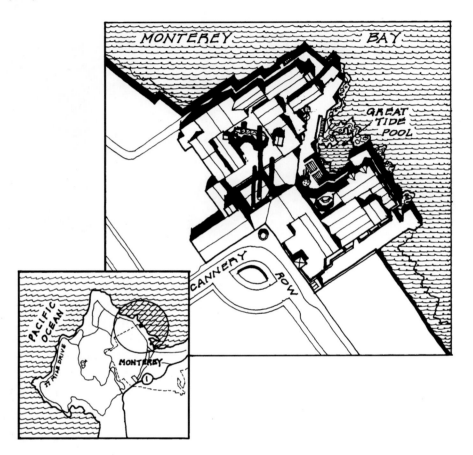

(*Harbourfront Centre*)

Programming Facilities
Harbourfront
Toronto, Ontario, Canada

Summary

One of the most ambitious waterfront programming venues anywhere, housed in three imaginatively reused industrial structures.

Description. The extensive programming/events activities of Harbourfront Corp., designed to lure citizens to an isolated and initially unwelcoming waterfront site, are based in three distinctive structures originally built for the shipping industry, plus adjoining outdoor space. The principal facilities are:

- York Quay Centre, a 50,000-square-foot former trucking warehouse converted to a venue for a mixture of arts, crafts, and performances, with adjoining park

- The Arts Complex, in a converted power plant and adjoining ice house now containing an art gallery and the du Maurier Theater Centre

- The Premier Dance Theater, on the third floor of Queen's Quay Terminal, a massive warehouse that is now a mixed-use complex (see Queen's Quay Terminal, Chapter 4).

The York Quay Centre is the focus of the events sponsored by Harbourfront Corp., originally an entity charged with development, management, and promotion of a 100-acre downtown waterfront site. Now, after years of controversy (see Chapter 1), it is involved only in cultural activities and public events. Its name is now Harbourfront Centre.

York Quay Centre houses the Studio Theater, the Water's Edge Cafe, and the Brigantine Room for special events. The center offers concerts, films, and live theater, as well as providing studio space for craftspeople. There's a special children's center also.

At its peak in the early 1980s, the events programming housed in the three facilities was exemplary. At one time Harbourfront Corp. had five programming departments that managed to fill the calendar 12 months a year, 7 days a week, and 16 hours a day. In all, Harbourfront Corp. ran as many as 4000 separate events that attracted 3[fr1/2] million people in one year.[7]

The events programming began in 1974, two years after Harbourfront Corp. was established as a Crown Corporation (i.e., an entity of the federal government). It set out to promote events that are not usually seen in Toronto. For instance, literary readings were offered in the 1970s, and by 1980 there was an International Festival of Authors at Harbourfront.

The Power Plant Gallery, opened in 1987, shows the work of contemporary Canadian artists. Modern dance is featured in the Premiere Dance Theater, opened in 1983.

The range of events extends far beyond cultural activity. Extensive use of the location by school children and festivals featuring various ethnic groups that make up today's Toronto have been part of the Harbourfront program as well. Other popular events range from a barbecue rib cook-off to a vegetarian fair, and from body-building tournaments to a New Year's Eve party.

Harbourfront Corp. ran into trouble in the mid-1980s, bumping into a recession at a time it was due to become self-supporting. Subsequently, all planning and development responsibility moved elsewhere. Harbourfront Centre still managed into the 1990s to host a major schedule of programmed events across a wide spectrum.

Appraisal. The economic and political difficulties encountered at Harbourfront should not detract from the bold and innovative programming that has occurred there for nearly 20 years, or the imaginatively adaptively reused spaces that house them. The pioneering programming contributions of the late Ann Tindall in her work at Harbourfront are particularly noteworthy.

Harbourfront Programming Facilities

Cost. $100 million total public investment, 1986

Dimensions. York Quay Centre, 50,000 square feet, including duMaurier Theatre, 416 seats; studio theater, 206 seats; Shipwreck Stage, accommodating 3300, plus crafts studio, 4000 square feet; Arts Complex, 3200 square meters; Premier Dance Theater, 446 seats; Ann Tindall Park, 3.5 acres

Established. 1976

Notes. Arts Center remodeled in 1991

Sponsor. William J.S. Boyle, general manager
Harbourfront Centre (formerly Harbourfront Corp.)
410 Queens Quay West, Suite 500
Toronto, Ontario, Canada M5V 2Z3
(416) 973-4955

Designer, arts complex. Peter Smith
Lett-Smith Architects
99 Crowns Lane, 5th Floor
Toronto, Ontario, Canada M5R 3P4
(416) 924-5780

Designer, York Quay Centre. Henry Schefter
Schefter & McCallum Architects
122 Pears Ave.
Toronto, Ontario, Canada M5R 1T2
(416) 922-4946

Designer, Premiere Dance Theater. Eberhard H. Zeidler
Zeidler Roberts Partnership
315 Queen St. West
Toronto, Ontario, Canada M5V 2X2
(416) 596-8300

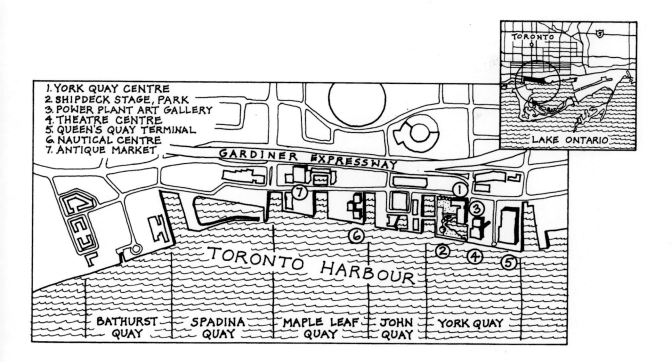

1. YORK QUAY CENTRE
2. SHIPDECK STAGE, PARK
3. POWER PLANT ART GALLERY
4. THEATRE CENTRE
5. QUEEN'S QUAY TERMINAL
6. NAUTICAL CENTRE
7. ANTIQUE MARKET

GARDINER EXPRESSWAY

TORONTO HARBOUR

BATHURST QUAY · SPADINA QUAY · MAPLE LEAF QUAY · JOHN QUAY · YORK QUAY

TORONTO

LAKE ONTARIO

Notes for Chapter 2

1. *The Wall Street Journal,* Nov. 22, 1985.

2. *The* (Baltimore) *Evening Sun,* Sept. 14, 1989, p. E1.

3. *The Washington Post,* May 4, 1992, p. B6.

4. Thomas Hoving, "Museum of the Sea," *Connoisseur,* March 1985, pp. 85, 87.

5. Press release, Monterey Bay Aquarium, Oct. 10, 1991.

6. Eleanor Smith, "Monterey's Natural Aquarium," *Oceans,* no. 6, 1984, p. 11.

7. The Waterfront Center, *Urban Waterfronts '86,* p. 61.

≈3≈

The Environmental Waterfront

Our eyes do not divide us from the world, but unite us with it. Let this be known to be true. Let us then abandon the simplicity of separation and give unity its due. Let us abandon the self-mutilation which has been our way and give expression to the potential harmony of man-nature. The world is abundant, we require only a deference born of understanding to fulfill man's promise. Man is that uniquely conscious creature who can perceive and express. He must become the steward of the biosphere. To do this he must design with nature.

IAN L. MCHARG,
*Design with Nature**

---

*The Natural History Press , Garden City, NY, 1969.

Hans Suter Wildlife Area, Corpus Christi, Tex. (*Malcolm Matthews*)

Hans Suter Wildlife Area
Ennis Joslin Road
Corpus Christi, Texas

Summary

Natural area near city center made accessible and informative.

Description/Design Features. For the modest sum of $250,000, the City of Corpus Christi has made a wetland area on Oso Bay readily accessible. The site, 22 acres along one of the major routes to and from downtown Corpus Christi, enables residents to easily explore a natural coastal area.

Facilities include parking, trails and a boardwalk, overlooks, and a sturdy, well-designed interpretive kiosk. In overall approach, natural values are emphasized and design intervention is kept to the minimum needed to enable people to explore the area. Parking is gravel, for instance, with paved accessways to the highway.

At the northern end is a boardwalk and viewing platform. Closer to Ennis Joslin Road is one of two parking areas feeding a hiking/biking trail. At the southern end is an additional small, but adequate, parking lot, a children's play area, and picnic spots.

The park, adjacent to a sewage treatment facility, contains a productive marsh area. Across the highway is a park with heavily used ballfields. The Suter Wildlife Area is home to a significant bird population.

Appraisal. This park demonstrates how useful a low-key, well-designed project emphasizing natural values can enrich a community's waterfront. Hans Suter Wildlife Area occupies a patch of land previously thought to be generally useless, if not positively dangerous, in an abandoned, out-of-the-way location.

The park transforms the area into a place used year 'round, for a variety of pursuits including nature education, birding, picnics, and walking. Neighbors who avoided the area before now feel comfortable walking in it at night.

Hans A. Suter Wildlife Area

Cost. $250,000
Dimensions. 22 acres
Completion date. May 19, 1987

Sponsor. Linda Strong, Corpus Christi City Council
340 Cape May
Corpus Christi, TX 78412
(512) 880-3105

Designer. Malcolm Matthews, landscape architect
City of Corpus Christi Park & Recreation Dept.
P.O. Box 9277
Corpus Christi, TX 78469
(512) 880-3464

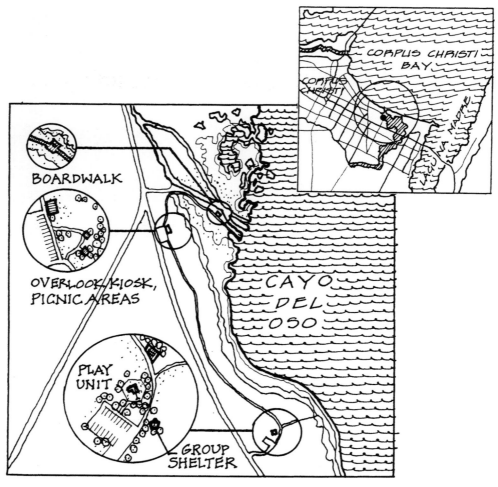

BOARDWALK

OVERLOOK, KIOSK, PICNIC AREAS

PLAY UNIT

GROUP SHELTER

CORPUS CHRISTI BAY

CORPUS CHRISTI

CAYO DEL OSO

Centennial Park, Howard County, Md. (*LDR International, Inc.*)

Centennial Park
Maryland Route 108
Howard County, Maryland

Summary

Open-space preserve with attractive appointments, acquired in advance of burgeoning suburbs between Baltimore and Washington.

Description. Once located amid rolling farmland, the 325 acres in Centennial Park are surrounded now by housing developments and are next to a busy intersection. County officials, anticipating the growth that has taken place, particularly since establishment of the nearby suburban new town of Columbia in 1967, began acquiring the site 25 years ago. The first purpose was flood control and protection of the Patuxent River watershed; initial planning was by the Soil Conservation Service. Site acquisition began with funds from a county transfer tax, aided by state and federal matching funds. Planning began in 1975, with a basic aim of retaining a bit of what rural Howard County was like before its recent development. Thus much of the land area is meadow and woodland.

The lake that is central to the park is from a flood-control dam on the eastern side of the site. A path circles the lake, frequently in woods, past boat launches, fishing spots, overlooks, and a natural preserve. Active sports facilities, such as tennis courts, are on the perimeter of the park, so as to be readily accessible to nearby homes, and leaving the center more natural.

Centennial Park, ranging as it does over a considerable rolling expanse, can and does handle a variety of activities. It's a favorite spot for runners, walkers, and strollers. There's fishing (the lake has small- and large-mouthed bass), a summer camp for kids, canoe and paddleboat rentals, a spot for lunch, and county-sponsored events.

There are also quiet areas and natural spots along the lake trail. The linear lake runs through the middle of the site and is almost constantly in view.

Design Features. The key design decision here was to minimize intervention on the land surrounding the new lake. There is thus a large meadow left intact, some of which is being let return to woodland.

The philosophy here is to create a preserve in a formerly rural county as major development spreads nearby. This allows visitors to experience, for instance, a farm pond and its community of wildlife and fish, as well as to be able to see the succession from a meadow to a woodland.

A key feature is picnic shelters and related structures scattered skillfully through the site. At the center of the park is a three-part shelter, with a concession stand and picnic seating built over the lake; a boat rental facility and restrooms adjoin, all of the same distinctive design, linked by a wooden walkway. Each structure has a peaked metal roof, tan plank siding, and is open

1. NATURAL RESERVE
2. ORGANIZED SPORTS
3. FISHING PAVILION
4. NATURE CENTER
5. BOAT LAUNCH
6. BOAT DOCK
7. AMPITHEATER
8. OVERLOOK
9. MEADOWS
10. PICNIC
11. POND

on all sides. At a cluster of five such shelters near a natural amphitheater, the principal building has a stone fireplace and angled decks overlooking the lake. The buildings manage to convey a rustic, summer camp feeling while being decidedly modern. After more than five years of use (the park was dedicated June 13, 1987), the structures are in excellent condition.

Appraisal. The county officials who in the early 1960s had the foresight to acquire this sizable watershed preserve are to be commended. That action made possible the distinctive, naturalistic approach employed later by the landscape architects here.

Where Centennial Park falls down is in the area of interpretation and explanation to the visitor of what has been preserved. The opportunity to acquaint the public, especially youngsters, with the richness of species, habitats, and wildlife contained in the park is missed here.

Also, there is no map at the main entry point, even though the park is in two parts and has several entrances. Directional signs are highway department style and don't fit with the more natural entrance signs, or the place itself.

Centennial Park
Cost. $6 million
Dimensions. 325 acres
Completion date. 1987

Sponsor. Rebecca Horvath, Director
Howard County Department Recreation and Parks
3300 North Ridge Rd., Suite 170
Ellicott City, MD 21043
(410) 313-7255

Designer. Donald F. Hilderbrandt
Land Design/Research, Inc.
9175 Guilford Rd., Suite 100
Columbia, MD 21046
(301) 792-4360

Lake Forest Park Beach Protection, Restoration and Recreational Development, Lake Forest, Ill. (Files of JJR)

Forest Park Beach Shoreline Protection, Restoration and Recreational Development Lake Forest, Illinois

Summary

Engineering solutions transform a dismal, diminishing shoreline beach into a multiuse recreation facility.

Description. The City of Lake Forest on Lake Michigan, north of Chicago, was in danger of losing its public lakefront beach and park to erosion. Continued high lake water levels, as well as wave and storm damage, had taken a severe toll, with resulting loss of beach, roadway, and boating areas.

In 1984 a 23-member Shoreline Restoration Advisory Committee began oversight of a plan process for the protection and restoration of 3400 linear feet of shoreline. Besides protecting the beach resource itself, the community wanted a usable park that incorporated the natural beauty of the area. The "forest" in Lake Forest aptly describes the heavily treed areas that grace the bluff areas above and along the shoreline. The entire park area consists of the breakwaters, the beach, the wooded bluff area, and a preexisting neighborhood passive park, Forest Park.

A total project cost of $9.1 million included the construction of a series of offshore breakwaters to absorb incoming waves and onshore revetments placed to protect the land behind them.

An extensive sand beach has been restored. Beach shelters, play areas, benches, walkways, boat launches and storage, other recreational facilities, parking areas, and new roads combine to make a multifaceted lakefront community recreational facility.

Design Features. In a departure from the perpendicular groins often used for shoreline protection, Lake Forest's rubble mound breakwaters run parallel to the shoreline with the appearance of artificial stone "sand bars." They are constructed in three layers, using quarry stones ranging in size from 1 pound to 10 tons. Pedestrian access by way of a jetty is provided on one of the breakwaters for fishing. The jetty facility also allowed construction of a protected small-boat harbor.

The restored sand beach undulates gracefully and includes a small play area. A concrete walkway alongside the beach provides joggers/bikers/strollers comfortable access near the lake. The lighting fixtures and benches (many with plaques indicating a local donation)

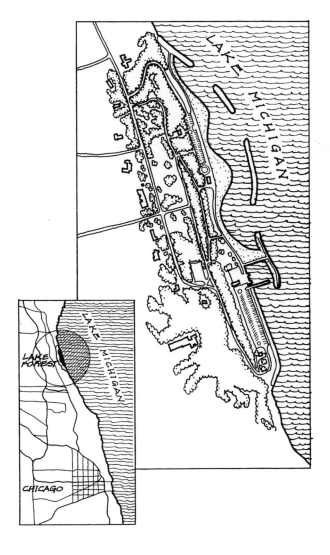

and all of the public buildings are of simple, attractive design. A full range of activities has been accommodated, from windsurfing to biking to winter uses, with appropriate facilities provided. On a cold, windy January day, resident walkers and joggers were using the park. Several were socializing around a blazing fireplace in one of the open-air shelters.

A 4-foot-wide timber walkway carries pedestrians through a heavily wooded bluff area connecting the beach with Forest Park above. Built-in benches and overlooks are provided as part of the walkway, with views out over the lake. Driveways allow cars to enter along paved surface at either end of the project.

Appraisal. In judging and appraising an engineering project such as this, lay opinions must rely on the documentation that the system was extensively tested in laboratories and that the project passed the necessary standards of the relevant environmental permitting authorities. Only time will tell, but for the moment this shoreline erosion-control technique appears to be successful.

Confident that shoreline erosion was under control, the community rescued a doomed beach and transformed the entire area into a very attractive community multiuse recreation facility. The diversity of environments—sandy beach, lakeside promenade, "catwalk" through the trees, lawns of the old park, provision for boating of all kinds, picnicking areas, and play space—all add to a broadly appealing environment.

Forest Park Beach is open only to the residents of Lake Forest. Without a local permit, parking is prohibited, effectively putting the area out of reach. Many community beaches in other parts of the country allow for day trippers who pay a fee. A provision for this eventuality did not appear on the signs.

Forest Park Beach
  Cost. $9.1 million
  Dimensions. 3400 linear feet
  Completion date. 1987

Sponsor. Robert Kiely Jr, City Manager
  The City of Lake Forest
  220 E. Deerpath
  Lake Forest, IL 60045
  (708) 234-2600

Coastal engineer. W. F. Baird
  W. F. Baird & Associates
  38 Antares Drive, Suite 150
  Ottawa, Ontario, Canada K2E 7V2
  (613) 225-6560

Engineer. Bruce A. Weber
  EWI Engineering Assoc., Inc. (formerly Warzyn Engineering)
  8383 Greenway Blvd.
  Middleton, WI 53562
  (608) 231-4747

Engineer. Fred Klancnik
  Johnson Johnson & Roy, inc.
  110 Miller
  Ann Arbor, MI 48104
  (313) 662-4457

Sellwood Riverfront Park, Portland, Ore. (*Mayer-Reed/Schwartz*)

Sellwood Riverfront Park
Willamette River
Portland, Oregon

Summary

A riverfront park in a floodplain, sensitive to natural values and conditions, created from an abandoned indusrial trcct

Description. Sellwood Riverfront Park is an 8-acre park on the Willamette River several miles from downtown, adjoining and serving the Sellwood neighborhood of Portland.

The site was used by one of the city's original sawmills, until fire destroyed the operation. The site remained in a derelict state for 40 years, during which time it was adopted by neighbors as an informal type of park, providing such features as a climbable tree, a pond with frogs, and blackberry-picking opportunities. The riverfront itself, however, was difficult to get to.

With a modest investment of $305,000, the City of Portland has succeeded in restoring the site to a more natural state, including a small pond and a wooded section. The small riverfront beach is now easily reached, and a viewing platform has been provided. A floating dock provides a boat tie-up and a chance to fish.

The edge is reinforced to sustain periodic flood waters.

Design Features. Principal among the features restored is a spring-fed pond and adjoining wetland. A walkway takes the visitor across the pond, at the edge of the landscaped portion of the park. There's also a path around most of the pond, allowing direct contact with its inhabitants. Beyond is a wooded area, a natural wildlife habitat that also has been enhanced. A path allows visitors to penetrate this area. At the river's edge are wildflowers and grasses.

A well-designed restroom facility is supplied, set amid an open area circled by pathways and well endowed with trees. A parking lot adjoins (charging a small fee during the summer), shared with an office structure. The park is also visible from a nearby bridge over the Willamette River.

Appraisal. Overall, the design and layout is straightforward, unpretentious, informal, yet sensitive to the site's natural values. The park designers aimed for what they termed a "Huckleberry Finn" atmosphere in what is a conscious preservation and enhancement project.

The strength of Sellwood Park is the bit of natural riverfront reestablished and made accessible, relatively close to the center of a major city. One can imagine its popularity with the nearby

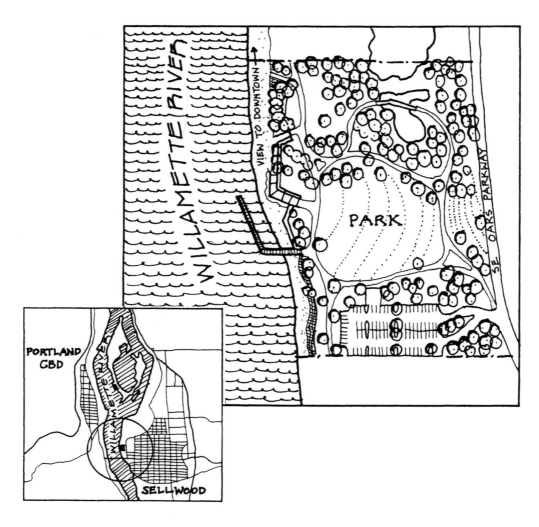

neighborhoods for picnics (facilities are provided), sunbathing, investigations of pond life and the woods, or just quietly watching the river.

The park serves as an effective balance to the nearby Portland Pioneer Park, which emphasizes traditional active sports facilities, and The Oaks Park, an amusement park.

Sellwood Riverfront Park makes for an impressive bit of waterfront carved out for the public, whose naturalness contrasts with the new, three-story office building beside it, River Park Center. Missed is an opportunity to supply interpretive material about the flora and fauna much in evidence, or about the ecology of the river.

Sellwood Riverfront Park
   Cost. $305,000
   Dimensions. 8 acres
   Completion date. 1986

Sponsor. John Sewell
   City of Portland, Bureau of Parks and Recreation
   1120 S.W. Fifth Ave., Room 502
   Portland, OR 97204
   (503) 796-5116

Sponsor. Commissioner Mike Lindberg
   City of Portland
   1220 S.W. Fifth Ave.
   Portland, OR 97204
   (503) 823-4145

Designer. Carol Mayer-Reed and Michael C. Schwartz
   Mayer/Reed Schwartz, Associated Landscape Architects
   319 S.W. Washington, Suite 820
   Portland, OR 97204
   (503) 223-5953

Part of the grading and excavation that went into the rehabilitation of the Harmon Meadows wetland. Machinery placed on a mat to minimize soil compression. (*Albert Cattan*)

Harmon Meadow Wetland Restoration
Hackensack Meadowlands
Secaucus, New Jersey

Summary

Three miles from Manhattan, a restored wetland flourishes beside massive mixed-use development.

Description. The Harmon Meadow wetland area is a huge, flat expanse split by the New Jersey Turnpike just outside Manhattan. Within the meadow beside the Hackensack River, on a total of 20,000 acres, is the Meadowlands Sports Complex, consisting of a stadium, arena, and racetrack.

The wetland restoration is immediately adjoining, and part of, a $1 billion complex built by Hartz Mountain Industries, Inc., one of the area's largest developers. The project and wetland restoration is in Secaucus.

In order to receive a permit to establish the Harmon Meadow complex of office, shopping, hotel, recreation, and, ultimately, residential uses on 127 acres of filled marsh, the developer agreed to restore to a biologically healthy condition a total of 158 acres of marsh. The first phases of this work, accomplished between 1984 and 1989, include 123 acres in two major sites straddling and visible from the Turnpike. A total of $7 million has been spent in the effort.

The condition of the meadowlands when work began was that of a degraded, abused area, dominated by the Phragmites reed that stifles other life forms. This common reed is an invasive species that becomes so dense that birds, animals, and other life can't compete. The meadowland had been visited by 150 years of pollution from municipal and industrial wastes and was used for years as a dump. It was drained, diked, and filled during times when wetlands were called swamps and their value as habitats poorly understood. Water flow was curbed by dams outside the area.

Several steps were needed in the restoration. One was to dig out canals to permit brackish water from the nearby Hackensack River to flow into the site and wash over the area at high tide. This was necessary to curb the Phragmites reed, which does not tolerate salty water well, and to encourage the better type of marsh grass that was planted, known as Spartina. To make daily flooding possible, part of the marsh was graded, taking off a top layer to lower the site so that the tide could reach it. A total of 89,000 cubic yards of dredged material were removed, without damaging the underlying soils. Pads were used for construction equipment, to prevent compression of organic materials below.

Monitoring since the restoration has established that expanded populations of various kinds of flora and fauna have taken up residence. An investigator with the Hackensack Meadowlands Development Commission found, at midpoint in the restoration work, a population explosion among worms, snails, and small crustaceans. In one square meter Dr. Mark Kraus counted an average of 5000 such creatures; in a control area in prerestoration condition there were 107.[1] Many birds are now found in the area, and as the waters are gradually cleaned up as a result of new treatment facilities, a more abundant fish population is expected. Canoeing is now a popular activity within this unique urban wild.

Design Features. The restoration of a portion of the Harmon Meadowlands to something like its original condition, flooded twice daily by tides from nearby Newark Bay, took sensitive engineering. Keys were the placement of the new canals and the determination of the new elevations in the area to allow normal wetland functioning.

Seeding with Spartina has been successful (10 seeds per square foot) in establishing this desirable species over most of the two principal sites. Little intrusion by the Phragmites reed is evident thus far. Dredged material was piled in knolls around the site, which have become rich habitats for birds and animals.

Because these techniques are relatively new, it will be necessary to keep a close watch on how the restored wetland fares over time. Environmental groups, state agencies, the development commission, local governments, the consulting engineering firm TAMS, and the developer, Hartz Mountain, all have a stake in the outcome.

Appraisal. A two-year monitoring program was completed in 1991, confirming earlier reports of a greatly expanded wildlife population in the mitigation area. Waterfowl, waders, gulls, terns, and shorebirds now are seen in significant numbers.

Billboards along the New Jersey Turnpike announce the restoration, but little appears to have been done otherwise to use the site for education. It was reported that a New York City high school class, studying engineering, was greatly interested in seeing the project firsthand. This suggests that more such educational work with area schools could employ the restored marsh with great impact. There is one point on the western site, for example, where a restored section adjoins the unrestored marsh; the contrast is vivid and readily makes the point about what constitutes a healthy wetland.

Looking across the marsh affords a dramatic sight: In the foreground is North Bergen, across the Palisades are the tops of the towers of Manhattan, clearly visible.

Harmon Meadow Wetland Restoration
  Cost. $7 million
  Source. 100 percent private financing
  Dimensions. 158 acres
  Completion date. April 1989

Sponsor. Ed Cole
  Hartz Mountain Industries, Inc.
  400 Plaza Drive
  Secaucus, NJ 07094
  (201) 348-1200

Sponsor. Anthony Scardino, Executive Director
  Hackensack Meadowlands Development
  Commission
  1 DeKorte Park Plaza
  Lyndhurst, NJ 07071
  (201) 240-1722

Civil and environmental engineers. G. Barrie
  Heinzenknecht
  TAMS Consultants
  655 Third Ave.
  New York, NY 10017
  (212) 867-1777

Horticultural consultant. Environmental Concern
  P.O. Box P
  St. Michaels, MD 21663
  (410) 745-9620

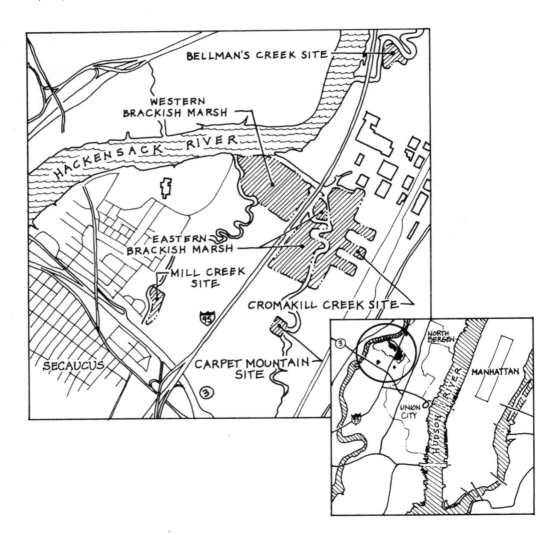

Marketing Corporation of America offices, Westport Conn.(*Environmental Design Associates P.C.*)

Marketing Corporation of America Headquarters 285 Riverside Avenue Westport, Connecticut

Summary

A disturbed wetland restored and made accessible as part of an office project.

Description. A five-building office park not far from the center of Westport occupies the site of a former car dealership. That use left a damaged Saugatuck River edge, where fill and trash had accumulated on 0.3 acre of the property. The fill was also a gathering spot for drainage from the car operations.

As part of a complicated and disputed approval process, Marketing Corporation of America agreed to restore the shore, build a pathway and boat launch, and plant new cordgrass as well as landscape the edge.

The restoration removed the fill and stabilized the boulders along the shore. After rough grading of the marsh area, salt marsh and salt meadow cordgrass plants were installed. Birds, waterfowl, and fish quickly found the restored marsh.

Design Features. There is now a 6-foot-wide gravel walkway, with benches, curving along the river, leading to a boardwalk that carries over the marsh, with a pier overlook and boat landing. On the north side of the five low-rise offices that constitute the firm's headquarters is another office, at whose river's edge is a continuation of the walkway, served by a restaurant/cafe.

Trees and plantings serve as a partial screen of the office campus from the river's edge. At the northern end, near the restaurant, there's a "Riverwalk" sign welcoming the public onto the site.

Appraisal. What this project demonstrates is that wetland restoration and public accessways can readily be required as part of project permits.

The walkway at Marketing Corporation of America could, one distant day, be part of a continuous public path from downtown Westport. Existing buildings crowd the shore; as they are modified in future years, Marketing Corporation's project creates a precedent for requiring walkway links that ultimately would provide a continuous path or type of greenway along an active, attractive urban river.

Marketing Corp. of America Headquarters
   Cost. $75,000 (wetland restoration)
   Dimensions. 3.4-acre site includes 48,400 square feet of office space, 194-car parking, 0.3 acre wetland

Sponsor. Marketing Corporation of America
   285 Riverside Ave.
   Westport, CT 06880
   (203) 222-1000

Architect. Environmental Design Associates, PC
   P.O. Box 247
   15 River Rd., Suite 200
   Wilton, CT 06897
   (203) 762-8020

Consultant. Leonard Jackson
   Leonard Jackson Assoc.

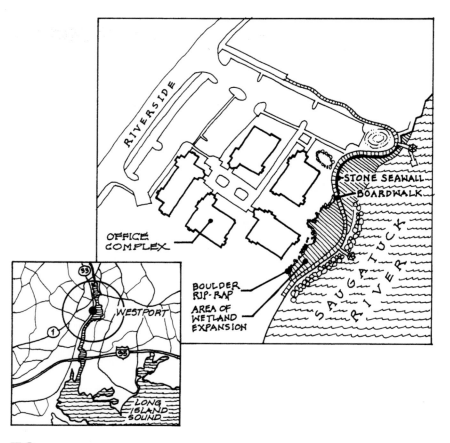

26 Skylark Dr.
Spring Valley, NY 10977
(914) 354-4382

Designer. Bruce Campbell Graham
Bruce Campbell Graham Associates
11 Grumman Hill Rd.
Wilton, CT 06897
(203) 834-1954

Consultant. Stanley White
Ocean & Coastal Consultants, Inc.
2225 Reservoir Avenue
Trumbull, CT 06611
(203) 372-9006

Note for Chapter 3

1. *The New York Times*, Jan. 3, 1987, p.25.

≈4≈

THE HISTORIC
WATERFRONT

The role of special waterfront features is to help each waterfront preserve its unique character. Without these special features, we simply have "malled the waterfront" in the same way that we have "malled" or "strip-developed" much of the suburban land in our country. Our waterfronts deserve better and the publics who ultimately own them deserve to experience the specialness which is, after all, what draws us to the waterfront in the first place.

PETER BRINK
Urban Waterfronts: Accent on Access*

---

*The Waterfront Press, Washington, D.C. 1989.

Brown's Wharf at Fells Point, Baltimore, Md.(*Baltimore Gas & Electric Co. Ed Howell*).

Brown's Wharf at Fell's Point
Thames Street at Broadway
Baltimore, Maryland

Summary

A sensitive, high-quality mixed-use project combining rehabilitation with
new construction in a historic working-class neighborhood.

Description. The Brown's Wharf project combines the restoration and conversion of four old warehouses, including two brick structures that date to the early 1800s, with sympathetic new construction. The bigger feat was to secure general community approval for the undertaking, in a prideful working-class area that feels threatened by new development.

Brown's Wharf occupies the central waterfront of Fell's Point, at the foot of its main thoroughfare, Broadway. It's beside the tug base that is at once the symbol of the area's long-standing ties to the harbor and the remnant of the working waterfront that was once dominant here. Brown's Wharf functionally integrates the main commercial spine of Fell's Point with a waterfront that in the past was largely off limits.

Fell's Point is about 1 mile from the Inner Harbor redevelopment and the central business district. Real estate speculation hit the area years ago, and signs of gentrification are not hard to locate. As a consequence, the neighborhood organized itself to resist being overrun.

It was in this context that Historical Developers, Inc., of Philadelphia came with not only the Brown's Wharf project, but plans including a still-larger development in the territory adjoining, 10 acres in all. Since then, local partner Constellation Real Estate Group, Inc., a subsidiary of Baltimore Gas & Electric Co., has acquired full interest in Brown's Wharf.

With careful attention to community groups, and a low-scale project featuring such public benefits as an open waterfront promenade where no access had existed for two centuries, Constellation won the support of the neighborhood.

The result is a sympathetic new construction fronting on Thames Street, combined with four rehabilitated buildings, plus a promenade with a small boat dock served by an alleyway off Thames. There's a total of 140,000 square feet, principally office, but with first-level retail and restaurants. Expansion plans are on hold, and the retail spaces have suffered with the recession of the early 1990s.

A water taxi service connects Fell's Point and the Inner Harbor, which in turn is minutes from downtown.

Design Features. The Brown's Wharf project succeeds in extending the fabric of the historic Fell's Point community to its heart, the waterfront. It does so with well-executed restoration

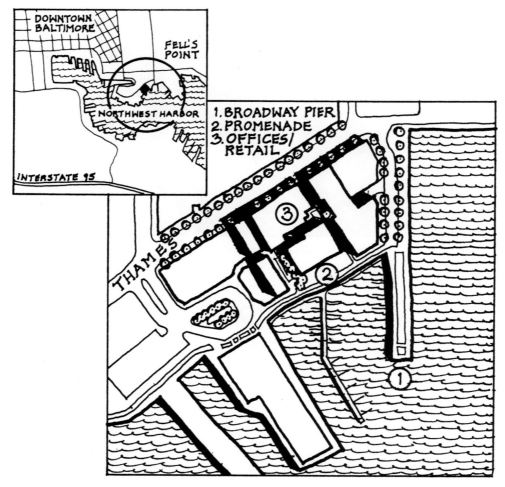

work and sensitive major new additions. A principal feature of the major addition is a roof line that echoes the shape of the dominant existing building. Windows in the new buildings are the same shape as in the old, brick is used throughout, and copper roofs and stone trim on the storefronts add to the compatible details in the additions constructed.

The frontage along Thames Street, the major waterfront street, is maintained at three stories, in scale with the stores, restaurants, and bars that are very much in evidence in Fell's Point.

At the same time, the development does not try to disguise new as old. What has been added is pretty clear, while maintaining its fit. One nice touch: The painted name of the past warehouse owner, Ruckert Terminals Corp., has been left on the waterfront side of one of the restored buildings.

Appraisal. Brown's Wharf at Fell's Point is a high-quality development, with careful attention to design in both the overall sense of careful siting and neighborhood fit, and in the details of execution. It makes a strong case that a quality approach is hardly inconsistent with for-profit development, and in fact, may contribute positively.

The developers here took care in their neighborhood relations. Fell's Point is a feisty, prideful community in which developers are viewed with suspicion. Beginning in 1967, citizens here successfully fought off a road proposal that would have decimated the area, helping to form a city-wide neighborhood group called Movement Against Destruction (MAD).

Constellation Real Estate and architects Bartley Bronstein Long Mierenda of Philadelphia evidently succeeded in winning over community groups. The Fell's Point Homeowners' Association endorsed the project.[1]

Brown's Wharf at Fell's Point
Cost. $17 million
Dimensions. 140,000 square feet, including 40,000 square feet retail and 100,000 square feet office; 27 slips
Completion date. June 1989

Sponsor. Florence Beck Kurdle
Constellation Real Estate Group, Inc.
250 W. Pratt St., 23rd Floor
Baltimore, MD 21201
(410) 783-2800

Designer. Frederick A. Long, Jr.
BBLM Architects, PC
924 Cherry St.
Philadelphia, PA 19107
(215) 625-2500

Long Wharf, Phase 1, Boston, Mass. (*Susan Duca*)

Long Wharf Reconstruction (Phase 1) Atlantic Avenue Boston, Massachusetts

Summary

The rescue of a deteriorating eighteenth-century industrial wharf provides a handsome public access point to Boston Harbor.

Description. The elegant appearance of the restored 1-acre end of Long Wharf masks the important restoration decisions and complicated engineering involved. On the surface, the visitor is treated to a stone and granite observation deck and boat landing, completely open to the public, in the center of Boston's downtown waterfront.

What's underneath is granite bulkhead construction dating back to 1711, obscured to citizens of Boston by 100-year-old wooden pilings. These had deteriorated significantly, and in 1976 Long Wharf was condemned.

A master plan prepared for the Boston Redevelopment Authority in 1979 called for restoration of Long Wharf. The plan was prepared by Sasaki Associates, Inc., whose responsibility the work on Long Wharf became 10 years later. The first-phase work was completed in the fall of 1989.

The basic decision was to retain and restore the granite structure on which Long Wharf stood, and to permanently remove the wooden deck and piling additions. To cut down on water washing over the wharf end during storms, it was necessary to raise the height of the wharf from as little as 8.5 feet above the mean low water mark to a uniform 13.5 feet.

Little of the original granite bulkhead, it turned out, had to be replaced, although additions to meet the new height were needed. Because of scouring at the base, it was necessary for divers to go below water to stabilize some sections. Replacing the center fill with a lighter-weight aggregate helped offset the weight the added stone walls contributed.

The surface, which is what the public enjoys, is attractive gray stone and granite, completely open to the harbor. The edge has large bollards with chains, similar to those featured at nearby Waterfront Park (see Chapter 6). The surface has a slightly higher center section, and stairs lead down to boat landings at intervals.

Design Features. The design theme here is ruggedness. Large granite blocks, with heavy black bollards, are principal features of the wharf edge.

The centerpiece is a beautiful, embedded compass rose with a white, red, and black graphic that dates to the early eighteenth century. There's an inlaid fleur-de-lis motif identifying north. The compass design comes from research at the Peabody Museum in Salem, Massachusetts, and is traced to craftsman Samuel Thaxter, who worked at a shop on Long Wharf in 1792.

The other three phases of the Long Wharf

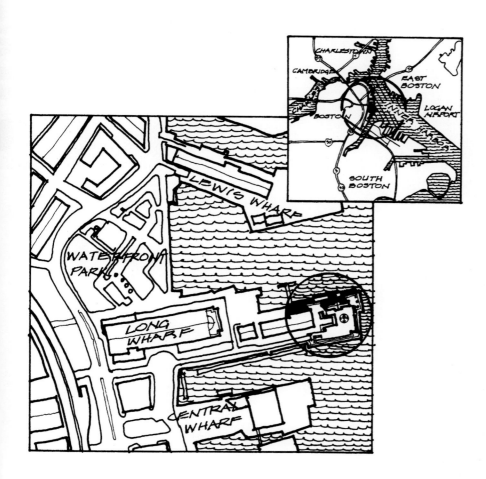

rehabilitation, identified in a plan approaching 15 years of age, call for restoration of the central portion of the wharf, additional access, establishment of a maritime exhibit, and other features. The wharf is now home to the Customs House block, restored for residences, offices, and retail, which dates from 1845, and a restaurant in a 1763 brick building. The landside end of the wharf is occupied by a hotel. The Waterfront Center award in 1991 was only for the wharf restoration.

Appraisal. The restoration of a storied feature of the Boston Harbor, shoring up its sturdy granite bulkhead walls, was worth the wait to have it done right. Helping make the case for keeping the original foundation was an estimate that doing so would be less expensive by several million dollars than replacing it with new sheet pile construction.

Visually and historically, the citizens of Boston benefited by bringing back the original construction. Long Wharf today thus is an honest heir to what was once the longest and busiest wharf of its time.

At a celebratory dinner in 1873, Oliver Wendell Holmes delivered himself of these lines:

While I turn my fond glance on the monarch of piers,

Whose throne has stood firm through his eightscore years,

My thought travels backward and reaches the day

When they drove the first pile on the edge of the bay.

Long Wharf Reconstruction, Phase 1
Cost. $7 million
Dimensions. Wharf end, 1 acre; width, 210 feet; length, 210 feet; total length of wharf, 820 feet
Completion date. 1989

Sponsor. Paul Reavis and Shirley Muirhead
Boston Redevelopment Authority
One City Hall Square
Boston, MA 02201
(617) 722-4300

Designer. Stuart O. Dawson FASLA and John Jennings
Sasaki Associates, Inc.
64 Pleasant Street
Watertown, MA 02172
(617) 926-3300

ELISSA, Galveston, Tex. (*Galveston Historical Society*)

1877 Barque *ELISSA*
Texas Seaport Museum,
Pier 21
Galveston, Texas

Summary

A remarkable feat of maritime preservation.

Description. Today the *ELISSA*, a restored 1877 sailing vessel, sits proudly at the heart of Galveston harbor. More than the beautiful tall ship she is, *ELISSA* symbolizes the passionate determination of people to work against odds to achieve a dream.

Galveston was the main port and financial center of Texas in the 1800s. In the early 1970s the Galveston Historical Foundation began work restoring nineteenth-century commercial buildings along The Strand, an area several blocks from the harbor. Preservationists were eager to obtain a typical sailing vessel as a living reminder of the city's maritime heritage.

Thus began the extraordinary saga of the *ELISSA*'s rescue and renovation. First, a word on the ship's lineage. Built in Aberdeen, Scotland, *ELISSA* was launched in 1877. She called on the port of Galveston twice, in 1883 and again in 1886, which makes the link with the seaport that was the determining factor in her survival. In 1898 her British owners sold her to Norwegians and she was renamed *FJELD*. In 1911, after being sold to Sweden, she became *GUSTAF*, and then, after a series of owners who made expedient alterations, in 1959 she was sold to Greek owners who called her *CHRISTOPHOROS*. She ended her days at sea smuggling untaxed ciga-rettes between Yugoslavia and Italy before being parked in Piraeus harbor awaiting the scrap heap.

In 1961, American maritime historians Peter Throckmorton and Karl Kortum discovered the remains of a ship named *CHRISTOPHOROS-EX-ELISSA* in the Greek harbor. After a series of complicated dealings, the ship passed hands from the San Francisco Maritime Museum to an owner in Victoria, B.C., whose heirs put her up for sale. She was finally purchased in 1975 by the Galveston Historical Foundation for $40,000. Initially, and naively, they thought they could restore the vessel in Greece for $250,000 and sail her home.[2]

The job turned out to be much, much bigger. In the words of one of the original crew members, "Everything was so ****** rotten!"[3]

The condition of the ship was such that she could only be towed back to Galveston. "When the 160-foot iron bark *ELISSA* was towed into Galveston Bay, Texas, in July, 1979, the overwhelming response of the city's residents was—utter disappointment. They hadn't expected the 102-year-old vessel to arrive in mint condition with all sails set, but neither were they prepared for the sight of the rusted, mastless, rotten-decked hulk that greeted their eyes."[4]

Rather than give up, the determined historical

The unbelievable condition of ELISSA before its rescue from a scrap yard in Greece and eventual restoration. (*Galveston Historical Society*)

foundation assembled a skilled team of restorers and expanded their fund raising efforts. *ELISSA* was to be a "Tall Ship for Texas." Close to $5 million was raised eventually. Roughly 10 percent came from public sources, including the U.S. Department of the Interior, the City of Galveston, a U.S. Housing and Urban Development Community Development Block Grant, the Governor's Discretionary Economic Development Administration Fund, and the Texas Department of Community Affairs. Businesses, corporations, foundations, and individuals contributed the lion's share.

The ship was effectively rebuilt after laborious research. Maritime craftspeople from all over the country came to Galveston to work. On July 4, 1982, *ELISSA* was opened to the public. She now is a totally restored, three-masted square-rigged sailing vessel 150 feet long on deck and 411 gross tons in weight. There are 19 sails (12,000 square feet), and the main mast rises 102 feet above the deck.

ELISSA is not only a floating museum that attracts approximately 100,000 visitors a year, but a roving ambassador for Galveston and Texas. In 1986 she was the oldest of the 23 Class A category of ships to sail into the New York Harbor for the Statue of Liberty celebration. She tests her seaworthiness with a crew of volunteer Texans regularly.

Because of her historic importance, *ELISSA* was listed in the National Register of Historic Places in 1977, and in 1990 was granted National Historic Landmark status. The ship is the chief artifact of the Texas Seaport Museum, whose new 11,000-square-foot facility covers in its exhibits the nineteenth-century working port, life at sea, and Texas naval history. An audio-visual presentation, "*ELISSA*: the Longest Voyage," and a computer database of U.S. immigrants through the port of Galveston—one of the country's main points of entry—are provided for visitors.

Appraisal. *ELISSA* dramatizes eloquently the special role that maritime heritage plays on many waterfronts and what a great contribution a restored historic vessel can make educationally, esthetically, and socially through volunteerism.

The story of the *ELISSA*'s rescue is one of the

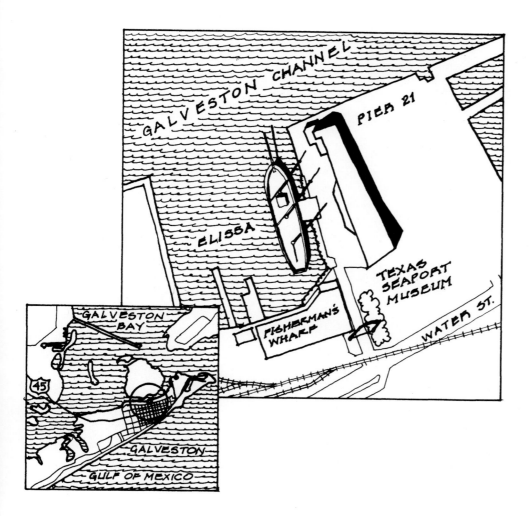

most inspiring grass-roots restoration tales of all times. The serendipity, the dreams, the naiveté, the determination, the passionate volunteerism and skilled professionalism, the years of effort, not to mention the money—ELISSA is a metaphor for many of the best in waterfront and community revitalization efforts.

1877 Barque *Elissa*
   Cost. $4.5 million
   Source. 10 percent public financing, 90 percent donations
   Dimensions. 202 feet overall length, beam 28 feet, 411 tons, draft 10.5 feet
   Completion date. July 1982
   Notes. Texas Seaport Museum: (409) 763-0027

Sponsor. Betty Massey, Executive Director
   (1990–present), Peter H. Brink (1973–1989)
   Galveston Historical Foundation
   2016 The Strand
   Galveston, TX 77550
   (409) 765-7834

Project director. David Brink
   229 Washington St.
   Bath, ME 04530
   (207) 443-2158

Technical consultant. Walter Rybka
   1256 W. 9th St.
   Erie, PA 16502

Volunteer leader. John Paul Gaido
   Gaido's Restaurant and Motor Inn
   3800 Seawall Blvd.
   Galveston, TX 77550
   (409) 762-9625

Roebling Bridge/Delaware Aqueduct, Lackawaxen, Penna. and Minisink, N.Y. (*Alan Schindler*)

Roebling Bridge/Delaware Aqueduct
Upper Delaware River
Lackawaxen, Pennsylvania, and Minisink Ford, New York
Top Honor Award, 1990

Summary

Careful restoration of the oldest existing suspension bridge in the United States, a forerunner of the Brooklyn Bridge.

Description. Measuring 540 feet in length, in four spans, the Roebling Bridge/Delaware Aqueduct has been carefully restored by the National Park Service. A National Historic Landmark, designated in 1970, the span was built in 1847 to transport coal along the Delaware and Hudson Canal from Pennsylvania to New York City. This structure was one of four that served the canal that operated from 1828 to 1898.

The aqueduct was made obsolete by train transportation at the end of the last century, after which it functioned as a highway toll bridge. The span connects New York and Pennsylvania northwest of Port Jervis, New York, and is within the Upper Delaware National Scenic and Recreation Area.

The bridge was closed in 1977 when a truck crashed through the roadway deck. Three years later the National Park Service acquired the structure and set about restoring it. A key decision, aggressively promoted by local residents, was to restore highway traffic as well as to allow pedestrian crossing. Some in the preservation community would have preferred pedestrians only; the prevailing argument pointed to an 18-mile detour as the result.

The bridge's five gray stone piers have been repaired. They are a distinctive triangle shape, the pointed end upriver to help deflect ice flows.

The superstructure has been rebuilt and rein-forced, using research into Roebling's original notes plus early photographs. The suspension cables were cleaned, rewrapped, and painted.

Architects Beyer Blinder Belle of New York had to conform to Park Service guidelines, stay within a $4.6 million budget, as well as meet local concerns. The restoration was completed and the bridge reopened to traffic in 1987.

The width of the bridge is about 17 feet. There is a one-way roadway, slightly below sidewalks on either side. Traffic lights regulate traffic.

On the eastern, New York, side, a former toll house has been restored and functions as the Park Service information building. Diagrams, early photos, and historic background are provided, and a ranger will answer questions for interested visitors. Overlooks and small picnic areas are provided on either side. The Delaware is actively used for recreation in this area.

Design Features. There is grace as well as power in the twin cables that run from the anchoring piers across the three mid-span piers. The cables are housed in a muted red casing that contrasts nicely with the wooden superstructure, black metal framing, and stone piers. The roadway is tinted a faint rose color, adding to the harmony.

At one end, a portion of the cable housing is enclosed in glass, to permit visitors to see the wire ropes inside. This small detail helps make understandable the principles of wire-rope sus-

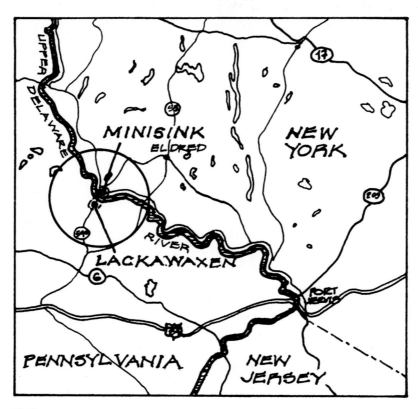

pension bridges, all the more dramatic considering that in 1883 the same principle made possible the Brooklyn Bridge, spanning 1595 feet over the East River in New York City in one of the great engineering feats of the world.

Appraisal. The Roebling Bridge/Delaware Aqueduct is a graphic reminder of the skill and daring that went into early water transportation systems. The nearly 150-year-old bridge, carefully repaired and revived, has the majesty that many good bridge structures possess, combining functionality and a rugged beauty.

It deserves its recognition as a civil engineering and historic landmark, as well as for architectural and waterfront accomplishment. As with much good historic preservation, the Roebling Bridge evokes the period of its initial industrial use and leaves us with a sense of respect for the skills embodied here.

Roebling Bridge/Delaware Aqueduct
 Cost. $4.6 million
 Dimensions. 540 feet, four spans
 Completion date. June 13, 1987

Sponsor. John Hutzky, Superintendent
 National Park Service, Upper Delaware Scenic
 and Recreational River
 P.O. Box C
 Narrowsburg, NY 12764
 (914) 252-7100

Designer. John Belle, FAIA
 Beyer Blinder Belle Architects and Planners
 41 East 11 St.
 New York, NY 10003
 (212) 777-7800

Engineers. Ed Cohen
 Ammann & Whitney Consulting Engineers
 96 Morton St.
 New York, NY 10014
 (212) 423-0307

Engineers. Abba G. Lichtenstein
 A. G. Lichtenstein & Associates Consulting
 Engineers
 17-10 Fair Lawn Ave.
 Fair Lawn, NJ 07410
 (201) 742-2345

The patio at Jackson Brewery atop the Mississippi River floodwall provides a dramatic river view. (*Breen/Rigby*)

Jackson Brewery
(Phase One)
Decatur Street at
Jackson Square
New Orleans, Louisiana

Summary

A pioneering project on the New Orleans riverfront, hurt by recession and rivals, may be revived by gambling.

Description. The Jackson Brewery redevelopment, aimed at turning a massive abandoned riverfront industrial eyesore at a corner of the French Quarter into a jazzy marketplace, is an architectural and historic preservation success story—and a financial dud, at least in the short term.

Opened with high hopes in 1984, with two subsequent additions, the phase one "brewhouse" reverted to New York Life Insurance Co. in 1988 when the original developers had to cancel a $20 million loan.[5] The phase one project involved a $5.5 million site acquisition and a major remodeling estimated at $14 or $15 million.

Original developers Darryl Berger and partner David Burrus arranged to lease nearby wharf space from the New Orleans Steamboat Co. and bought other lands from the city to assemble a 22-acre parcel. They had ambitious plans in the early 1980s for a bold scheme to remake a major portion of the downtown New Orleans riverfront. The phase one "brewhouse" occupies 4.5 acres. The partners are still owners of the phase three portion, housing a Hard Rock Cafe.

When Jax Brewery reopened its doors on October 27, 1984, the 1984 World's Fair was upriver. A portion of the fair site was converted in 1986 to Riverwalk, a 160-store "festival marketplace," by the Rouse Co. The rival marketplace, plus upscale stores in nearby Canal Place—not to mention the French Quarter—together with a drastic decline in the Louisiana economy in the mid-1980s, sapped the vitality at Jax Brewery.

What's forgotten about the Jax Brewery project—named for the beer made on the site between 1891 and 1974—is that it was a pioneer riverfront project in downtown New Orleans. Previous riverfront development had been restricted to a hotel and office. Additionally, the developers contributed to a subsequent change of attitude on the state Dock Board toward more public uses of its extensive holdings up and down the riverfront. Since the Jax initiative beginning in 1982, the Dock Board has become considerably more receptive to expanded uses, which now include an aquarium and a park.

Jax Brewery contains 65,000 square feet of retail and restaurant space, on six levels. In its first several years of operation, it remained popular with visitors and, despite turnover, its space was substantially leased. It was consciously modeled on the Ghirardelli Square (San Francisco) and Quincy Market (Boston) festival marketplaces, which were very much in vogue for a time in the mid-1980s.

Still operating as a "festival marketplace" despite its ownership shift, the brewhouse was sold to two developers in February 1992. Daniel Robinowitz of Dallas, a New Orleans native, and Christopher Hemmeter of Los Angeles, signed a contract to purchase the structure. The developers are said to be interested also in acquiring "Millhouse," phase two of the Jackson Brewery development, a new structure built to harmonize with the historic brewhouse, which contains an additional 70,000 square feet of shops.

They are also reported to have obtained additional nearby waterfront property, in a bankruptcy proceeding involving the Canal Place project, with an eye on the prospect that land-based gambling will come to New Orleans at a nearby site.

In the meantime, a crafts shop has opened on the third floor of the Millhouse, allowing local artists and craftspeople to demonstrate their skills and sell their wares. As of the end of 1991, "Louisiana's Living Treasures" listed 42 participants.

Design Features. In execution, the conversion of the brewery had many standout features. Where the monolithic brewery completely walled off Decatur Street and the French Quarter from the river, the conversion reopened Wilkinson, Toulouse, and St. Louis Streets to the river for the first time in the twentieth century. Inviting accessways, from which river views are possible across the flood levee, are featured.

Original architect Dietrich Einseidle designed the brewery in the 1890s to face the river. Here was elaborate fenestration and millwork, now restored. Over the years, additions and changes dictated by the brewery meant that for decades the city saw a virtual blank wall when it looked toward the Mississippi.

The project's emphasis on "opening to the river" was carried out at the multiple levels of the structure. Decks are provided to take in splendid views of the Mississippi River as it makes a dramatic turn in front of New Orleans. Visitors can use these lookouts on levels 2 through 6 without purchasing food or drink.

On the river side, a 300-foot-long promenade was built at the second-story level. This permits strollers and café goers to see the river over a concrete floodwall.

The exterior of Jax Brewery was restored to its romantic, castlelike Romanesque Revival style. The interior, meanwhile, was completely gutted and a new, six-story glass atrium structure was built inside. In part the gutting was dictated by the fact that several walls did not meet municipal code requirements.

Appraisal. The instinct here—to open up to the river and convert an idle brewery next to the heavily visited French Quarter—is hard to argue with.

Nor can the general care and sensitivity of the restoration of the main building in phase one be faulted in bringing back to life a romantic, 100-year-old riverfront structure. The course chosen for the interior was less successful, however, being done in a very glitzy style.

Aside from the economic downturn that affected not only retail, but New Orleans business in general during the mid-1980s, in hindsight other factors can be cited in the failure of the execution.

As in Minneapolis, where two riverfront "festival marketplaces" were placed in competition with each other, causing one to fail and seriously injuring the other, so in New Orleans. A market already saturated with the lively shops of the French Quarter would, in retrospect, seem unlikely to be able to absorb Jax Brewery, Canal Place, and Riverwalk, all within blocks of the Quarter and each other. For a time, however, such was the strength of the "festival marketplace" concept that the backers of each thought they all could make it.

The irony about the Jackson Brewery is that just up the street from it now is a popular new attraction—a "micro" brewery selling a product made on the premises. Had there been another vision for the phase one Jax Brewery, more along the lines of reviving its original function rather than making it a "festival marketplace," who knows what the outcome might have been.

Two facts remain. One is that the original developers had the vision that the New Orleans riverfront was an exciting opportunity for varied public uses—and took action on that vision—well in advance of most others in the city, certainly its officials and planners. And second, the quality of the restoration at Jax Brewery, assisted by the preservation tax credits in place at the time, remains a striking monument to that vision for residents and visitors to enjoy today.

Jackson Brewery (Phase One)
Cost. $15 million
Dimensions. 85,000 square feet (overall site, 4.5 acres)
Completion date. October 27, 1984
Note. Property now owned by Daniel Robinowitz and Christopher Hemmeter

Sponsor. Darryl Berger
Darryl Berger Investment Corp.
P.O. Box 57329
New Orleans, LA 70157
(504) 581-4082

Architect. Steven Bingler
Concordia Architects
621 Decatur St.
New Orleans, LA 70130
(504) 525-1862

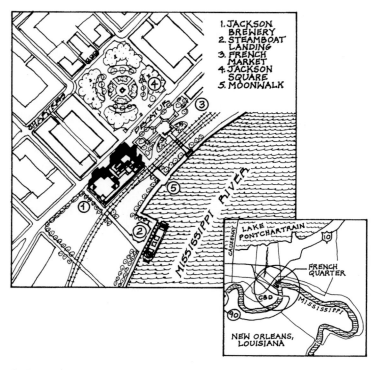

1. JACKSON BREWERY
2. STEAMBOAT LANDING
3. FRENCH MARKET
4. JACKSON SQUARE
5. MOONWALK

NEW ORLEANS, LOUISIANA

Ellis Island National Museum of Immigration, Ellis Island, N.Y. (*Beyer Blinder Belle/Notter Finegold + Alexander*)

Ellis Island Museum of Immigration
New York Harbor
New York, New York

Summary

Ambitious, well-executed restoration of one of America's notable icons; evokes a sense of awe at the millions of immigrants who were processed here.

Description. Arrival at the Main Building of Ellis Island by boat from Manhattan—just like the 26 million immigrants who passed through here from 1900 to 1924—places you in front of a majestic structure. A turn-of-the-century building with four copper-clad turrets and three arched portals, the Main Building was meant to inspire, if not intimidate. Brought back by a meticulous, $156 million restoration, it continues to inspire today.

The decision by the National Park Service to rescue the structure, abandoned and deteriorating since 1954, came in the early 1970s as the nation's Bicentennial approached. Also, Ellis Island, which began operating as New York's point of entry for foreigners in 1892, had a centennial coming up. By the time America clamped down on immigration in 1924, 71 percent of all those who came to this country's shores had been processed here.

Funds to restore Ellis Island's principal structure and heating plant, and to stabilize the laundry/kitchen facility, were raised by the Statue of Liberty-Ellis Island Foundation, Inc., Lee A. Iacocca, Chairman. All but 20 percent of the restoration cost was donated.

Reopening came in September 1990. The Park Service anticipated that 1.75 million people would visit during a year. The estimate for 1992 was 3 million visitors, requiring some adjustments in boat frequency, movie reservations, and other aspects of crowd handling. A controversial proposal, pushed by the New Jersey congressional delegation, is to build a bridge from Liberty State Park to the island. It is opposed by those fearing that cars, not just pedestrians, will eventually make their way to Ellis, and that a land bridge means people won't have the sense of arrival a boat provides.

The Main Building, containing 220,415 square feet, is experienced now as new arrivals to America did. From the wide, handsomely paved dock area, entry is under a canopy. This feature, built in the exact footprint of an original metal arrival shelter, is rendered in modern materials. Plexiglass permits light and allows the visitor to take in the huge eagles and other architectural details of the imposing facade.

(Breen/Rigby)

Canopy at front entrance to Main Building is a replacement of the original. (*Breen/Rigby*)

Inside, on the first of three levels, is the restored baggage area, now a combination information center, tour assembly point, movie theater (two, each with 140 seats), and display of the history of U.S. immigration.

The Registry Room on the second level is the most inspiring single feature. Dominated by a tiled ceiling carefully restored to its 1918 splendor (despite the building's abandonment, only 17 of the nearly 29,000 individual tiles had to be replaced), the room provides a moving experience. With the aid of large photographs on the walls throughout the museum, it is not hard to imagine a hall filled with nervous immigrants awaiting their fate.

Originally there were metal pipes in this large hall (measuring 160 feet long and two stories high) that marked the area in which immigrants stood while awaiting processing, usually for three to five hours. Later, in 1909, benches were provided, and some of these are in place at one end of the room to help the imagination fill the whole space, as well as provide a place to sit.

As a museum, Ellis Island is packed with well-displayed information. There are four major exhibition rooms in the corners of the second floor, including processing rooms as they appeared circa 1920, additional displays in the third-floor corners, a sample dormitory room, and another displaying articles, letters, and other memorabilia of the immigrants. A balcony around the third floor provides an overview of the Registry Room.

At the first level is a cafeteria. Here stools are placed at the windows to allow spectacular views of Manhattan to be enjoyed; an outdoor patio does the same. Throughout, because of the hard surfaces, the Museum of Immigration is noisy. Instead of being a negative, that seems fitting, because Ellis Island once must have been bedlam, processing as many as 7500 persons a day.

The outside of the Main Building includes a promenade, overlooking Manhattan, and in and of itself is splendid space.

Design Features. An imposing French Renaissance-style brick edifice, with limestone, terra cotta, and granite accents, the Ellis Island Main Building was finished on June 3, 1900, at a cost of $1.5 million. The architects were Boring & Tilton of New York, a small firm that beat better-known architects in a competition.

This original facade, restored to a deep brick red with careful steam cleaning, features four copper-clad corner towers. Soaring 100 feet, they mark a building elaborately decorated with sculptures, stone work, and three arches at the front, echoed in three peaks in a red tile roof.

In all it's a magnificent sight, reminiscent of old train or ferry stations, with which it has much in common.

The interventions by the team of architects Beyer Blinder Belle/Notter Finegold + Alexander, Inc., Architects, working with several engineering firms plus Hanna Olin and Bruce Kelly, landscape architects, are relatively limited. A new stair replaces the one immigrants climbed to the Registry Room (no plans of the original could be found), and glass encloses what had been outdoor space on the third floor, to create more display rooms. The canopy at the entrance has drawn mixed reviews, but it functions well.

Phase II is controversial because the proposal as it stood in mid-1992 called for demolition of 12 structures at the southern end of the island, away from the Main Building, to allow a conference center. The National Trust for Historic Preservation (opposed) is pitted against the developer, architects (Beyer Blinder Belle), and the National Park Service (in favor).

Appraisal. There's no question that the Main Building and its ancillary structures have been brought back to life with a high standard of restoration. The design team is reported to have assembled 12 volumes of historic materials about the original structures.

In another time, Ellis Island easily would have been a candidate for demolition—particularly with a price tag of $156 million that still leaves many buildings of the complex untouched.

It says something about the power of this structure on our imaginations, and of our respect for our history, that Ellis Island as well as the nearby Statue of Liberty have been carefully restored, to enable them both to be available for future generations.

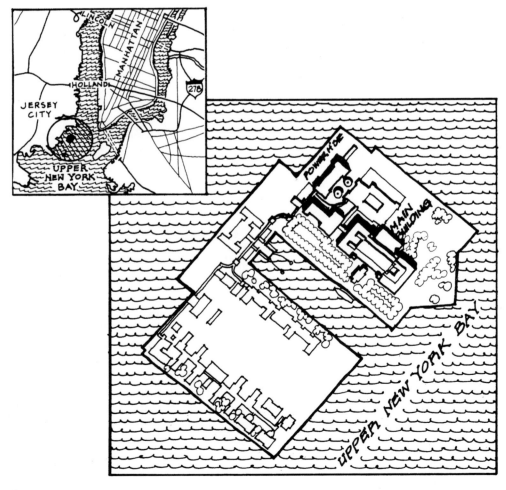

Ellis Island Museum of Immigration
  Cost. $156 million
  Source. 20 percent public financing, 80 percent private donation
  Dimensions. Main Building, 220,415 square feet
  Completion date. 1990

Sponsor. Stephen Brigante, President, Statue of Liberty/Ellis Island Foundation
  52 Vanderbilt Ave., 4th Floor
  New York, NY 10017
  (212) 883-1986

Sponsor. Michael Adlerstein, Chief, Urban Projects National Park Service, Office of Urban Projects
  26 Wall St.
  New York, NY 10005
  (212) 264-8711

Sponsor. Herbert S. Cables, Deputy Director National Park Service, U.S. Dept. of the Interior
  P.O. Box 47127
  Washington, DC 20213
  (202) 208-3100

Designer. John Belle, FAIA, RIBA
  Beyer Blinder Belle, Architects and Planners
  41 East 11th St.
  New York, NY 10003
  (212) 777-7800

Designer. James G. Alexander, FAIA
  Notter Finegold + Alexander, Architects
  77 North Washington St.
  Boston, MA 02114
  (617) 227-9272

Architectural lighting design. Jules Fisher + Paul Marantz, Inc.
  126 Fifth Ave.
  New York, NY 10011
  (212) 691-3020

Designer. Bob Hanna
  Hanna/Olin, Ltd.
  41 Chestnut St.
  Philadelphia, PA 19106
  (215) 440-0030

Civil engineer. Martin Solomon
  Lockwood, Kessler & Bartlett
  One Aerial Way
  Syosset, NY 11791
  (516) 938-0600

Structural engineer. Robert Silman
  Robert Silman Associates
  88 University Pl.
  New York, NY 10003
  (212) 620-7970

Mechanical engineer. Howard Rosenfield
  Syska & Hennessy
  11 West 42nd St.
  New York, NY 10036
  (212) 921-2300

Historic landscape architect. Bruce Kelly
  532 Broadway, 10th floor
  New York, NY 10012
  (212) 941-8440

Harbour Place, Portsmouth, N.H. (*Robert Karosis*)

Harbour Place
Bow Street
Portsmouth, New Hampshire

Summary

Adaptive reuse of abandoned riverfront industrial structures fits nicely with the city's historic emphasis.

Description. The City of Portsmouth, so the story goes, woke up in the late 1950s to the fact that its stock of historic structures was being lost. The triggering moment is said to have been a speech in 1957 by the city librarian to the Rotary Club, which sounded the alarm.[6]

In fact, in an old waterfront section near the site of Harbour Place, an urban renewal program was poised to level a neighborhood that included homes built as early as 1695. The area was dilapidated, with many an eyesore among the older buildings.

The city rallied and called off the bulldozing in favor of a selective clearing and ultimate restoration of old homes, which became the Strawbery Banke historic district. Its success helped set the tone for Portsmouth, which has gone on to revive its downtown and other areas in celebration of its rich history, much of which revolves around the waterfront.

Harbour Place takes its cue from this preservation and rehabilitation effort, and combines with it an emphasis on waterfront access, both physical and visual.

Harbour Place forms a transition between a largely residential area to the south and a commercial area to the north. Its immediate neighbor is a theater. The project fits onto 1.5 acres. Across Daniel and State Streets to the south—parallel roadways to Memorial Bridge, which forms the backdrop for Harbour Place—are Prescott Park and the Strawbery Banke historic area, a prime visitor destination.

Industrial buildings once used for a power plant and machine shop were restored, while three stories were added to the principal structure on the Piscataqua River. In all, 120,000 square feet of office space is included, along with 230 parking spaces. Local law firms are the main tenants.

Three additional components comprise the mixed-use package, total cost $20 million, completed in the mid-1980s. They are a walkway with a small marina, a new condominium complex, and a plaza.

The walkway runs along the river's edge and is completely accessible. It runs into a gate at the next property. Docking space for about 24 vessels is available. The 18 condominiums, immediately adjacent to the office building, are new construction, but of a character that complements the brick plaza and offices.

Design Features. An open, brick plaza is readily accessible to Bow Street, which in turn leads to the center of downtown Portsmouth. There is a handsome stairway leading down to the walkway and the river. A view of the river is maintained through the center of Harbour Place, with offices to one side, condominiums to the other. An addition to the original building was removed, helping to make possible part of the riverfront plaza as well as a second entrance. The plaza contains colorful plantings that serve to brighten it up.

Along the walkway in front of the condominiums are large archways, which might have been made into a pleasant sitting area. Handsome light fixtures have been used.

The provision for public access is generous, and the fact that the river walkway is not continuous or connected to downtown is outside the project's purview. The opportunity exists, however, for the City of Portsmouth, with some investment and cajoling of property owners, to put in a riverfront walkway that would connect Memorial Bridge with a row of restaurants farther up Bow Street in the heart of the downtown.

Appraisal. Harbour Place is an imaginative adaptive reuse, fitting in its overall approach and bold in its three-story addition to the old powerhouse. This virtual doubling of the building area blends well with historic Portsmouth. A slope on the site means that much of the old powerhouse at the river's edge is below grade level.

Because Harbour Place is slightly removed from the center of Portsmouth's business district, it has a bit of an isolated feel to it, at least in the nonsummer seasons. Space for parties, a market, or other events exists both along the walkway and in the plaza area above. At the same time, the quietness may well suit the condominium residents and law office users.

Adding to the empty feeling of the plaza area is an absence of benches. Nonetheless, one imagines that the plaza fills up on pleasant days with office workers, residents, and an occasional visitor taking in the river views for lunch or a similar occasion.

Parking is handled well, tucked under the plaza and into the lower level of the old power plant and machine shop structures. It's virtually unnoticeable from Bow Street, the entrance being located around the corner on Daniel Street.

Harbour Place

Cost. $20 million
Source. Fleet National Bank, Providence, RI
Dimensions. 1.5-acre site, including 120,000 square feet of offices, 18 condominiums, a 23,000-square-foot plaza, and 230 parking spaces
Completion date. 1986

Sponsor. Seaboard Development Corp.
2 Stamford Landing, Southfield Ave.
Stamford, CT 06902
(203) 357-1600

Designer. Frank J. Gravino Associates
 319 Peck St.
 New Haven, CT 06513
 (203) 787-7469

Structural engineer. Weidlinger Associates
 44 Brattle St.
 Cambridge MA 02138
 (617) 876-9666

Mechanical/electrical engineer. Cosentini Associates
 44 Brattle St.
 Cambridge, MA 02138
 (617) 876-3830

Landscaping. Kimball Chase Co., Inc.
 P.O. Box 537
 Portsmouth, NH 03802
 (603) 431-2520

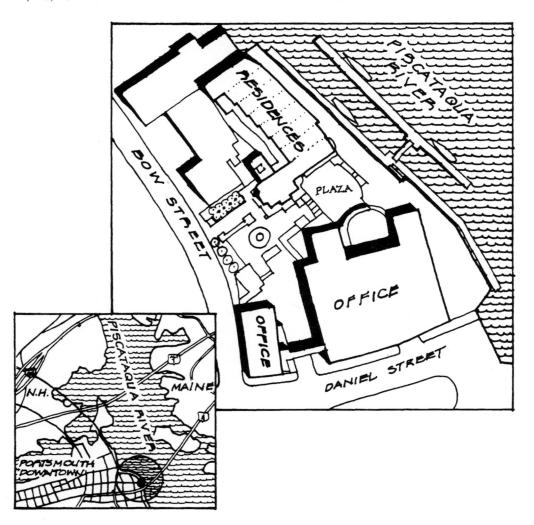

(Ned Ahrens)

Waterfront Streetcar
Alaskan Way and Main Street
Seattle, Washington

Summary

A colorful, enjoyable, *and* practical transportation link on the downtown Seattle waterfront.

(Renee Montegelas)

Description. Vintage green and yellow street-cars now run daily for 2.1 miles along the core area of the downtown Seattle waterfront.

Opened on Memorial Day in 1982, the street-car proved its usefulness to the extent that a half-mile addition was undertaken, for $6.5 million, and completed in June 1990.

Originally, the Waterfront Streetcar ran a straight, 1.6-mile route along the downtown waterfront, using a track leased from the Burlington Northern Railroad. In 1988, agreement was reached to reroute freight traffic, giving the streetcar the exclusive use of the track closest to the waterfront.

The run begins on the north at Myrtle Edwards Park. Stations serve such attractions as Pier 69, where ferry service to Victoria, B.C., Canada, departs; the Seattle Aquarium and Waterfront Park; Pike Place Market, reached by nearby stairs; the Washington State ferry terminal at Pier 52; historic Pioneer Square; the Kingdome arena, and the International District and Metro bus tunnel station. The last three stops are on the streetcar route extension of 1990. Parking is provided at the northern end.

By all accounts, the impetus for the streetcar project came from a member of the city council, George Benson, an admitted trolley buff. In fact, it was Mr. Benson who personally went to Melbourne to select the cars to be used in Seattle, after the Australian city submitted the winning bid to supply the cars.

The Seattle Waterfront Streetcar now serves 220,000 riders per year. It is supported by retailers and property owners along the route, a number of whom were tapped in the original project as part of a local improvement district tax. A principal benefit is the reduction in people trying to get to the downtown waterfront in a car.

Originally a project of the City of Seattle, operated by the transportation agency Metro (Municipality of Metropolitan Seattle), ownership of the entire undertaking was turned over to Metro in 1986.

The present fare covers about 25 percent of the annual operating cost, approximately $900,000, with the subsidy coming from Metro. The current (1992) fare is 75 cents during peak hours, 55 cents at other times.

Design Features. The trams used on the Seattle Waterfront Streetcar are 1927 class W-2 trams. The car interiors are appointed with interiors of Tasmanian mahogany and white ash. The cars have large windows, arched doorways, and comfortable wooden benches. They seat 52 each, plus standing room for 40. The traditional architectural style of the stations complements the streetcars.

Included in the refurbishing of the cars (the fleet now numbers five, with three in service, one restored as a backup, and the fifth in reserve) was making them accessible to persons in wheelchairs. This was accomplished by building up the station platforms to the entrance level of the cars, and supplying tie-downs inside.

Appraisal. The Seattle Waterfront Streetcar is now an integral part of the experience of that city's downtown waterfront. The conductors, a colorful lot, add to visitors' enjoyment.

A key to the evident success is the choice of vintage cars, obtained for $25,000 each. These are classics and, after their refurbishment, contribute significantly to the area's ambience.

The streetcar's 20-minute journey makes it practical for city users and a pleasant way for visitors to see and move along the Seattle waterfront, as well as to gain ready access to it and such nearby features as Pioneer Square.

When first put forward in 1974, many no doubt viewed the idea as quixotic. The quick popularity of the streetcars not only stilled whatever debate there may have been, but contributed to early planning (1983) to extend the line. Support in the late 1980s was garnered to finance a short spur through Pioneer Square to hook up with Seattle's bus tunnel, a complicated engineering and traffic management proposition. This action affirms the hold the streetcar has on

the business community and public transportation users in Seattle.

The Seattle Waterfront Streetcar served as a model for a similar riverfront trolley that now operates along the Mississippi River in New Orleans. And likewise, there are proposals to extend the present service along the Mississippi to link additional attractions to the downtown waterfront.

Waterfront Streetcar, Seattle

Cost. $3.4 million (original); $6.5 million for extension (1990)

Source. Original, one-third each, Urban Mass Transportation Administration, City of Seattle, and Local Improvement District

Dimensions. 1.6 miles (before extension) with 0.5 mile extension = 2.1 miles

Completion dates. May 1982; 1990

Sponsor. City Councilman George Benson
Municipal Building
600 4th Ave.
Seattle, WA 98104
(206) 684-8801

Sponsor. Andrea Tull, Project Manager
Municipality of Metropolitan Seattle (METRO)
821 2nd Avenue, MS 51
Seattle, WA 98104
(206) 684-1642

Civil/structural engineer. Ejner Handeland
Tudor Engineering Co.
801 2nd Ave., Norton Building, Suite 516
Seattle, WA 98104
(206) 682-4915

Engineering. City of Seattle Engineering Department
Municipal Building
Seattle, WA 98104
(206) 684-5087

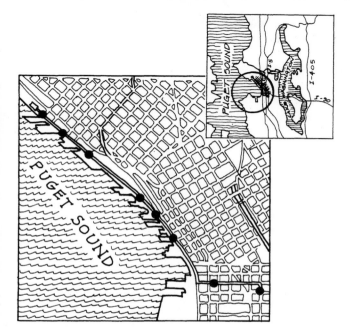

(*Zeidler Roberts Partnership/Architects and Panda Associates*)

Queen's Quay Terminal
Queen's Quay West,
Harbourfront
Toronto, Ontario, Canada

Summary

Impressive transformation of a massive warehouse into a mixed-use attraction that dominates Toronto's central waterfront.

(*Zeidler Roberts Partnership/Architects and Fiona Spalding-Smith*)

Description. Built in 1927 when the Port of Toronto was thriving, the Terminal Warehouse contained 1 million square feet of storage space. Handling dry goods on its eight floors, the terminal was flanked by deepwater docks and served by rail lines. The builder was Canadian Rail and Harbour Terminal Ltd.

The transformation began in 1980 under the auspices of Harbourfront Corp., a federal planning and development entity established in 1972. (See Chapter 1 for more on Harbourfront Corp.) A development competition for the warehouse was won by Olympia & York Developments Ltd., with the Zeidler Roberts Partnership as principal architects.

Opened in 1983, the Art Deco-styled warehouse has been transformed into a retail, office, and condominium mixed-use destination, yet it retains much of its industrial character. While four glass-enclosed levels were added at the top in a major addition, the facade on Queens Quay West was retained largely intact, including its signature clock tower.

On the first two levels is an enclosed retail mall. On the east side, a glass atrium puts passers-by in direct touch with the shops within. In nice weather, tables and chairs are set out for waterfront cafés.

The middle six levels are offices, built around three central atriums carved from the poured-concrete structure that penetrate from the roof through to the shopping areas. The developer notes that no office is more than 35 feet from a window.

On top are 72 luxury condominiums on four levels, all with views of Lake Ontario and greenhouses. Terraces sealed from their neighbors are another feature. The condominiums are arranged around a waterfall and pool.

The prime feature of Queen's Quay Terminal is the atrium at the southern, lakefront, end of the building. A glass-enclosed opening was cut into the southwest corner of the building, including the removal of some floor slabs to help open up the interior. A wide, two-level promenade fronts the lake. As with the eastern side, there are major plantings, flags, and varied seating areas along the building perimeter. On the third floor is the 450-seat Premier Dance Theater (see Chapter 2, Programming Facilities, Harbourfront).

The remodeling cost about $50.5 million (1983 U.S. dollars) and provides 148,000 square feet of retail and restaurant space, 400,000 square feet of office space, plus the theater and condominiums. One feature in the retail area is extensive use of the "incubator" concept, where local

(Zeidler Roberts Partnership/Architects and Fiona Spalding-Smith)

craftspeople, artists, and designers are encouraged to display. In 1989, half of the shops were occupied in this manner, enabling the retail area to escape the sameness of some waterfront retail centers.

Design Features. Perhaps the outstanding characteristic of the renovation of Queens Quay Terminal is the extensive use of green-tinted glass. The top, condominium floors are dominated by glass, and major glass features have been added to the east, south, and part of the western sides of the building. This has the effect of opening up and making penetrable what had been a monolithic structure that was not especially inviting. In warm weather, the building seems to spill out onto the promenade that surrounds it because of this extensive use of glass. During winter the atriums help lighten the interior and give shoppers and diners a feel for the lakefront outside.

Likewise, the three atriums in the interior, bringing light from above through the center of the structure, brighten the feeling inside for both office tenants and retailers.

Appraisal. This is a well-done conversion of a huge waterfront warehouse, creating a lively centerpiece for Harbourfront and the downtown Toronto waterfront. It likely will remain the major attraction here no matter what future course is chosen.

Retaining this old industrial structure is an important, visible link to the city's recent past, a lively reminder of another waterfront era.

Queen's Quay Terminal is an eloquent argument in opposition to those who would segregate such uses as housing and retail; the mixture of activities works here, with each component contributing to a dynamic, urban center that ably serves multiple functions, with different daytime and seasonal rhythms.

Queen's Quay Terminal
  Cost. $50.5 million (U.S.) 1983 dollars
  Dimensions. 880,000 square feet, including 72 condominiums and 148,000 square feet of retail space
  Completion date. November 1983

Sponsor. Ron Soskolne, Senior Vice President
  Olympia & York Developments Ltd.
  2 First Canadian Place, Suite 2700
  Toronto, ON, M5X 1B5, Canada
  (416) 862-6100

Sponsor. Harbourfront Centre
  410 Queen's Quay West, Suite 500
  Toronto, ON, M5V 2Z3, Canada
  (416) 973-4600

Architect. Eberhard H. Zeidler
  Zeidler Roberts Partnership, Architects
  315 Queen Street West
  Toronto, ON, M5V 2X2, Canada
  (416) 596-8300

Structural engineer. Barry Charnish
  Yolles Partnership Ltd.
  163 Queen St. East, Suite 200
  Toronto, ON, M5A 1S1, Canada
  (416) 363-8123

Mechanical engineer. Lorne Mitchell
  The Mitchell Partnership Ltd.
  285 Yorkland Blvd.
  Willowdale, ON, M2J 1S5, Canada
  (416) 499-8000

Electrical engineer. Husayn Banani
  Mulvey & Banani
  44 Mobile Drive
  Toronto, ON, M4A 2P2, Canada
  (416) 751-2520

Designer. Ted Baker
  Baker Salmona Associates Ltd.
  10 Kingsbridge Garden Circle, Suite 800
  Mississauga, ON, L5R 3K6, Canada
  (416) 568-4375

Notes for Chapter 4

1. Letter to Waterfront Center, Maryrose Whelley, Secretary, May 21, 1990.

2. Karen Lord, "Galveston's Ship Has Come In," press release, Galveston Historical Foundation, July 1982.

3. Brian Toss, "Craftsmanship and Fate Assisted the Longevity of Galveston's *Elissa*," *National Fisherman*, July 1982, p. 33.

4. Ibid.

5. Bruce Eggler, "Developers Buy Tax Brewhouse," *The Times-Picayune*, February 1992, p. C-1.

6. Lewis J. Lord, "Old England Port Rescues Its Vanishing Charm," *U.S. News & World Report*, Oct. 19, 1981, p. 89.

≈5≈

THE MIXED-USE WATERFRONT

A waterfront is a significant resource and a challenging opportunity for a city; a chance to be an escape valve for the pressure-cooker of crowded city life, a chance to be a bright, breathing edge of city living.

ARTHUR COTTON MOORE,
*Bright Breathing Edges of City Life. Planning for Amenity Benefits of Urban Water Resources**

Humankind has progressively discovered its intellectual and emotional wealth through the unpredictable encounters and confrontations made possible by life in the city.
RENÉ DUBOS: A Collection from His Writings

---

*National Technical Information Service, Springfield,Va., 1971

The Inner Harbor Shoreline, Baltimore, Md. (*Baltimore Development Corporation*)

Baltimore Inner Harbor Shoreline
Inner Harbor
Baltimore, Maryland

Summary

The model urban waterfront transformation of the time, and still growing.

(Baltimore Development Corporation)

Description. The Inner Harbor shoreline at the doorstep of downtown Baltimore is probably the best-known piece of redevelopment real estate in the world. Cities and developers from around the globe have come to see the miracle of recovery and rebirth in the heart of Baltimore. There's many a U.S. mayor who has resolved to "do something like Baltimore" after a visit.

Because of the visible and apparent success of what is present today, it's difficult to imagine the poor prospects that faced downtown business interests when they coalesced in 1955 to take action. The previous year had seen the closing of O'Neill's Department Store, one of the city's largest, capping years of decline in the retail core. Around the harbor, the Chesapeake Bay steamers that once left from the docks along Pratt and Light Streets had gone, many piers had been torn down, and warehouses stood abandoned. There had been no new construction downtown for 30 years, property values were falling, vacancy was high.

David Wallace, of Wallace McHarg Roberts and Todd of Philadelphia, who was brought in to prepare a downtown plan, recalled, "We soon realized that unless something drastic was done in the form of an immediate project, we would lose our investors." The planning was launched with $225,000 in private funds, raised by two business committees formed to organize the rescue. The idea of developing a comprehensive downtown plan was set aside for the moment in favor of immediate action, so dire were the straits of Baltimore felt to be. The "something drastic" was the mixed-use, public/private megaproject Charles Center, 2 million square feet in all, the first of its kind in a downtown.[1]

Phase two of the downtown rescue was the Inner Harbor. While Charles Center was primarily an office project, the Inner Harbor was seen as a more public place, beginning with a harbor's edge promenade.

Cleanup of the Inner Harbor dates to 1950, after which there was landfill and then a roadway. In its first days of renewal, the harbor's edge was a parking lot. Not all here was torn down in the 1950s, but many of the structures left behind simply deteriorated. As a consequence, there's little of the original Inner Harbor left intact from its flourishing days. One surviving structure, the McCormick & Co. headquarters, subsequently was torn down by the Rouse Co. The smell of the firm's spices no longer scents the air here.

The Inner Harbor rebirth was launched officially in 1963 by Mayor Theodore McKeldin. The Wallace-prepared plan followed in 1964. The vision called for the "best use of water and open land in post-war U.S. urban renewal. Instead of cutting the water off from the city as almost all cities do, Baltimore will thrust the living, 24-hour-a-day city into intimate, vivacious contact with the harbor whence it sprang."[2]

Underlying this striking vision for a downtrodden city was the basic fact that the Inner Harbor adjoins the central business district. This fundamental fact of geography made the vision of a lively, working city embracing its historic harbor a realistic goal. Many see today's array of attractions and yet fail to perceive the significance of being able to stroll across the street to enjoy the harbor from a downtown office or a nearby condominium, without an expressway or railroad barrier.

The core of the Inner Harbor project is 95 acres surrounding the small harbor basin on three sides. The larger context includes 240 acres. From the beginning, planners saw the Inner Harbor as a whole. The upland areas adjoining have played a role in that new and rehabilitated residences, particularly in Inner Harbor West, were developed at the same time as the public attractions lining the harbor were being assembled.

In part because of the Inner Harbor, existing nearby neighborhoods, such as Federal Hill, were also discovered. East of the harbor are new condominium units, a vibrant Little Italy, and the historic, partially gentrified, Fell's Point neighborhood.

The Inner Harbor redevelopment began with a brick promenade that surrounds this intimate water body. It is 35 feet wide, handsomely paved,

the south side lined with trees. The water's edge is completely open. It has been a magnet since construction in 1975, especially as discovered by citizens at such events as the annual City Fair and the spectacular Tall Ships visit during the Bicentennial year of 1976.

If in the past the intersection of Pratt and Light Streets at the corner of the Inner Harbor was the front door to Baltimore, it is no less so today. A large, inviting public space—Constellation Plaza—occupies the corner. The Inner Harbor attractions are arrayed to either side of this key juncture. A water sculpture/fountain named for Mayor McKeldin adds interest nearby.

What makes the Inner Harbor the successful attraction it continues to be (the claim is that 23 million people visited the Inner Harbor in 1987) is its mixture. This includes office towers, such as the USF&G and IBM buildings and federal offices along Pratt Street; the Hyatt Regency Hotel; the nearby Baltimore Convention Center; the World Trade Center on the Inner Harbor itself, with an observation deck on top and an open first level (I. M. Pei, architect); the Maryland Science Center opened in 1976 (Edward Durrell Stone, architect); the frigate *U.S.S. Constellation*, the very first public attraction placed here, in 1972; the promenade; a boat rental concession, including paddle and electric

(Cy Rhode)

An early event in Baltimore—part of a conscious effort by the city to bring people to the developing waterfront before all its attractions were in place. Spice factory in background has since been torn down. (*Breen/Rigby*)

versions that enliven the harbor in good weather; a marina/restaurant combination; a playing field, a children's play area with a carousel and garden below Federal Hill, itself an Inner Harbor attraction with commanding views; the National Aquarium at Baltimore (see Chapter 2), opened in 1981; the Pier Six Pavilion, a music venue at pier's end that seats 2000 under a tensile structure; Harrison's Inn plus restaurant and cafe; the *Pride of Baltimore II*, the lightship *Chesapeake*, and the submarine *U.S.S. Torske*, on display at the Baltimore Maritime Museum; the Public Works Museum and Streetscape, in and adjoining the ornate Eastern Avenue Pumping Station; the newest nearby facility, Oriole Stadium at Camden Yards, from which the Inner Harbor can be seen; and, lastly, the twin pavilions of Harborplace.

What's seen here represents an investment of $2.5 billion, 25 percent or $625 million in public funds, much of it from an array of federal grants, occurring over nearly 30 years. This recent figure is from the City of Baltimore Development Corp., successor organization to Charles Center-Inner Harbor Management Inc.

Harborplace was the culmination of the Inner Harbor redevelopment, while the public promenade is the unifying link. The immense amount of publicity surrounding the Harborplace opening on July 2, 1980, when 50,000 people showed up, has tended to overshadow the complex of features that make up the Inner Harbor.

Despite its key site at the juncture of Pratt and Light Streets, the Harborplace location went begging for development interest for years. In the absence of development, a park along the Light

Street side of the harbor was established, and enlarged when the roadway of the 1950s was removed. The public, including residents of nearby moderate- and lower-income homes, became attached to this rare in-city open green space. The planned replacement of some of this greensward with the shops and restaurants of Harborplace met citizen opposition.

The result was a referendum in 1978 on whether or not Harborplace should be built. The tally was 54 to 46 percent, in favor, after a major campaign for it by city and business interests. Opposition came in part from the black community, which expressed fear that Harborplace shops would not offer it much. Today such opposition is considerably reduced, in part because of a good-faith effort by Harborplace developer Rouse Co. to sponsor minority merchants, to feature a full range of ethnic foods, and, not incidentally, to hire a black as the first manager. Also, as many as 40 percent of the 2000 employees are said to be minority group members.

Harborplace, in a now-familiar pattern, includes a lively mixture of shops, restaurants, overlooks, and pushcarts. One tally lists 130 shops in the twin structures, including 20 food markets, about 40 small eateries, plus 12 restaurants and cafes. Ten years later, Galleria at Harborplace, with more upscale shops, opened in a new development across Pratt Street.

Design Features. The first feature to cite is that the Inner Harbor Shoreline was developed according to a plan generated by the downtown Baltimore business community. From the beginning, this was a public/private undertaking, with business and political leadership united. Baltimore, with a strong mayor form of government, has had a succession of willful mayors, with William Donald Schaefer presiding at the most dynamic time of the Inner Harbor redevelopment.

An underlying factor propelling this collaboration was, simply put, desperation—the sense that without drastic action, the downtown area would be lost to all but the most marginal enterprises. Coupled with strong pride in their city, it moved the civic leadership to act.

The Inner Harbor promenade is the real symbol of the transformation there. This public facility ties together the myriad features. Its distinguishing characteristic, besides its generous width, is an open edge. This was a deliberate decision by designer David Wallace, who argued successfully that this kind of edge served a maritime function by making vessel loading and unloading possible. Two lawsuits against the city, and Wallace's firm, have followed, but the edge

remains marked only by a shift from brick paving to granite.

The National Aquarium at Baltimore is the dominant design feature (see Chapter 2). The twin Harborplace structures (Benjamin Thompson & Associates, Cambridge, Massachusetts architects) helped set the standard for this genre. The green-roofed pavilions are open, light, industrial-looking, with harborside walkways and upstairs seating and overlooks, many banners, tile floors—very colorful.

There are other individual components of distinction: The clean-lined World Trade Center by Pei is open in part at the lower levels to allow views of the harbor from downtown; the 1896 power plant, site of a failed venture by Six Flags Corp. in the mid-1980s, is a powerful, dark brick structure; and Edward Durrell Stone's science museum avoids the monolithic appearance of some such facilities.

Most compelling of all, however, remains the original concept of involving the City of Baltimore intimately with its core harbor area. The one-and-a-half-mile-long promenade is the heart and soul of the undertaking.

Appraisal. The combination of Charles Center and the Inner Harbor redevelopment literally saved downtown Baltimore. They gave a boost to civic morale that is difficult to convey. Suddenly, "Washington's Brooklyn" was a star. It is not accidental that the Charles Center-Inner Harbor office publishes a list of the international delegations that have visited, ranging from Antioch, Turkey, and Asyut, Egypt, to Vienna, Austria, and Wellington, New Zealand. Twenty-five or so years ago, few people from anywhere chose to visit Baltimore.

The lessons here for city planners and developers are myriad, not all of them readily apparent. Baltimore's "formula" has been attempted elsewhere, with varying degrees of success; Cleveland for a time even called its planned lakefront redevelopment the Inner Harbor.

People looking for a quick fix sometimes fasten onto some of the features here, overlooking the social, geographic, financial, and political circumstances that, together, combined with luck, fashioned today's most dramatic waterfront transformation.

Inner Harbor Timeline[3]

1954   Retail Merchants Committee for Downtown formed

1955   Greater Baltimore Committee formed

1956   "Prospectus for Downtown" by Planning Director Arthur Mcvoy published; private Planning Council formed

1959   Plan for Charles Center approved by city council

1960	Charles Center Management Office established; Charles Center project begun
1963	Mayor McKeldin establishes Inner Harbor as major development objective
1964	Inner Harbor plan by Wallace McHarg Roberts & Todd published; bond issue for Inner Harbor of $2 million approved
1965	Charles Center-Inner Harbor Management, Inc., established
1966	Inner Harbor Project 1 Plan published; voters approve loan of $12 million
1968	Inner Harbor project under way; federal grant of $22.4 million released
1972	U.S.S. *Constellation* moved to new pier
1973	Fourth Annual City Fair moved to Inner Harbor
1975	Shoreline promenade completed
1976	Maryland Science Center opens; athletic field completed; Tall Ships visit for two weeks
1977	World Trade Center office tower completed
1978	Marina opened
1978	Harborplace wins voter approval
1979	Baltimore Convention Center opens
1980	Harborplace opens
1981	National Aquarium in Baltimore opens
1984	Redevelopment of Piers 5 and 6 begins

Baltimore Inner Harbor Shoreline

Cost. Estimated $2.5 billion, $625 million in public funds

Dimensions. 95 acres overall, 1.49 miles (7910 linear feet)

Completion date. 1975 (promenade)

Sponsor. Honora M. Freeman, President
City of Baltimore Development Corp.
36 S. Charles St., Suite 1600
Baltimore, MD 21201
(410) 837-9305

Designer(master plan). Wallace Roberts Todd
260 South Broad St.
Philadelphia, PA 19102
(215) 732-5215

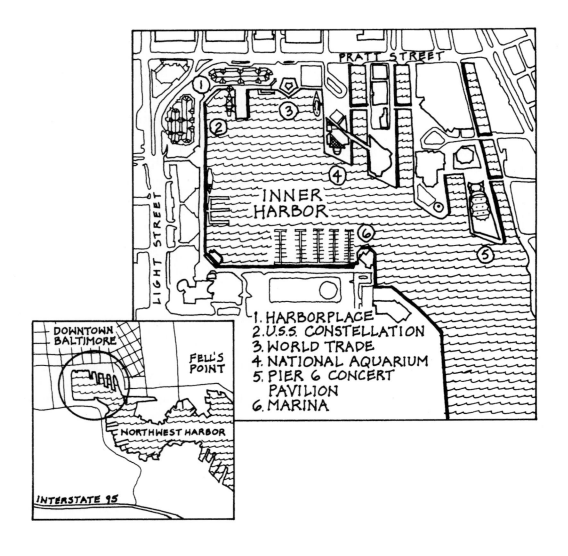

1. HARBORPLACE
2. U.S.S. CONSTELLATION
3. WORLD TRADE
4. NATIONAL AQUARIUM
5. PIER 6 CONCERT PAVILION
6. MARINA

Rowe's Wharf, Boston, Mass.

Rowe's Wharf
Atlantic Avenue
Boston, Massachusetts

Summary

Exemplary mixed-use project, now the new gateway to downtown Boston;
a triumph of contextualist design.

Water taxi to Logan Airport from Rowe's Wharf, an attractive way to
avoid tunnel traffic tieups. (*Jim Harrison*)

Description. Rowe's Wharf is a large project,
containing a total of 665,000 square feet of
office, hotel, residential, dock, and retail space
on a 5½-acre site. But because of skilled attention to its massing and design details, the project not only isn't overlarge, it manages an elegant "fit" into the tight confines of downtown
Boston and its historic central waterfront.

The $193 million undertaking, finished in
1987, mixes interesting public space with high-
income office, hotel, and condominium residences, no mean feat. That Rowe's Wharf is not
a totally private-feeling project is in good part
because the land belonged to the city, in the
hands of the Boston Redevelopment Authority
(BRA). And because the Boston real estate market was "hot" in the early 1980s, the BRA could
be demanding.

Rowe's Wharf is the result of a BRA-organized
competition. The winner, developer Beacon
Companies and its architect, Skidmore, Owings

& Merrill (SOM) of Chicago, spent two years
with the agency and a committee of Boston
architects working out the final design. The
guidelines established such basic issues as height
(a 15-story limit), the use mix, general style, and
public access. They reflected lessons the BRA
learned from its early days, when the approach
was to build big and modern to overcome the
Central Artery highway barrier between the
waterfront and downtown. The twin Harbor
Towers next door, 40 stories high, boxy, concrete,
and sited in a way that blocks access and views,
are products of the earlier era (they were erected
in 1971).

Rowe's Wharf has five components, woven
together so that it's not obvious which is what.
At the front, Atlantic Avenue side, the structure
has two 15-story wings, housing the Boston
Harbor Hotel on one side and residences on the
other. In between, at nine stories, are offices.
Three structures are built onto piers; these step

down in height from seven stories and are surrounded by a public walkway. One of these finger pier buildings is completely condominium, the other two mix hotel and office functions plus support for the docks.

The fifth element of Rowe's Wharf relates most directly to the waterfront. Along the 500 feet at the water's edge is a busy ferry dock; a water ferry service to Logan Airport docks here, providing a dramatic and attractive entry to downtown Boston. There's also a yacht basin. Commuter services to the South Shore, for instance, leave from here.

The centerpiece tying the project together is a 3½-story archway on Atlantic Avenue. This provides unobstructed harbor views from downtown and is the public's invitation to enter. When the elevated expressway in front of Rowe's Wharf is buried, the drama of the arch will be even more obvious and enjoyable, and the pull toward the water stronger.

Atop the arch is a copper dome, echoed in a symbolic gazebo at water's edge that serves as a shelter for ferry passengers and strollers. There's also an observatory on the top level of this central portion of the project, of questionable use to the general public, but enjoyable for hotel or office visitors.

The brick construction, with finely detailed concrete accents, enables Rowe's Wharf to blend with nearby downtown Boston. In this approach, pushed by the BRA, it stands as a philosophic departure from the I. M. Pei-designed Harbor Towers.

With Rowe's Wharf's opening, with its walkway from one side to the other around the perimeter of its three piers, as well as through the center, a long-standing interruption of a waterfront walk next door was finally opened in the fall of 1988.

Another BRA guideline required a significant amount of open space. The guideline called for 50 percent, the developer claims two thirds. The ground-level space is accommodating, and has an open feel about it when the enclosed water area is taken into account. The perimeter walkway is adequate as opposed to outsized.

Two major changes occurred in working out the design. One was the addition of the domed arch. The other was the addition of the hotel, which adds a destination and activity center to

(Breen/Rigby)

what otherwise would have been predominantly residential and office uses. Not all public/private collaborations have such sanguine results, and no doubt the process was frustrating. In the end, the developer, architect, and public entity spoke highly of each other and the give-and-take they went through together to produce Rowe's Wharf.

A less obvious result of the public/private collaboration here is a donation of $2.1 million by the developer to low- and moderate-income housing in the city.

Design Features. Along Atlantic Avenue, the brick facade of Rowe's Wharf curves gently to fit the street. This, together with the low height, basic red brick construction, and rich detailing, may be why people say the project looks as if it's been there for years.

The design approach is consciously contextual. The collaboration of the SOM office, headed by Adrian Smith, a design committee named by the Boston Society of Architects, the design team from the BRA, headed by Robert Kroin, and representatives of the developer worked out an approach that has won general critical plaudits. The BRA's "design concept" stated on page 1 that it was looking for a facility "exhibiting a strong architectural relationship with the abutting properties, the artery, the downtown urban matrix and waterfront development."

One of the significant features of Rowe's Wharf is a stepping down from the street to the waterfront. From its 15-story maximum, the project has a break at nine stories, to echo nearby structures, then gradually drops to seven stories, then three, and finally to a walkway at harbor's edge. The stepping makes Rowe's Wharf the inviting entry point it is from the water, accentuated by the huge archway opening directly in its middle. From the water there are glimpses of the richness of Boston's downtown, one of the most dramatic points of arrival in North America.

Foster's Arch, as the centerpiece is called (it is named for the other wharf that, with Rowe's, was built here in the 1760s), is topped by a glass dome that lets in soft light. The entire 10,000-square-foot space has a monumental feeling, and is elegantly detailed.

Appraisal. In overall execution, Rowe's Wharf is one of the outstanding mixed-use waterfront projects of the 1980s. It successfully fits its context—an active harbor presence and a historic financial district—without being overly fussy.

There's real public accessibility, including a portion of a walkway along the downtown waterfront edge. Visually, by virtue of its dramatic archway, Rowe's Wharf connects the city and the water and is welcoming. Psychologically, the lux-urious feel of the place may be offputting; on the other hand, Bostonians are not shy people.

Probably the feature that is most obviously lacking is a lower-level cafe/restaurant and shop scene, particularly in the vicinity of the ferry docks. This was in the original plans, and would add to the overall liveliness of Rowe's Wharf. As it is, a visitor is greeted by handsome, formal space along the water, with benches but little else. Hotel facilities also do not take maximum advantage of the water.

Rowe's Wharf has been called "sensationally good city-making" by *The Boston Globe* architectural critic Robert Campbell. Paul Goldberger of *The New York Times* labeled Rowe's Wharf a "triumph of urban design, not the least because it strikes a nearly perfect balance between the needs of the people who enter it every day and the needs of the people who walk past it, around it and through it." A sour note came from Ellen Posner of *The Wall Street Journal*, who found the project unimaginative, overly private-feeling, and uninteresting. "A rim of pleasantly designed masonry-clad buildings isn't the worst thing that could happen to the waterfront, but it isn't necessarily the best," she wrote.

We think that Rowe's Wharf is in fact one of the best.

Rowe's Wharf

Cost. $193 million

Source. Equitable Real Estate Investment Management

Dimensions. 5.4-acre site, including 665,000 total square feet with 230 hotel rooms; 330,000 square feet of office space; 10,000 square feet of retail space; 700-car parking; 100 condominiums; and 38 boat slips

Completion date. Fall 1987

Sponsor. Dr. James M. Becker
Equitable Real Estate, The Beacon Companies
75 State St., No. 2450
Boston, MA 02109
(617) 330-1400

Sponsor. Bernard Dreiblatt
Rowe's Wharf Associates
50 Rowe's Wharf
Boston, MA 02110
(617) 330-1400

Sponsor. Stephen Coyle
Boston Redevelopment Authority
One City Hall Square, No. 910
Boston, MA 02201
(617) 722-4300

Designer. Adrian Smith
Skidmore Owings & Merrill
224 S. Michigan Ave.
Chicago, IL 60604
(312) 554-9090

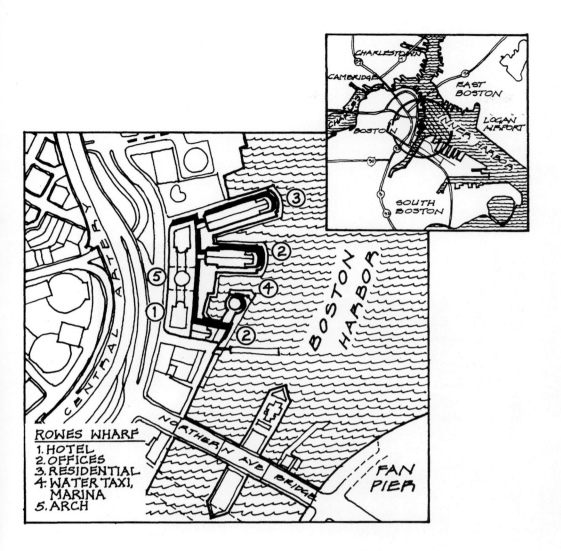

ROWES WHARF
1. HOTEL
2. OFFICES
3. RESIDENTIAL
4. WATER TAXI, MARINA
5. ARCH

Lechmere Canal Park, East Cambridge, Mass. (*John Gustavsen;. Carol R. Johnson & Associates*)

Lechmere Canal Park
Lechmere Canal
East Cambridge, Massachusetts

Summary

Well-designed park around the canal is a focal point for major commercial, mixed-use revitalization.

Description. Carved from an abandoned, weed-infested industrial canal, the restored Lechmere Canal Park brings to life a water feature that had been all but forgotten by its community.

As the industry of East Cambridge left the area after World War II, in a now-familiar pattern for waterfronts, there was left behind 40 acres of empty warehouses and parking lots around a leftover canal that connected to the nearby Charles River.

The turnaround began in 1978 with issuance of the *East Cambridge Riverfront Plan*, developed by city planners and the neighborhood, and subsequent adoption of zoning to carry it out. The story since then, of which the canal park is the symbolic and physical heart, has been a methodical, 12-year revival of the area, capped in 1990 with the opening of a splashy mall, CambridgeSide Galleria.

Before this investment, and numerous others in apartments, condominiums, office space, and retail use, came the plan and the critical up-front public investments. The key early components, made possible with the help of federal grants, in addition to the canal cleanup and beautification, were a public parking garage, road improvements, and modernization of the transit system's Lechmere station.

The most visible of the changes, keyed to a fountain whose spray reaches as high as 160 feet, is the restored Lechmere Canal. The dredged canal was returned to a 100-foot width. It measures 500 feet in length and has a basin that is 240 feet in diameter. The site is very visible, crossed by busy Commercial Avenue, which runs along the Charles, near the campus of the Massachusetts Institute of Technology and across the river from downtown Boston.

In all there are about 4 acres of carefully bermed green space surrounding the canal, landscaped with trees and shrubs, a total project of about 7 acres. The cost of the park was $10 million, out a total of some $50 million invested in public funds in the area, said to have generated about 10 times that in private investment.

Since its opening, the canal park has been a popular attraction, both for pedestrians who are now able to enter from paths along the river, and for boaters. A Charles River cruise boat based at the nearby Science Center makes a stop in the basin for passengers from the Galleria. Skating in the winter and model boat races in warm weather are additional activities sparked by the canal's restoration. The residents adjoining the park, and in revived nearby East Cambridge districts, have adopted the area as their window on the Charles.

Design Features. Around the canal is a brick walkway up to 14 feet in width, without railing. A pavilion is another centerpiece, with photographic details of early days in East Cambridge etched into its glass canopy.

Details in the park design are consciously meant to reflect the area's industrial heritage—which included the Davenport sofa company and the forerunner of the Libby glass company, now in Toledo—in such details as park furniture with iron patterns based on the factories, benches resembling old trolley seats, and compatible light fixtures and rails. Rugged stone is used around the basin edge and for steps and other components.

Another feature of Lechmere Canal Park is the incorporation of art work, under a program in Cambridge as in certain other jurisdictions, where 1 percent of public works projects are set aside for art. Three artists' works are in place here, including the "Stepping Stones" by David Phillips, which are bronze medallions in the paving under the pavilion that suggest the earliest days of the site, when it was a tidal marsh, shellfishing site, and in the very earliest times, part of the ocean floor.

One key design feature, reflecting the stated desire of the neighborhood, is the absence of a railing around the basin (the depth varies from 4 to 8 feet), and steps along part of the basin edge that lead directly to the water. This allows canoes and paddleboats to land easily. Another aspect is the lighting, which helps to make the basin a magical place at night.

Appraisal. This small gem of a water body, seemingly undiscovered by the outside world until a shopping mall was sited beside it, stands on its own as a finely detailed restoration. It is described in official documents as the "heart" and "focal point" of the major redevelopment that has taken place in an old, decayed industrial neighborhood—accurate enough descriptions in this instance.

The total turnaround here is dramatic and would probably be better recognized in some place other than Boston, where the emphasis is generally on the harbor. Lechmere Canal Park set a high standard of quality for the entire undertaking.

The community and its planners deserve credit for developing a lofty vision and, more important, seeing it through. It's not perfect, of course. It has been noted, for instance, that the Filene's store in the Galleria refused to have doors opening to the canal park, preferring that its customers enter only from within the mall. This kind of problem results when suburban models are applied in city areas; the general view of the

Galleria, and especially its splendid park setting, is sanguine.

Lechmere Canal Park
Cost. $10 million
Source. 90 percent public, including an Urban Development Action Grant, U.S. Dept. of Housing and Urban Development
Dimensions. 7 acres
Completion date. 1985

Sponsor. Michael H. Rosenberg, Assistant City Manager; J. Roger Boothe, Director of Urban Design
Cambridge Community Development Department
57 Inman St.
Cambridge, MA 02139
(617) 349-4600

Designer. Carol R. Johnson, William Taylor
Carol R. Johnson & Associates, Inc.
1100 Massachusetts Ave.
Cambridge, MA 02138
(617) 868-6115

Designer. Dennis J. Carlone
Drill Campbell Carlone
130 Prospect St., 3rd Floor
Cambridge, MA 02139
(617) 492-8400

Water engineering. HMM Associates, Inc.
196 Baker Ave.
Concord, MA 01742
(617) 371-4000

Marine/structural engineer. Childs Engineering Corporation
541 Main St.
Medfield, MA 02052
(508) 359-8945

Architectural consultant. Laurence Rubin, AIA
381 Congress St.
Boston, MA 02210
(617) 542-6243

Civil/mechanical/electrical engineer. Fay, Spofford & Thorndike, Inc.
191 Spring St.
Lexington, MA 02173
(617) 863-8300

Geotechnical engineer. Haley & Aldrich, Inc.
58 Charles St.
Cambridge, MA 02141
(617) 494-1606

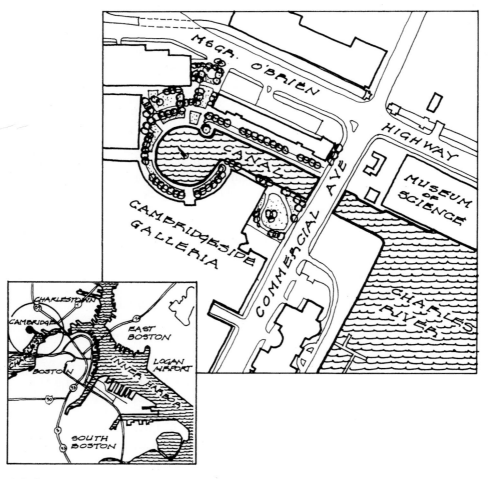

Riverfront Park, Chicago, Ill. (*Breen/Rigby*)

Riverfront Park
Chicago River between Clark
and Dearborn Streets
Chicago, Illinois

Summary

A high-quality stretch of riverfront public access provided as part of a
major new mixed-use development in the heart of the city.

Description. Riverfront Park is a 10-acre public-amenity portion of a large mixed-use development on the north bank of the main branch of the Chicago River. Quaker Tower, headquarters of Quaker Oats Company, is a 35-story, 1-million-square-foot building that sits next to the 425-room, 20-story Nikko Hotel. The two separate owners cooperated on the design and execution of the multilevel park space in front of their buildings.

A tree-lined promenade runs 300 feet on the lower level between bridge abutments on Dearborn and Clark Streets. Beautiful stairways descend to the river level from both streets. The bridge tower building on Clark Street contains an elevator, providing handicapped access to the river. In good weather, a restaurant on the river level further animates the promenade with an outdoor cafe. A low, limestone wall does not block views. The terraces above the river level are open to the public and landscaped with evergreens that provide year-round color.

Design Features. The Chicago River is one of the most exciting urban rivers anywhere. Ten bridges cross it in the downtown area from the mouth of Lake Michigan to where it branches off near the Merchandise Mart. Stunning skyscrapers line the banks, but access to the river was somewhat limited for many years.

Friends of the Chicago River, a nonprofit citizen's organization founded in 1979, has been promoting public accessibility to the river and has been a catalyst for adoption of riverfront zoning and design guidelines (Chapter 8, Chicago River Urban Design Guidelines). Riverfront Park is an example of developers working with the city to achieve not just public access, but quality public space complete with handsomely detailed terraces, stairways, and a promenade embellished with lush plantings and enlivened by eating areas. The Nikko Hotel lobby, appropriately enough, opens onto a Japanese garden.

The Nikko Hotel went one step further and donated $200,000 toward the $450,000 cost of another riverfront garden and walkway on the south bank of the river, across from Riverfront Park and the hotel/office tower. Noted architect Kenzo Tange designed the 9000-square-foot Japanese garden there.

Appraisal. Riverfront Park set a standard and was a major breakthrough for Chicago River advocates. In 1988, Elizabeth Hollander, city planning commissioner, put it this way:

> I think especially what the Nikko Hotel and the adjacent Quaker Tower office development did on the river, with their restaurants and park, represented a major breakthrough for developing the river into a tourist attraction. It created a whole

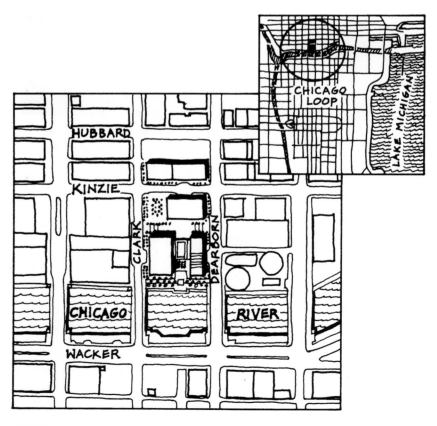

new positive attitude among developers about what can be done along the river. I foresee the river becoming a major tourist attraction within the next five years. I think the public will take to the river the same way they now take to the lakefront.[4]

This park/walkway eloquently demonstrates that such facilities can be incorporated as part of private commercial projects in densely built-up, high-rent downtown areas.

Riverfront Park
Cost. $280 million (entire project)
Source. Aetna Insurance Co., Hartford; Sumitomo Life, Tokyo Dimensions. 10 acres; 300 linear feet of riverfront
Completion date. 1987

Sponsor. Daniel T. McCaffery
  BCE Devel. Properties, Inc.
  737 North Michigan Ave., Suite 2050
  Chicago, IL 60611
  (312) 944-3777

Sponsor. Tishman Realty and Construction Corp.
  321 N. Clark St., Suite 2800
  Chicago, IL 60610
  (312) 930-2080

Sponsor. Chicago Department of Planning
  City Hall, 121 N. LaSalle, Room 1000
  Chicago, IL 60602
  (312) 744-4190

Designers. Bruce Graham, Diane Legge
  Skidmore, Owings & Merrill
  33 W. Monroe St.
  Chicago, IL 60603
  (312) 641-5959

Bayside Marketplace, Miami, Fla. (*Steve Rosenthal*)

Bayside Marketplace
Miamarina at N.E. 4th Street
Miami, Florida

Summary

Perhaps the most successful of the new "festival marketplace" designs.

(*Steve Rosenthal, Benjamin Thompson & Associates*)

Description.   Bayside Marketplace consists of twin two-story, tin-roofed structures centered on a courtyard. It's a now-familiar formula that architect Benjamin Thompson & Associates of Cambridge, Massachusetts, and The Rouse Co. of Columbia, Maryland, have repeated on a number of waterfronts. This model resembles most closely their marketplace in Baltimore, versus the restoration at historic Quincy Market in Boston.

That said, however, this installation has strengths its predecessors lack, as well as one fundamental problem that many of the other "festival marketplaces" don't face.

The style with which Bayside is done is standout. Its openness, orientation to the water (it's wrapped around a marina), accessibility to excursion vessels, significant landscaping, and colorful details may make it the best of the Thompson/Rouse installations built from scratch.

Its biggest problem is that it is isolated from downtown Miami. There's a six-lane major roadway, plus a parking median, between Bayside and the city. To the north is a blank park; south is another park, equipped with an amphitheater, a waterfront promenade, a fountain sculpture by Isamu Noguchi, and a large InterContinental Hotel. Thus Bayside, for all of its liveliness,

openness, and simulated urbanity, is relatively isolated.

Contributing to this isolation is a 1200-space parking garage that adjoins it. Local design critic Beth Dunlop called it "inexcusable dead space in a city that needs as much life as it can get."[5] Another part of her complaint is that the city's People Mover monorail is blocks away, as a result of a route choice that was not coordinated with downtown's major public attraction.

As parking garages go, Bayside's is one of the better-looking models. Its four levels are well screened with palms and other landscaping, and from the south it is relatively unobtrusive. Its existence would seem to be a necessity for an installation that must appeal to suburbanites to make its living. The garage feeds directly into one of the two structures (the north building)— the one with what might be termed the "serious" shops. The City of Miami spent $19 million on the parking structure, a familiar pattern in deals with the Rouse Co.

Bayside's construction cost was $93 million. It opened its doors to enthusiastic crowds on April 8, 1987.

Just as the parking garage is, relatively speaking, hidden and unobtrusive, the same can be said for Bayside as a whole. Approaching it from

(*Steve Rosenthal, Benjamin Thompson & Associates*)

the south, it is hidden by a landscaped berm that is the backside of the amphitheater. Approaching along the wide promenade at bay's edge, you are fairly onto Bayside before its flags and characteristic peaked roofs come into view.

The dock here is served by excursion boats that pick up and drop off from Bayside. The area, leading directly into the south building, is also where tour buses circle. Thus Bayside serves the larger Miami economy by providing a safe downtown destination for visitors. It seems evident, however, that the bus- and boat-transported visitors generally do not venture into downtown.

The two marketplaces contain 235,000 square feet. The overall site is 20 acres. Typical of such marketplaces, there's a high turnover of shops and an inevitable amount of what's called "remerchandising." In 1989, a major shift was made away from food toward more retail.[6] Shops at Bayside are 50–50 national chains and local stores. When it opened, 77 of the 156 merchants were members of minorities, The Rouse Co. reported.[7] Many later went out of business, victims of their own inexperience and hard retail times.[8]

In numbers of visitors, Bayside was reported in mid-1989 to be serving a mix of 55 percent tourist trade, 45 percent locals. On a visit in early 1992, the mix was evident: At midday there was a crowd dressed in everything from shorts to gray suits. Bayside is also apparently a hit with the singles crowd working downtown; a Dick Clark American Bandstand two-level bar is reported to be a lively after-work spot, especially on Fridays and again on Saturday afternoons.

Design Features. Some of the construction cost is in the details. For instance, there are tile accents with a deep blue band above a mottled brown/tan-colored tile along the pastel salmon-colored stucco walls. The buildings are predominantly white, with turquoise shutters.

Each building has two decked platforms built slightly into the marina. These spaces provide public seating, which affords excellent views across the marina into Biscayne Bay. There is another large public area at the center of the twin structures, Bayside's events place. The market is heavily programmed to induce South Florida residents to visit.

Another characteristic detail is the industrial-looking railing and stairs to the second level; somewhat nautical-looking wires are used with metal or wooden railings. The trash receptacles are handsome and, typical of such marketplaces, there are omnipresent cleanup crews.

In 1991 Bayside underwent an $11 million renovation. Some of this was to correct what the current manager describes as design flaws, namely, the difficulty in getting traffic to the ends of the two upper stories. Part of the solution was to relocate the escalators from the center to the ends of the twin pavilions. Another aspect of the renovations was the opening up of the lower levels to the marina-side walkway, with doors, windows, and cafe tables.[9]

Appraisal. Bayside is, altogether, the best of this newly built genre of waterfront installation. It has created a lively destination in a downtown crying out for more of the same. The location, astride a recreational marina and with ample overlooks of the harbor, is dramatic. (Problems with the marina are apparently on their way to being worked out.)

In execution, Bayside's combination of South Florida and Caribbean colors and motifs distinguishes this "festival marketplace." Its landscaping and siting behind screens of palm trees are uncharacteristic of such installations. It may—or may not—be the financial boon projected (it's hard to get accurate data), but it has succeeded in bringing people into downtown Miami, even at night—many, no doubt, for the first time in years.

The pity about Bayside is the decision made years ago to run a major north–south highway along the edge of downtown, separating it from Biscayne Bay. Bayside and the refurbishing of neighboring Bayfront Park are a spirited attempt to bridge the gap.

Bayside Marketplace

Cost. $93 million
Dimensions. 20-acre site; 234,408 square feet with 180 shops, 1200-space garage
Completion date. May, 1987

Sponsor. Laurin B. Askew, Jr., Director of Design
The Rouse Company
10275 Little Patuxent Pkwy.
Columbia, MD 21044
(410) 992-6000

Sponsor. Bayside Center Ltd./Rouse Miami, Inc.
Miamarina at N.E. 4th St.
Miami, FL 33132
(305) 577-3344

Designer. Ben Thompson and Bruno D'Agostino
Benjamin Thompson & Associates
One Story St.
Cambridge, MA 02138
(617) 876-4300

Designer. Hilario Candela, FAIA; Walter Fleck, PE
Spillis Candela & Partners, Inc.
800 Douglas Entrance
Coral Gables, FL 33134
(305) 444-4691

Designer. Albert R. Perez, ASLA
Albert R. Perez Associates
801 Madrid St.
Coral Gables, FL 33134
(305) 445-9223

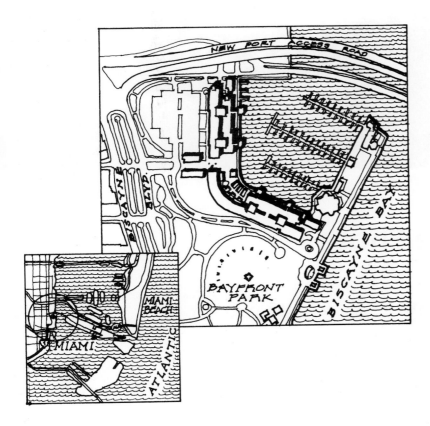

Aker Brygge Phase II, Oslo, Norway. (*Bengston/Solvang/Winsnes*)

Aker Brygge Phase II
Stranden 1
Oslo, Norway

Summary

Dazzling transformation of a former shipyard in downtown Oslo.

(*Bengston/Solvang/Winsnes*)

Description. Phase II of the Aker Brygge project is a dramatic four-building project that effectively extends the center of Oslo to its waterfront.

A key to the project, following the closing of the shipbuilding industry by the Aker Company in 1981, was the decision to replace a major roadway that split the city center from the waterfront with a tunnel. This project, begun in the 1980s but not due for completion until 1992, set the stage for an "ideas competition" for the shipyard.

The competition, held in 1982, was called "The City and the Fjord Oslo Year 2000." Plans for a 65-acre site were developed in the following years, and, with a vibrant real estate development market, action followed rapidly in three phases in the late 1980s. Phase II, detailed here, was completed in 1989. Phase III followed, but a Phase IV aquarium has been postponed.

Among the principles enunciated as a result of the design competition was that there should be a mixture of uses, including housing; that it should fit into the existing city street grid, which is very pronounced in adjoining parcels; that there should be strong connections to the docks and the bay; and that the work should be phased. Key design features that needed to be taken into

account were a nearby castle, the City Hall Square, and Pipervika Bay. Unstated, but obviously a given, was a policy that the water's edge should be publicly accessible.

In a pattern familiar to many city waterfronts in the United States, an early action, in 1984, was a major festival. Called "Culture Is Alive," it impressed on the citizens that changes were imminent, and that public cultural attractions were to be a part of what was to be built at the shipyard.

Following the renovation of three warehouses, with varied uses including offices, shops, restaurants, a theater, and exhibit space, the stage was set for new construction in Phase II. First came construction of the wide, brick promenade along the bay in the project area, completed in 1986. Also during Phase I, a ferry dock, with service connecting Oslo with Nesodden, was moved to the promenade.

In Phase II the emphasis is on housing on the upper levels, plus strong street-level activity on the first floors, and maximum connections to the waterfront. Phase II faces the waterfront on two sides, in fact. The promenade runs along one side, while the spine of Phase II—a magnificent public plaza—leads physically and visually to a former drydock and, beyond, to the working port and fjord. The drydock has been converted into a private marina.

The four buildings of Phase II cluster around a large plaza. There's an additional "fjord alley," lined with trees, that brings pedestrians into the middle of the plaza. Other openings also connect to the surrounding city, providing a rich mixture of intimate spaces, wide avenues, and a grand piazza-type space. Underneath the project is a large parking garage, with direct access by elevators to the floors above.

Two buildings front the bay, Dokkbygningen and Kaibygning II. The former is four stories, with a lower section cantilevered slightly over the dock it oversees. Kaibygning II contains shops and a restaurant facing the tree-lined walkway, the Fjordalléen, with the five levels above containing offices, and the top levels, residences.

The other two buildings, Fondbygningen— distinguished by a bold glass facade—and Kaibygning I, have shops and upper-level residences. The whole residential precinct is connected with an overhead walkway on the sixth levels. The height and siting of the buildings serve to maximize harbor views.

Design Features. Aker Brygge Phase II does a number of things well. It presents a harmonious profile along the promenade and bayfront. Decidedly modern, with extensive use of glass,

the bayfront facades also emphasize brick, in keeping with two converted warehouses adjoining. The roofs here pick up the profile and forms of their historic neighbors.

Inside Phase II, the metal and glass of the focal-point building of the Fjordalléen walkway—Fondbygningen—establishes its own sprightly mood. Inside are terraced levels, including a restaurant. An art exhibition space is here as well, plus a theater that seats 645. Paving on the carefully landscaped walkway combines traditional slate-gray granite sidewalks and a main alley of paving bricks.

A water sculpture at the heart of the wide, brick plaza has rounded walls, a snail-like feature, an obelisk, and a spray, and it makes an inviting kid's play area. Visually, it is the focal point of the upper end of the plaza, facing the drydock and waterfront beyond. The plaza itself is lined with cafes in warm weather. Perhaps because of the climate, there's little in the way of permanent seating.

Kaibygning I is distinguished by a glass atrium six stories high, into which offices protrude. A spiral staircase occupies one corner of an altogether sleek space. The atrium is actually a glass roof that connects two parts of the structure.

The building closest to the dock will be part of a future development. It has a white marble and

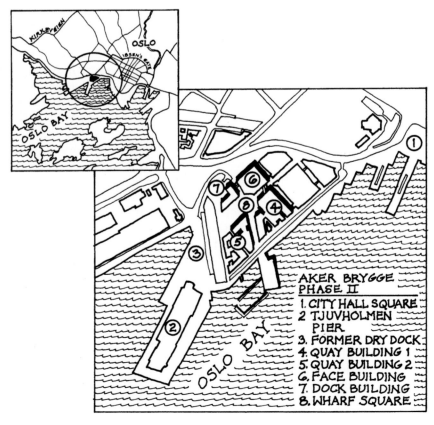

AKER BRYGGE
PHASE II
1. CITY HALL SQUARE
2. TJUVHOLMEN
   PIER
3. FORMER DRY DOCK
4. QUAY BUILDING 1
5. QUAY BUILDING 2
6. FACE BUILDING
7. DOCK BUILDING
8. WHARF SQUARE

green steel frame, intended to set it off from the warm bricks of the plaza and to reflect the industrial past of the site.

Appraisal. There's a liveliness here and a welcoming atmosphere for a project that contains significant amounts of office and residential space among its 250,000 square meters. The public promenade at one side is a major open space for Oslo, and the nearby cafes and shops work together with it. The plaza in the middle of Phase II is another major public area, and is the site of concerts.

The architecture is bold but in scale and harmony with traditional Oslo, a neat feat. There's a bit of a light-hearted air to the entire project, perhaps best captured in the plaza fountain—a whimsical installation, fairly small as fountains go, but playful, inviting, and well placed. It's a good metaphor for Aker Brygge Phase II.

Aker Brygge Phase II

Cost. $450 million

Source. Aker A.S. 75 percent, Den Norske Bank 25 percent

Dimensions. 170,000 square meters; overall site, 2.5 acres

Completion date. Late 1980s

Sponsor. Aker Brygge ANS
Fjordalléen 16
0250 Oslo Norway
(011-47-2) 601840

Designer. Niels Torp
Niels Torp A/S Arch. MNAL
Industrigt 59, Postbox 5387, Majorstuen
0304 Oslo Norway
(011-47-2) 601840

Designer. 13-3 Landscape Architects A/S
Grensen 5/7
0159 Oslo Norway

Structural engineer. Ingeniørene Bonde & Co. AS
Treschowsgt. 2B
0477 Oslo Norway

Mechanical engineer. Erichson & Horgen
Hansteengt. 5
0253 Oslo Norway

Electrical engineer. Rasmussen & Strand
Drammensvelen 130C
0277 Oslo Norway

Geotechnical engineer. Geoteam
Hoffsjef Lovenskioldsv 31C
0382 Oslo Norway

RiverPlace, Portland, Ore. (*City of Portland Development Commission*)

RiverPlace
S.W. Harbor Way
Portland, Oregon

Summary

Well-designed mixed-use project anchors a key portion of Portland's Willamette River waterfront and has become a city hallmark.

Description. It is not to minimize the skilled design and quality execution in evidence here to begin instead with its context. For what is most remarkable is that RiverPlace exists where once the Harbor Drive Expressway ran.

The decision to remove the Robert Moses-designed highway along the Willamette River in downtown Portland is credited to the late Tom McCall, one-time governor; Neil Olson, a former mayor; and businessman Glenn Jackson.[10] Olson was part of a city club committee stocked with local architects that wanted to remove the road. McCall and political opponent Bob Straud agreed on the idea one day while driving together on the opposite side of the Willamette. In any case, the road removal became official with adoption of the city's Downtown Plan in 1972 and constitutes a relatively rare civic assertion of its values.

In place of the expressway, described as Portland's busiest (the traffic was moved to the other side of the river), is 1 mile of linear riverfront park adjoining the central business district. Work on the park began in the 1970s, and by 1979 a plan had been adopted to develop a portion as a mixed-use project, from a total park of 73 acres.

Since 1958, the driving force downtown had been the Portland Development Commission, originally an urban renewal agency, and it was this body that prepared and carried through the South Waterfront Project, of which RiverPlace is the major commercial component. One key to moving the project forward was the city's gradual acquisition over time of the property involved.

First came public improvements to the site, representing a total investment of about $6 million and focused on a downtown marina, made possible by twin breakwaters. Other site improvements included a park extension, a walkway, shore stabilization, and roadway construction, and set the stage for developers to compete.

The marina, covering about 5 ½ acres, officially opened in 1985. The facility includes a floating restaurant, a rowing school, docks for about 200 boats, and an open, accessible breakwater that serves as a walkway and fishing pier.

The development commission chose Cornerstone Columbia Development Co. of Seattle, a creation of Weyerhaeuser Co. and Portland General Corp. For the developer, the commission's design controls meant it knew exactly what was expected of it, it had an active city partner, and, important to the speed with

(City of Portland Development Commission)

(City of Portland Development Commission)

which RiverPlace moved from plan to construction, all permits for in-water activity had been secured.[11]

The result, in two phases, consists of 150 residential units in part one, a deluxe hotel with 75 rooms, a promenade lined with small shops and anchored by restaurants, underground parking, office space, an athletic club, and recreational facilities. Phase one was completed in August 1985. Included is a combined office/residential building on S.W. Harbor Way.

The second phase, immediately adjacent, is an apartment complex, on 6 acres, with 108 units, associated parking, and retail spaces along the lower, riverfront level.

The tallest building is four stories, meaning that the entire undertaking has a low profile along the very visible riverfront. RiverPlace appears to nestle into its setting, with the taller buildings of the central business district behind it and forming a backdrop, and Tom McCall Waterfront Park stretching along the river beside it.

The 25-foot-wide brick promenade is an active spot, lined with cafe tables in good weather (the season is generally May to September).

The condominium units are behind and above the shops, their entranceways gated but accessible to a degree.

The housing surrounds interior courtyards and conveys a sense of privacy and security even though it is adjacent to a busy public space. Noise created a problem in housing over one restaurant. The solution was to convert three units to office space.[12]

Ownership has been transferred to Sansei America, Inc., since Cornerstone Columbia Development Co. has been dissolved. The new owner paid $34.4 million for an 85 percent share in 1989, and was ordered by a court in April 1992 to complete the buy-out for another $7.4 million.[13] The first two phases of RiverPlace cost a total of $44 million.

Design Features. Notable is the construction of the condominium housing in wood. This was a developer/architect decision to both hold down the costs and reflect the Pacific Northwest heritage of Portland. The units, in seven separate buildings, are constructed on a concrete lid over a 433-space parking garage. In part, the concrete pad is a fire-protection element.

The triangular site, wedged between Front

Street and the river as it curves past downtown, was once occupied by a sawmill. This posed a particular challenge in that as much as 40 feet of sawdust were left behind. This necessitated that pilings be driven deep into the ground to anchor the complex.

The Portland Development Commission, as the lead public partner, provided design and performance guidelines in 20 areas, including what was wanted at street level, namely, activity focused on the pedestrian. Guidance included the minimum number of residential units in the first phase (150), aimed at a moderate price level. Two major restaurants were to anchor the retail area along the water's edge, with shops in between, and a functioning marina was to occupy the foreground.

Cornerstone added to the mix a small, European-style hotel, the Alexis, at the apex of the triangular property. Its wide porches recall old-time Northwest hotels. The distinctive roof shape helps define RiverPlace and establishes an image for the entire project. Gabled and sloping roofs characterize the residential quarter, making for a far more visually interesting project than flat roofs would have provided.

The developer proposed, and accomplished, the floating restaurant in the marina to add to its liveliness. This required a waiver of state poli-cy against a "non-water-dependent water coverage component" and has been very popular. Adjustments came during the development process; for instance, a mid-rise housing tower was dropped in favor of a lower building with a mixture of office space and housing, in response to market conditions.

Pedestrian access to the site is provided from downtown as well as along the riverfront. Service and trash handling to the site is complicated. The design decision was to concentrate all such activity on one street; congestion is said to occur.

The detailing along the generous promenade is excellent, extending to tree grates, lampposts, and railings. Another standout feature is the use of colors in the buildings. In one structure fronting the promenade, there is brown stone at eye level, tan wood above, with white and red accents.

The promenade is curved, a simple but extremely effective detail. Reflecting the river, the curve enables people at any point along the way to have a good view of the entire scene; a straight, linear design would not allow this.

RiverPlace has experienced heavy parking and traffic demand at times, exceeding capacity, attesting to the pulling power of a well-executed project that mixes public open space and commercial offerings along a water body.

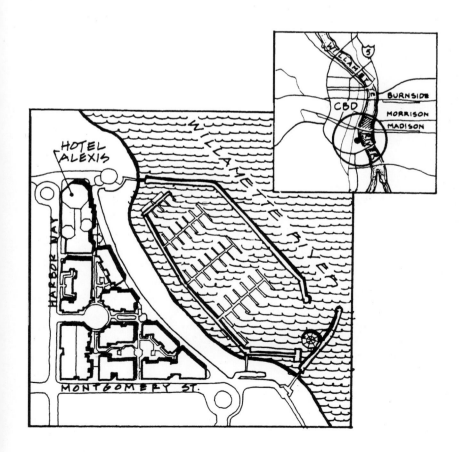

Appraisal. The book, *Images of Portland*, carries RiverPlace on its cover. This attests that the low-profile, peaked-roof design, with public attractions amid housing and offices and a lively marina, have won wide acceptance in Portland. RiverPlace now anchors one end of the well-used Waterfront Park in one of the country's most distinguished waterfront transformations. Well conceived, embodying a successful public/private collaboration that promoted a quality design and execution, it is a model for such undertakings.

It is significant that, in a city with a strong open-space commitment, part of the riverfront opened up by expressway removal has been employed for commercial purposes, with apparently wide support. For instance, the Portland Friends of the Willamette Greenway, often at odds with developer proposals, backed RiverPlace.[14]

RiverPlace

Cost. $200 million
Dimensions. 8.7-acre site; Phase I, 150 residential units, retail and esplanade, 75-room hotel, athletic club, 41,900 square feet of office space, 200-slip marina
Completion date. Phase I, 1985; Phase II, 1987

Sponsor. Commissioner's Office
City of Portland Development Commission
1120 S.W. Fifth, Suite 1102
Portland, OR 97204
(503) 823-3200

Sponsor. Dennis O'Neill
Cornerstone Columbia Development Company
1011 Western Ave., No. 500
Seattle, WA 98104
(206) 623-9374

Designer. Olson Sundberg Architects
108 First Avenue South, 4th Floor
Seattle, WA 98104
(206) 624-5670

Designer. Alan Grainger
GGLO Architecture & Interior Design
1008 Western Ave.
Seattle, WA 98104
(206) 467-5828

Designer. David Wright, FAIA
Bumgardner Architects
101 Stewart St.
Seattle, WA 98101
(206) 223-1361

Salford Quays, Salford, England. (*Ian Beesley*)

Salford Quays
Trafford Road
Salford, Greater Manchester,
England

Summary

An ambitious rejuvenation of massive docks along the Manchester Ship Canal has bolstered the image of Salford, known in song as a "dirty old town."

(Ian Beesley)

Description. The Salford Docks were a principal feature of Manchester's 35-mile canal and dock system, which opened in 1894. The system succeeded in making the inland city a major port, third largest in the country, where industry and commerce flourished through World War II. Trade peaked in 1958, and the docks began a gradual decline for the same reasons similar facilities around the globe fell into disuse.

The docks were shut in 1982, but early efforts to interest investors were largely unsuccessful, even with the establishment of an "enterprise zone" providing various incentives. The area in the early 1980s was unpromising: The hinterland was said to exhibit "all the hallmarks of urban decay and loss of confidence." A nearby area, once the largest industrial estate in Britain, was a "desultory shadow of its former glory." Some signs of rebirth in the area were evident, however, including private investment interest in an area to the north of the docks, and in a small portion of the Salford Docks site, both with enterprise zones.[15] The stage was set for the next phase.

In 1984 the Salford City Council acquired most of the docklands property— some 75 acres, including 3 miles of open waterfront—from the ship canal company owner, using assistance from the national government. A master plan for the entire property was launched, the feeling being that the docks had to be addressed as a whole rather than approached piecemeal.

The Salford Quays redevelopment plan was adopted in May 1985, and a commitment was made by the city council to invest in infrastructure improvements to induce the desired private-sector involvement. The plan, by Shepeard, Epstein & Hunter of London, aided by engineering consultants Ave Orup & Partners, identified four major areas for improvements: the water, about 40 percent of the site; roads and services; public access and landscaping, opening up docks that had been impenetrable by the public in the past; and other infrastructure improvements.

The water in the Manchester Ship Canal, as a City of Salford document describes it, was severely polluted, one of the worst in Britain. It contained "foul odors from gases bubbling in profusion to the water surface." This, it was noted dryly, was a deterrent to potential developers.

The scheme called for sealing off three of the four water bodies between the docks, with dams that would serve as roadways. The water left inside was treated, using a system of air pumps to aerate the oxygen-poor waters. The sealed water bodies were interconnected by new canals cut through the docks. One water area was left connected to the ship canal, for a marina.

To open up the docks to development, a circulation system of roads was established, looping around the site and connecting to Trafford Road, a major thoroughfare.

The edges of the docks, the plan stated, should

be landscaped promenades and walkways, to allow public circulation along the docks and pedestrian connections between them.

The additional infrastructure improvements included reworking outmoded service ducts that ran under the dock structures. Considered a health hazard, they have been made over to carry electrical lines and to serve as tree planters.

This preliminary work was substantially completed by 1990. The city estimates the total public expenses at only about $70 million. A key source of initial funding was the national Department of the Environment, whose regional office was said to see the need for a high-quality public investment.

In the meantime, a number of private projects were built, beginning with an eight-screen movie house in 1986 that seats 1808 (with parking for 300). Additional investments, bearing out the plan's call for a mix of uses, followed. Copthorne Hotel opened in June 1987, with 166 rooms, four-star quality, and banquet and restaurant facilities.

Office developments in a number of locations, restaurants/pubs, and housing developments have followed. Outside the Salford Quays site, across Trafford Road, a major office project is well developed; projected employment at Exchange Quay is 1000. This is in addition to the 1245 permanent jobs listed within the project as of April 1991. Overall projected private investment is put at $680 million, making for a very high private-to-public investment ratio of nearly 10 to 1.[16]

At the beginning in 1992, in addition to the movie house and hotel cited above, there were 500 housing units at Salford Quays, a 76-berth marina, 1.6 million square feet of office space, nine wine bars/restaurants/pubs, and around 100,000 square feet of retail space.

In the planning stage, at a key site on the largest pier, is the municipally financed Salford Centre for the Performing Arts and Heritage Centre. This is billed as the centerpiece of the entire undertaking, and the city hopes for at least a partial opening in 1994–1995. It's envisioned as a facility for both resident and touring companies, especially ballet, and as gallery space for the city's collection of the works of local artist L. S. Lowry (1887–1976), noted for depicting often bleak scenes of Manchester. The heritage centre will focus on the history of the Manchester Ship Canal. Also projected is a link to Manchester's Metrolink rapid transit system.

With the cleansed waters came boating activi-ties inside the basins, and a fish-stocking program. The city aims to establish a community water sports program.

Teaching aids used in the school system focus on the work, past and present, at Salford Quays. There's also an effort at oral history, to collect remembrances of the days when the docks employed 3000 workers.

Design Features. In a physical sense, the Salford Quays project fits into the generally low profile of Salford and next-door Manchester. It avoids the outsized presence of its larger counterpart project in London, the bankrupt Canary Wharf.

There is an attention to quality in the work here. Granite boulders, matching the walls of the dock areas, edge the shoreline. There's solid brickwork in the paving, recycled bollards along the edges, plus lighting fixtures and benches chosen with an eye to fit the industrial past. A major amount of landscaping has been installed, especially on the walkways.

The city has employed local artists and crafts-people since the beginning. As a result, there are public sculptures throughout the project. Another detail deserving praise is the presence of stepped levels at the water's edge, allowing direct contact with the water.

Two cranes from the active days of the port have been kept, as symbolic reminders of the past. Likewise, an old railway swing bridge was floated to a new location and now is a pedestrian passageway between two docks. It is 93 meters in length.

Appraisal. There's little question about the psychological impact of the Salford Quays project. A major mixed-use development that is bringing new office, housing, and public attraction investments to an area rendered obsolete by technology shifts is an obvious boost for a gritty manufacturing area such as Salford/Manchester.

In fact, a city brochure talking about the "new era" in Salford highlights the quays project as the "most exciting development" in the city. Although there are differences in estimates of the number of jobs that will eventually result here, it's clear that substantial employment is now located at Salford Quays.

There is a question whether this employment matches the needs in Salford, or whether the jobs are filled from outside the city. As with all enterprise zones, there's the related question of whether the jobs are genuinely new or merely relocated.

Still, Salford Quays is a remarkable achievement, taking a virtual blank piece of territory beside a foul waterway and turning it into a place of considerable potential. When the performing arts center opens, Salford Quays will no doubt affirm itself with an appreciative public as a well-done conversion of a territory rich in memories.

Salford Quays

Cost. $750 million
Source. 9.5 percent public financing, federal government; 90.5 percent private financing
Dimensions. Overall site, 60 hectares (including 25 hectares water); hotel, 166 beds; cinema, 1808 seats; 500 housing units; 76-berth marina; 1.6 million square feet of offices; up to 100,000 square feet of retail space
Completion date. 1990

Sponsor. W. A. K. Struthers, City Technical Services Officer
City of Salford
Salford Civic Centre, Chorley Rd, Swinton
Salford, Greater Manchester, M27 2AD, England
(011 44 61) 794-4711

Designer. J. Thacker
Shepheard, Epstein & Hunter
14-22 Canton St.
London, W1V 1LB England
(011 44 71) 734-0111

Engineer. J. Morgan
Ove Arup & Partners
13 Fitzroy St.
London W1P 6BQ England
(011 44 71) 636-1531

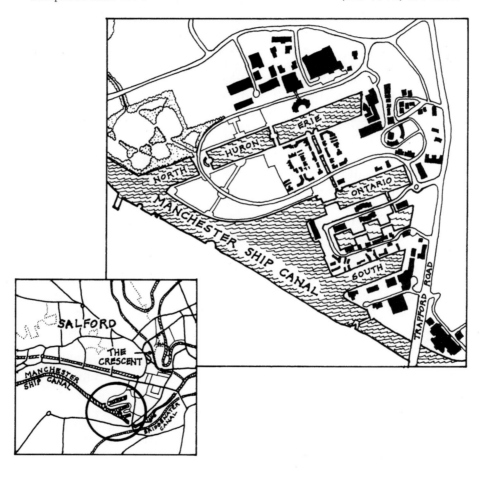

Water sculpture and landscaped pathway help overcome highway barriers that divide Darling Harbour's two precincts.(*Breen/Rigby*)

Darling Harbour
Pyrmont
Sydney, New South Wales,
Australia

Summary

Audacious makeover of a former industrial harbor area is one of the foremost waterfront redevelopments of the time.

The "Tidal Cascade" is a dramatic and well-used water feature in front of the Convention Centre. Design by Robert Woodward. (*Breen/Rigby*)

Description. In just a few years, Darling Harbour near the central business district of Sydney has firmly established itself as a prime visitor destination, the third-ranked attraction in all of Australia by one count. Over 14 million people, 70 percent of them locals, went to Darling Harbour in 1990–1991, the high end of early projections.[17] And this was before significant additions—recently opened, under construction and planned—have taken their place in the array of attractions here.

Darling Harbour was an industrial area as recently as 1982, when the state government ordered the State Rail Authority to move its facilities elsewhere. Another decision that year, to keep a historic bridge crossing the middle of the harbor, effectively barred new shipping terminals beyond it, and left a 134-acre site largely in government hands awaiting a future.

The decision to redevelop was made in 1984 by the state government. On May 1, the premier declared that Darling Harbour would be made over in time for the Australian bicentennial in 1988. This deadline became a driving force behind the project; Darling Harbour was to be the contribution of New South Wales to the country's anniversary celebration.

The decision did not come out of the blue. A City of Sydney plan as early as 1971 had suggested a bicentennial park at Darling Harbour. Two additional studies in the 1970s pointed to varied new uses, and contributed to development by the New South Wales government of such facilities as a Power House Museum, an Institute of Technology, and an auditorium immediately south of the site. A state Department of Environment and Planning study in 1982 called for an educational-entertainment park at Darling Harbour, to include a Chinese garden, housing, retailing, a waterside promenade, and a maritime museum, much of which would come to pass.

In 1984 the prospects at Darling Harbour itself would have to have been judged to be mixed. While it is somewhat near the central business district, the site was effectively isolated. Surrounding a water body, Cockle Bay, a portion of the land was fill and unsuitable for building. Expressways ran overhead and alongside. Much of the immediate neighborhood was in decline.

A Darling Harbour Authority was set up in September 1984 by special state legislation and given considerable power. Principal among these was effective exemption from the usual local or state controls, a type of "enterprise zone" approach. The key management decision of the authority was to establish a working collaboration with two private components, one a lead design firm, the other a lead contractor. As described by Barry Young, design director with MSJ Keys Young, the trio worked as one team rather than in a hierarchical manner. Construction deadlines drove the design process.[18]

By June 1985, a concept plan had been agreed to, major buildings sited, and a process established by which individual components would be designed and constructed, either privately or by government, and coordinated with the development of a considerable public realm. In all, about 50 percent of the total site has been left open; some parcels are set aside for later private development. Overseeing the process was a Quality Review Committee, with eminent architectural and design professionals appointed by the cabinet minister in charge.

The givens the design team had to work with included installing a number of major facilities to establish the public attraction mix at Darling Harbour. These included three museums, a major exhibit hall, a convention center, a hotel, a retail center, a Chinese garden, and parks, all of which have been built.

There are two focal points at Darling Harbour. The first is the harbor itself, horseshoe-shaped, around which a collection of major "people attractions" is arrayed. The second is a large, circular park.

The largest structure on the harbor is Harbourside, a festival market modeled after facilities in the United States such as Harborplace in Baltimore or Bayside in Miami.

In fact, one of the marketplace designers is the firm of RTKL Associates, Inc., of Baltimore; James Rouse of Columbia and Baltimore, Maryland, served as a consultant. Unlike its U.S. counterparts, which are usually housed in twin pavilions, Harbourside is one large structure, joined at the center by a huge, arched glass centerpiece. It contains 147,500 square feet of retail and restaurant spaces on three levels. The design orients toward the harbor and the generous brick promenade, as wide as 90 feet here. A lively mix of cafes and restaurants fronts the harbor.

Under historic Pyrmont Bridge, which dates from 1902, is the Australian National Maritime Museum, built by the national government. Designed by Philip Cox and Partners, it displays Australia's rich seagoing history in a dramatic structure at water's edge. It has in-water exhibits associated with it, which relate to nearby displays in and near the water at the Sydney Maritime Museum Wharf. The museum contains 86,500 square feet of space.

Pyrmont Bridge, which once used electricity to open, is a pedestrian-only link to downtown and supports a monorail that runs between Darling Harbour and the central business district.

A third major harbor attraction is the National Aquarium, located across from the mar-

(Breen/Rigby)

(*Breen/Rigby*)

itime museum and Harbourside, but linked by a ferry. Containing 54,900 square feet of space on a leftover pier, with a floating addition, it was developed privately by Jonray Holdings Pty. Ltd. and designed by Philip Cox, Richardson, Taylor and Partners.

At the foot of the bay is a carnival–amusement park. It sits under overhead expressways, but its noise and bright lights help to screen pedestrians from traffic noise. Also here is a major Convention Centre of 80,700 square feet, capable of holding 3500 people inside its main hall. The structure, designed by John Andrews International, is cylindrical, to fit a curving expressway ramp that runs beside it. There are bars, restaurants, and a foyer that open to the harbor in an otherwise internally oriented building.

Along the eastern promenade of the harbor is a development site that is ultimately to be joined to an office tower under construction in 1992. Near here there's a new Nikko Hotel.

The other Darling Harbour focal point is a centrally located park. The Tumbalong Park precinct, with a lake and other water features, unites the land-locked portion of the project, south of the freeway that splits it in two. The park is visible from, and is linked to, the harbor area by the continued brick promenade and such devices as a linear water feature that pulls pedestrians under overhead highway ramps.

Features of the park include an informal performance area, a "hooked stream" of water in a circle that helps define the park space, terraces, and a well-used play area. The latter receives such active use that it has been refurbished three times. A pond with a curved walkway is to one side. A sports center with restaurant, a portion of which is decked over the pond, takes advantage of the waterside location.

A walled, 2-acre Chinese Garden is also a feature here, from New South Wales's sister-state of Guangdong Province, China. Inside are winding paths around and across pools, streams, and waterfalls, surrounded by shrubs and trees that allow a quiet interlude from the busy city, including nearby Chinatown.

Also in this portion of the Darling Harbour project is a giant Exhibition Centre, containing 366,500 square feet of display space, plus a service structure, located under the highway ramps, that also serves the convention building. Designed by Philip Cox and Partners, the exhibit hall is five separate, connected units that help break up the mass, a provision of the design guidelines. The white glass and steel structure is dominated by masts and cables that permit column-free interior spaces, and give the entire building a nautical aspect. The Exhibition Building, with its own 1000-car park spaces, is screened from the public walkway and a children's play area by of trees and shrubs.

At the southernmost end of Darling Harbour are the Power House Museum and Entertainment Centre, or auditorium (dating from 1983), plus a "micro" brewery housed in a old pumphouse.

The pedestrian entrance into Darling Harbour was enhanced by raising the Pier Street overhead roadway. A water sculpture helps mask the highway noise, public art is on display, and the brick promenade that knits together the disparate pieces of Darling Harbour is here as well.

Appraisal. To merely list the components of Darling Harbour misses several of its major motifs. One is a very high standard of quality, evident in the public realm and carried on by the private sector. The two new hotels at the edge of the project, for instance, are four-star quality. The exhibition hall is an exceptional design. Smaller features such as the Chinese Garden and brewhouse are also very well done.

There is an evident attention to design, in the large, master plan sense, and in the details. A water sculpture in front of the Convention Centre is a gem—a simple circle with water flowing along steps that ring the inside is a favorite of children. The bollards that line the harbor promenade are originals. There's a wooden edge of the promenade that is a nice touch.

The overall atmosphere is very urban, and very welcoming. There are few of the "don't do this and don't do that" signs that predominate many U.S. public areas.

The water orientation around Cockle Bay is notable. Even the Convention Centre orients toward the harbor it sits beside.

There were no doubt complaints as this project was put together—particularly over the removal of local controls. At the same time, there was not a neighborhood here, or even significant industrial displacement in that this had already occurred in response to market forces.

The existence of the Power House Museum and maritime museum are obviously meant to assuage those of a historic bent. There is a working port immediately adjacent to the new public realm at Darling Harbour, at least for the near

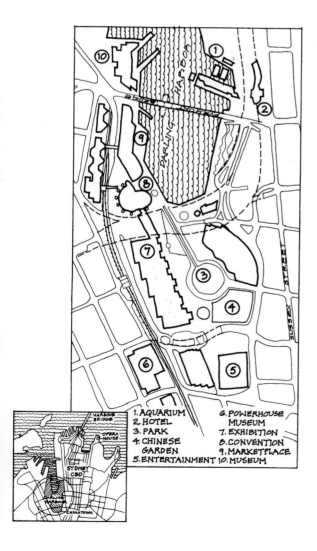

1. AQUARIUM
2. HOTEL
3. PARK
4. CHINESE GARDEN
5. ENTERTAINMENT
6. POWERHOUSE MUSEUM
7. EXHIBITION
8. CONVENTION
9. MARKETPLACE
10. MUSEUM

term. There are no doubt those who wish more of the industrial heritage—the piers, warehouses, and railroad structures—had been left in place, rather then living on only as artifacts in museums.

It's a relatively small quibble for a project that stands as a model with a rich mix of elements adding up to a public, entirely pedestrian-oriented, facility. When coupled with Sydney's historic area near the Central Quay, called The Rocks, and its fabulous Opera House, Darling Harbour helps give Sydney a collection of downtown waterfront attractions that few cities anywhere can match.

Darling Harbour

Cost. $2.5 billion (U.S.)

Source. Public financing, $853 million; private investment, $1.6 billion

Dimensions. Site area, 148.2 acres; existing buildings total 1,694,000 square feet, including 1,000,000 square feet of office space, 366,500 square feet of exhibition centre space, 80,700 square feet of convention centre with a capacity of 9500 people; Harborside, 147,500 square feet; hotel rooms on or adjacent to the site, 2000; car-park spaces, 6000

Completion date. January 1988

Sponsor. T. W. Jones
Darling Harbour Authority
Level 16, 2 Market St.
Sydney, NSW 2000 Australia
(011-61-2) 286-0100

Designer(*master plan*). Barry Young
MSJ Keys Young/The MSJ Group
35 Richards Ave.
Surry Hills, NSW 2010 Australia
(011-61-2) 361-4301

Designer (*exhibition centre*). Cox Richardson Taylor & Partners Pty. Ltd.
477 Kent St.
Sydney, NSW 2000 Australia

Designer (*convention centre*). John Andrews International Pty. Ltd.
1017 Barrenjoy Rd.
Palm Beach, NSW 2108 Australia

Designer (*promenade*). MSJ Group

Designer (*Harborside*). Clarke Perry Blackmore

Architecture Oceania
RTKL Associates, Inc.
Baltimore, MD

Designer (*National Maritime Museum*). Cox Richardson Taylor & Partners Pty. Ltd.
477 Kent St.
Sydney, NSW 2000 Australia

Designer (*Tumbalong Park*). MSJ Group

Designer(*Aquarium*). Cox Richardson Taylor & Partners Pty. Ltd.
477 Kent St.
Sydney, NSW 2000 Australia

Portside Festival Market/Festival Park/Trinity Plaza, Toledo, Ohio. (*R. Greg Hursley*)

Portside Festival Market, Park, and Plaza
408 N. Summit Street
Toledo, Ohio

Summary

Bold attempt at downtown waterfront redevelopment an economic failure, at least in the short term.

Description. A key component of the major remake of the former industrial waterfront along the Maumee River in downtown Toledo is the Portside Festival Market. It is a direct clone of generally successful marketplaces in Baltimore and Norfolk (note different corporate sponsorship), but it failed to attract the traffic needed and shut six years after opening in May 1984.

It was developed by the Enterprise Development Co., headed by James Rouse after his mandatory retirement from the company bearing his name.

More successful has been the adjacent Festival Park and riverfront promenade. The park is particularly known for its Friday afternoon "TGIF" parties, and the promenade's docking facilities have become a destination for recreational boaters in the area. Similarly, the park is where Fourth of July and Labor Day festivals are held.

Portside was not alone in bearing overblown expectations. A $27 million Hotel Sofitel likewise failed and was converted to a more modestly priced chain hotel. Part of its problem, beyond a luxury style that may not have been appropriate for the city, was the late arrival of a downtown convention facility.

The Portside market began with 80 shops in a single, 80,000-square-foot structure, situated perpendicular to the river to accommodate the site and hotel nearby. It featured a variety of food establishments, general boutique retail, and several restaurants, on two levels.

Festival Park, part of the major public open-space investments on the river, covers 3 acres, is terraced, and functions as an amphitheater. It is on a 20-foot graded slope, and provides a physical and visual link from the downtown street above to the Maumee River. Nearby Trinity Plaza is a 12,000-square-foot park above a garage, serving Portside and the Episcopal church that developed it.

The major public/private investments along the waterfront—Portside cost $14.5 million; the Festival Park and promenade $8 million; Trinity Plaza, housing a parking garage, $1 million; plus a $100 million Owens-Illinois headquarters office—may well pay off in the future. When the city arrives at a solution for what to do with a large abandoned power plant (designed by Daniel Burnham) that is a major presence along the river, for instance, it will help determine how the riverfront evolves.

In the early 1990s, Portside, sometimes occupied by homeless people, was seen as a possible science museum or similar facility.

Design Features. Portside has a tin roof (blue) and an industrial-feeling interior typical of many such marketplaces. The Festival Park beside it is an engaging, sloped open space leading to a wide, inviting promenade.

One interesting detail here is the art work of school children cast in bronze and embedded

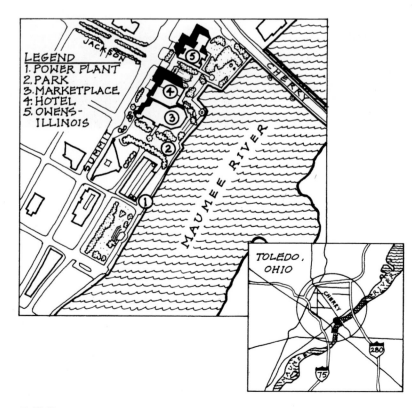

into the pavement. Metal interpretive plaques are a nice touch along the promenade. The transient docking facilities were an important addition, making it possible for the first time for boaters to come to downtown Toledo.

Appraisal. The Toledo example made clear that a festival marketplace is not a cure-all answer to a downtown's needs, by itself or even in combination with significant investment in attractive public open space. The market analysis that justified the festival marketplace on the river here was clearly marked by wishful thinking. Five or ten years from now, with adroit choices, downtown Toledo's waterfront could again be a success story and Portside enjoying new, and perhaps longer-lasting, life.

Portside Festival Market, Park, and Plaza
  Cost. Portside, $14.5 million; Festival park, $1.8 million; Trinity Plaza, $1.0 million
  Source. Trust Corp. of Toledo (now Society Corporation)
  Dimensions. Portside, 80,000 square feet; Festival Park, 3 acres; Trinity Plaza, 12,000 square feet
  Completion date. May 1984

Sponsor. Wayman Usher
  City of Toledo, Economic Development Division
  One Government Center, Suite 1850
  Toledo, OH 43604
  (419) 245-1470

Sponsor. Mike McCall
  Enterprise Development Co.
  600 American City Bldg.
  Columbia, MD 21044
  (410) 964-3600

Sponsor. Michael John Young, Principal Planner
  Toledo-Lucas County Plan Commissions
  One Government Center, Suite 1620
  Toledo, OH 43604
  (419) 245-1200

Sponsor. George Mather, Sr., Warden, Trinity
  Episcopal Church
  316 Adams
  Toledo, OH 43604
  (419) 243-1231

Designer. Robert A. Fessler, AIA
  The Collaborative, Inc.
  P.O. Box 1317
  Toledo, OH 43604
  (419)242-7405.

Anderson's Restaurant/False Creek Yacht Club, Vancouver, B.C.(*Simon Scott*)

Anderson's Restaurant/False Creek Yacht Club
1661 Granville Street
Vancouver, British Columbia, Canada

Summary

Successfully mixes industrial and nautical design motifs in bold, under-bridge structure.

Description. Sheathed in glass and metal and built on a concrete base, this three-level restaurant and private yacht club maximizes a waterfront site on False Creek. Overhead, about 12 stories tall, is the Granville Street Bridge, one of the principal connections to downtown.

The restaurant/club fits into its unlikely site at a 45-degree angle; it appears to, and does to a degree, jut into the creek. Views of the city's nearby English Bay are maximized by this siting.

The appearance entering from under the bridge is to a somewhat abstract, metal-clad structure featuring portholes. The view from the creek and beyond is, by contrast, dominated by green-tinted glass on the top two levels. A circular outdoor patio, very pleasant in good weather, surrounds the lower-level cafe.

At the base, beside pilings, is a floating dock. A small ferry connects during the day to the Granville Island complex (see page 158). A pedestrian/bike path runs along the shore here, and new apartment towers form part of the backdrop, along with the girders of the Granville Street Bridge.

Functionally, the False Creek Yacht Club occupies the top, 385 square meters, with an outdoor deck and large and small meeting spaces. Anderson's Restaurant, with white table cloths and seating for 150, is on the middle level, and Riley's Cafe, a more informal venue, is on the lower level, with seating for 80 both indoors and outside. The restaurants together occupy 930 square meters.

Design Features. The mix of materials at Anderson's Restaurant/False Creek Yacht Club is exceptional. Metal cladding dominates the entrance from the parking lot, across a walkway that is part gangplank, while glass and concrete are dominant elsewhere.

The nautical motif is subdued, incorporated into a modern design rather than taking it over. Thus portholes are discrete, poles on the top level are relatively tasteful mastlike objects.

Anderson's Restaurant is a standout interior space, with a decor in warm browns and maroons that does not compete with the fine views afforded in the huge, wraparound tinted glass windows. Tables are oriented toward the views of False Creek and beyond, to a bay and the entrance to Vancouver's busy harbor.

Appraisal. The Anderson's Restaurant/False Creek Yacht Club building is decidedly modern, very bold, and yet a good "fit." The imagery successfully mixes metaphors—the complex can be seen as a moored boat, and also conveys an industrial feel.

The site, in part directly under a major highway bridge and across from Granville Island,

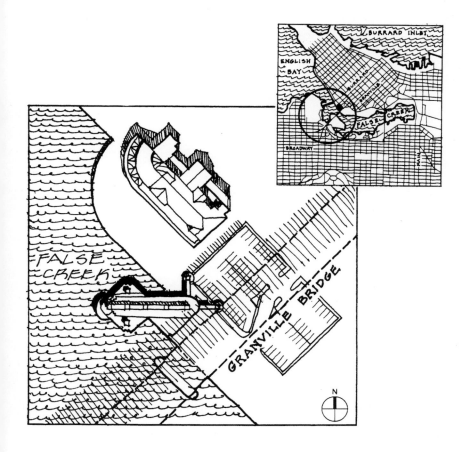

whose own imagery is powerful, calls for a vivid design, and gets it here. Overall, the industrial nature of Anderson's/False Creek Yacht Club blends well with iron girders above, the operating cement plant with barges across the creek, and, indeed, all of Granville Island itself.

Anderson's Restaurant/False Creek Yacht Club

Cost. $2.2 million

Dimensions. Restaurant (two floors), 930 square meters, 310 seats; yacht club, 385 square meters

Completion date. 1990

Sponsor. Glen Anderson Holdings
1661 Granville St.
Vancouver, BC, V6Z 1N3, Canada

Designer. Bing Thom
Bing Thom Architects, Inc.
1430 Burrard Street
Vancouver, BC, V6Z 2A3 Canada
(604) 682-1881

Structural engineer. C. Y. Loh Associates Ltd.
1863 Powell St.
Vancouver, BC, V5L 1H8, Canada
(604) 254-0868

Mechanical engineer. Yoneda and Associates
204-1159 West Broadway
Vancouver, BC, V6H 1G1, Canada
(604) 733-3412

Electrical Engineer. Schenke/Bawol Engineering Ltd.
200-1281 West Georgia
Vancouver, BC, V6E 3J7, Canada
(604) 688-8008

Canada Place, Vancouver, B.C. (*Timothy Hursley, Downs Archambault/Musson Cattell Mackey Partnership and Zeidler Roberts Partnership/Architects*).

Canada Place
999 Canada Place,
foot of Howe
Vancouver, British Columbia,
Canada

Summary

A former World's Fair pavilion lives on as a resplendent mixed-use development providing major public access and outstanding harbor views.

(*Downs Archambault/Musson Cattell Mackey Partnership and Zeidler Roberts Partnership/Architects*)

Description and Design Features. Canada Place, with its towering, white fabric sail-inspired roof that juts boldly into Vancouver harbor, started life as the Canadian pavilion during Expo '86. It is built on the old B.C. Pier, a historic docking place of ships coming from the Orient.

In addition to a 175,000-square-foot cruise ship facility, the 1.8-million-square-foot, mixed-use project also houses a trade and convention center, a 500-room luxury hotel, offices, a 480-seat IMAX theater, parking for 770 cars and a bus terminal for cruise ship passengers. Public plazas, promenades, retail outlets, and restaurants complete the picture.

Canada Place is a bold structure with a high-tech, distinctly nautical flavor. Five enormous Teflon-coated fiberglass fabric "sails" rise on the roof and dominate this harbor much as the peaks of the Sydney Opera House do. In overall shape the structure resembles in part a cruise liner, in part a sailing vessel, especially when seen from a distance.

Canada Place provides plentiful waterfront access in a section of the city where the shoreline is largely cut off by rail lines, industry, and port uses. Extensive walkways extending 1000 feet into the harbor echo the feel of being on a ship's

deck, reinforced by the detailing in the railings. The decks and walkways offer spectacular views of the harbor, nearby mountains, and the downtown skyline.

The outdoor space comes alive with the drama of cruise ships entering or leaving the harbor and terminal. Massive Canada Place is suddenly dwarfed when these huge vessels are parked alongside. Five cruise vessels can be accommodated at one time. The entire cruise ship operation, from passengers embarking and departing to the activities of the forklifts and cranes, can be viewed by the public from the walkways above.

A series of well-designed informative and commemorative plaques has been installed along the public promenade. Portions of the history of Vancouver are told through photographs, colorful artwork, and text that have been enameled onto sturdy white molded metal stands. White mesh metal seating and trash receptacles are plentiful and attractive. Restaurants and snack bars are strategically placed for harbor vistas.

Total cost of the project was $307 million, half of which came from the Canadian government.

Appraisal. Apart from being a spectacular icon in the Vancouver harbor, and a project that incorporates many different functions well, Canada Place should be lauded for the amount and quality of public access and its interpretive elements. It is fast becoming a symbol and a gateway for a special waterfront city, particularly for those arriving by sea.

Canada Place

Cost. $307 million (U.S.) 1986

Source. 50 percent Government of Canada (Trade and Convention Center), 50 percent Tokyo Corp. of Japan (Pan Pacific Hotel)

Dimensions. 1,780,000 square feet, including 505 hotel rooms, 770 parking spaces, 134,000 square feet of public space; Trade and Convention Center includes 100,000 square feet of exhibition space and 30,000 square feet of meeting rooms; cruise ship terminal, 176,000 square feet; offices, 250,000 square feet; theater, 480 seats; bus terminal for 11 buses

Completion date. 1986

Sponsor. Kenneth G. Bream (formerly Canada Harbour Place Corp.)
Pan Pacific Development Corp.
650 W. Georgia St., 33rd Floor
Vancouver, BC, V6B 4N9 Canada
(604) 681-1000

Sponsor. Nobuo Kitsuda, President
Tokyo Canada Corp.
999 Canada Place W.T.C., Suite 515
Vancouver, B.C., V6C 3E1, Canada
(604) 682-7391

Designer. Eberhard H. Zeidler
Zeidler Roberts Partnership, Architects
315 Queen Street West
Toronto, ON, M5V 2X2 Canada
(416) 596-8300

Designer. Barry V. Downs
Downs, Archambault & Partners
1014 Homer St., Suite 200
Vancouver, BC, V6B 2W9 Canada
(604) 685-6312

Designer. John Marchant
Musson Cattell Mackey Partnership
555 Burrard St., 1825 Two Bentall Centre
Vancouver, BC, V7X 1M9, Canada
(604) 687-2990

Structural engineer. Read Jones Christoffersen Ltd.
210 West Broadway, Suite 400
Vancouver, BC, V5Y 3W2, Canada
(604) 872-0391

Mechanical/electrical engineer. MCW Consultants Ltd.
1650-1500 W. Georgia
Vancouver, BC, V6G 2Z6, Canada
(604) 687-1821

Granville Island Redevelopment, Vancouver, B.C. (*Hotson Bakker Architects, Dennis France*)

Granville Island Redevelopment 1592 Johnston Street Granville Island, Vancouver, British Columbia, Canada

Summary

A landmark urban waterfront project where new commercial and cultural uses fit harmoniously with industry, past and present.

Description. A key fact about Granville Island is that it is not an island; rather, it is a peninsula, linked to the nearby neighborhoods by roadway.

This is not idle information, because central to the redevelopment strategy for the project was that it should first and foremost serve nearby residents. That Granville Island has become heavily visited by the greater Vancouver population and tourists is by and large a happy accident. In 1986, 81 percent of the visitors were local and regional in origin.

The goal for Granville of serving residents set the tone for what has come. It is a real place, symbolized by an active, not to say hectic, farmers' market, a feeling promoted by deliberately narrow aisles. In style the market is a throwback to earlier facilities where farmers brought their fresh goods to the city to sell directly to customers. It is in fact the prime generator of traffic at Granville Island and was grossing about $30 million in 1986.[19]

Because Granville Island overall has a feeling of authenticity, which is furthered by the low-key industrial design and the continued existence of active industry, it has become enormously popular. *The Vancouver Guide*[20] describes it as "peculiar, easygoing and friendly." Visitation is an estimated 8 million a year for 1992, according to the island information office. One consequence is that weekend traffic is "horrendous," and visitors are advised to use a bus, ferry, or to walk.

The history of the island dates from 1913, when it was created out of the dredged material from False Creek, an inlet that divides it from downtown. It was established as an industrial park, probably one of the first of its kind. In its day, Granville Island was a manufacturing area, transforming goods arriving by barge into products that were shipped out by rail.

Eventually it became an overlooked, outmoded industrial area, until the federal government took control in 1972 and directed its redevelopment. The Canada Mortgage and Housing Corp., a federal entity, was placed in charge (it still is today). A master plan effort was launched.

According to Norman Hotson, of Hotson Bakker Architects of Vancouver, the project urban designers, there was considerable pressure to make the island a park. They chose instead an approach they term an "urban park," consisting of a blend of new commercial/cultural and existing industrial uses with an overall aim of creating an array of attractions that would appeal to a wide range of people. The philosophy was to define public recreational pursuits so as to include not only walking or jogging, but shopping or drinking in a pub.

Because it was a federal project, including ownership of the land, redevelopment proceeded more smoothly than it might otherwise have. Work began in late 1976, free of local zoning controls, but according to a city-approved concept plan. The island was broken into activity zones, or realms, which permitted a healthy mixture on the ground. By the mid-1980s there was established a total of 750,000 square feet of space,

Located near a farmer's market and theater, a pier conveys part of the industrial feel of Granville Island. (*Breen/Rigby*)

both old and new, housed on 42 acres (including 4 acres in the water).

The redevelopment was launched with a capital grant from the federal government of $19.5 million. Over the years this was augmented by another $20 million or so in public funds, including for educational and cultural facilities. Private investment is put at $30 million in the buildup of the island's facilities (all figures are in Canadian dollars).

If the farmers' market is the main attraction, it is one among many. An arts club theater and cabaret are immediately next to the market. Underneath Granville Bridge is a restaurant and a cluster of gift shops. On the same, northern, side of the island, where two water ferries carry passengers along False Creek, are a working cement plant, a major art and design college, a landscaped parking lot (with an industrial crane artifact), and a small, European-style hotel.

Walkways of various sorts wind around most of the perimeter of the island. Attractions along the way include a water park and a marketplace for kids, a "micro" brewery, a community center, rowing school, and tennis courts, parking, a man-made hill with an amphitheater for events, restaurants, and multiple other attractions, including an "arts umbrella," an art center for young people, which had been expanded since its establishment.

There's also a multifaceted marine center, dubbed the "maritime market," where retail space is combined with boat repair and outfitting facilities—all accessible to a public encouraged to walk about the entire island. This encouragement includes a designated walkway through an enclosed outdoor patio of a restaurant, appropriately called the Boardwalk Cafe.

Retail space, including the market, occupies over 100,000 square feet. Other large uses are cultural and educational facilities, 135,000 square feet; industry, 91,000 square feet; parking, 110,000 square feet; arts and crafts, 58,000 square feet, and restaurants, 57,000 square feet.

The arts school plans a major addition, as of 1992, of approximately 60,000 square feet in a new, five-story building across from its present site. Interior parking will be included. The Emily Carr College of Art and Design brings 800 students to the island daily, plus another contingent of night students.

To the rich mix of facilities is added an array of events and a lively cultural offerings. A 1991 calendar at Granville Island ran to 30 pages. The second quarter, for instance, began with the 10th Annual Fools parade on April 1; other offerings included a sugaring off, a high tea matinee, a floating boat show, a bluegrass festival, authors' series, and a two-week jazz festival. The summer schedule was even more extensive, with 18 events.

According to *The Vancouver Guide*, Granville has several of the city's "superlative attractions," including Water Park, called one of the most imaginative playgrounds in the city; "the best beer in British Columbia," served at the

The view from the Granville Island Hotel patio, punctuated with a crane from the island's earlier industrial days. (*Breen/Rigby*)

(*Breen Rigby*)

Granville Island Brewery; and one of the best bookstores in the city, Blackberry Books.

Design Features. Perhaps the most striking design approach at Granville Island, beyond its conscious integration of the industrial past and today's commercial mix, is the accommodation of the car. Building on the island's past, when no curbs existed, Granville Island today has no curbs, no gutters, and no sidewalks, just streets meant to serve both cars and pedestrians. There is a good deal of parking, as many as 1400 spaces, much in heavily landscaped surface lots.

The car was seen as a given and a positive, adding to the ambience. The street feels very comfortable to the pedestrian; cars move through generally slowly, but are very much part of the active scene.

A unifying treatment, simple but effective, is a system of piping that runs between the buildings along the street, as well as into buildings. Its bright color adds to a bit of dash; the pipes function in various ways, as something on which to hang signs, plants, or mailboxes, or as a place for a canopy. There are blue railings at docks and boat ramps. Overall, in fact, Granville is a very colorful place, with bold and imaginative uses of color throughout.

Water accessibility is another unifying element throughout the island. False Creek is never very far from view. There are walkways along the edge, restaurant patios overlooking the creek, and a host of boating activities available. The latter, beside rentals of various craft (kayaks, motorboats, canoes), includes a tiny "Sea Village" of floating homes and a floating school, on a barge. There are public docks for visiting boats and a

major anchorage along the western shore.

In design approach, many of the new buildings are clad in corrugated metal, in the spirit of the industrial predecessors. This includes the Granville Island Hotel, 58 rooms, whose glamorous interior is belied by its outside industrial appearance.

Appraisal. The total package here is what makes Granville Island a stunning achievement. The design is low-key in the extreme—some buildings are virtual sheds. But it all works to establish a feel of robust vitality, with a strong link to the past industrial reality.

The mixture of uses combines a stimulating amount of commercial activity with a considerable educational, cultural, and public recreational realm. It's not everywhere that a brewery has a gallery attached to it, down the street from a water park for kids.

In its continued industrial activity—a cement plant and boat repair facilities—and celebration of its industrial heritage rather than its obliteration, Granville Island ranks as a top waterfront redevelopment achievement. No matter that some of this was strict pragmatism—moving the cement plant would have taken half the original capital improvement budget, so it was a relatively easy decision to live with it. Still, the instinct of many others would have been to secure the funds to relocate it and to begin with a cleaner slate.

Granville Island Redevelopment
  Cost. $70 million (Can.)
  Dimensions. 42 acres, including 38 acres land, 4 acres water; 260 businesses, 248 berths, 750,000 square feet of buildings
  Completion date. 1979 (public market)

Sponsor. Government of Canada
   Canada Mortgage & Housing Corporation
   1661 Duranleau St.
   Vancouver, BC V6H 3S3, Canada
   (604) 731-5733

Designer. Norman Hotson
   Hotson Bakker Architects
   406-611 Alexander St.
   Vancouver, BC V6A 1E1 Canada
   (604) 255-1169

Notes for Chapter Five

1. Eugene Carlson, "Revival of Baltimore's Core Took Lots of Work and Time," *The Wall Street Journal*, Sept. 22, 1981, p. 29.

2. Baltimore Dept. of Planning, *The Baltimore Harbor*, 1985, p. 81.

3. Adapted from 1985; Baltimore City Department of Planning, *The Baltimore Harbor*, Inner Harbor chapter prepared by the Waterfront Center.

4. Stanley Ziemba, "Chicago's Lakefront May Have New Rival," *Chicago Tribune*, Oct. 9, 1988, p. 1

5. Richard Wallace and M. Dion Thompson, "Festive Spirit Fills New 'Wonderful' and Patrick May, "Marketplace Charms First Wave of Visitors," *The Miami Herald*, Apr. 9, 1987, p. B-1.

6. Cindy Krischer Goodman, "Reuse Makes Physical Promotional Changes at Bayside" *Today's Business*, Nov. 16, 1989, p. 8.

7. Ellen Livingston ,"77 Minority Shops Sign at Bayside," *The Miami Herald*, Apr. 12, 1987, p. 1B.

8. Gregg Fields, "Bayside Mall Bustles with a New Attitude," *The Miami Herald*, Apr. 6, 1992, Business Section, p. 7.

9. Ibid.

10. The Waterfront Center, *Urban Waterfronts '87*, chap. 1, "Portland: A Riverfront Reclaimed," Washington D.C., 1988."

11. Ibid., p. 18.

12. Urban Land Institute, Project Reference File, vol. 18, no. 3, January–March 1988.

13. Steve Law "Japanese Investor Ordered to buy Out RiverPlace Partner," *The* (Portland) *Business Journal*, Apr. 13, 1992, p. 1.

14. The Waterfront Center, *Urban Waterfronts '87*, op. cit., p. 12.

15. Ove Arup & Partners, *Arup Journal*, Autumn 1987.

16. City of Salford, Annual Review, April 1991.

17. Darling Harbour Authority, private communication, Feb. 14, 1992.

18. Peter Webber, *The Design of Sydney*, Law Book Co., Sydney, 1988, chap. 11, "Darling Harbour: A New City Precinct," pp. 191–213.

19. The Waterfront Center, *Urban Waterfronts '86*, "Waterfront Character: What Is It and Will Any Be Left?," p. 39, Washington D.C., 1987.

20. Terri Wershler, *The Vanconver Guide*, 3d ed., Douglas & McIntyre, Vancouver, 1991.

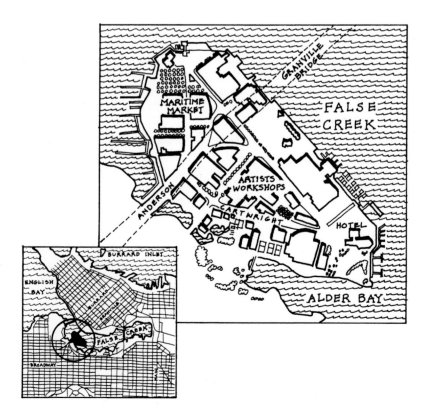

≈6≈

THE RECREATIONAL WATERFRONT

The public view of most city-bound rivers has often been restricted because of the rigid viewpoints of many public servants who are considered the overseers of our waterways. In their narrow-mindedness the officials more often than not have considered only one of the two possible sides of the streams they tend. They have thought of rivers only as utilitarian water courses and drainageways and have forgotten, indeed rejected, the classic notion that urban watercourses might also be amenities for people. The hidebound official view has consigned urban rivers to serving as water carriages for disposal of city sewage wastes, drainageways for stormwater runoff from streets and parking lots, sources of cooling water for electrical generators and other industrial machinery and, in the West, lifelines for agricultural irrigation. With this outlook firmly set by the passage of decades, it has long been forgotten that the same rivers may even serve cultural roles, purposes pleasurable and satisfying to the people—places to boat, sites for riverside picnics, lovely parts of communities for walking or biking, backgrounds for concerts and other performing arts, natural places for gardens and parks, indeed, pleasant refuges inside the very noisy city itself where one may find a quiet place of ground and greenery amenable to thinking.

JOE SHOEMAKER WITH LEONARD STEVENS
Returning the Platte to the People

---

*The Platte River Greenway Foundation, Denver, 1981.

Allegan Riverfront Renaissance, Allegan, Mich. (*O'Boyle, Cowell, Blalock & Associates, Inc.*)

Allegan Riverfront Renaissance Park Allegan, Michigan

Summary

An elegant small-town riverfront renaissance triggered by saving a historic iron bridge.

Description. The Allegan Riverfront Renaissance Park represents an impressive return to the riverfront on the part of this 4500-person community situated along the Kalamazoo River.

In the early 1980s, having successfully waged a battle with the Michigan Department of Transportation to save a historic iron bridge that spans the river close to the downtown, the city and its citizens decided to bring life back to their portion of the Kalamazoo River. Planning for the 2.5 miles of central riverfront which circles the historic downtown began in 1984. The slogan and name "Riverfront Renaissance" was officially adopted and used to promote the project.

The resulting park, opened in 1986, includes walkways, overlooks, a play area, an amphitheater, a gazebo, a water garden, a canoe launch, a picnic shelter, and several floating fountains. It ties together the historic iron bridge, the downtown, and the city library and auditorium. The cost of the project was $1.1 million, of which $150,000 came from a local fund-raising campaign. A Vietnam Veterans Memorial was added in 1989, and additional play equipment was installed in 1991.

The revived riverfront is used for festivals, concerts, and other events and is enjoyed on a daily basis. Many downtown businesses have improved their back, or riverside, facades. Some have opened entrances to face the river.

Design Features. An 800-foot wood and brick walkway which cantilevers over an existing steel sheet pile wall, adjacent to a modest parking area, is the key connector of the project. To one side it links with a half-acre park and garden which features a gazebo/bandshell and a grassy amphitheater. To the other side it links with community cultural facilities, a canoe launch, and play areas by way of an inviting 300-foot, over-water pedestrian bridge.

Handsome ornamental iron handrails, inspired by the detailing of the historic bridge, are complemented by period lighting fixtures and attractive benches. The use of wood echoes the town's historic roots in the lumber industry. The brick reflects many of the old buildings found throughout the downtown. The water garden features a number of plantings, and several floating fountains are illuminated at night in seasonable weather. An ornamental iron and canvas canopy covers a former alleyway to highlight the pedestrian link to the riverfront from downtown.

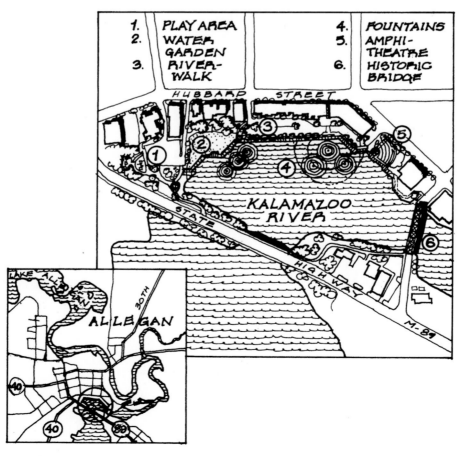

1. PLAY AREA
2. WATER GARDEN
3. RIVER-WALK
4. FOUNTAINS
5. AMPHI-THEATRE
6. HISTORIC BRIDGE

Appraisal. The Allegan Riverfront Renaissance Park, and the earlier saving of the historic iron bridge by the city and citizens, shows the powerful determination of people to connect with their cultural and natural heritage. While it is relatively small in scale, the low-key elegance and attention to detail and diversity of experience here make this riverfront turnaround an exemplary smaller-community project.

The pedestrian bridge, a very nice design feature, allows for a continuous walkway along the riverbank (where shoreline rights of way on the riverbank itself may not have been feasible because of private ownership). It thus serves as an example of how to overcome a barrier encountered in many cities attempting to create continuous access. Interpretive signage explaining historic and environmental features is missing.

Allegan Riverfront Renaissance Park

Cost. $1.1 million
Source. Includes $150,000 in donations
Dimensions. 1300 linear feet
Completion date. 1986

Sponsor. Aaron Anthony, City Manager
City of Allegan
112 Locust Ave.
Allegan, MI
(616) 673-5511

Designer. Eric Lyons, ASLA
O'Boyle, Cowell, Blalock & Associates, Inc.
521 South Riverview Dr.
Kalamazoo, MI 49004
(616) 381-3357

Structural engineer. Carl Walker Engineers, Inc.
445 W. Michigan, Suite 101
Kalamazoo, MI 49007
(616) 381-2222

Electrical engineer. Kingscott Associates, Inc.
229 E. Michigan, Suite 335
Kalamazoo, MI 49007
(616) 381-4880

Marine engineer. c/o Spalding DeDecker & Associates, Inc.
McLavry Engineering Associates
Madison Heights, MI 48820
(517) 669-2515

(Ken Graham)

The Anchorage
(Tony Knowles) Coastal Trail
Upper Cook Inlet
Anchorage, Alaska

Summary

A major urban trail accomplishment affording year-round coastal access and recreation.

Description. Anchorage, Alaska, with its more than 225,000 residents, is the state's largest city. Its setting on Cook Inlet with surrounding mountains makes for spectacular scenery.

The $11 million Anchorage Coastal Trail in place today is the product of considerable detailed planning work to overcome the not insignificant problems faced. Among them were extremely high tidal ranges and winter coastal storm surges, including possible scouring by tank-sized ice flows, railroad and industrial uses, residential neighborhoods that required buffering, and sensitive habitats.

The width of the 14-mile trail varies from 8 to 11 feet, depending on the extent of use along its sections. Users include bikers, joggers, hikers, and skiers. Tunnels and bridges are used to overcome barriers and sensitive habitats.

A local community group, the Coastal Trail Commandoes, sponsors running events, periodic maintenance, and a newsletter.

Schools use the trail for interpretive nature walks focusing on the extensive birdlife and marine ecosystems. Interpretive kiosks have been installed in Earthquake Park, site of damage caused by a 1964 earthquake, to explain that phenomenon and the resulting natural landscape.

Design Features. On any waterfront walkway, one of the most—if not the most—interesting features is the variety of experiences to be accessed and enjoyed. The success of the design, then, is how it enhances or detracts from people's enjoyment of the surroundings and the views. The Anchorage Coastal Trail does not fall short. The vistas and experiences to be had along the way are nothing short of spectacular: Cook Inlet mudflats, expanses of water, the skyline of the city, magnificent mountains, coastal bluffs, dense woodlands, and beautiful skies.

Basic blacktop is the dominant paving chosen, no doubt for its durability. Interesting is the use of heavy wooden timbers for bridges, with bright blue pipe railings. The same blue accent color is used on other fencing along the route, which successfully incorporates chain link—a notable accomplishment. Chain-link "panels" topped with gray metal piping fit discreetly into concrete posts that subdivide the fencing sections. Wooden benches of simple, straightforward design are placed along the walkway.

Appraisal. A major attribute of any significant waterfront trail is, first, its very existence. Achieving a continuous accessway in an urban area is no mean accomplishment, with property acquisition, easements, barriers of various sorts, and sensitive terrains to contend with. In Alaska, the design also had to take into account severe weather conditions.

The Alaska Coastal Trail is a brilliant effort,

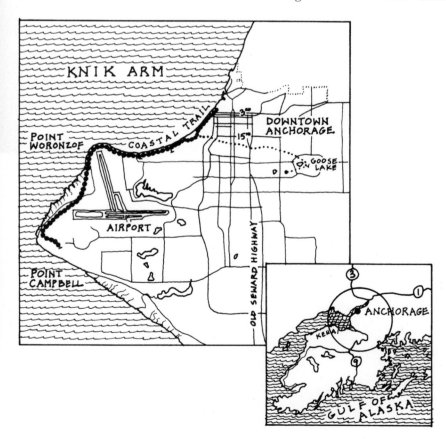

enabling residents and visitors alike a chance to enjoy a beautiful, fascinating coastline.

The Anchorage (Tony Knowles) Coastal Trail

Cost. $11.4 million
Dimensions. 14 miles
Completion date. 1987
Notes. Trail extension to downtown area completed since 1988

Sponsor. Dave Gardner
Cultural and Recreational Services Department
Municipality of Anchorage
P.O. Box 196650
Anchorage, AK 99519
(907) 343-4521

Sponsor. Michael J. Meehan
Economic Development and Planning
Department

Municipality of Anchorage
P.O. Box 196650
Anchorage, AK 99519
(907) 343-4865

Designer. Ken Morton and Don Vogan
Burns and Peterson (formerly Burns, Clarke & Vogan)
3301 C Street, Suite 220
Anchorage, AK 99503
(907) 563-1942

Consulting engineers. Peratrovich, Nottingham & Drage, Inc.
1506 W. 36th St.
Anchorage, AK 99503
(907) 561-1011

Engineering. Coffman Engineers, Inc.
550 West Seventh Ave., Suite 700
Anchorage, AK 99501
(907) 276-6664

Dramatic transformation of the Battle Creek, Michigan, riverfront. Battle Creek Linear Park, Battle Creek, Mich.(*O'Boyle, Cowell, Blalock & Associates Inc.*)

Battle Creek Downtown Riverfront Park and Linear Park Battle Creek, Michigan

Summary

A formal downtown riverfront park and promenade at the heart of a city-wide linear trail system.

Photo of same location as previous page before transformation . (*O'Boyle, Cowell, Blalock & Associates Inc.*)

Description. Battle Creek, a town of 56,000, is the birthplace of ready-to-eat breakfast cereals (Dr. John Harvey Kellogg and his brother, H. K. Kellogg, invented the corn flake in the late 1800s). In the early 1980s the Kellogg Company decided to move downtown from its suburban location. Construction of its $75 million headquarters in downtown Battle Creek helped spur the revitalization of the city and the riverfront. The Kellogg development allowed the city to leverage an $11 million Urban Development Action Grant from the U.S. Department of Housing and Urban Development, which it used to construct streets, parking lots, mini-parks, and other amenities.

The Downtown Riverfront Park embraces formal promenades on either side of the Kalamazoo River in a key section of central Battle Creek. Several small gardens adjoin the walkway. A pedestrian bridge links uses on the north side of the river—the public schools administration building, the high school, the Kellogg Auditorium, and a historic train depot—to those on the south side, including a commercial area, a hotel, and the Kellogg Company Headquarters.

In 1991 the W. K. Kellogg Foundation opened its new headquarters building on the riverfront adjacent to the park. The foundation also relocated a historic home of W. K. Kellogg and installed flower gardens and a walkway across the river from its headquarters building.

The Downtown Riverfront Park serves as a main site for Battle Creek's "International Festival of Lights" holiday display. In 1992, Clara's Riverfront Restaurant was slated to open in the train depot and 120 units of market-rate rental apartments were to commence construction.

The 14-mile Battle Creek Linear Park, of which the Riverfront Park is the centerpiece, offers a variety of experiences for the user. A paved path runs alongside the Kalamazoo and Battle Creek Rivers and loops through various parts of the city connecting schools, parks, and neighborhoods. The trail is patrolled by motor scooter.

Students in vocational education classes built portions of the railings used in the system. During construction, hundreds of area youth were provided employment. In 1991, at Horseshoe Bend Park, play equipment and a river-edge viewing deck were installed.

The 1500 linear feet of the downtown park and the 14 miles of trails throughout Battle

Creek were supported by $3.47 million from Kellogg and a total of $1.6 million from the Urban Development Action Grant.

Design Features. While the 14-mile linear park is an informal paved trail, punctuated with picnic areas and overlooks, the Downtown Riverfront Park makes a more formal statement.

Battle Creek's logo is a semicircle incorporating a stylized wheat flower. The walkway on both sides of the river between McCamly Street and Capital Avenue incorporates many elements of this motif in the paving patterns and layout, the seating, decorative arches, and the lighting fixtures. Circular overlooks rhythmically punctuate the walkway and help break the monotony of concrete bulkhead. The area is well landscaped; fountains add interest in season.

The recent installation of the W. K. Kellogg historic home with surrounding gardens, and the continuation of the walkway on the north bank of the river, is commendable. Unfortunately, the design of the Kellog Foundation headquarters on the south bank does not take full advantage of the river setting. Instead, its large blank white wall obscures parking, presumably, but presents a large, windowless facade. The linear trail does not continue on this side of the river, and public access is completely blocked off.

Appraisal. Battle Creek's Linear Park is a very good example of a community providing an open-space trail system, large portions of which run next to the river, connecting educational and cultural facilities while providing for recreation and commuting. The downtown portion creates a formal park, walkway, and gathering spot for community events.

While it is outside the purview of this project, any visitor to the area will observe nearby flaws. The Kellogg Foundation's blocking of public access on one side of the riverbank is a missed opportunity. The destruction of a nearby park that once physically and visually connected downtown commercial uses to the riverfront, in order to build a parking lot, is regrettable. The Linear Park logo and locational signage is attractive, but could be larger.

Battle Creek Downtown Riverfront Park and Linear Park

Cost. $5.07 million
Source. 32 percent public financing ($1.6 million UDAG Grant); 68 percent private ($3.47 million grant from W. K. Kellogg Foundation).
Dimensions. 14 miles of linear park completed; 1500 linear feet downtown
Completion date. 1985 (downtown park)

Sponsor. Rance Leaders, City Manager
City of Battle Creek
P.O. Box 1717
Battle Creek, MI 49016
(616) 966-3378

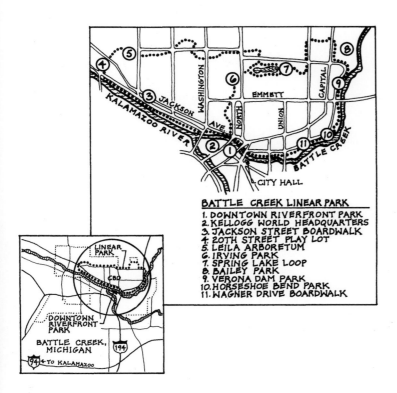

BATTLE CREEK LINEAR PARK
1. DOWNTOWN RIVERFRONT PARK
2. KELLOGG WORLD HEADQUARTERS
3. JACKSON STREET BOARDWALK
4. 20TH STREET PLAY LOT
5. LEILA ARBORETUM
6. IRVING PARK
7. SPRING LAKE LOOP
8. BAILEY PARK
9. VERONA DAM PARK
10. HORSESHOE BEND PARK
11. WAGNER DRIVE BOARDWALK

Landscape architect. Robert L. O'Boyle, Sam Lovall
O'Boyle, Cowell, Blalock & Associates, Inc.
521 South Riverview Drive
Kalamazoo, MI 49004
(616) 381-3357

Structural engineer. Carl Walker Engineers, Inc.
445 W. Michigan, Suite 101
Kalamazoo, MI 49007
(616) 381-2222

Electrical engineer. Kingscott Associates, Inc.
229 E. Michigan, Suite 335
Kalamazoo, MI 49007
(616) 381-4880

Engineering Department, City of Battle Creek
P.O. Box 1717
Battle Creek, MI 49016
(616) 966-3343

Newcastle Beach Park, Bellevue, Wash. (*Jones & Jones. Linda Feltner*)

Newcastle Beach Park
Lake Washington
Bellevue, Washington

Summary

A community lakefront park celebrates its Northwest heritage and preserves a major amount of open space.

(*Jones & Jones. Linda Feltner*)

Description. Newcastle Beach Park occupies a 29.4-acre site on the shores of Lake Washington, in Bellevue, Washington, a suburb of Seattle. Purposefully, over 20 acres of the site remains natural. As a result, the park represents 6.6 percent of the amount of undeveloped land on the lake.

An entry road to the park, which links up with existing bike paths, passes through a preserved woodland before reaching the formal recreation area. A meadow, a children's play space, and parking areas make up the major part of the formal park. A beach and dock offer water access and views across the lake. A wood dock extends into the water, where it deflects at a 45-degree angle to protect the shoreline from eroding. A lifeguard office and observation deck, a bathhouse with rest rooms and changing facilities, and a pier with swimming floats punctuate one end of the beach.

Canada geese vie with members of the Bellevue community to enjoy the open meadow. Maintenance crews use a special outdoor vacuum to clean up after the geese.

Design Features. The lake setting and the natural features are beautiful, but the building forms and detailing make this park particularly outstanding. The design interprets typical rural Northwest structures built by European and Asian workers who settled around Puget Sound. The simple lines of the narrow wooden structures and the wide overhanging eaves of the park buildings embody this design type. The use of gray, aqua, and blue colors echo the water and blend with the surroundings. The yellow accents on the window trim add the right touch of contrast. The tall, narrow buildings are extremely functional looking and at the same time elegant.

In other detailing, small, square blue tiles are embedded in one of the cement retaining walls near the beach. Handsome trash receptacles and wooden benches show care in their selection, an often-overlooked detail.

Appraisal. This park combines sensitivity for natural features and conditions with a respect for the built environment. Rather than the uninspired service buildings found in many otherwise gorgeous parks and wilderness areas, the Newcastle bathhouse and lifeguard station enhance their setting and provide visitors to the park with beautiful, uniquely designed structures and features to match the surroundings. Handsome, interpretive display plaques that depict both the natural and human history of the area are commendable as well.

Newcastle Beach Park

Cost. $2 million
Dimensions. 29.4 acres
Completion date. 1988

Sponsor. Department of Parks and Recreation
City of Bellevue
13204 SE 8th Pl.
Bellevue, WA 98005
(206) 455-6881

Designer. Jones & Jones, Architects and Landscape
Architects
105 South Main St.
Seattle, WA 98104
(206) 624-5702

Civil/structural engineer. TAMS Consultants, Inc.
999 Third Ave.
Seattle, WA 98101
(206) 296-0700

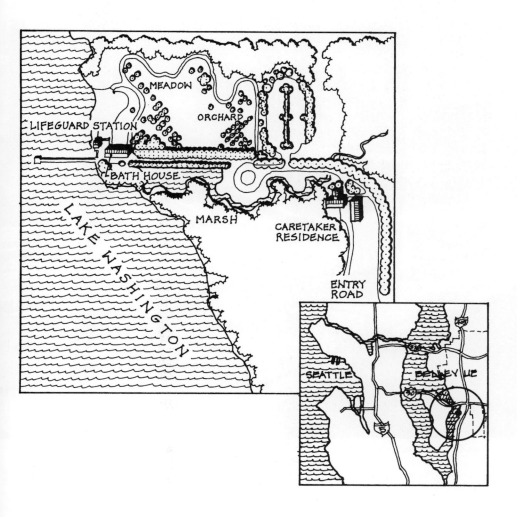

Waterfront Park, Boston, Mass. (*Cymie Payne*)

Waterfront (Christopher Columbus) Park Atlantic Avenue Boston, Massachusetts

Summary

The essential public opening to the harbor in the heart of Boston's central waterfront.

Description. Waterfront Park occupies a critical 4.5 acres of the center city waterfront. It is the conscious terminus of a pedestrian path from nearby Government Center via Faneuil Hall/Quincy Market to the waterfront, dubbed the "walk to the sea." It likewise is a north–south link, tying together the bustling North End neighborhood with some of the newer waterfront installations such as the New England Aquarium and Rowe's Wharf (see Chapter 5).

The park opened at the same time the immensely popular Quincy Market restoration was completed, in the Bicentennial year of 1976. That was also the year the Tall Ships rode into Boston Harbor, drawing people by the thousands to various vantage points. The combination of the spectacular event, a well-designed public waterfront park, and a popular marketplace has had an indelible impact not only on Boston, but on the planning, design, and development communities of the United States and the world.

The park, built for a cost of $2.5 million, is singular in that it owes its relative spaciousness in the cramped downtown of Boston to moving a major road. To make space for this park, Atlantic Avenue was swung away from its course along the shore. Since the park's establishment, a large hotel has been built beside it and the Rose Fitzgerald Kennedy Rose Garden has been built within it.

The park's views to the harbor are neatly framed between Long and Commercial Wharves.

Design Features. There is a wide promenade and cobblestone plaza with seating at the shore, and distinctive bollards and large chains at the water's edge. Seating, an imaginative play area built around a "crow's nest," open green lawn, and a fountain people can splash in are included. There's also a grove of locust trees.

The signature of Waterfront Park is a striking, 340-foot-long trellis that runs across the middle. Curved and 20 feet high, covered with wisteria vine, it is a prominent visual element, providing shade and interesting shadows. The walkway underneath is lined with wooden benches, choice spots for reading or harbor viewing.

Details used here are well chosen: The granite, brick, cobblestone, and wood features are both rugged and handsome, reflecting the area's early days as a prosperous port.

Appraisal. Waterfront Park is an obviously well-enjoyed facility, for residents, office workers, and visitors alike. Its opening simultaneous-

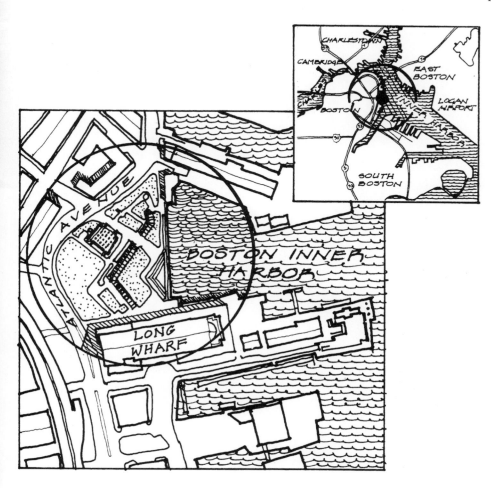

ly with Quincy Market paired the very urban intensity of the marketplace with a quiet, expansive green "window" on the harbor. The combination is powerful, aided by the careful attention to detail.

Waterfront Park, like so many such places, misses the opportunity to educate the visitor about the rich maritime history here, the nature of the harbor, and plans for the future. Common, not to say ugly, trash barrels mar the park's beauty.

Waterfront (Christopher Columbus) Park

Cost. $2.9 million
Dimensions. 4.5 acres
Completion date. 1976
Note. An Adjacent parcel developed as the Rose Kennedy Fitzgerald Park in 1987 for $1 million

Sponsor. Homer Russell, Director of Urban Design
Boston Redevelopment Authority
City Hall, Room 900
Boston, MA 02201
(617) 926-3300

Architect. Stuart O. Dawson, FASLA, and John R. Jennings
Sasaki Associates, Inc.
64 Pleasant Street
Watertown, MA 02172
(617) 926-3300

Lighting consultants. William M. C. Lam
Lam Partners, Inc.
84 Sherman St.
Cambridge, MA 02140
(617) 354-4502

Burlington Community Boathouse, Burlington, Vt. (*Barbara Leslie*)

Burlington Community Boathouse
Foot of College Street
Burlington, Vermont

Summary

A central, symbolic feature of what has come to be known as "The People's Waterfront of Burlington."

(*City of Burlington*)

Description. To see the Community Boathouse in action is to belie the somewhat tortuous path taken to establish this feature. Burlington, like many cities, has gone through fits and starts—and generated considerable controversy—on its way to settling finally in 1990 on a Waterfront Concept Plan.

One of the notable success stories in the course of a 20-year debate was establishment of the floating boathouse on the central waterfront, not far from Main Street. Opened on July 4, 1988, the boathouse had been approved by voters a year earlier, after several defeats of earlier waterfront plans.

And even while the boathouse was opening, private property owners were before the Supreme Court contesting a related waterfront bike path (the city won its case in 1989).[1]

The boathouse is built on a barge, attached to a new dock facility by twin ramps that handle a lake fluctuation of 10 feet. A 4.5-acre park leads to the boathouse, linked to the city's 9-mile waterfront bike path. College Street, one of Burlington's principal east-west streets, feeds into the boathouse/park and is one block from Main Street.

The boathouse contains 6700 square feet of space on two levels. There's an outside deck around both levels, and mooring space on either end. It was built, to locally generated design, in Texas and towed to the site.

The Burlington Community Boathouse func-tions year-round. Operated by the City Parks and Recreation Department with leases to private vendors, it is home to a variety of activities, many involving active water use, but a number otherwise. In the latter category, for instance, are such functions as weddings and community-sponsored concerts.

The Community Boathouse offers boat rentals of various types, bike and scuba gear rentals, a snack bar, and an upstairs function room. Views from the deck of Lake Champlain and the Adirondack Mountains are spectacular, and available to the public even after the facility is closed. A program of musical and community events such as a Thursday evening barbecue bring people to the boathouse and pier.

Design Features. The Burlington Community Boathouse is a functional design, dominated by a red tin roof with dormer-style skylights. The red is continued as the accent color around windows and doors, balanced with gray and tan tones, to give the boathouse a coordinated color scheme that fits the site. There was a predecessor boathouse in Burlington that is recalled in the design approach, but not replicated.

A dominant feature is the wraparound deck on both levels. Especially from the second story, this provides a splendid viewing platform. The first-level deck is more functional, especially in season, with moorings at either end and a boat tie-up dock along the middle.

Appraisal. After years of controversy, it must have been with a sense of relief that Burlington opened a facility that met with widespread community approval. As one indication, an initiative in November 1988 to buy park land near the boathouse was approved by a 74 percent margin, only three years after voters defeated a city-backed initiative for another bond issue. The earlier bond was for $6 million in support of a large, mixed-use project, while the park site near the boathouse cost $2 million and was strictly for public facilities.

While the city and its citizens were hammering out an agreement on the future of their waterfront in the late 1980s, including some commercial development, an "urban reserve" of 45 acres, and continued park development, the boathouse emerged as a well-appreciated symbol of a waterfront on its way to becoming a major community space.

Burlington Community Boathouse

Cost. $1.19 million
Source. General Obligation Bond
Dimensions. 6700-square-foot boathouse, 5000-square-foot pier, 4.5-acre park
Completion date. 1988

Sponsor. Mayor Peter Clavelle
City of Burlington, City Hall
Burlington, VT 05401
(802) 865-7272

Sponsor. Betsy Rosenbluth
Community and Economic Development Office
Room 32, City Hall
Burlington, VT 05401
(802) 865-7144

Sponsor. Don Bessler
Burlington Parks and Recreation Department
216 Leddy Pk. Rd.
Burlington, VT 05401
(802) 864-0123

Designer. Marcel Beaudin
Beaudin Associates
435 Main St.
Burlington, VT 05401
(802) 862-9633

Consulting engineer. John B. Stetson
Thermo Consulting Engineers
P.O. Box 784
Williston, VT 05495
(802) 879-7733

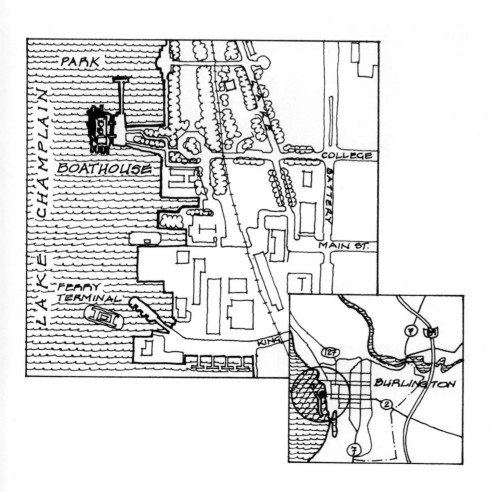

Waterfront Park, Charleston, S.C. (*Stuart O. Dawson*)

Charleston Waterfront Park Vendue Range and Concord Street Charleston, South Carolina Top Honor Award 1992

Summary
A showcase waterfront park designed in harmony with a historic setting and built to withstand coastal storms.

Description. The Charleston Waterfront Park, which opened in May 1990, comprises a key 12-acre site in historic downtown Charleston on the Cooper River, stretching from Adger's Wharf to Vendue Range.

The upland area along the waterfront contained rubble fill, deposited there after a turn-of-the-century fire had destroyed much of Charleston's wharfs and industry. By the mid-1970s, when philanthropists Charles and Elizabeth Woodward donated money for the reconstruction of historic Adger's Wharf, the area was derelict. In 1979 the city acquired the future site of the park, and by September 1980 a master plan for the park had been prepared with the goal of providing citizens and tourists additional open space in the densely developed downtown.

The park today provides about 3500 linear feet of public access along the shoreline close to the center city. A 400-foot wharf/fishing pier juts out over the water, affording excellent views of Charleston Harbor. Care was taken during construction to protect and enhance existing marsh vegetation in front of the park. The city also created new marsh, off-site, at a 2:1 ratio to make up for any lost during construction. The 3-acre park is divided into several distinct areas, from the expanses of green lawns to the secluded seating areas to the centerpiece fountain. In the water itself, old

pilings—remnants of the historic wharves—have been selectively retained as artifacts.

The potential damage that could occur due to hurricanes and coastal storm surges was one of the biggest planning concerns. While cost prohibited designing the entire park to withstand storms, certain measures were taken. Wave energies, storm surges, and distances between wave crests were calculated, and a thorough range of directions, fetches, and water depths were studied. Analyzing and taking these factors into consideration, the T-shaped fishing pier and reinforced seawall were carefully designed to take the brunt of the attacks. In th fall of 1989, Hurricane Hugo roared through Charleston with 135-mile winds and storm surges of as high as 12 feet to test the park's mettle. While the hurricane caused a setback and $1 million worth of damage, the park was not dealt nearly the severe blow that it might have been. The pier structure interacted with the storm exactly as anticipated.

The park was 80 percent publicly funded and cost $13 million, of which $3.3 million came from an Urban Development Action Grant. Another $2.5 million came from private donations.

Design Features. This project—which is really two linked parks, Charleston Waterfront Park and Adger's Wharf Park—offers a rich variety of experiences for the visitor. The entire park is

(*Breen/Rigby*)

(Breen/Rigby)

built up from the street level, so the waterfront itself cannot be viewed from afar.

The entry plaza at the terminus of Vendue Range is announced by flags and a focal-point water fountain. A fishing pier is the major feature at this end of the park. Its inclusion in the design was the result of community wishes expressed during public hearings in the planning for the park. Wooden planking is traditional, and three large, handsome pavilions on the pier provide seating and protection from sun and rain. Big, swinging benches hooked to beams in the pavilions are a hit with young and old alike. Free telescopes are in place to enhance the viewing experience of the harbor.

The fishing pier is a major plus, because it provides recreational access over the water for anglers as well as general visitors. The design of the pier and waterfront promenade relate visually and functionally to the water: They are sturdy and simple. Between the pier and the promenade, four interpretive bronze relief maps depicting the development history of the city have been installed on good-sized stone blocks.

The waterfront promenade runs along the entire river, highlighted by impressive rows of native palmettos. It orients the walker to an expanse of wetlands, old piles, and views of the harbor. The promenade changes character as it approaches Adger's Wharf Park; the path here is closer to the water and grasses, and has a more informal feel, as was requested by the adjoining neighborhood.

Typical of the other, more formal areas of the main park area is a large, central ornamental fountain reflecting the beauty, charm, and character-full architecture of Charleston. The centerpiece design keys off of the pineapple—a symbol of hospitality. The fountain, surrounded by green lawn and colorful plantings and flowers, is framed by stone steps and walls, and is dramatically lit at night.

The city edge of the park relates to the elegance of the historic city and its handsome homes. The fencing and gates are formal and intricate. The slate, gravel, and brick-patterned walkways weave among a number of intimate garden "sitting rooms." Classic Charleston Battery benches have been arranged differently in each space. These well-shaded and beautifully planted niches provide a series of private, flower-scented refuges on a hot South Carolina day.

Appraisal. Charleston's Waterfront Park is a primier example of how to take a derelict strip of waterfront and transform it into a major civic asset. It is destined to become a classic urban waterfront park, taking its place with Charleston's Battery Park.

Helping to distinguish this park from others is its provision of a handsome fishing pier and the careful environmental planning that went into the design and construction—in wetland preservation/mitigation and the built-in flood/hurricane–protection measures.

Additionally, the park handles well the challenge of addressing the water, the waterfront, and its historic context in different ways, through the excellent design detailing. Mayor Joseph Riley, who predicted on opening day that the park "will be something every citizen will cherish," was more than a driving force. He was "actively involved in the planning and construction of the park down to the minor details. He helped sample 50 types and colors of gravel for the walkways, finally settling on a mixture of 10 different ingredients. He personally selected the bright pink petunias in the flower beds."[2] This attention to detail is telling and points up the importance of having an educated "client" to work with designers.

While the park in fact retains many of the pilings that remained from early warehouses and pier facilities as artifacts, and has reconstructed historic Adger's Wharf for public enjoyment and put in interpretive maps, there is not a great amount of explanatory material on site. Given this city's rich maritime history and the environmental elements here, and the industrial activity of the port nearby, much more educational material could be displayed and celebrated in this splendid space.

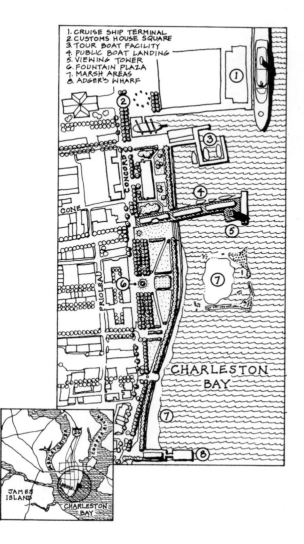

1. CRUISE SHIP TERMINAL
2. CUSTOMS HOUSE SQUARE
3. TOUR BOAT FACILITY
4. PUBLIC BOAT LANDING
5. VIEWING TOWER
6. FOUNTAIN PLAZA
7. MARSH AREAS
8. ADGER'S WHARF

Charleston Waterfront Park

Cost. $13.5 million
Source. 20 percent ($2.5 million) private donations; 80 percent public financing, including a $3.3 million Urban Development Action Grant, U.S. Dept. of Housing and Urban Development
Dimensions. 12-acre site including 1500-foot promenade, 400-foot wharf, 300-foot fishing pier
Completion date. May 1990

Sponsor. Mayor Joseph P. Riley, Jr.
City of Charleston
P.O. Box 304
Charleston, SC 29402
(803) 577-4727

Sponsor. Trident Community Foundation
456 King St.
Charleston, SC 29403
(803) 723-3635

Designer. Stuart O. Dawson, FASLA
Sasaki Associates, Inc.
64 Pleasant St.
Watertown, MA 02172
(617) 926-3300

Designer. Jacqueline T. Robertson
Cooper, Robertson & Partners
311 W. 43 St.
New York, NY 10036
(212) 247-1717

Geotechnical engineers. Law Engineering Testing Co.
7316-A Pepperdam Ave.
Charleston, SC 29405
(803) 767-0100

Consultant. Edward Pinckney
Edward Pinckney Associates, Ltd.
P.O. Box 5339
Hilton Head Island, SC 29938
(803) 785-4265

Cincinnati Gateway, Riverwalk and Bicentennial Commons at Sawyers Point, Cincinnati, Ohio. (*Rick Bieser*)

Bicentennial Commons at Sawyer Point, Cincinnati Gateway, and Riverwalk
Pete Rose Way
Cincinnati, Ohio
1989 Top Honor Award

Summary

In celebrating the city's bicentennial year, Cincinnati achieved three separate but integrated projects as part of a popular, monumental riverfront improvement, outstanding for its educational/interpretive elements.

Gateway to Bicentennial Park is crowned with flying pigs atop riverboat smokestacks. A Noah's Ark caps a flood marker. (*Greater Cincinnati Bicentennial Commission*)

Description. Bicentennial Commons at Sawyer Point is named for the late Charles Sawyer, a local philanthropist who donated a million dollars, later matched by a Department of the Interior Land and Water Conservation Fund grant. Together with $1 million of city money, the funds were used to acquire an old riverfront scrapyard and clear it.

The 22-acre site is east of and adjacent to the central waterfront, with a stadium, coliseum, public landing for riverboats such as the *Delta Queen*, Serpentine Wall with its curving steps into the river, plus several park areas. Contributions from more than 500 area corporations, foundations, and government agencies, keyed to the city's bicentennial anniversary, made this $14 million project a reality. Over 33,000 individuals also paid $35.00 each to purchase brick pavers with their names inscribed, which are laid on a promenade.

Bicentennial Commons is a community and family recreation space emphasizing a wide range of sports, education, and cultural activities. Parking facilities for 383 cars have been provided along Pete Rose Way. The entrance is marked by the stunning Cincinnati Gateway, a 300-foot-long environmental sculpture by artist Andrew Leicester. Eighteen different design features woven into the piece depict aspects of Cincinnati's history and its ties to the river.

Passing through the gateway, the visitor comes to open areas and views of the Ohio River from a 400-foot-long, tree-lined plaza/promenade. A brick plaza that can house booths and displays during events works well with the grassy Great Lawn, which seats 5000 and provides space for informal picnics or large festivals. A large tensile structure, the Procter & Gamble Performance Pavilion, backs up to the river and is used for musical and other entertainment events. This major event venue is complemented by a more intimate performance area, the Harold C. Schott Foundation Amphitheater.

For exercise enthusiasts there are eight lighted

championship tennis courts, two volleyball courts, a par-course fitness area, an all-year-surface skating rink for both ice and roller skaters, and a boathouse, home to an Olympic rowing training center and a state-of-the-art fitness centers. Restaurant facilities are housed in the upper stories of the boathouse, revenues from which help support the rowing facility. Besides a children's play area, ample walkways, and open green space, there is also a fishing pier.

Four overlooks provide views of the river. One of these, the Arches Overlook, is a historic restoration of a brick viaduct, a remnant of an old railroad bridge. Another overlook provides outstanding views of the skyline and river. Metal/photo plaques are embedded in the stone railings here, depicting the early river and steamboat eras of the city.

Along an 1800-foot stretch of the Riverwalk, a geologic timeline is engraved in the paving, interpreting 450 million years. It gives the stroller a living history lesson in the geology of the earth in general, and the Ohio River Valley in particular. School children are brought to this feature to give them a graphic sense of history and time.

The geologic timeline forms part of a 4-mile heritage trail that connects the riverfronts of Cincinnati, Ohio, and Covington and Newport, Kentucky. In all there are 36 historical stations along the trail; some are commemorative statues, others, like the timeline, are interpretive. The riverwalk crosses the Ohio on the Roebling Suspension Bridge, built in 1866 (see Chapter 4).

On the Kentucky side, the riverwalk meanders through a historic riverfront section along Riverside Drive in Covington and across the Licking River to Newport. A more informal route goes past Riverboat Row, where a number of dinner boats are docked, and then across the Central Bridge back to Cincinnati.

Design Features. The most outstanding design feature of the Bicentennial Commons is the Gateway Sculpture. It is a combination gate, pathway, viewing platform, and dramatic sculpture. A long grass and shrub berm extends the full length (except for the main entry area) of the piece, which is located on both sides of rail tracks that run along the riverfront and separate the park from the upland areas. What distinguishes the Gateway is the richness of the interpretive material employed throughout. Not your standard plaque/representational sculpture, it presents information in a splendidly imaginative, and sometimes whimsical, manner. The design elements can be enjoyed on their own. The interested viewer can try to figure them out, or refer to the bronze key near the entrance.

At one end of the sculpture are Serpent Steps,

A geologic timeline is a popular feature of Bicentennial Park. It depicts in text and images the 440 million years since the creation of the Ohio River basin. (*Greater Cincinnati Bicentennial Commission*)

Riverwalk on the Kentucky side of the Ohio River is lined with sculptures of historic figures of the area. James Audubon is in foreground. (*Greater Cincinnati Bicentennial Commission*)

reminders of the Serpent Mound in Peebles, Ohio, which dates back to 100 B.C. These lead to a triangular-shaped abstraction of the source of the Ohio River (the confluence of the Allegheny and Monongahela Rivers at Pittsburgh). A scale-model replica of the 981-mile-long river is carved into a red-paved walkway along the top—it can be walked beside. Midway along this "river" is a bridge across the opening in the berm—the actual entry gate. The bridge's wire rope cables pay homage to John A. Roebling, whose suspension bridge crosses the Ohio nearby. Bronze fish heads at the base of each bridge column secure the cables, which stretch to the top of four tall smokestacks, symbolic of the riverboats that were the major form of transport and commerce in the 1800s. Geological and historical features related to the city and the site are depicted in tile murals and other details.

Atop each smokestack is a winged pig, recalling Cincinnati's heyday as "Porkopolis." In the mid-1800s the city was the principal hog market of the world. There were several hundred slaughterhouses then, and hogs were said to have run in the streets. The pigs—and questions about the city's dignity—stirred up major controversy, as well as considerable local and national publicity. At a climactic public meeting at City Hall, the "Flying Pigs" were ultimately unanimously endorsed. Today they have become an emblem of the city and appear on all sorts of merchandise, from charms to T-shirts.

The park itself repeats round structures and forms: the overlooks, the boathouse, the skating rink, and the plazas, for example. This theme is said to have been inspired by the curves of the shoreline. The landscaping, including trees, flowers, and shrubbery, much of it donated by civic clubs, is also notable. Remnants of the old waterworks pumping station and a railroad bridge are interesting features.

The geologic timeline which constitutes the first 1800 feet of the Riverwalk is enhanced by the 440 granite panels that represent the 440 million years before the settlement of the city. Flora and fauna from these eras are inscribed into some of the panels, and are suitable for artistic rubbings.

The course of the 4-mile Riverwalk is identified by a distinctive logo, which is embedded on the walkway and on signposts and banners along the way. Maps are placed in strategic locations to inform pedestrians where they are and how their position fits in with the whole. The Covington, Kentucky, portion of the walk includes the Riverside Historic District. Here care has been taken to use brick walkways, period lighting, and benches—a sharp contrast to the more modern treatment on the Ohio side. Seven representational bronze statues by different artists punctuate the walk in a historic hall of fame. Personalities represented include John R. Roebling, John J. Audubon, Miami Indian Chief Little Turtle, and the founder of the Boy Scouts of America, Daniel Carter Beard.

Appraisal. The significant riverfront accomplishments made in connection with the city's bicentennial—the park, the Gateway sculpture, and the Riverwalk— stand heads above many other equally beautiful waterfront parks in part because of the strong educational features. The amount and range of interpretive materials provided in many different media is exceptional—in both expected ways, as in the representational sculptures and historic photos, and in unexpected ones, such as the timeline and the Gateway.

The collaboration among two states and three cities to achieve the Riverwalk is notable. The collective energy expressed in corporate, civic, and individual contributions to the entire undertaking is impressive. It speaks of community pride and determination, as well as the power of the river.

Bicentennial Commons at Sawyer Point

Cost. $22 million
Source. 64 percent public, including City of Cincinnati/Cincinnati Recreation Commission; 36 percent contributions administered by Bicentennial Commission
Dimensions. 22 acres, performance pavilion for 5000
Completion date. June 1988
Notes. Currently expanding volleyball facilities and children's Fantasy Play
Contact. Ann C. Sternal, (513) 352-4026

Sponsor. Richard Greiwe, Executive Director
Greater Cincinnati Bicentennial Commission, Inc.
I.D. Group (present)
Cincinnati, OH 45201
(513) 721-0104

Sponsor. Ronald W. Chase, Director
Cincinnati Recreation Commission
644 Linn Street, Suite 411
Cincinnati, OH 45203
(513) 352-4000

Designer. Arthur A. Hupp, III
Glaser Associates
2753 Erie Ave.
Cincinnati, OH 45208
(513) 871-9111

Designer. M. Paul Friedberg & Partners
41 East 11 St.
New York, NY 10003
(212) 477-6366

Designer. Eric Doepke
Eric Doepke & Associates
2712 Erie Avenue
Cincinnati, OH 45208
(513) 321-1133

Mechanical/electrical engineer. Fosdick & Hilmer, Inc.
4th and Walnut Building
Cincinnati, OH 45202
(513) 241-5640

Tensile structure. Nicholas Goldsmith
FTL Associates
157 Chambers St.
New York, NY 10007
(212) 732-4691

Structural engineer. Graham, Obermeyer and Partners, Limited
205 West 4 Street
Cincinnati, OH 45202
(513) 621-7073

Cincinnati Gateway

Dimensions. 300 feet by 50 feet
Completion date. 1988

Sponsor. Richard J. Greiwe
Greater Cincinnati Bicentennial Commission, Inc.
I.D. Group (present)
Cincinnati, OH 45201
(513) 721-0104

Designer. Meyer Scherer & Rockcastle Ltd.
325 2nd Ave. North
Minneapolis, MN 55401
(612) 375-0336

Artist. Andrew Leicester
1500 Jackson St. NE
Minneapolis, MN 55413
(612) 781-7422

Artists. Dept. Design, Architecture & Planning
University of Cincinnati, Room 710/ML 016
Cincinnati, OH 45221
(513) 556-4933

"Flying Pig" and fish head shrouds artist. Douglas Freeman
Sculpture Studio
310 North 2nd St.
Minneapolis, MN 55401
(612) 339-7150

Riverwalk

Dimensions. 4 miles
  Completion date. October 1988

Sponsor. Richard J. Greiwe
  Greater Cincinnati Bicentennial Commission, Inc.
  I.D. Group (present)
  Cincinnati, OH 45201
  (513) 721-0104

Project designer. Pamela Rogow
  R + B Design
  5971 West Third St.
  Los Angeles, CA 90036
  (213) 936-9916

Graphics. Schenker, Probst, Barensfeld
  2728 Vine St.
  Cincinnati, OH 45219
  (513) 221-1977

Consultant. I.D. Group
  P.O. Box 1256
  Cincinnati, OH 45201
  (513) 352-6197

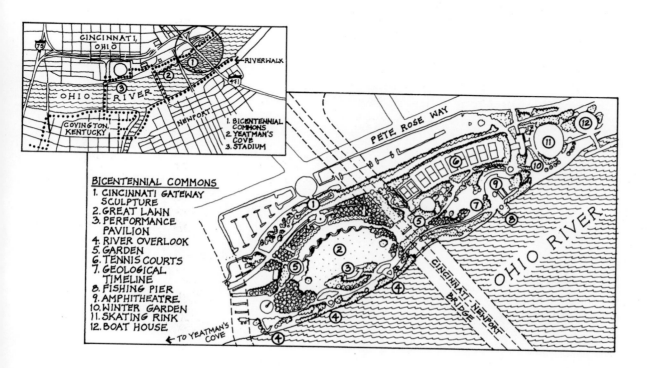

BICENTENNIAL COMMONS
1. CINCINNATI GATEWAY SCULPTURE
2. GREAT LAWN
3. PERFORMANCE PAVILION
4. RIVER OVERLOOK
5. GARDEN
6. TENNIS COURTS
7. GEOLOGICAL TIMELINE
8. FISHING PIER
9. AMPHITHEATRE
10. WINTER GARDEN
11. SKATING RINK
12. BOAT HOUSE

Riverdesign Dayton, Dayton, Ohio. (*Breen/Rigby*)

Riverdesign Dayton/River's Edge Park
Great Miami River at Main Street
Dayton, Ohio

Summary

Sculptural park carved from floodwall, focal point of 8-mile downtown riverfront effort.

Description. River's Edge Park took a blank concrete floodwall and transformed it into a sculpted series of steps, seating areas, and walkways down to the river's edge. At the almost completely open edge, a stage in the shape of a boat was installed in the river, reached by an arched wooden bridge.

The park, in the central riverfront of downtown Dayton, was constructed in 1980 following two earlier riverfront studies. The first, in 1972, The Great Miami River Study, was by Dan Kiley Associates, Landscape Architects, and led to development of what is now a significant walkway and bikeway system at two levels. The upper level is a well-marked Riverwalk.

The second effort, called Riverdesign Dayton, was finished in 1977 and carried the earlier work a major step forward. Collaborating on this work were Centerbrook, architects of Essex, Connecticut, and Lorenz and Williams, Inc., of Dayton, sponsored by the Chamber of Commerce river committee. (At the time the work was accomplished, the firms were, respectively, Moore Grove Harper of Essex, and Lorenz, Williams, Lively, Likens and Partners, Dayton.) River's Edge park was executed by Lorenz and Williams and dedicated in 1980.

The park, still predominantly concrete, effectively opens to the public a key section, closest to downtown offices. New townhomes are now located immediately adjacent, and apartments are present in the 12-story YMCA structure, one of Dayton's major buildings, beside the park.

Running along the top of the park is a gravel walkway lined with trees. Because the river floods periodically, the park and bikeway at river's edge are bereft of plantings. The walkway's trees provide the shade here, and in fact on a sunny day, picnickers congregate at the upper levels.

A fountain is built into the base of the steps, providing welcome water noise beside the still waters of the Great Miami.

Design Features. The 10 rows of steps to the river are alternately plain concrete and a pebbled surface to provide visual relief. The risers are high, and in fact a series of steps is provided to make passage to and from the walkway easier.

There are also paths carved out that can be used by bikes or wheelchairs. Visually these serve to break up the mass.

At the river's edge, where the flat area is wide enough in places for separate biking and hiking trails, additional interest is provided in the form of a flat concrete pad in the shape of a vessel, accessible by foot bridge.

Riverdesign Dayton in the late 1970s used innovative techniques of public participation, including a downtown store location where people from all walks of life were encouraged to drop in, and television programs where ideas were solicited. Suggestions during one of the latter events were grouped by major user groups, such as children, the elderly, "brown baggers," nature lovers, and people with $2.00 to spend, with viewers calling in suggestions for each. The public participation identified the central riverfront between the bridges as the first area of opportunity, with River's Edge Park the outcome. (See bibliographic citation, Riverdesign Dayton.)

Appraisal. River's Edge Park is a punctuation point in a years'-long effort to make a recreational and economic development asset out of the Great Miami River as it swings around downtown Dayton. This effort goes at least as far back as 1968, when a River Corridor Committee was established by the Dayton Area Chamber of Commerce. The river bikeway along the river was dedicated in 1984 to the committee's first chairman, Horace Huffman, Jr. The chamber's effort to fashion an asset out of the river came years after flood-protection levees and walls had been installed, following a major flood in 1913.

While River's Edge Park is on the section of the Great Miami River closest to downtown, it is far enough away and with significant enough vacancy intervening to give it a somewhat isolated feeling. Also, the absence of a cafe along the top (in part a function of the relative isolation) cuts down on the amount of active use on a day-to-day basis.

River's Edge Park is enjoyed at lunchtime, for quiet contemplation during the day, and no doubt for special occasions. The walkway above and bikeway below, repeated on both sides of the river for miles, draw many users.

The major amount of concrete, absent a single tree near the river, gives the park a somewhat bleak appearance; but considering it was developed from a blank concrete wall, its curves, steps, and boat feature make it an inviting exception to traditional flood-protection walls.

Riverdesign Dayton/River's Edge Park

Cost. $1.4 million
Dimensions. Trail, 8 linear miles, 3 acres
Completion date. 1980

Sponsor. James L. Rozelle, General Manager
The Miami Conservancy District
38 East Monument Ave.
Dayton, OH 45402
(513) 223-1271

Sponsor. H. M. Huffman, Chairman
Dayton Area Chamber of Commerce
111 W. 4th St.
Dayton, OH 45402
(513) 226-1444

Architect (master plan). Chad Floyd, FAIA
Centerbrook Architects
P.O. Box 955
Essex, CT 06426
(203) 767-0175

Architect (park). Stephen J. Carter, AIA
Lorenz and Williams, Inc.
120 West Third Ave.
Dayton, OH 45402
(513) 223-6500

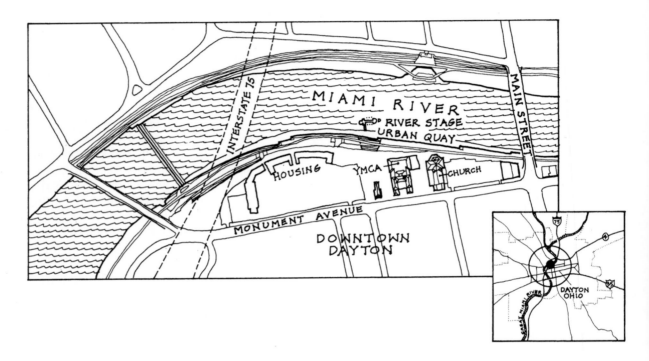

Platte River Greenway, Denver, Colo. (*Breen/Rigby*)

Platte River Greenway
South Platte River
Denver, Colorado

Summary

Ten miles in length and years in the making, a model greenway project carved from a neglected river resource .

(*Robert Searns*)

Description. The South Platte River in the 1970s was known as Denver's "blighted, degraded river—little more than an open sewer," among other, negative things. Its restoration to civic health, and later extension to communities outside Denver, is a dramatic story, with many players and just as many lessons for others.

What the greenway accomplished, in action that dates from 1974, is the linking of two state parks north and south of the city. The step-by-step course that the transformation entailed—a deliberate strategy borne of necessity and a conscious, politically adept policy—resulted in development of a green amenity at the edge and readily accessible to downtown Denver. In all there are 400 acres of trails, parks, picnic grounds, amphitheater, and other amenities along a continuous hiking and biking trail.

Such an accomplishment was at best a glimmer on a day in June 1974 when the mayor met with his recent political opponent and set in motion the Platte River Development Committee. Mayor William H. (Bill) McNichols (Democrat) was planning a river committee when Joe Shoemaker (Republican), defeated mayoral candidate, one-time state senator, and former city public works director, approached him with the identical idea. Shoemaker was named chairman on the spot, and from this unlikely marriage came unprecedented action after years of stalling.[3]

The diverse, nine-member committee was initially supported by $1.9 million in city revenue-sharing monies, enough to get planning and early action going. In fact, so intent was the committee on not falling into the trap of a predecessor body appointed after a disastrous flood in 1965 that in February 1975, scant months after its establishment, the committee had a ceremonial ground-breaking. That spring, 1000 volunteers were enlisted in a huge river cleanup, helping to pave the way for a Labor Day 1975 opening of the first segment of the Greenway, Confluence Park, at the site where the Platte and Cherry Creek come together and where Denver was founded in 1859.

While a project such as the Platte River Greenway is in some senses never "completed," it is generally thought to have reached a point of maturity by the mid-1980s and to have succeeded in its goal of linking the 10.5 miles of river within the city limits, with an extension along Cherry Creek. By 1987, a total of $14 million had been spent, much of it donated by industries and citizens. The mature Greenway is actively used by thousands of people each year for such recreational pursuits as rafting, kayaking, jogging, biking, picnics, fishing, horseback riding, and more.[4]

By 1982 there was support to extend the Greenway south into Arapahoe Valley. Whereas the initial work on the Platte was assisted by federal funds, later extensions are backed by local and state money. For instance, state lottery proceeds are shared with local governments, and committed local officials saw to it that the South Platte Greenway Extension got its share.[5] Littleton, Colorado, has acquired 640 acres for a South Platte Park, and Englewood has a golf course and refuge along the river. By the late 1980s the original greenway had grown into a 30-mile network of recreational trails.

The revitalization took more than an energetic committee, committed volunteers, and ingenuity in getting things done, although each was a factor. Flood-control measures were also planned. Reflecting this concern, a two-year master drainage study was undertaken in 1983, covering 40 miles of the river's course. This study, for the Urban Drainage and Flood Control District, made recreational opportunities a twin goal along with flood protection, a measure of the impact of the Greenway in a relatively short time.

Another feature is the Greenway Trail Ranger Program, charged with maintenance. The idea

was to have people actively looking after the facility even if there was not a nearby neighborhood to assume that function, as was the case for stretches of the river within Denver.

Currently, it is reported that pedestrian use of the Greenway has increased since the late 1980s by as much as 50 percent. The Greenway is also in use as a biking commuter link to downtown.

Design Features.   The Greenway's design approach includes many, sturdy signs. These are both directional—such as street signs along the path telling hikers which crossing they are approaching—and interpretive—explaining natural or man-made phenomena. Signs also explain industry along the trail so that it will be more understandable.

The Greenway's trail system and its structures use wood and warm-toned concrete to blend with the natural environment. Pedestrian bridges at various points are attractive wooden structures, for instance. Berms have been built to screen unsightly areas, such as nearby highways, on occasion using rubble pulled out of the river

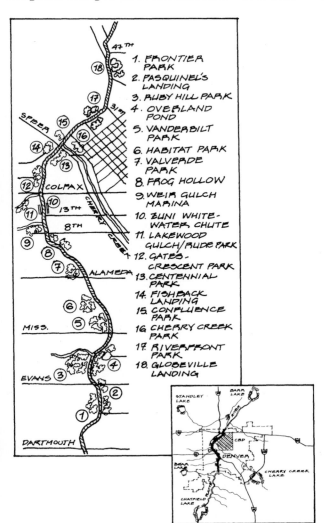

1. FRONTIER PARK
2. PASQUINEL'S LANDING
3. RUBY HILL PARK
4. OVERLAND POND
5. VANDERBILT PARK
6. HABITAT PARK
7. VALVERDE PARK
8. FROG HOLLOW
9. WEIR GULCH MARINA
10. ZUNI WHITE-WATER CHUTE
11. LAKEWOOD GULCH/RUDE PARK
12. GATES-CRESCENT PARK
13. CENTENNIAL PARK
14. FISHBACK LANDING
15. CONFLUENCE PARK
16. CHERRY CREEK PARK
17. RIVERFRONT PARK
18. GLOBEVILLE LANDING

bed. Attention was also paid to engineering design that will withstand the strong natural forces of the river.

Confluence Park, the beginning point of the Greenway, has a dramatic boat chute carved from the rubble that clogged the Platte. It's used by rafts, canoes, and kayaks. The Greenway as a whole features numerous boat landings, introducing an activity that was unthinkable when the Greenway committee was launched.

Appraisal. Joe Shoemaker tells the story of how he, like many others, was inspired by visiting the San Antonio Riverwalk to do something with the derelict Platte River in his home city. Today, the Platte River Greenway, whose initial development he helped guide, can likewise be visited for inspiration and specific, transferable ideas on how to transform an urban river from dumping ground to playground.

One technique used by the committee in its early days reflects the political nature of its leadership. After any segment was completed, signs were immediately put up crediting everyone who had played a role. Celebrations were held frequently, to help fix in the public's mind that real change was under way, after years of discussion but no action. Likewise, events were established along the newly cleaned-up river area for the same purpose.

The Platte River Greenway is testament that virtually anything is possible if—a big if—the local leadership is skilled and persistent. The Platte Greenway naturally encountered setbacks and opposition. The committee moved quickly to accomplish, promoted its accomplishments widely, and no matter what, kept moving.

The result is an urban greenway that is now an integral part of Denver, a virtual institution in that community. As interest in greenways spreads in the United States, the Platte Greenway story will no doubt be retold frequently.

Platte River Greenway

Cost. $14 million
Source. 40 percent public financing
Dimensions. 10.5 miles
Completion date. 1985

Sponsor. Mayor Wellington Webb
City and County of Denver
Denver, CO 80202
(303) 640-2721

Sponsor. Joe Shoemaker, Executive Director
Platte River Greenway Foundation
1666 South University Blvd.
Denver, CO 80210
(303) 698-1322

Designer. Kenneth Wright
Wright Water Engineers
2490 West 26 Ave., Suite 100A
Denver, CO 80211
(303) 480-1700

Consultant. Robert Searns
Urban Edges, Inc.
1401 Blake Street, Suite 301
Denver, CO 80202
(303) 623-8107

Emeryville Peninsula Park & Marina, Emeryville, Calif. (*Hansen/Murakami/Eshima Inc*)

Emeryville Peninsula Park and Marina
San Francisco Bay—East Shore Freeway and Powell Street
Emeryville, California

Summary

Underutilized, barren strip of land becomes a well-loved community park and marina.

Description. The Emeryville Park and Marina are located on an artificial peninsula that extends approximately [fr3/4] mile into San Francisco Bay. The peninsula was created to provide an East Bay dock location for the once-extensive bay ferry system. It became outmoded with construction of the Oakland Bay Bridge in the mid-1930s and was underutilized territory for many years. In the 1960s a large apartment complex was built at the base of the peninsula. Later, the city expanded the peninsula and built a marina.

In the mid-1970s the city hired a consultant and began working collaboratively with a number of government agencies having jurisdiction over the project to create a development plan. These included the Bay Conservation and Development Commission (BCDC), the Army Corps of Engineers, the California Boating Department, and the Wildlife Conservation Board. All of these agencies were actively involved in the design process to upgrade the 12-acre site, as well as in the funding.

Besides the large park, the $1.7 million project today includes a 750-foot fishing pier, picnic benches and barbecues, pedestrian and bike trails, a boat launch, a new restroom facility, and parking areas. One hundred new berths were added to the marina facilities as part of the expansion project, making a total of 350. Three existing buildings were upgraded.

The views of downtown San Francisco and the bay are spectacular. The creation of the park enables residents and visitors alike a chance to get onto the bay and to enjoy the setting.

Design Features. The understated design serves to highlight the natural beauty that surrounds the peninsula. Wooden benches and tables are rustic. Cypress and poplar trees, Monterey pines, native grasses, and ice plant provide lush contrast to the grassy lawns. Pines and cypress shelter many of the picnic areas. Some feature sand barbeque pits encircled with large stones, a more naturalistic touch than more typical grills.

Where the shoreline is not rip-rapped for protection against the harsh bay conditions, marsh grasses and plantings give a wild feel. The fishing pier is a particularly nice addition. The lighting, railing, and gate treatment of the marina areas is low-key, and while not inspired, it is of better caliber than is typically found.

Appraisal. The City of Emeryville took an underutilized peninsula of man-made land and turned it into a major community asset that can be enjoyed by a wide variety of users. Rather than converting it into a private marina or

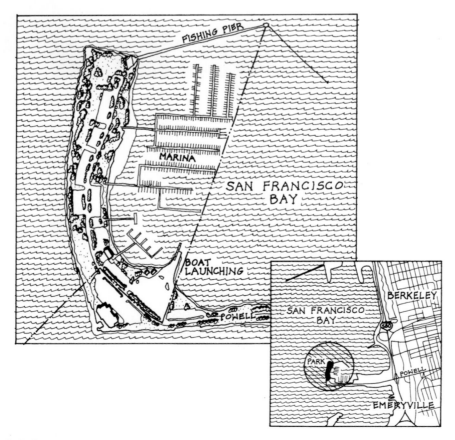

yacht club, this spectacular spot, with its glorious views, has been put into the public realm.

Emeryville Peninsula Park and Marina

Cost. $1.7 million
  Dimensions. 12 acres
  Completion date. late 1970s

Sponsor. John A. Flores, City Manager
  City of Emeryville
  2200 Powell St.
  Emeryville, CA 94608
  (510) 596-4370

Sponsor. California Department of Boating and
  Waterways
  1629 S Street
  Sacramento, CA 95814
  (916) 445-2651

Designer. Mike Murakami, John Nelson
  Hansen/Murakami/Eshima, Inc.
  100 Filbert St.
  Oakland, CA 94607
  (510) 444-7959

Designer. The SWA Group
  2200 Bridgeway Blvd.
  Sausalito, CA 94965
  (415) 332-5100

Hackensack River County Park, Hackensack, N.J. (*Breen/Rigby*)

Hackensack River County Park
Riverside Square Mall, State Highway 4
Hackensack, New Jersey

Summary

A wetland area, once an illegal dump, transformed to green open space adjoining a shopping mall.

Description. The 30-acre site at the rear of Riverside Square Mall provides a parcel of green, open space carved from a highly developed area of northern New Jersey. Nearby are mid-rise offices along a busy state highway. The park is the first step toward what the county hopes will one day be a 12-mile river greenway corridor linking 12 communities along the Hackensack River.

The park is deliberately designed for passive enjoyment, with an emphasis on education about the nature of the tidal river environment. To this end, paths wind along the shore and through wetland areas, with river overlooks at strategic points, equipped with interpretive plaques.

The park is a dramatic reclamation of territory once used as an illegal dumping site and motorcycle track. One of the principal project aims was to restore the area to a healthy condition; paths are located on damaged areas where possible, and the shore has been stabilized.

Parking is provided by agreement with the adjoining shopping mall; 90 spaces are allotted on the ground level of the four-level parking deck at the rear, river, side of the mall. Stairs permit park access from all parking levels.

Design Features. Hackensack River County Park mixes very formal elements with more natural features. The centerpiece is an entryway directly behind the parking deck that has classical overtones, including a curved marble balustrade with flagstone paving, leading to a wooden overlook, with seating, that is directly on the river.

Curved paths emanate from this centerpiece along the fairly narrow (80 feet) site to river overlooks surrounded by natural vegetation. A variety of paving material is used in the park, including stone, gravel, boardwalk, flagstone, and wood chips.

Well-done interpretive plaques at the overlooks illustrate and explain features of the environment, including waterfowl, other birds, and plant life. For instance, at the southern overlook there are five sturdy poles with laminated reprints from an illustrated textbook, with a citation, which provide good information on such features as marshlands, egrets, and ducks.

There is significant landscaping, now somewhat overgrown and perhaps ambitious for the site. Lack of maintenance is today very evident, with the formal planting beds suffering as a result.

Appraisal. This is a commendable first step in the ambitious goal of linking communities along the Hackensack River within Bergen County by a greenway. Such a feature, as is evident at the Hackensack River County Park

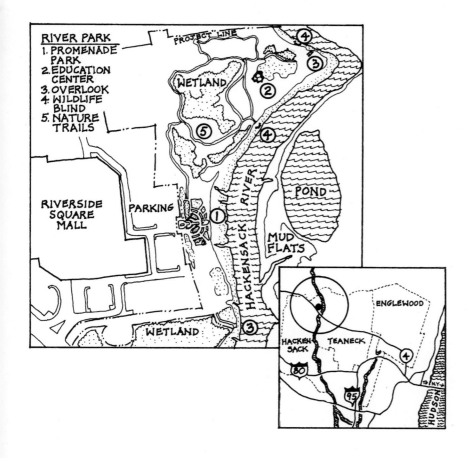

behind Riverside Square, would bring natural open space within ready reach of thousands in New Jersey's most populous county. This initial portion, begun in 1989, cost $1.5 million.

To make the existing facility more effective, considerably better signs and directions are needed. There is no notice about the park within the parking deck or the nearest stores, and its visibility is limited. Some users have obviously found it and enjoy the area for lunch, strolling, or observing the fairly natural-appearing river, but better announcement of its availability might increase use without unduly burdening the resource.

The natural area and interpretive features are well executed. The more formal areas are overdesigned and seem fussy. In some areas, the pathway stones, while visually interesting, are difficult to walk on.

Hackensack River County Park

Cost. $1.5 million
Source. Green Acres Program loan, $500,000; Bergen County bond, $1 million
Dimensions. 30 acres
Completion date. 1990

Sponsor. C. P. Mattson, Director
Bergen County Dept. Planning and Economic Development
21 Main Street, Court Plaza S., Admin. Bldg.
Hackensack, NJ 07601
(201) 646-2896

Sponsor. Wolfgang Albrecht, Jr., Director
Bergen County Dept. of Parks
21 Main Street, Court Plaza S., Admin. Bldg.
Hackensack, NJ 07601
(201) 646-2680

Designer. Dana Jay Hepler, RLA
Hepler Associates, Landscape Architects & Planners
94 Tyrconnell Avenue
Massapequa Park, NY 11762
(516) 797-4300

Structural engineer. Tom Reilly, P.C.
4 Bezel Lane
Smithtown, NY 11787
(516) 724-7888

Surveyor/engineer. Boswell Engineering
330 Phillips Ave.
South Hackensack, NJ 07606
(201) 641-0770

A water feature represents the Tijuana Estuary, which flows into the nearby Pacific Ocean. Pier Plaza, Imperial Beach, Calif. (*Campbell & Campbell*)

Imperial Beach Pier Plaza
Imperial Beach, California

Summary

Imaginative reworking of an entranceway to a standard municipal pier.

Description. The redesigned entrance to the Imperial Beach Pier combines benches, rocks, a fountain, and a graceful stream, with landscaping and curving walls that transform what was no doubt a traditional approach to a recreational pier.

The design came about after consultation with the citizens of Imperial Beach, a blue-collar community south of San Diego. As many as 600 took part in articulating what was important about their community: namely, the beach itself, the site of the successful Imperial Beach Sandcastle Competition; the nearby Tijuana River Estuary, one of the dominant features of the landscape; and the offshore Coronado Islands. The extensive public participation in establishing some of the design features reflects the project's sponsorship by the California Coastal Conservancy of Oakland.

With rocks symbolizing the offshore Coronado Islands, tile streams built into the pavement that model the Tijuana Estuary, plus an overall welcoming setting for entrance to the beach, the design attempts to articulate the community's expressed desire to evoke the city's significant natural features.

A landscaped area, shaded by palms, and numerous seating opportunities on both walls and rocks, round out the remade entrance.

Design Features. The entrance centerpieces are Zen-like boulders and a carefully designed fountain. Water jets that can be activated are set among the four boulders. They are a favorite play area of the kids, and are used by young and old for sitting.

The fountain, when it is working, overflows periodically, sending streams down miniature river courses along ribbons of blue and green tile. This gives a soothing and symbolic point of entrance to the pier.

Accent tile is a feature of the undulating brown, concrete seating wall that sets off a small grassy area beside the beach. Another feature of note is the use of strip lighting under the wall's edge, which accents the curves at night. Groves of Mexican fan palms mark the plaza's edges.

Appraisal. The Imperial Beach Pier Plaza demonstrates the difference a carefully designed approach can make in municipal installations that are usually noted for their solid mundaneness. With a modest budget, an installation that the public enjoys at various levels, and no doubt feels some pride in, has been created from a parking lot.

Somewhat jarring is a pre-existing bathhouse of standard cinder block painted institutional yellow. Maintenance of the fountain may be a problem; it was not working in November 1991.

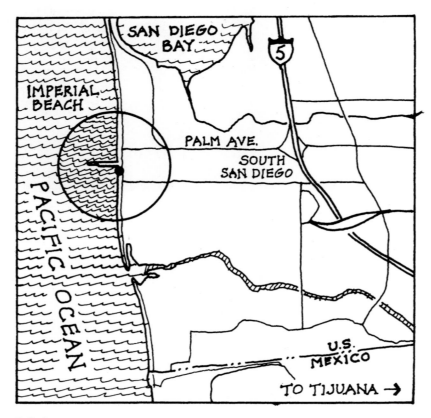

Imperial Beach Pier Plaza

Cost. $786,856 ($600,000 from California Coastal Commission)
Dimensions. 32,000 square feet
Completion date. 1988

Sponsor. City of Imperial Beach
825 Imperial Beach Blvd.
Imperial Beach, CA 91932
(619) 423-8300

Sponsor. Peter Grenell, Executive Officer
California Coastal Conservancy
1330 Broadway, Suite 1100
Oakland, CA 94612
(415) 464-1015

Architect. Regula and Douglas Campbell
Campbell & Campbell
1425 Fifth St.
Santa Monica, CA 90401
(310) 458-1011

A canopied shelter and over-water pathway are features of the Southbank Riverwalk.
Downtown Jacksonville is across the river. Southbank Riverwalk, Jacksonville, Fla.
(*Breen/Rigby*)

Southbank Riverwalk
St. John's River
Jacksonville, Florida

Summary

A central, downtown riverwalk, built largely over water, affords excellent
pedestrian and boater access with views to match.

Description. The St. John's River runs through the heart of Jacksonville, a city of 500,000, originally the site of a French Huguenot settlement in 1564. Today's very modern skyline, testimony to an ambitious downtown redevelopment program focused largely on the riverfront, belies the city's long history.

Before the creation of the Southbank Riverwalk, over 4 million square feet of office, hotel, commercial, restaurant, and recreational facilities had been developed along the banks of the St. John's. However, there was little access to the water or linkage between the facilities. The 1.1-mile Southbank Riverwalk, opened in 1984, is a 20-foot-wide walkway, built mostly over the water on piles. Hugging the shoreline, it created a new, uninterrupted edge and access points along this side of the riverfront with views across the river to the central business district and the port.

This major achievement of public/private partnership in gaining permits and easements was spearheaded by the Downtown Development Authority, which worked with private property owners and Florida permitting agencies.

Space for transient docking and water taxis that ferry visitors across the river at regularly scheduled intervals is provided. Several very contemporary-looking shelter areas are located at key spots, and no doubt provide welcome shade in the hot Florida months. Several double as performance pavilions.

Apart from the shelters, what landscaping there is has been provided in planters and does not offer much shade. Public restrooms and a security office are located near a large observation platform with stepped seating and a Navy war memorial. On either side of the Main Street Bridge, fountains have been installed around the pavilions to help muffle the traffic noise. The bridge, a classic lift structure, allows pedestrians to cross and connects the north and south riverfronts.

The main attractions along the north bank today are the restaurants, bars, and shops of Jacksonville Landing. The hotels and restaurants on both sides of the river, the ability to walk across and along both sides, combined with the presence of the water taxis, make it attractive for visitors and locals who want to enjoy the nightlife. Plans are under way to expand the riverwalk on the north bank.

Design Features. The walkway, by its extension over the water and the way it works around the Main Street Bridge, brings the visitor in close contact with the St. John's River and provides striking views of downtown. The most domi-

nant and successful design feature of the riverwalk is its use of wood. Heavy, treated pine planks are employed throughout for the nicely patterned decking, for railings, and for backless benches—which double in many areas as a kind of wall along the water's edge—and have an authentic nautical, industrial feel to them, like solid old piers. Given the amount of port activity that is visible along the river, they are all the more appropriate.

Bold steel bridges crossing the St. John's add drama to the scene. Contemporary-looking shelters and pavilions trimmed with red piping, with neon accents for nighttime drama, may not be to everyone's liking. Repeated use of blue tubular steel piping in the detailing and for the lighting fixtures echoes the bridges and industrial motif.

Appraisal. This riverwalk is a model for other cities in the way it has created a wonderful pedestrian precinct and brought focus to the river. A formerly inaccessible edge now affords spectacular views of the river and downtown, and provides space for civic festivities and public recreation both day and night. The numerous light fixtures, trash receptacles, and sturdy benches amply supplied are plus factors.

Missing are interpretive elements or public art to explain and celebrate the river, the industry, and the port just across the way. At Jacksonville Landing, by contrast, are nicely designed plaques giving some of the area's history. The only artwork on the walk is the Navy war memorial. Directional signs are weak, and the riverwalk logo, featured on such things as telephone kiosks and banners, is a very stylized "rw," which looks a bit like a bolt of lightning.

Southbank Riverwalk

Cost. $5.5 million
  Dimensions. 1.1 miles long, 20 feet wide
  Completion date. 1984

Sponsor. Frank R. Nero
  Downtown Development Authority
  128 East Forsyth Street, Suite 600
  Jacksonville, FL 32202
  (904) 630-1913

Designer. Robert Perkins
  Perkins and Partners, Architects-Planners
  1661 N. Claiborne Avenue
  New Orleans, LA 70116
  (504) 837-0642

Designer. L. Azeo Torre
  Design Consortium, Ltd.
  5005 Magazine Street
  New Orleans, LA 70115
  (504) 899-2932

Engineer. Al Hammack
  Bessent, Hammack and Ruckman
  1900 Corporate Sq. Blvd.
  Jacksonville, FL 32216
  (904) 721-2991

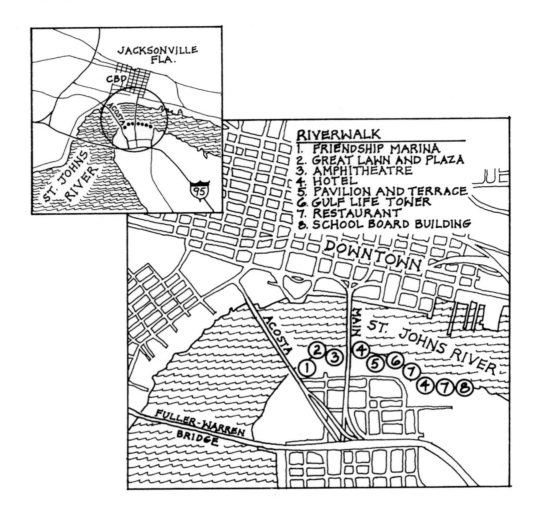

St. Andrew's School Boathouse, Middletown, Del. (*Alexander Nitsch, Swallow's Studio*)

St. Andrew's School Boathouse
Noxontown Pond
Middletown, Delaware

Summary

A beautifully crafted boathouse built to function efficiently, designed to reflect the romantic tradition of the genre.

Description. The impressive St. Andrew's School is located on 2-mile-long Noxontown Pond. Devotees of the movie *Dead Poets Society* may recognize the college preparatory campus.

The boathouse, which replaces an earlier 1947 structure, is built in a heavily wooded gully, previously the location of a now-abandoned on-site sewage treatment facility.

A new boat basin was dredged to extend the water area farther inland to put it in close to the boathouse. This lengthening doubles the amount of docking space and makes water a central feature within the entire setting.

The 4800-square-foot building fits snugly at the end of the new cove. It houses the boating functions (storage for 20 racing shells and maintenance) on the lower level and a "team room" with an outdoor covered porch on an upper story. The building abuts a hill. Stairs from the cove ascend to the second story, patio, porch, and clubhouse.

The entire project—boathouse, site work, dredging, new bulkhead, and dock—cost $780,000.

The pond itself, a major feature of the campus, is used as a living laboratory for study of life sciences. The school has traditionally encouraged fishing and boating activities on the pond. No gates or sentries prevent a visitor from entering the campus to enjoy access to the water's edge.

Design Features. This building harmonizes with both its natural setting and the nearby structures. The craftsmanship throughout is exquisite—evident even to the knobs on the wooden screen doors to the clubhouse. A close inspection reveals even more beautiful detailing, from crystal-like beveled glass windows to intricate lattice woodworked ceilings in the storage sheds and the "Team room" porch. Windows in the roofs allow filtered light to reach the interiors.

A small flagstone patio and porch provide good viewing of the pond beyond. Clover-shaped arches, the pillars and balustrades of the porch, are embellished with intricately carved woodwork.

The Vermont slate roof and some of the windows of the two-story clubhouse echo the nearby

(*Breen/Rigby*)

campus buildings. The colors of the wood stain of the clapboard siding and trim seem to key off the stone work, all of which blend nicely with the woods and water.

Missing are benches. The functional, but ugly, trash cans located at various spots mar the overall beauty of the place.

Appraisal. In the great tradition of Philadelphia's Boathouse Row along the Schuylkill River and the grand old structures along the Charles River in Boston, St. Andrew's School Boathouse goes well beyond providing a mere shed in which to store and repair boats. Rather, it houses them handsomely and provides a beautiful, sociable setting for people who take pleasure in this strong and graceful sport.

St. Andrew's School Boathouse

Cost. $780,000
Dimensions. Boathouse, 5000 square feet, holds 20 racing shells

Completion date. 1990

Sponsor. R. Elliott McBride, Business Manager
St. Andrew's School
Middletown, DE 19709
(302) 328-9511

Designer. Richard Conway Meyer
Richard Conway Meyer, AIA
1704 Walnut Street
Philadelphia, PA 19103
(215) 546-8790

Structural engineer. The Keast & Hood Company
400 Market St.
Philadelphia, PA 19106
(215) 625-0099

Mechanical engineer. The Energy Consortium
114 Chestnut St.
Philadelphia, PA 19106
(215) 923-5115

Geotechnical engineer. N. T. H. Russell
West Chester, PA 19381
(215) 524-2300

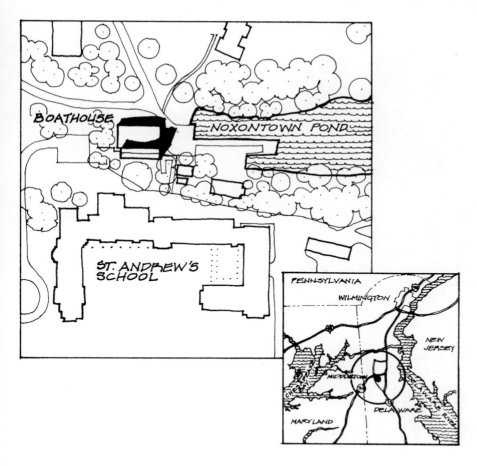

Monterey Peninsula Recreation Trail, Monterey, Calif. (*Breen/Rigby*)

Monterey Peninsula Recreation Trail Roberts Lake to Cannery Row Monterey, California

Summary

An urban coastal trail that links natural and built-up areas.

Description. The Monterey Peninsula Recreation Trail is a 3 ½-mile route that runs more or less uninterrupted from one end of the city of Monterey to the other, north to south along Monterey Bay. It affords the walker or biker a wide variety of experiences along the way. At one end—flanked by highways—sits Roberts Lake, with wetland grasses and open water. At the other end is Monterey Bay Aquarium and a cypress-punctuated shoreline.

Beginning at Roberts Lake and for approximately one-third of the way is the more "wild" portion of the trail as it runs past industry, Navy property, housing, and conservation areas. Except for a few posted California Coastal Conservancy coastal access points, one cannot reach the water along here. A beautiful eucalyptus grove is a high point along the way. There's an unsigned fork in the pathway that leads over a dune and offers a special view of Old Monterey harbor, and then along the beach, a sea-swept alternative route for walkers.

The official trail follows upland of the beach and leads to the Fisherman's Wharf area. By summer of 1992, beautification and improved pedestrian circulation systems around the historic Custom House and construction of a pedestrian causeway along the harbor were scheduled for completion, formally linking the two existing segments of the urban trail. The transition, between Fisherman's Wharf and Cannery Row, is enhanced by beautiful vistas of the rocks, sea, and harbor activity. Seating areas and lookouts are provided.

Once inside the Cannery Row district, the trail becomes decidedly more urban as it cuts between rows of industrial, commercial, and residential structures until it finally reaches the shopping/tourist core. From here it continues past the Monterey Bay Aquarium (see Chapter 2) and joins with the neighboring Pacific Grove trail system. The Monterey Bay trail in Cannery Row is very heavily used by tourists and locals alike.

The project cost $3.8 million, funded by a cooperative effort of the city, the Monterey Peninsula Regional Park District, and the California Coastal Conservancy.

Design Features. The trail, designed for multiple use by walkers, joggers, and bicyclists, has a hard surface throughout. When it passes through the more natural areas, there is little in the way of street furniture. In the more urban portions, very nice, simple wooden and black metal lighting fixtures, in keeping with an industrial or railroad motif, are used. Natural, unvarnished wood benches provide seating. A plentiful array of native plantings and vegeta-

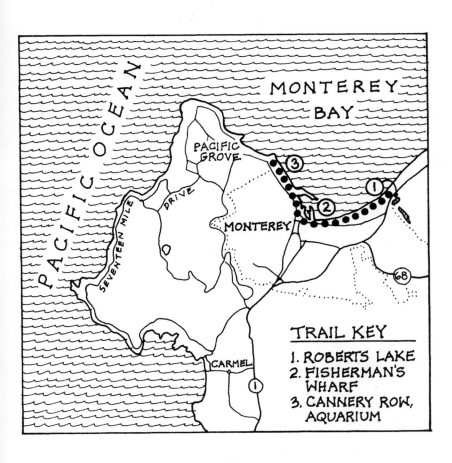

TRAIL KEY
1. ROBERTS LAKE
2. FISHERMAN'S WHARF
3. CANNERY ROW, AQUARIUM

tion in the urban portions of the trail was carefully chosen with an eye to reduced water consumption.

One nice touch in the heart of the Cannery Row district is the use of an old rail car as a visitor information center and post office. As much of the trail has been constructed on old railroad right-of-way, this provides a visible, usable tie with the past. A small, historical interpretive exhibit is housed in the center.

The largest criticism of the entire system has to do with the signage or lack thereof. The trail system is not strongly identified: no logo, no maps, no arrows when needed, no leaflets. While experientially the trail offers a great deal, given the cultural and industrial heritage of the city—not to mention the environmental aspects of the bay, including the dunes and vegetation—much more could be done in the way of interpretive

and directional materials along the trail.

Appraisal. This trail shows what the rails-to-trails concept can provide within a city as it traverses not just through the less developed areas, but also through the residential, commercial, and tourism heart of the city.

Monterey Peninsula Recreation Trail

Cost. $2 million
Dimensions. 3 ½ miles long
Completion date. 1988

Sponsor. City of Monterey
City Hall, 546 Dutra St.
Monterey, CA 93940
(408) 646-3885

Designer. Callander Associates
299 Cannery Row
Monterey, CA 93940
(408) 646-1383

Battery Park City Waterfront Plaza, New York, N.Y.(M. *Paul Friedberg & Partners)*

World Financial Center Plaza
Battery Park City
New York, New York

Summary

A formal, urban plaza, lauded for its collaborative design process among artists, architect, and landscape architect, offers an interesting range of experiences.

Description.   One among a collection of public open spaces within the Battery Park City development (see Chapter 8), the 3 ½-acre World Financial Plaza is positioned at the center and is the most formal of the public spaces.

It is surrounded by the buildings that comprise the 6-million-square foot World Financial Center, a mixed-use complex housing offices, shops, and eating establishments. The dramatic Wintergarden, a large indoor atrium dominated by palm trees, has massive windows facing onto the plaza, with stunning views of the Hudson River. The plaza itself surrounds the indented North Cove yacht basin.

The plaza provides a front porch and terraces for the World Financial Center's 30,000 employees, the 100,000 people who work in the nearby World Trade Center, the millions of Wall Street workers, plus tourists and the thousands of nearby residents. For those who are not inclined to cross at the lighted intersections across West Street, two enclosed pedestrian walkways complete with escalators bring visitors here.

The plaza also connects with a distinguished waterfront promenade and eventual pedestrian connections with the Battery to the south and walkways, a new high school, and North Park to the north. It is located at the terminus of North and South End Avenues, the main spines running through Battery Park City.

The plaza itself can accommodate large numbers of people in three distinct kinds of spaces, plus the walkway areas. On the one hand are quiet, gardenlike spaces, contrasted with the elevated terraces used in season for outdoor cafes among trees that overlook a very open, paved main forecourt. Public seating areas have been provided in the commercial cafe areas where people can relax with bag lunches and books.

The World Financial Center Plaza, completed in 1986 for a cost of $13 million, is the result of the winning design in a limited competition sponsored by the Battery Park City Authority in 1982. Seven artists were formally invited to participate. The idea of a collaboration between architect Cesar Pelli and the artists was met with some hesitancy. When first proposed, Pelli told Richard Kahan, then chairman of the authority, that he thought it was a terrible idea. In the end he said that it was "rewarding, challenging and vivifying." The winning artists were Siah Armijani and the late Scott Burton. Like many of their colleagues, these public artists place

(M. Paul Friedberg & Partners)

(Breen/Rigby)

heavy emphasis on the "public" or user, and design with this in mind.

Design Features. Battery Park City has a series of parks and open spaces, each with its own character and function; South Cove Park, the North Park, the Promenade, the Rector Gate, and the Upper Room street-end sculptures are all commendable for their style and imagination.

The World Financial Center Plaza functions as the formal entry point and major celebration space within this mixture of spaces. It "announces" the waterfront and withstands the hardest use.

Running along the cove edge in the main part of the plaza is a curved, black, wrought-iron poetry fence. Inscribed in shiny brass letters are two quotations:

City of tall facades of marble and iron—proud and passionate city—mettlesome, mad, extravagant city! (Walt Whitman)

One need never leave the confines of New York to get all the greenery one wishes. (Frank O'Hara)

In a sense, the plaza is an expression of these two phrases.

The first overall impression of the plaza as it faces the riverfront is its hard, bold, formality.

Massive, one could say extravagant, amounts of granite and marble dominate both the paving and the street furniture. High-backed benches function almost as "outdoor sofas" where people can sit close to the edge and look out over the river toward New Jersey. These benches, others close to the South Garden, even the drinking fountains, are made of a mottled pink-and-gray marble. In the case of the "sofas" the marble is highly glossed, shiny like water. A massive, torchlike column is a visual focal point among the benches, perhaps as a nod to Lady Liberty's torch, within view in the harbor.

On the plaza level, close to two cafe terraces, is a transition area. Small granite "tables and chairs" are located at regular intervals in front of steps that also provide informal seating space and lead up to linear reflecting pools. The small, round tables and chairs—backless, steplike affairs—miss the mark functionally. People seem more apt to use the tables than the chairs for sitting. Traditional black iron street lights echoing those along the esplanade are used here.

The twin pools reflect light beautifully and mark a transition between the two areas. Water spills over the edge, creating a pleasant sound and a handsome fountain wall. Rows of plane trees canopy the sidewalk cafes on the paved terraces above and in front of the office buildings. The cafe furniture is brushed silver industrial steel whose shapes are strong.

The tree-lined cafe and promenade area could be said to be a transition to the garden areas—O'Hara's green—which stand in sharp contrast to the rest of the plaza. Groves of birch trees, a grass lawn, clipped hedges, flowers, plantings, teak garden benches, and handsome iron gates are formal, in keeping with the plaza as a whole. The garden offers a lush retreat.

The areas on either side of the North Cove yacht basin are far less interesting than the main sections of the plaza. They lead pedestrians to a very handsome waterfront promenade to the south, and to a ferry dock to the north.

Appraisal. The collaborative design process that included artists as an integral and equal part of the team is one of the most important aspects of the World Financial Plaza. People can quibble over individual pieces—whether it's animated enough, whether this or that bench is appropriate—but as a whole, it offers room enough for major gatherings, plentiful public access, and magnificent views of the Hudson River and harbor scene. People are able to eat, drink, read, and relax here in a variety of ways.

World Financial Center Plaza

Cost. World Financial Center Plaza, $13 million
Dimensions. 92 acres overall; public space and promenade at North Cove, 3 ½ acres
Completion date. 1986

Sponsor. David Emil, President
Battery Park City Authority
1 World Financial Center
New York, NY 10281
(212) 416-5300

Sponsor. John Caiazzo
Olympia & York
425 Lexington Ave.
New York, NY 10017
(212) 477-6366

Designer. Cesar Pelli & Associates
1056 Chapel St.
New Haven, CT 06510
(203) 777-2515

Designer. M. Paul Friedberg
M. Paul Friedberg & Partners
41 East 11th St.
New York, NY 10003
(212) 477-6366

Artist. Siah Armijani
602 North First St.
Minneapolis, MN 55401
(612) 332-1234

Artist. Scott Burton, deceased

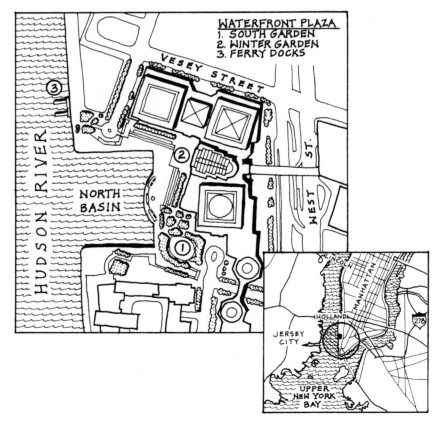

WATERFRONT PLAZA
1. SOUTH GARDEN
2. WINTER GARDEN
3. FERRY DOCKS

VESEY STREET

WEST ST.

HUDSON RIVER

NORTH BASIN

LINCOLN
MANHATTAN
HOLLAND
278
JERSEY CITY
UPPER NEW YORK BAY

Japanese American Historical Plaza, Portland, Ore. (*Robert Murase*)

Japanese American Historical Plaza
Tom McCall Waterfront Park
Portland, Oregon
1991 Top Honor Award

Summary

A poetic, meditative riverfront park memorializing the internment of Japanese-Americans during World War II.

Description. The Japanese American Historical Plaza is a 1.65-acre park set along the Willamette River within the 1.2-mile Tom McCall Waterfront Park and riverfront promenade in downtown Portland. The park was conceived as a memorial to recognize the internment of over 110,000 Japanese-Americans during World War II. It is also celebrates the Japanese-American story, and the Bill of Rights, which protects people's freedom.

The spirit with which the park was created is expressed in these words, inscribed on the dedication plaque:

> *Let all who visit this plaza partake in the delight of the cherry trees, the texture of the stones,*
>
> *the flow of the Willamette, and hear the voices of the story—an American story of Japanese descent.*
>
> *Come enjoy the beauty of this place, and come celebrate with us.*
>
> *Join us in the wish that all Americans may always be free.*

Between 1880 and 1924, many Japanese immigrants settled along the Pacific Coast. Most Nisei, the term for first-generation Japanese-Americans who grew up in America, were born between 1910 and 1930.

In March 1942, all persons of Japanese descent living in Oregon, California, and Washington State—about 125,000 people—were notified that they must move out of their homes. Seven out of 10 were American-born citizens. By November 1942, over 100,000 internees had been put behind barbed wire in isolated areas in six western states and Arkansas, where they would remain for three years.

In addition to the loss of personal liberty was the loss of businesses, farms, homes, and personal property. When at last they went home, it was to "a bitter freedom." It took more than a year to empty all the camps. Given train fare and $25, the evacuees returned to the Coast, many to learn that their goods had been stolen or lost, their land had been seized for unpaid taxes, or strangers had taken possession of their homes. Jobs were plentiful, but not for the returning detainees, who were met with notices, "No Japs Wanted."

Meanwhile, the Japanese-American 442nd Regimental Combat Team fought in Europe and received over 18,000 individual decorations for

(Breen /Rigby)

bravery and sacrifice. Another 6000 served in the U.S. Military Intelligence Service in the Pacific.

The park displays bronze plaques with the words of the Bill of Rights, an August 1988 Congressional statement declaring that a grave injustice had been done, and a letter of apology from President Ronald Reagan to the Japanese-Americans. It is the first major memorial to honor these citizens and their contribution to American society, and to tell a unique story of people whose rights were tragically ignored, in hopes that it will never happen again.

The main physical feature within the space is a chest-high, 275-long berm. On one side a grass bank slopes to the riverfront walkway, and on the other, gray, roughhewn, basalt stonework forms a background for 12 standing granite stones strategically placed, each etched with a haiku poem. The granite for the poetry stones came from the nearby Cascade Mountains..

The park site was a previously derelict portion of the riverfront. It is adjacent to the historic Japan Town or old Nihonmachi across Front Avenue, once the location of over 100 Japanese merchants.

The park cost $500,000, over 90 percent of which came from private funds. Money was raised by the nonprofit Oregon Nikkei Endowment, which built and maintains the project. The plaza has been donated to the city of Portland.

Design Features. The overall aura of the place, echoing traditional Japanese design principles, is one of calm and meditation. The plaza is a kind of wayside retreat along a heavily used, straightforward-looking riverfront walkway. Even without knowing the story, the space itself exudes a meditative aura. The plaques and the haiku poems are powerful. The designer calls them "talking stones." Listen, for example, to the voices of a newcomer and an internee:

> *Mighty Willamette!*
> *Beautiful friend,*
> *I am learning, I am practicing*
> *to say your name.*

> *Rounded up*
> *in the sweltering yard*
> *Unable to endure any longer*

> *Standing in line, some collapse.*

A "camp stone" is engraved with the names of the 10 relocation camps. Two large circular columns close to Front Street form a gateway to the park and connect with the old Japan Town area. Relief sculpture on one column shows an elderly man and his grandchild, newly arrived immigrants coming off a ship, and a woman working on a farm. The other shows children being evacuated, a mother and baby in camp,

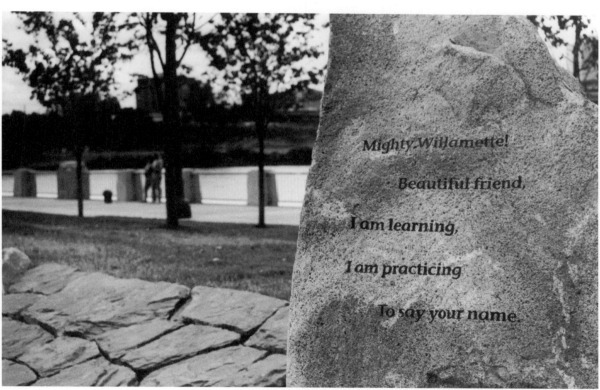

(Breen Rigby)

and a group of Japanese-American soldiers from the 442nd Regiment.

A pathway between the columns leads to the river and cuts through the wall/berm. The break in the wall is meant to signal the internment as a dividing point. The "talking stones" on one side tell the story of the immigration and war years, and on the other the return home and the rebuilding process. The skilled use of stone in both the paving and sculpture is beautiful.

Appraisal. This dignified, rather solemn, park is a counterpoint to many of the other areas along the downtown Willamette River, such as RiverPlace (see Chapter 5) and a large playful, waterfront fountain. While there are plenty of green, wild, wooded, and landscaped areas along the river for reflection, the Japanese American Historical Plaza, through its artful design, creates a very special meditative atmosphere.

The exquisite craftsmanship of the stonework throughout the park makes the preexisting adjacent walkway along the river look quite plain by comparison.

Japanese American Historical Plaza

Cost. $500,000
Source. 8 percent public financing, 92 percent private
Dimensions. 1.65 acres, 480 feet long, 150 feet wide
Completion date. 1990

Sponsor. Henry Sakamoto, President
Oregon Nikkei Endowment
P.O. Box 3458
Portland, OR 97208
(503) 233-2001

Designer. Robert Murase
Murase Associates
1300 NW Northrup
Portland, OR 97209
(503) 242-1477

Sculptor. Jim Gion
3831 S.E. 82nd
Portland, OR 97266
(503) 282-0109

Poet. Dr. Lawson Inada, Southern Oregon State College
1250 Siskiyou Blvd.
Ashland, OR 97520
(503) 552-7672

Graphic designer. Elizabeth Anderson
Anderson Krygier, Inc.
519 SW Third Ave.
Portland, OR 97204
(503) 243-2060

Historical research. Mark Sherman
55 W. Burnside
Portland, OR 97209
(503) 245-0571

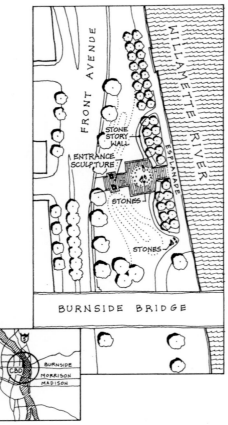

Racine Harbor/Marina Development, Racine, Wisc. .

Racine Harbor/
Marina Development
Racine, Wisconsin

Summary

An attractive, full-service marina combined with a public lakefront park,
part of a downtown economic development strategy.

Description. Racine, Wisconsin, birthplace of Johnson's Wax, is an easy drive from two large Midwestern metropolitan areas, Milwaukee and Chicago. Like many other industrial cities, by the early 1980s the city and its downtown were in dire need of an economic turnaround.

In 1982 the Downtown Racine Development Corporation was formed. One of the early strategies to diversify its economic base was to turn the existing commercially oriented harbor into a major recreational boating center to serve metropolitan Lake Michigan's large boating population. Key to achieving this was the creation of a safe harbor of refuge, which involved upgrading existing breakwaters. By an Act of Congress, the project was declared "nonfederal," thus enabling Racine County to take over and save time. Normally such activity is the responsibility of the Corps of Engineers.

To protect against the fierce waves of Lake Michigan, the old 450-foot harbor entrance was narrowed to 200 feet. The engineers used a stone berm to modify the old breakwaters, using carefully graded stones from locally available quarry materials.

The completed 110-acre harbor was funded by $4.7 million of county general-obligation bonds, with an additional $3 million contributed by the city, and other smaller grants from the University of Wisconsin Waterways Commission, Community Development Block Grant funds, the Coastal Breakwater Improvement Program, and the Local Park Aids Program.

The 921-boat marina with service buildings, said to be the largest privately operated facility on Lake Michigan, cost $9 million. The marina contributes about $300,000 annually in tax revenues to the community. The marina enjoyed full occupancy until the recession of the early 1990s, when it dropped to 80 percent. The 17-acre county ReefPoint Park was created from material dredged from the harbor bottom to provide desired water depths in the harbor.

Service buildings house toilets, showers, snack bars, and observation areas. One near the main marina entrance offers fuel to both transient and resident boaters. The main administration building features a public restaurant on the second floor with excellent views of the lake and harbor. Well-equipped, covered fish-cleaning stations serve the anglers who have been provided ample access to the lake along one of the breakwaters.

The harbor/marina project is a major component of a $100 million redevelopment effort. Lakefront revitalization projects in place nearby include a municipal Festival Park used for programming and events, boat-launching facilities, Lakeshore Towers of Racine condominiums, and Gaslight Pointe townhouses.

Design Features. The Racine Harbor/Marina is a model of handsome design detailing throughout, and public accessibility. The heavy, wrought ironwork used in the railings, gates, and other design details, along with the light stanchions, are all painted a bright aqua and provide a unifying theme throughout the project. The red-roofed, concrete service buildings are of straightforward, attractive design, accented with the aqua ironwork. Clear, well-designed signs point out the facilities and access areas. An overlook has been provided at the end of the park area and serves as a visual focal point.

Appraisal. Many marina facilities use ugly chain-link fences trimmed with barbed wire. Others are often very exclusive domains, offering little or no public access to the waterfront. The Racine Harbor/Marina development is noteworthy from a design and access viewpoint, as well as serving as a catalyst for the revitalization of the community's entire waterfront.

Racine Harbor/Marina Development

Cost. $20 million
Source. 60 percent public financing
Dimensions. 110 acres, including 921 boat slips, 16-acre park
Completion date. Spring 1988

Sponsor. Mayor N. Owen Davies
City of Racine
730 Washington Ave.
Racine, WI 53403
(414) 636-9111

Sponsor. Arnold Clement, Director
County of Racine, Planning and Development
14200 Washington Ave.
Sturtevant, WI 53177
(414) 886-8470

Engineer. Greg Hofmeister
EWI Engineering, Inc.
8383 Greenway Blvd.
Middleton, WI 53562
(608) 836-4450

Engineer. Larry W. Ryan, formerly Warzyn Engineering, Inc.
Johnson Johnson & Roy, inc.
110 Miller Ave.
Ann Arbor, MI 48104
(313) 662-4457

Coastal engineering. W. F. Baird & Assoc. Ltd.
38 Antares Dr., Suite 150
Ottawa, ON, K2E 7V2, Canada
(613) 225-6560

Designer. Torke/Wirth/Pujara Ltd.
933 Mayfair Rd.
Wauwatosa, WI 53226
(414) 453-4554

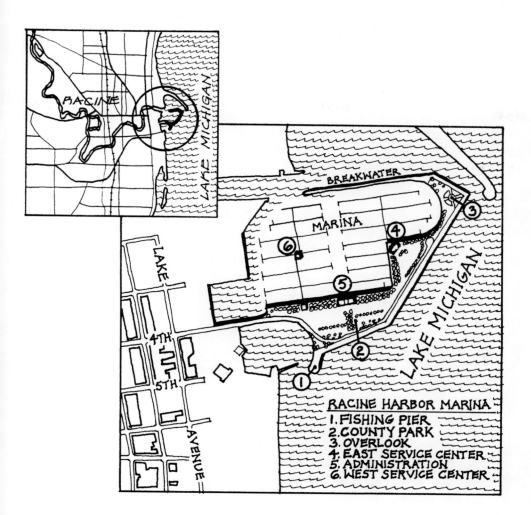

RACINE

LAKE MICHIGAN

BREAKWATER

MARINA

LAKE MICHIGAN

LAKE AVENUE

4TH

5TH

① ② ③ ④ ⑤ ⑥

RACINE HARBOR MARINA
1. FISHING PIER
2. COUNTY PARK
3. OVERLOOK
4. EAST SERVICE CENTER
5. ADMINISTRATION
6. WEST SERVICE CENTER

Gene L. Coulon Memorial Beach Park, Renton, Wash. Jones & Jones. (*Randy L. Shelton*)

Gene L. Coulon Memorial Beach Park Lake Washington Renton, Washington

Summary

Dramatic transformation of a former industrial waterfront into a dynamic, well-designed recreational space.

Description. The 57 acres along the shore at the southern end of Lake Washington in the Seattle area was a major industrial facility from the late 1800s up through the 1950s. The linear stretch was first a loading dock for coal barges from nearby mines. Later came a succession of log dumping, shipping, sawmill, and wartime activities to confirm the industrial heritage.

With abandonment of the site by its railroad owner came the opportunity for transformation. The process took fully 15 years, and included close consultation with the community as to what kinds of facilities were wanted. The result was voter approval of a $7.8 million bond issue to acquire the site for park development.

Planning work began in 1979, and the park was opened in 1982. Subsequently, a swimming and diving pier was added.

Design Features. The centerpiece of the park is a "waterwalk" feature, with a pilot house and two picnic pavilions, built into the lake and forming a lagoon. Adjoining it is a boathouse, a restaurant pavilion, and a large picnic shelter. The boat harbor adjoins, served by a large boat-launch parking area as well as a general parking lot.

The architectural style of the structures reflects turn-of-the-century, Victorian waterfront boathouses and pavilions, providing both consistency and appropriateness in the park's buildings. The structures are also on the rugged side, to absorb the heavy use. Carefully selected details, such as railings, benches, trash receptacles, and tables, echo the industrial uses of the past.

Besides active recreational areas, there are significant natural segments. There is a cattails area, for instance, at the southern end, near a protected swimming beach. The northern end of the park, where a pedestrian trail begins, is in a natural state, landscaped with native trees such as silver poplar, copper beech, and hemlock. A fishing pier and canoe launch are provided along the northern shoreline of the park.

Appraisal. A well-planned and well-executed transformation, reflecting close consultation with affected community groups, makes this a special park. The architecture has a handsome, rugged feel of the Pacific Northwest to it, while the landscaping treatment of parking areas and other sites is likewise fitting.

Today's park setting is dramatized by the nearby location of major manufacturing facilities. What has been carved out here is a mile of shoreline under total public ownership, offering varied recreational experiences from the most passive to active. The inclusion of a restaurant and concession enrich the enjoyment and utility of the park, and no doubt contribute to its maintenance. Well-designed educational materials and signs throughout the park are excellent, and models for other parks.

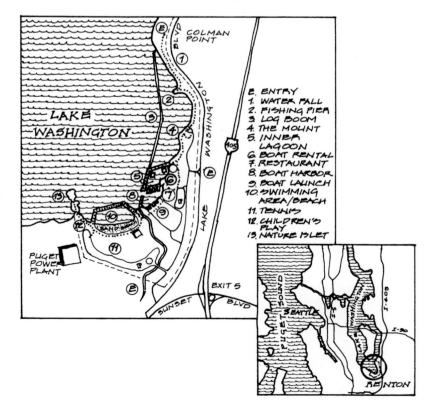

E. ENTRY
1. WATER FALL
2. FISHING PIER
3. LOG BOOM
4. THE MOUNT
5. INNER LAGOON
6. BOAT RENTAL
7. RESTAURANT
8. BOAT HARBOR
9. BOAT LAUNCH
10. SWIMMING AREA/BEACH
11. TENNIS
12. CHILDREN'S PLAY
13. NATURE ISLET

Gene L. Coulon Memorial Beach Park

Cost. $7.8 million
Dimensions. 57 acres; 1 mile of shoreline
Completion date. 1982
Notes. Swimming and diving pier added

Sponsor. Department of Parks & Recreation
City of Renton
200 Mill Ave. South
Renton, WA 98055
(206) 235-2568

Designer. Jones & Jones, Architects and Landscape
Architects
105 South Main St.
Seattle, WA 98104
(206) 624-5702

Engineer. KPFF Consulting Engineers
1201 3rd Ave., No. 900
Seattle, WA 98101
(206) 622-5822

Pier 7, San Francisco, Calif. (*Breen/Rigby*)

Pier 7
The Embarcadero
San Francisco, California

Summary

An elegant public recreation pier enhancing the waterfront experience as
only a pier can.

Description/Design Features. Pier 7, dedicated in October 1990, is a new structure, 845 feet long and 25 feet wide, adjacent to the Ferry Building on the downtown San Francisco waterfront. The first and the longest pier built on the waterfront since the 1940s, it affords spectacular views across the bay and back to the city skyline. This ability to get out over the water, while obvious, is what is unique and special about a pier experience.

Usually piers are a bit rough hewn. Not this one. Elegant, ornamental metal railings, classic lighting, graceful wood and iron benches, and wooden decking lend an old-fashioned, but sophisticated, air to the pier. A series of semicircular viewing platforms—like small balconies—punctuates the promenade, allowing the visitor a chance to gaze out over the water uninterrupted. At the end of the pier is a small, T-shaped "plaza" to accommodate larger numbers of people and, not incidentally, the fishing community. Wider spaces are also provided at the beginning and midway along the promenade deck.

The sense of entrance is heightened by two pieces of sculpture called "Bay Bench," by artist Steve Gilman. The works are square-shaped bronze grids that are meant to be reminiscent of both the cobblestones that once paved the old waterfront and of hatch covers. The $60,000 piece was commissioned under the San Francisco Art Commission's Public Arts Program. The work allows viewers to see through to the water below. Responding to criticism often provoked by public art, local reporter Margot Doss had this to say:

> *Forget the critics who say they look like giant hibachis. If you feel inspired some lunchtime when the day is blue and gold, take off your shoes and dance barefoot with the sunshine on the grids. No one will object, especially not the sculptor, who wanted the viewers to feel close to the water. Any closer and you'd be wet.*[6]

Eight years in the making, the pier cost $6.5 million. The Port of San Francisco contributed $2.7 million, the San Francisco Recreation and Park Department $2.9 million, with the balance from the California State Department of Fish and Game, the California State Coastal Conservancy, and the National Park Service.

Appraisal. Pier 7 is a beautiful, urbane, romantic city recreational pier that offers that unique experience of walking out over water—seeing it, smelling it, nearly tasting it. In city after city, many of these special waterfront features have been allowed to rot, forcing their removal. Once gone, they may never be replaced, either because of the expense or because in many jurisdictions environmental regulations disallow such structures. Pier 7 is a gem worthy of emulation.

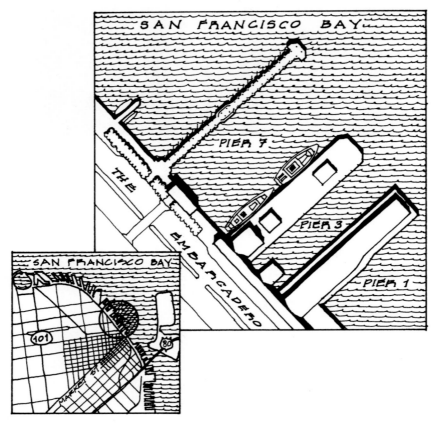

Pier 7

Cost. $6.5 million
Source. Port of San Francisco, $2.7 million; San Francisco Recreation and Park Department, $2.9 million; balance from California State Department of Fish and Game, California State Coastal Conservancy, and National Park Service
Dimensions. 845 feet long, 25 feet wide
Completion date. Oct. 26, 1990

Sponsor. Michael P. Huerta, Executive Director
Port of San Francisco
Ferry Building, Suite 3100
San Francisco, CA 94111
(415) 274-0404

Sponsor. Mary E. Burns, General Manager
City and County of San Francisco Recreation and Park Dept.
McLaren Lodge, Golden Gate Park
San Francisco, CA 94117
(415) 666-7080

Sponsor. San Francisco Arts Commission
25 Van Ness St., Suite 240
San Francisco, CA 94102
(415) 554-9671

Designer. Boris Dramov/Bonnie Fisher
Roma Design Group
1527 Stockton St.
San Francisco, CA 94133-3305
(415) 616-9900

Structural engineer. TY Lin International
315 Bay St.
San Francisco, CA 94133
(415) 291-3700

Electrical and mechanical engineer. YEI Engineers, Inc.
28996 Hopkins St.
Hayward, CA 94545
(510) 887-4200

Sculptor. Steve Gillman
1765 12th St.
Oakland, CA 94607
(510) 763-8313

Santa Monica Pier Carousel Park, Santa Monica, Calif. (*Campbell & Campbell*)

Santa Monica Pier Carousel Park Santa Monica, California

Summary

Carousel Park is an imaginative new entryway to a beloved 85-year-old institution undergoing gradual restoration.

(Campbell & Campbell)

Description. The new entranceway, children's park, pavilion, and amphitheater, the heart of this project, are a piece of a much larger story.

Carousel Park derives its name and much of its design from a carousel that sits resplendently at the entrance to Santa Monica Pier. The park is to the side and below the carousel—in effect, the pier's second entrance, the connection between a linear oceanfront walkway and the pier.

The $1.1 million carousel restoration and construction of Carousel Park came about in the mid-1980s after an emotional debate about the pier. From its rescue in 1973 to participatory design workshops in the early 1980s and major storm damage in 1983, the pier's modern history has been turbulent and has featured strong public intervention.

A citizen's uprising in 1973, sparked by the group, Save Our Pier Forever, tossed out a city council that had voted to demolish the pier, then a faded remnant of its glory days in the 1920s and 1930s. In the subsequent election, a new council pledged to save the pier was elected.

With a grant from the California Coastal Conservancy, an extensive public planning process was begun. Design guidelines issued in 1982 as a result are models for their spirit and sensitivity. The Santa Monica Pier, the guidelines declared, "is an organism that already has a very lively life of its own, one that is participated in by many people. These guidelines seek to join and enrich that life, not replace or fundamentally alter it. The process for Santa Monica Pier must be accretive and enhancing."[7] *Los Angeles Times* critic Sam Hall Kaplan noted that the citizens were consciously avoiding attractions that would appeal to what he dubbed the "quiche and Perrier crowd," said to populate waterfront attractions in San Francisco and Baltimore.[8]

In 1983, five teams of architects and landscape architects, selected by the new Santa Monica Pier Restoration Corp. set up by the city, were charged with organizing a competitive public planning exercise to design the new entranceway and an overall pier master plan. The event, which occurred over three days, resulted in rival schemes, based on the guidelines, that were presented to the community on the final day. From this the citizens and jury elected the team of Campbell and Campbell, landscape architects, and Moore Rubell Yudell, architects, both of Santa Monica, to design the carousel park.

The final result, in overall size about 47,500 square feet, transforms what had been a patch of dirt into a whimsical, multifaceted feature that does much more than provide steps to the pier. In time this entranceway will gain additional importance, as the guidelines call for eventual removal of all parking from the pier; as of late 1992 there was still a parking lot near the carousel.

Part of the carousel project was the addition of what was to have been additional commercial space along the walkway under the pier, joining a group of vendors now operating there. What has evolved for the time is a children's arts center. For whatever combination of reasons, restoration work on the pier itself, set back by the damage suffered in 1983, has proceeded slowly.

Design Features. The Santa Monica Pier Carousel Park includes an extension of the pier, by approximately 50 feet, to provide seating and two pavilions that are prime viewing spots. Whimsical pelicans perched on top echo the carousel architecture. The area below contains an informal amphitheater and volleyball courts. It was once a "muscle beach" scene, where Jayne Mansfield was said to have been carried about by bearers. The deck is a children's amusement area during the summer. Concrete seahorses stand guard on either side of the steps leading to the pier.

Carrying out one of the pier design guidelines is an imaginative children's play area of about 5000 square feet, about one-quarter of the project, with a sandy area and play sculptures. A huge, fierce-looking dragon's head, with wide-open jaws, is part of the sand pit. A boat-shaped play feature has a water valve tucked away waiting to be discovered. When it is pressed, spray comes out of the dragon's nostrils!

Appraisal. The Carousel Park and the careful restoration of the nearby carousel are both well done and in keeping with the clearly—not to say emphatically—stated popular preferences for enhancing Santa Monica Pier. Newspaper stories about the emotional testimony before the city council when the pier was damaged in 1983 attest to its strong hold on the public, a sizable segment of which sees the pier as providing a recreational outlet for the less well off in Santa Monica. Its restoration is thus the subject of intense scrutiny, which may help to account for why, 10 years later, much remains to be done.

What has been accomplished at Carousel Park is first-rate design, capturing architectural details and reflecting the area landscape (the trees planted at the children's park recall the classic Palisades Park on the cliff above the pier).

The guidelines of the Pier Restoration and

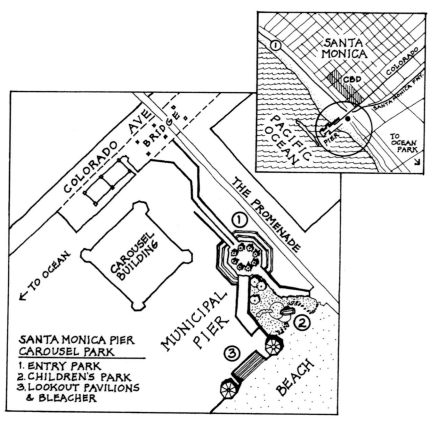

Development Task Force are a model. Some work to date on the pier, unfortunately, does not reflect the high standards of this effort. Carousel Park and the carousel itself, on the other hand, do reflect the best in projects in which the public takes an active, direct part, and demonstrate the validity of this approach. The creativity and humor evident in the children's play area is not found everywhere and is especially commendable.

Santa Monica Pier Carousel Park

Cost. $1.1 million
Source. California Coastal Conservancy no-interest loan and City of Santa Monica
Dimensions. 47,500 square feet
Completion date. 1986

Sponsor. John Jalili, City Manager
City of Santa Monica
1685 Main St.
Santa Monica, CA 90401
(310) 458-8301

Sponsor Peter Grenell, Executive Director
California Coastal Conservancy
1330 Broadway, Suite 1100
Oakland, CA 94612
(415) 464-1015

Designer. Douglas & Regula Campbell
Campbell & Campbell
1425 Fifth St.
Santa Monica, CA 90401
(310) 458-1011

Designer. Moore Rubell Yudell
933 Pico Blvd.
Santa Monica, CA 90404
(310) 450-1400

Meewasin Valley Project, Saskatoon, Saskatchewan. (*Meewasin Valley Authority*)

Meewasin Valley Project
South Saskatchewan River
Saskatoon, Saskatchewan,
Canada

Summary

An exemplary river corridor conservation, recreation, and education effort, overseen by an authority implementing a visionary, conceptual master plan.

(Meewasin Valley Authority)

Description. The Meewasin Valley Project involves a series of accomplishments carried out within the context of an overall 100-year conceptual master plan.

The City of Saskatoon, with a population of 150,000, has a long history of devotion to the river which runs through its center. An 1883 plan set aside land as a public reserve, which was followed by a 1930 comprehensive zoning plan that dedicated almost the entire riverbank to public use. Development pressures in the 1960s and 1970s led the Province of Saskatchewan, the City of Saskatoon, and the University of Saskatchewan (whose campus abuts the river) to reconfirm civic commitment to the river.

In 1979, a 100-year conceptual master plan for 80 kilometers of the South Saskatchewan River Valley was commissioned. The long-range view provides a high degree of adaptability to changing circumstances and the ability to evolve and improve with periodic reviews. The underlying principle of the plan is to assure physical health of the river system and all its components. A theme of linkage calls for ties between urban/rural and natural systems, between people, and between past, present, and future.

The same year the provincial legislature passed the Meewasin Valley Authority Act, creating a special-purpose agency called the Meewasin Valley Authority to carry out the mandate of the plan. The board of directors consists of 12 members, four each from the city, the province, and the university. The authority relies heavily on volunteers and on charitable grants and donations for its programming and projects.

From the outset this authority, with its broad powers of planning, project review, and coordination, was charged with protecting the natural resources and providing recreational opportunities as well as preserving the cultural heritage and educating the public. The authority was also charged with making the river accessible to everyone in all seasons and to allow for maximum amount of public participation in the decision making.

Between 1979 and 1989, statutory funding for the Meewasin Valley Project was approximately $21 million, with an additional $8 million raised from a combination of sources including foundations, clubs, and other special funding. The money was used to oversee action along 45 miles of river, river channel, shoreline parks, and university and Crown lands encompassing approximately 24 square miles.

The many accomplishments that have occurred include planting of approximately 20,000 trees and shrubs a year, riverbank stabilization, and ongoing river cleanup. Three parks, Meewasin, Victoria, and Gabriel Dumont, are in place, the latter being an urban natural-habitat landfill reclamation. The Mendel Gallery and Meewasin Valley Centre offer indoor interpretive and educational opportunities. Annual visitation to the centre by tourists, locals, and school children in 1989 was put at 22,000.

Meewasin has restored and renovated the Marr Residence, the oldest building on its original foundation, for interpretation. The authority also developed self-guided trails and an interpretive centre at the Beaver Creek Conservation Area. Wanuskewin Heritage Park, another multi-million-dollar interpretive center opened in June 1992. It is designed as a spiritual place to celebrate Plains Indian culture and history.

The authority has so far implemented a continuous, paved 16-kilometer pathway on both sides of the river in central Saskatoon, and it continues to add segments. The heavily used trail serves both pedestrians and cyclists.

Downtown, on the banks of the river in front of the historic Besborough Hotel, between the University Bridge and Broadway Bridge, is an area where many festivals and events are held. Walkers have the option of using a sidewalk along charming Spadina Drive, the paved Meewasin Trail, or a dirt path. Where the dirt paths occur within the system, they often go closer to the river or through brush, offering the hiker a more "wild" alternative.

The pathway crosses over a railroad bridge, offering breathtaking views of the falls created by a nearby weir, and enables users to make a continuous loop.

Design Features. The Meewasin Valley Trail, with its blacktop paving and dirt byways, meanders along the riverbanks and leads the explorer through the formal downtown area, into wooded areas, alongside some dramatic falls, up bluffs and down next to streams. In short, it allows people to get close to the natural environment. The design of the path is low-key and respects nature.

Making it outstanding are educational and cultural features that have been included within the system. One glass-roofed shade/shelter facility is trimmed with rich red metal to harmonize with the same treatment used in the railings on the boardwalks, an overwater deck, and boat ramps. A representational statue of a local figure, Gabriel Dumont, and a more modern "Tribute to Youth"—a circle of children dancing to commemorate the Canada Summer Games of 1989—are among the public art installations that enrich the trail.

Notable are clearly lettered directional signs and easy-to-read maps posted on the walkway, particularly on the west bank. Interpretive signs are posted all along the trail. Simple but attractive overlooks and rest areas are provided at intervals.

(Breen/Rigby)

(*Breen/Rigby*)

Appraisal. The Meewasin Valley Trail, part of a long-term, far-reaching plan, is notable for its sensitivity to the environment; inclusion of interpretive elements; quality signage, maps, and graphics; and attention to the design of seating, overlooks, and pavilions.

Meewasin Valley Project

Cost. $29 million (Can.)
Source. 75 percent public financing
Dimensions. 45 miles of river, river channel, and shoreline; riverbank parks, university and Crown lands, approximately 24 square miles
Completion date. Begun in 1979, ongoing
Notes. Since 1990, Meewasin Valley Trail has been extended 800 meters.

Sponsor. Fred Heal, Executive Director
Meewasin Valley Authority
402 Third Ave. South
Saskatoon, SK, S7K 3G5 Canada
(306) 665-6887

Designer. Raymond Moriyama
Moriyama & Teshima, Architects & Planners
32 Davenport Rd.
Toronto, ON, M5R 1H3 Canada
(416) 925-4484

Designer. Hildeman, Witty, Crosby, Hanna & Associates
504 Queen St.
Saskatoon, SK, S7K OM5 Canada
(306) 665-3441

Consultant. Delcan Western Ltd.
108-3502 Taylor St. East
Saskatoon, SK, S7H 5HN Canada
(306) 721-4805

Engineer. UMA Engineering Ltd.
200-2100 8th St. East
Saskatoon, SK, S7H OV1 Canada
(306) 955-3300

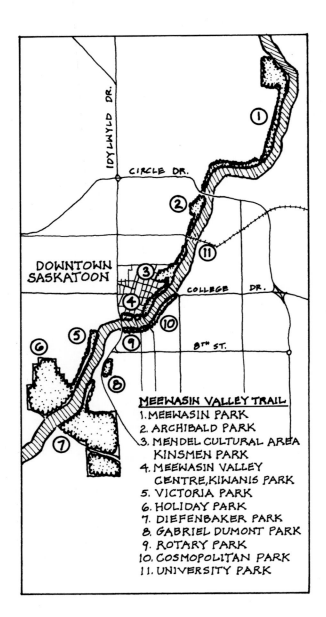

MEEWASIN VALLEY TRAIL
1. MEEWASIN PARK
2. ARCHIBALD PARK
3. MENDEL CULTURAL AREA
   KINSMEN PARK
4. MEEWASIN VALLEY
   CENTRE, KIWANIS PARK
5. VICTORIA PARK
6. HOLIDAY PARK
7. DIEFENBAKER PARK
8. GABRIEL DUMONT PARK
9. ROTARY PARK
10. COSMOPOLITAN PARK
11. UNIVERSITY PARK

Savannah Riverfront Redevelopment, Savannah, Ga. (*Breen/Rigby*)

Savannah Riverfront Redevelopment
Savannah River between Jefferson and Lincoln Streets
Savannah, Georgia

Summary

A promenade/park built out over the river expands the riverfront experience and enhances the historic warehouse setting.

Description. Savannah, founded in 1733, is considered America's first planned city. It is home to some of the most interesting historic neighborhoods and stately squares in the country. During the nineteenth century it was a major cotton port, which accounts for the row of three-story warehouses that line the Savannah River.

Beginning in the early 1960s intrepid entrepreneurs began opening bars and shops in what was a decaying, but colorful, set of structures. A Savannah Waterfront Association was founded in the early 1970s, and the city began to move to enhance the area.

Over $7 million was raised to create the half-mile promenade, which covers 8 acres and varies in width from 100 to 180 feet. The funding came from a variety of sources: the U.S. Department of Housing and Urban Development (Urban Development Action Grant, $4.3 million; Community Development Block Grant, $1.9 million); the Environmental Protection Agency, $160,000; general obligation bonds, $420,000; revenue bonds, $70,000; the Savannah District Authority, $266,000; and adjoining property owners, $210,000.

Design Features. The design and engineering of this facility not only provided expanded public space along the riverfront, it accomplished other infrastructure improvements as well. Bulkheading to prevent further erosion of the derelict riverbank was put in place. Sanitary sewer lines that were spilling raw sewage into the water were collected into a new sewer trunk main. At the same time, electrical wires and new water and gas lines were installed.

To create the promenade, a 100-foot platform was constructed over the river so that in fact the river flows beneath the walkway. Brick, slate, and granite paving elements have been used to blend with the historic character of the warehouses. In contrast with the tree-lined and landscaped areas adjoining River Street and the warehouses, the shore edge has the open feel of an ocean boardwalk This openness allows for unobstructed views of the water and the working river's interesting traffic. The railings and lighting bollards are low. Large granite blocks double as seating. Three mooring facilities that accommodate various types of boats have been incorporated.

Three small, recessed and screened parking areas are located at either end of the promenade. Rousakis Plaza (named for the mayor who championed the project), along with its covered stage and arbor, provide space for public festivals and gatherings.

Old cotton warehouses, now a lively cluster of bars, restaurants, and shops, give the Savannah riverfront a distinctive flavor.

Six small "squares" echo the famous landmarks of urban Savannah. These miniparks dot the walkway and provide fountains, "tot lots," seating, and planting. Reflecting the maritime motif, a miniature tug has been provided for kids to play on. The backdrop of shops, offices, restaurants, and hotels housed in the old buildings enlivens the scene.

Appraisal. Overall, this ½-mile stretch of waterfront accommodates pedestrians, cars, bikes, boats, trains, people of all ages, festival goers, lovers, and tourists—in short, a little bit of everything.

Visually, the almost stark simplicity of the Savannah riverfront promenade park contrasts with the feel of the old industrial warehouses and provides a frame for these distinctive, textured buildings. Functionally, it creates quality recreational spaces where people can enjoy the river. A Hyatt Regency Hotel's rude, cream-colored, boxy intrusion onto the walkway is a major visual flaw. Contextual design this is not, while it no doubt contributes to tourism and the economy.

While care has been taken to incorporate historic and maritime artifacts, an opportunity was missed to educate visitors even more about the richness of Savannah's history and the activity along the river today.

Savannah Riverfront Redevelopment

Cost. $7.33 million
Source. 97 percent public financing: Urban Development Action Grant, $4.3 million, Community Development Block Grant, $1.9 million, both U.S. Department of Housing and Urban Development; EPA, $160,000; property owners, $210,000; bonds, $490,000; Savannah District Authority, $266,000
Dimensions. 8 acres; ½ mile
Completion date. 1977

Sponsor. Ed Wolverton, Downtown Programs
  Coordinator
  City of Savannah
  City Hall
  Savannah, GA 31401
  (912) 651-6520

Designer. Eric Meyerhoff
  Gunn & Meyerhoff AIA Architects, PC
  425 E. President St.
  Savannah, GA 31401
  (912) 232-1151

Engineers. Hussey, Gay, Bell and DeYoung
  329 Commercial Dr.
  Savannah, GA 31416
  (912) 354-4626

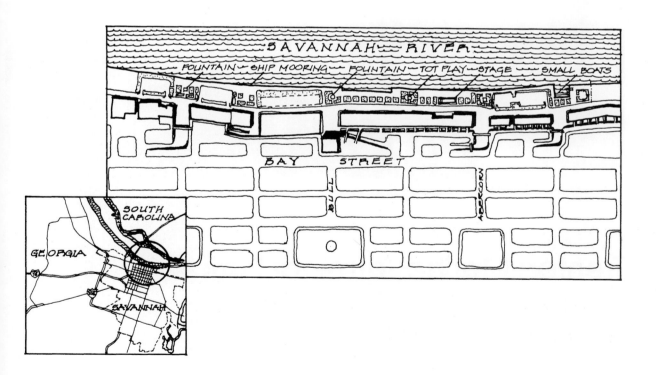

Trenton Marine Terminal Park, Trenton, N.J. (*Janet M. Gnall*)

Trenton Marine Terminal Park
Lamberton Road
Trenton, New Jersey

Summary

A park in an unlikely setting celebrates the industrial past and provides fishing and boating access.

Description. The Trenton Marine Terminal Park on the Delaware River, somewhat removed from downtown Trenton, was built in 1980 on a 2.6-acre site that was part of the former Marine Terminal facility. Industrial activity was greatest during the 1930s and 1940s, when the Port of Trenton was in its prime.

The new development was the first stage of a 27-acre rehabilitation meant to transform a derelict industrial area for commercial revitalization. As of 1992, only the park and the terminal building had been put to new use. The Trenton Marine Center occupies an old terminal shed beside the park, and serves as a boat sales, repair, and marina facility. Food concessions, restaurants, shops, and a farmers' market, along with other commercial facilities, were planned for the area but have not materialized.

A riverfront promenade, a children's play area, a picnic grove, restrooms, open space, industrial artifacts, and parking are the pieces that comprise the park. Floating docks, to allow for boating and marina use, are in place. They have been moved from their original location, and the breaks left in the handsome railing look rather like wounds.

Indeed, the whole park suffers from serious lack of maintenance—a victim, no doubt, of municipal budget cutbacks in recent years. Broken glass, trash, and disrepair have taken their toll. The imaginative quality of the design and the use of handsome trees have saved this recreation space from being a total disaster. Even on a weekday afternoon, people use it—particularly fishermen.

Design Features. A key decision in the design of the park was the retention and celebration of the industrial heritage of the site. Rather than simply remove the old gantry cranes—which in fact are registered historic landmarks—these relics have been incorporated and become massive black iron "sculptures" within the park. Another sad note is that the arm of one of the cranes has fallen over and is now surrounded with yellow plastic police ribbon.

In a departure from "authenticity," one speed crane has been painted bright red and is the main feature of a children's play area/sand pit. It is the first thing one sees upon entering the park.

A 10-foot-wide promenade runs beside the Delaware and, despite obvious neglect, is still quite romantic. Part of the walkway is boardwalk, bordered by crushed stone that recalls the rail beds that were once part of the area. A double row of plane trees form a lush canopy along most of the distance, echoing mature rows of these trees occurring along Lamberton Road, which leads to the site. The beauty of the tree-lined road contrasts sharply with the chain-link fence

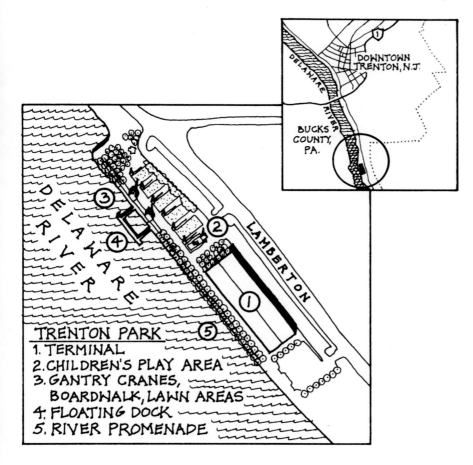

TRENTON PARK
1. TERMINAL
2. CHILDREN'S PLAY AREA
3. GANTRY CRANES, BOARDWALK, LAWN AREAS
4. FLOATING DOCK
5. RIVER PROMENADE

that surrounds the Marine Terminal itself. The fence was no doubt necessitated by fear of vandalism and crime. The park gates close at 10:00 p.m.

The edge treatment along the river is very nautical: precast concrete with steel wire cable railings—the latter meant to avoid blocking the views of those seated on the many benches along the promenade and throughout the park.

Appraisal.   The Trenton Marine Terminal Park is exemplary for its retention of industrial artifacts, use of trees, and good detailing. It is also a poignant example of how the best-designed park can suffer from neglect. It is why "friends of the park" groups are formed, and why maintenance budgets should be required as part of funding.

The whole project—a bold attempt to turn around an old industrial area—is an idea whose time may still come. In time, Marine Terminal Park can be returned to its earlier glory.

Trenton Marine Terminal Park

Cost. $800,000
Dimensions. 2.6 acres
Completion date. 1980

Sponsor. Alan Mallach, Director; Diane Strauss, Senior Planner
City of Trenton, Dept. of Housing and Development
City Hall Annex
Trenton, NJ 08608
(609) 989-3604

Sponsor. New Jersey Economic Development Authority
200 South Warren St.
Trenton, NJ 08625
(609) 924-4047

Designer. Henry F. Arnold
Arnold Associates
40 Witherspoon St.
Princeton, NJ 08542
(609) 924-4047

Designer. Arthur Lutzker
226 Park Avenue
Oakhurst, NJ 07755
(609) 924-4047

Portside Park, Vancouver, B.C., Canada. (*Brent Hamblin Photography*)

Portside (C.R.A.B.) Park
0 North Foot Main Street
Vancouver, British Columbia,
Canada

Summary

A neighborhood park responding to community needs offers shoreline access and views of the nearby port.

Description. Local representatives from this downtown, industrial neighborhood, close to the Port of Vancouver, lobbied both the federal and city governments to create badly needed open space along the water for community use. The 6-acre Portside Park is the result.

Numerous meetings with various interest groups and a committee called "Create a Real Available Beach" (C.R.A.B.) resulted in wish lists and helped shape the final plan. The park, developed at a cost of $1.5 million paid for by the City of Vancouver and the Vancouver Ports Corporation, sits on land owned by the federal government (Ports Canada) and leased to the city. To guard their prized park from outsiders, the only access to the park is by way of an overpass that is an extension of Main Street—a long walk from downtown offices or the historic area of Gastown. Rail lines prevent entrance from other points along the way.

Portside Park offers a variety of experiences, including a seniors' center, horseshoe pitches, outdoor chess and checkerboard on paving, a "tot lot" with a sand pit, an older children's play space with climbing gear, a bandshell, an informal amphitheater, a timber observation pier, a water's edge pathway, grass lawns, a beach, and a wetland area. It is a significant piece of green open space set amid a working port area.

Design Features. One unusual feature of this park is that it was designed to encourage contact with the water's edge, but not physical interaction because the water quality is not suitable for swimming or fishing. Thus a cobble beach strewn with logs and an observation pier enable people to get close to the water. In keeping with the port setting, natural, heavy timbers are used in the design of sturdy-looking benches, the bandshell, and play equipment. The blue roof of the simple, attractive Senior Center harmonizes with the industrially inspired blue metal lighting fixtures.

Besides different areas and activities for various age groups, changes in the landscape offer a variety of experiences within this relatively small park. The beach and the lawn are expansive and open, while a small garden area and the children's play space afford a level of privacy. A Japanese garden and stone lantern, donated by the Port of Yokohama and the Vancouver Port Corporation, lend an elegant, meditative touch. The wetland area created within the park provides a small, wild, nature preserve, and is in sharp contrast to all the surrounding industry. The observation pier enables people to get out over the water and view the harbor, the mountains, the city, and the port.

Appraisal. Portside Park is exemplary for responding so effectively to a community consensus and shows how welcome green, recreational space can be carved out of an industrial shoreline.

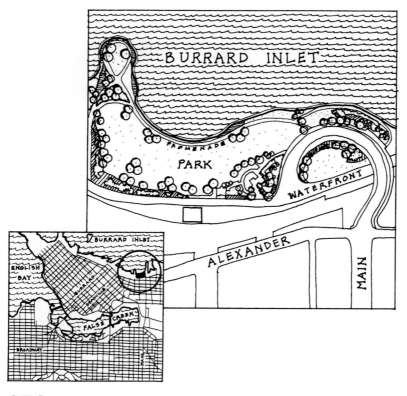

While providing ample opportunity to view the port and the comings and goings in the harbor, more could be done to explain the activity, identifying the vessels and cargo. The wetlands also offer an opportunity for education that is not taken.

Portside (C.R.A.B.) Park

Cost. $1.5 million
Source. City of Vancouver; Vancouver Port Corporation
Dimensions. 6 acres
Completion date. 1987

Sponsor. Nancy McLean, BCSLA, Park
Development Manager
Vancouver Board of Parks and Recreation
2099 Beach Ave.
Vancouver, BC, V6G 1Z4 Canada
(604) 681-1141

Sponsor. Jim Green
Downtown Eastside Residents Association
9 East Hastings St.
Vancouver, BC, V6A 1M9 Canada
(604) 682-0931

Sponsor. Don Larson, President, Create a Real Beach
Committee (C.R.A.B.)
60A Alexander St.
Vancouver, BC, V6A 1B4 Canada

Designer. R. Kim Perry & Brian F. Guzzi, BCSLA
Guzzi Perry and Associates, Inc.
134 Abbott St., No. 304
Vancouver, BC, V6B 2K4 Canada
(604) 685-41122

Designer. Larry Diamond
Sharp and Diamond
29-1551 Johnston
Vancouver, BC, V6H 3R9 Canada
(604) 681-3303

Coastal engineer. Hay and Company, Consultants, Inc.
One West 7th Ave.
Vancouver, BC, V5Y 1L5 Canada
(604) 875-6391

Electrical engineer. Nemetz Flagell Engineering Ltd.
960 Quayside Drive, No. 405
New Westminster, BC, V3M 6G2, Canada
(604) 525-4601

Watkins Glen Waterfront, Watkins Glen, N.Y.(*Breen/Rigby*)

Seneca Lake Pier
and Pavilion
Foot of Franklin Street
Watkins Glen, New York

Summary

Pier provides public focal point of slowly redeveloping downtown waterfront.

Description.   Where the town of Watkins Glen meets Seneca Lake, once a largely industrial tract, there is now a well-used public pier and a marina. The beginnings of a planned waterfront park are here.

Jutting 330 feet into the lake, where it ties to a $1 million breakwater that is the other visible municipal investment to date here, the Seneca Lake Pier lures the public out to enjoy a special place. For Watkins Glen is at the base of Seneca Lake, the largest of the 11 Finger Lakes that give this region its identity.

The pier, 14 feet in width, is straightforward planking on concrete pipe. At the end is its distinguishing pavilion, whose wooden slats are painted an unusual burnt orange. The small, glass-enclosed shelter and fishing access make it enjoyable in varied ways, especially during the May-to-September season.

The breakwater itself does double duty as a fishing platform and boat shelter. The marina and a commercial tour boat operation are the other waterfront attractions. A planned park is just that, with only three small trees, three benches, and two flower pots at present. Otherwise the downtown waterfront is unpaved parking, an unrestored train depot in a key location, and abandoned industrial buildings. One

such structure, the former Schuyler Iron and Agricultural Works, was converted to a market-place but has since been closed and abandoned (as of July 1992). The main street leading to the waterfront is lively. An active rail line runs past the waterfront.

Design Features.   The small pier-end pavilion is fairly simple and clean-cut in design approach. It features a shelter that is partially protected with windows, a bench, and a cupola with a spire. It embodies a Victorian style reminiscent of area boat houses.

There are two benches in front and additional seating on the lake side. The pier has standard-issue gray piping for rails, topped with nautical lights and dressed up in season with flower boxes.

Outstanding is the vivid hue of muted orange chosen for the pavilion's color. This enables the structure to stand out on the lake without seeming garish.

Appraisal.   The popularity of the Seneca Lake Pier, on a waterfront that is very much still in the making, is a testament of the powerful lure of such features.

The pier is not visible from the town's main street. There are no signs directing people to it. Some of its immediate neighbors are not inspiring—a cinder-block restroom, a train depot in

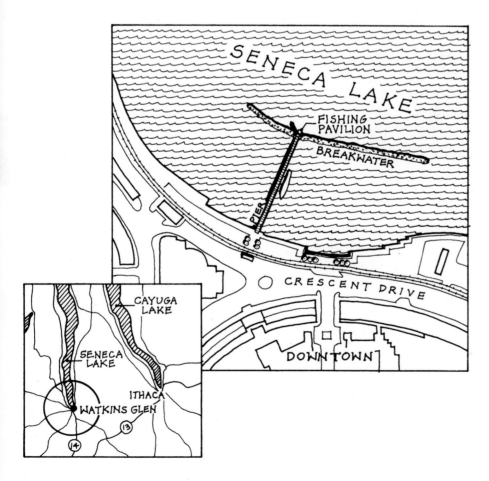

disrepair, and abandoned industrial buildings surrounded by parking—but the pier and pavilion are strong enough attractions to overcome the setting. Helping out is a popular tour boat operation next to the pier.

The investment begun here—the pier cost $450,000, the marina $150,000, in addition to the breakwater, and additional funds have been spent on acquiring land from the railroad—is a major commitment by the town to reviving its waterfront. That it has a long way to go, and that planning dates back to 1981, should be no surprise.

The pier and pavilion celebrate the lake setting and stand as a signal accomplishment for a community making the transition from an industrial base to an agricultural/tourist economy.

Seneca Lake Pier and Pavilion

Cost. Marina, $150,000; pier, $450,000; breakwater, $1 million
Dimensions. Pier, 330 feet; breakwater, 680 feet; marina, 120 slips; planned Seneca Harbor Park, 6 acres
Completion date. 1981

Sponsor. David Kelly, Director of Planning and Economic Development
Schuyler County Industrial Development Agency
208 Broadway
Montour Falls, NY 14865
(607) 535-7391

Designer. Chad Floyd, FAIA
Centerbrook Architects & Planners
P.O. Box 955
Essex, CT 06426
(203) 767-0175

Structural engineer (pier). Lozier Engineers
1050 Pittsford Victor Rd.
Pittsford, NY 14534
(716) 381-2210

Structural engineer. Besier Gibble Norden, Consulting Engineers, Inc.
130 Elm St., P.O. Box 802
Old Saybrook, CT 06475
(203) 388-1224

Notes for Chapter 6

1. Peter Clavelle, " The People's Waterfront of Burlington," *Waterfront World*, vol. 11, no. 1, Spring 1992, p. 11.

2. Kerri Morgan, "It's a Dream Realized," *Charleston News & Courier*, May 11, 1990, p.1.

3. Joe Shoemaker, *Returning the Platte to the People*, Tumbleweed Press, Westminister, Colo., for the Greenway Foundation, 1981.

4. Platte River Greenway Foundation, 1987.

5. The Waterfront Center, *Urban Waterfronts '86*, Chap. 11, "Urban Rivers: A Recreation Resource," p. 80.

6. Margot Patterson Doss, "A Classy City Pier," *San Francisco Chronicle*, May 19, 1991.

7. Thirteenth Street Architects, *The Santa Monica Pier Design Guidelines*, Santa Monic Pier Restoration Corporation, Santa Monica, CA.

8. Sam Hall Kaplan, "The Pier Pressure in Santa Monica," *Los Angeles Times*, Sept. 13, 1982, part V, p. 1,

≈7≈

THE RESIDENTIAL WATERFRONT

"You must think me very rude; but all this is so new to me. So–this–is–a–River!"
"The River," corrected the Rat.
"And you really live by the river? What a jolly life!"
"By it and with it and on it and in it," said the Rat. "It's brother and sister to me, and aunts, and company, and food and drink, and (naturally) washing. It's my world, and I don't want any other. What it hasn't got is not worth having, and what it doesn't know is not worth knowing. Lord! the times we've had together! Whether in winter or summer, spring or autumn, it's always got its fun and excitements...."

—KENNETH GRAHAME,
*Wind in the Willows**

---

* Charles Scribner's Sons, New York, 1991 edition.

Charlestown Navy Yard Rowhouses, Charlestown, Mass.(*Steve Rosenthal*)

Charlestown Navy Yard Rowhouses Charlestown Navy Yard Boston, Massachusetts

Summary

Affordable housing is a harmonious fit within a major waterfront redevelopment effort.

Description. Overall, this is a small project, containing 50 newly constructed townhomes in a historic Navy Yard. The yard, closed in the 1970s, is being redeveloped into a largely residential precinct with striking views across Boston Harbor to downtown, a few minutes away by ferry service.

This housing, sponsored by the Bricklayers and Laborers Non–Profit Housing Co., Inc., is at the eastern end of the still–developing yard; there are plans for more housing on adjacent property, now abandoned. Across the street are warehouses, some of which have been converted to condominiums.

The Charlestown Rowhouses are on a narrow, 350–foot–long site that runs perpendicular to the harbor. The structure fronts First Street, the principal avenue of the Navy Yard. Here the project is seven stories, with a gabled roof to echo the existing warehouses along the street. The mass is broken by an arcade two stories high over the sidewalk, and by handsome multicolored brickwork.

The center section, by contrast, is three stories in height, leading down to the water where a turret–shaped end unit is canted to front the public walkway in place along the harbor. The turret recalls New England seacoast forms and gives the project a distinctive presence on the harbor.

Units were priced very modestly, well below market rates for such a location. In 1989, for instance, a two–bedroom unit cost $100,000 or less.[1] Some of the subsidy came from the landowner, the Boston Redevelopment Authority (BRA), which made the site available for $1.00 and also assisted with the copper roofing. The BRA puts the public portion of the $6.5 million project at 18 percent.[2] Still another factor in the pricing was the ability of the nonprofit, union–backed housing corporation to obtain low–interest loans.

The homeowners (the project is 100 percent occupied) nearly all have harbor views. Some units have small patios; they all relate well to their surroundings. In fact, it is architect William Rawn's philosophy that a successful housing project not only provides comfortable living quarters, but beckons people outdoors, to interact and establish a sense of community.[3]

Design Features. The Charlestown Rowhouses are a very conscious fit into the Navy Yard fabric. Looking along First Avenue from either direction, the seven–story frontage takes its place on the street among a stately line of brick Navy Yard structures.

Likewise, at harborside, the turret–shaped end piece fronts the walkway and serves as the project's punctuation. The linear middle section can be taken as reflecting a typical wharf building.

All three components reflect a thoughtful analysis of the site and the surroundings and are a successful embodiment of a design approach that is no mere imitation of neighboring structures, but respectful of them in a contemporary idiom.

Another feature is the skilled use of brick. Two bands of different colors are used throughout the project, plus a distinctive cross–hatched pattern along the second level. At the base, there's a course of bricks designed to shed rain, a nice detail.

The units themselves are not grand. Kitchens, in fact, are said to be small. But the space is flexible, the views are splendid, and there's no doubt the families here appreciate being early residents on the Charlestown Navy Yard's redeveloping waterfront.

Appraisal. There's not a great deal of affordable housing along the downtown Boston waterfront, or on many waterfronts refurbished or otherwise. The Charlestown Navy Yard Rowhouses prove that, under special circumstances, it can happen.

The approach here adds to the equation that when this special occasion occurs, it can be of top–quality design and execution. "Affordable housing" does not have to be synonymous with "cheap-looking."

Charlestown Navy Yard Rowhouses

Cost. $6,537,176
Source. 18 percent public financing; U.S. Trust Company, Quincy, MA, lender
Dimensions. 350 feet long
Completion date. 1988

Sponsor. Tom McIntyre
Bricklayers & Laborers Non–Profit Housing Corp.
P.O. Box 1140
Boston, MA 02130
(617) 277–8014

Sponsor. Stephen Coyle
Boston Redevelopment Authority
One City Hall Square
Boston, MA 02201
(617) 722–4300

Designer. William L. Rawn III, AIA
William Rawn Associates, Architects
101 Tremont St., Suite 201
Boston, MA 02108
(617) 423–3470

Landscape architect. Michael Van Valkenburgh
231 Concord Ave.
Cambridge, MA 02138
(617) 497–2042

Structural engineer. LeMessurier Consultants
1033 Mass Ave.
Cambridge, MA 02138
(617) 868–1200

Mechanical engineer. C. A. Crowley Engineering
40–48 North Main St.
Middleboro, MA 02346
(617) 947–6888

Geotechnical consultant. McPhail Associates
30 Norfolk St.
Cambridge, MA 02139
(617) 868–1420

Civil engineer. C. A. O. Planning
and Engineering, Inc.
88 Stiles Rd., Suite 203
Salem, NH 03079
(603) 893–3515

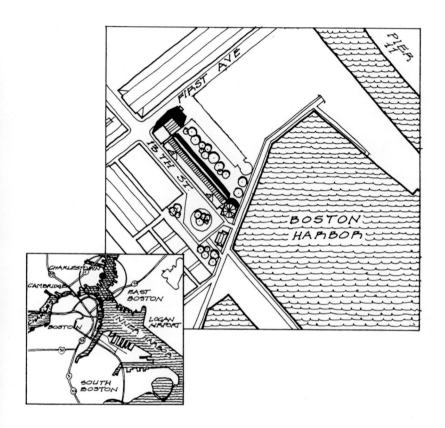

Part of Harbour Town, Hilton Head, S.C., showing environmentally sensitive development, set back from the shoreline to the right of the photo, which was taken from the top of the project's signature lighthouse. (*Breen/Rigby*)

Harbour Town
Sea Pines Plantation
Hilton Head Island,
South Carolina
Top Honor Award 1987

Summary

A forerunner in environmentally sensitive coastal development, including an enclosed harbor that has been much emulated.

Description. Harbour Town is the commercial/residential/boating center of Sea Pines Plantation, the first resort development on Hilton Head Island, near Savannah, Georgia. Since construction began here in 1968 (planning dates from the late 1950s), the island population has grown significantly.

Harbour Town has become a classic, often–imitated resort for many reasons. Its symbolic lighthouse, circular boat harbor ringed with condominiums and a small commercial area, and its uncluttered architecture with subdued colors have become major resort design precedents. Many waterfront projects, for instance, introduce a small body of water to provide a focus, as Harbour Town's recreational boat basin does.

Harbour Town occupies the central 100 acres of Sea Pines Plantation, a basically suburban–style resort totaling 5200 acres. The plantation as a whole involved precedent–setting covenants governing land development, and strict design guidelines with a review process.

At Harbour Town itself, in a combination rare for the 1960s, shops were built with residences, offices, and conference space upstairs. This natural mixture continues today. The ambience of the harbor is accented by ample, two–level public walkways, with benches, plus rocking chairs on the porches of the shopping structures looking out over the harbor. Around the condominiums the walkway is of a concrete mixed with oyster shells, typical of the area.

A 90–foot lighthouse, dubbed Fraser's Folly at first, in a reference to developer, Charles Fraser, was built to serve as a beacon for passing boat traffic on the Inland Waterway. It has since become the trademark of the entire project, if not of Hilton Head Island itself. The views over a bay from the lookout on top are a major visitor attraction.

Design Features. The architecture of Harbour Town and its colors have been chosen to blend into the low country island landscape. Colors emphasize earth tones, including grays, gray–greens, and browns with red accents. The buildings around the harbor are no higher than five stories, with significant numbers of trees and plantings surrounding them, enabling them to nestle comfortably into the setting.

In what is now a generally accepted approach to coastal development but was then precedent shattering, buildings are set behind the dune line along the shore. Paths to the shore are carefully built on walkways to minimize disturbance of the dunes. The project as a whole features a large amount of open space, in addition to that devoted to golf courses.

Typical of the sensitive approach taken here, the more remarkable given the predominant development values of the time, was configuring

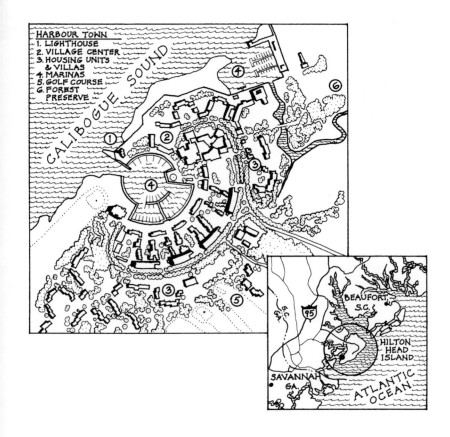

the harbor to accommodate an old tree, the Liberty Oak. This feature means that the circumference is a variation on the circle, giving the excavated harbor a visual point of interest and adding a romantic touch.

Appraisal. Harbour Town stands out today on Hilton Head Island, and relative to standard waterfront resort development, as a reflection of unusually sensitive planning, design, and execution. The fact that much of the later development on Hilton Head did not achieve as high a standard is regrettable.

Hilton Head as a whole, including Sea Pines Plantation and with it, Harbour Town, has a very private air. Entrance to Harbour Town costs $3.00 and requires passage through a gate with uniformed guards. Gated, for–fee entrances are offputting; they give a community a feeling of exclusivity as well as security.

Once within Harbour Town itself, the space is very welcoming. Here a sense of community is achieved, where people walk or bicycle to shops and then pause to socialize. Other projects on Hilton Head appear to lack such a viable community center; residents instead must do their shopping and mingling at numerous roadside malls, more tasteful than most, but still malls isolated among parking lots, distant from residences.

Harbour Town Sea Pines Plantation

Cost. Not available
Source. Travelers Insurance Company
Dimensions. Total for Sea Pines, 5200 acres; Harbour Town, 100 acres
Completion date. 1968

Sponsor. Charles E. Fraser, Founder, Sea Pines
Plantation Co.
The Fraser Group
P.O. Drawer Nine
Hilton Head Island, SC 29938
(803) 785-4643

Sponsor. Travelers Insurance Company
One Tower Square
Hartford, CT 06115
(203) 277-0111

Designer. Stuart O. Dawson, FASLA
Sasaki Associates, Inc.
64 Pleasant St.
Watertown, MA 02172
(617) 926–3300

Thomas Place Properties, Rowayton, Conn. (*Tyler Resch*)

Thomas Place Properties
Bluff Avenue
Rowayton, Connecticut

Summary

Homes carefully set on a wooded, rocky shore, including schoolhouse renovation; public access token.

Description. A 7–acre site on Wilson Cove, off Long Island Sound, once a private school ground, has been transformed into a sensitively sited housing development.

New homes are fit onto a slope that leads to a cove, equipped with a private boathouse and gazebo relocated from a nearby estate. Most of the tall trees have been retained, large boulders are worked around, and one-half of the acreage is left open. Across the sound is a yacht club.

The development's style is keyed to the former Thomas Schoolhouse, a combination of field stone and gray clapboard. When fully developed, there are to be 13 new residences, four condominiums in the former school, and three existing homes renovated. The recession of the early 1990s stopped the development short of its completion.

The existing structures, summer homes for the Thomas family, are retained and house family members today.

Design Features. The project is impressive in its preservation of the landscape and the careful way the homes are oriented to the water views.

The renovation of the former schoolhouse is a sympathetic adaptive reuse, preserving a classic New England shore structure in a new guise. The old Thomas School style was consciously adopted in the homes erected to date. The shades of gray and brown that dominate the development harmonize with the surrounding woodlands..

Appraisal. The care and sensitivity of the development to fit the setting here is exemplary.

The weakest aspect of Thomas Place Properties is the provision of public access, which according to a representative of the owning family will come only when the development is fully built, in the indefinite future. In the meantime, the entry is marked "private road," and a public parking lot and waterfront access exists only in planning documents.

It's a good question whether a bit of token public access in an area that is overwhelmingly private in feel and reality—and which may never be an actuality—represents a successful exercise of public permit leverage, or whether the City of Norwalk wouldn't have been better off requiring that the developer provide some meaningful public shore facility off-site. The second lesson might be that when a jurisdiction requires public access, it should insist on its actual provision at the outset of the project.

Thomas Place Properties

Cost. School remodeling, $1.69 million
Dimensions. 7 acres
Completion date. Incomplete

Sponsor. Thomas Properties, Inc.
Jonathan Lovejoy
Lovejoy, Hefferan, Rimer & Cuneo
148 East Ave.
Norwalk, CT 06852
(203) 853–4400

Designer. A. Robert Faesy, Jr.
Robert Faesy Associates Architects
523 Danbury Rd., Box 445
Wilton, CT 06897
(203) 834–2724

Landscape architect. Jerzy Hajduczyk
16 Ninth Ave.
Danbury, CT 06810
(203) 792–6227

Mechanical engineers. Lois Roberts Consulting
Engineers
16 Bridge Square
Westport, CT 06880
(203) 227–5570

Town of Seaside, Florida. (*Breen/Rigby*)

Town of Seaside
Seaside, Florida

Summary

Small resort embodying traditional town values has major impact on contemporary planning and development.

Description. Seaside sits astride a nondescript, two–lane county road. It is immediately and indelibly different from neighboring developments in myriad ways—it is compact, colorful, determinedly Victorian. More fundamentally, Seaside is by and large built on the land side of the roadway. The "towns" that string along Route 30A from Panama City, by contrast, have houses and condominiums built helter–skelter along the shore side of the highway.

Fundamental to understanding Seaside is its setting. The white sand beach and lovely green Gulf water, in a section of Florida as yet lightly developed, is the lure around which Seaside is built. It is the attraction which led developer Robert Davis to attempt his project in the first place, recalling family visits as a youngster, and remains the principal magnet today.

The layout of Seaside is simple, with subtle details. The 80 acres of Seaside include a beach-front that is largely undeveloped except for "honeymoon cottages" and a tiny segment of beach-front shops/restaurant, and a wooded area at the back that is to remain largely unchanged.

Each neighborhood street leading to the beach across the county road features its own pavilion of distinctive design. These are set atop the dunes, with walkways from the road and down to the beach; Seaside itself fronts 2300 feet of beach. Most of the vegetation here is undisturbed; the cottages are built behind the dunes. From the shaded seats in Victorian pavilions, lovely views up and down a quiet stretch of beach are possible.

Inside Seaside, lots are small, streets are narrow (18 feet), picket fences of varied designs are in front of all single–family homes. There's a commons, or town center, that is fully laid out and serves as the focal point of Seaside. The commercial center is only about one-third developed after 10 years, but is a likely focus of near–term development.

Seaside is now strictly a resort, and for upper-income families. Its lots (50 by 100 feet is good–sized) were going for $75,000 in 1988, and homes for a lower range of $130,000 to $200,000, with some approaching the $500,000 mark.[4] As of late 1991, according to Davis, of the approximately 200 homes in place, only 12 or so were for year-round residents. The sense of resort is furthered by the busy rental office/visitor center, and the home towns listed on owners' signs in front of many of the homes. Nighttimes at Seaside are quiet.

One indication of a future direction for Seaside comes from Davis. After a six–month sabbatical at the American Academy in Rome, he returned inspired with the idea of establishing

Porches and fences are the hallmark of Seaside. (*Breen/Rigby*)

a "Seaside Institute" for the arts and education, modeled on such facilities as those at Tanglewood, Massachusetts, and Aspen, Colorado. This activity would be located at the town center and contribute to its invigoration.[5]

Two main streets converge on a central square, which fronts the county road. The commercial core will surround this center, with its amphitheater. Today there is one, somewhat modern, three–story structure, with a corrugated exterior, housing a grocery/deli and a few other shops/restaurant; residences are on the top. There's also a restaurant building and a classic Post Office rounding out what is clearly a slow–to–develop commercial center.

One major street, Seaside Avenue, leads straight to a swimming pool. The other, Smolian Circle, is shaped like a horseshoe focused on the town center.

Seaside works in its objective of establishing an intimate, walkable town where the car is subdued. While some still drive to the town center, others obviously use the strollable streets to shop or visit the beach. The attractiveness of the setting, with colorful homes in tropical pinks, greens, purples, and salmon, all with white trim, encourages walking.

While most homes are single–family, there is a section of townhouses in Seaside. These are about 22 feet wide and contain some of the most distinctive individual architecture. One such structure sports a purple door, white frame, yellow and orange sills, plus green siding, and manages to pull it off without seeming garish.

Besides the walkable streets and walkways, which feature gazebos, seating, and other features that encourage their active use, the community realm of Seaside includes a pool, tennis courts, and a croquet court, all set among trees.

As Seaside has slowly filled out, it is taking on more of the aspects of a real town. A milestone of sorts in this regard was the election in early 1992 of a town council to be the governing body of Seaside. It takes over from nine neighborhood associations and the Seaside Community Development Corp., which had handled maintenance. The population by the time of the transfer, February 1, was around 1000.

Design Features. The principal factor operating here is the layout, a compact, urbane, walkable town, with housing and shopping located together. The design philosophy stands in contrast to standard suburban subdivision zoning, which separates functions and dictates automobile use. The design principles can readily be applied to nonresort settings, as they have been

The commercial heart of Seaside—the architecture here is in sharp contrast to the Victorian homes in the background. (*Breen/Rigby*)

(*Breen/Rigby*)

in more than 40 places by the Seaside architects/planners. In these applications, employment may well be housed within a community.

Design controls, drafted by the town's designers, architects Andres Duany and Elizabeth Plater–Zyberk of Miami, are in graphic rather than strictly narrative form. They prescribe such things as front porches (minimum of 8 feet) and picket fences for single–family homes, the size of townhomes and overall heights, but do not govern styles. There is nonetheless a Victorian–style sameness to much of the housing (all of the roofs are tin and have the same pitch), while the townhomes exhibit the more flamboyant styling to date. Overall, Seaside is characterized by what one writer has called "harmonious diversity."[6]

On the small lots there are no grass lawns. Front yards instead are covered by pine needles. In addition to walkable streets, with sidewalks, there are alleys behind homes, creating a network of paths that connect all parts of Seaside.

There are no curbs. This tends to put pedestrians and cars on a more equal footing than usual. Brick pavement serves to slow down the traffic. Seaside achieves its objective of establishing a walkable settlement.

Appraisal.   This small project on the Florida Panhandle coast takes its place with Sea Pines Plantation in South Carolina (see Harbour Town, above) and Sea Ranch, California, as a landmark post–World War II resort development.

Its planning principles have burst on the current architectural/planning scene as something "new." The inspiration, however, is the traditional town. The degree to which this appears new is a function of how far most developments of recent years have strayed from a sound design approach that responds to basic human needs for socialization.

Because of its striking contrast with its neighbors—such as next–door Seagrove, with its large lots, streets without sidewalks, lawns, and isolated, standard–issue vacation homes—there's a bit of a precious feel to Seaside, as if it were a bit of a fantasyland.

The layout is very practical. Although it is strictly a resort, the idea of a traditional town center within walking distance, where employment, shops, and housing are mixed together, is eminently transferable. Given a gasoline shortage, the principles of Seaside could become orthodoxy in short order.

Even without such an impetus, Seaside has managed to touch a nerve in the architectural and development communities. It may be a bit precious, but Seaside has power as well.

Town of Seaside

Cost. $75 million (when completed, private homes not included)
   Dimensions. 80 acres, approximately 1000 residents
   Completion date. Begun 1982

Sponsor. Robert S. Davis
   Seaside Community Development Corporation
   P.O. Box 4730
   Seaside, FL 32459
   (904) 231–4224

Designer (*master plan*). Andres Duany, Elizabeth
   Plater–Zyberk
   Duany, and Plater–Zyberk Architects
   1023 SW 25 Avenue
   Miami, FL 33135
   (305) 644–1023

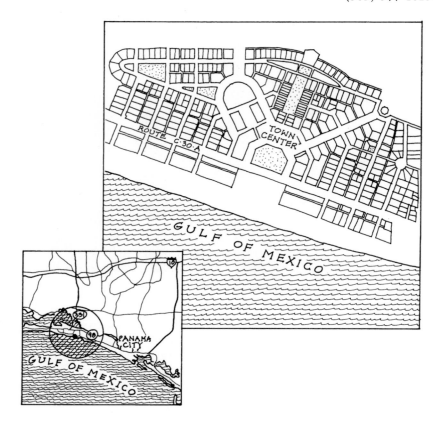

Notes for Chapter 7

1. Robert Campbell, "Remarkable Rowhouses" *The Boston Globe,* Mar. 21, 1989, p. 25.

2. Communication from Boston Redevelopment Authority, January 1992.

3. S. Avery Brown, "Architect's Focus: A Mix of Old and New,"*The Boston Globe,* May 29, 1987, p. 57.

4. Philip Langdon, "A Good Place to Live," *The Atlantic Monthly,* March, 1988, p. 45.

5. "Robert Davis Returns from Italy," *The Seaside Times,* Fall 1991, p. 1.

6. Philip Langdon, op. cit., p. 42.

≈8≈

WATERFRONT PLANS

The Lakefront by right belongs to the people. It affords their one great unobstructed view, stretching away to the horizon, where water and clouds seem to meet. No mountains or high hills enable us to look over broad expanses of the earth's surface; and perforce we must come even to the margin of the lake for a survey of nature. These views calm thoughts and feelings, and afford escape from the petty things of life....In every aspect it is a living thing, delighting man's eye and refreshing his spirit. Not a foot of its shores should be appropriated by individuals to the exclusion of the people. On the contrary, everything possible should be done to enhance its natural beauties, thus fitting it for the part it has to play in the life of the whole city. It should be made so alluring that it will become the fixed habit of the people to seek its restful presence at every opportunity.

DANIEL BURNHAN
*Plan of Chicago**

---

*The Commercial Club, Chicago, 1909.

Chicago River Urban Design Guidelines, Chicago, Ill. *(Breen/Rigby)*

Chicago River Urban Design Guidelines Chicago River Chicago, Illinois 1991 Top Honor Award

Summary

Development guidelines promoting an accessible riverfront are a model of clarity and ambition.

Description. As major development projects began to sprout along the long-neglected downtown Chicago River, the need for controls became increasingly apparent to river advocates during the 1980s.

The resulting *Chicago River Urban Design Guidelines* for the core 6-mile downtown section of the river are a signal accomplishment of the Friends of the Chicago River. The guidelines were prepared by this citizen's group in collaboration with the City of Chicago, specifically the Chicago Plan Commission and City Planning Department. The collaboration reflects a close working relationship between the citizen's group and city officials.

Mayor Richard Daley endorsed the guidelines publicly in 1990, declaring that the river should be the "centerpiece, not the edge, of downtown development," reflecting the expansion of downtown highrises beyond the river to the north and west of the traditional core.[1] The Chicago Plan Commission officially adopted the guidelines on June 14, 1990, giving them official standing.

The objectives of the guidelines are clearly stated:

- To establish a continuous riverside walkway throughout the downtown river corridor.

- To create oases of quiet green space easily accessible to central area workers and visitors.

- To transform the downtown portion of the Chicago River into a high-profile tourist attraction and recreational amenity, thereby enhancing Chicago's image as a desirable place to live, work and visit.[2]

Two other aims are to reinforce the city's architectural gems along the river, and to make the river the development centerpiece.

The "teeth" of the guidelines are that all developments subject to the plan commission's review must conform. An additional effort was to be made to incorporate the guidelines into Chicago zoning law.

The guidelines were drafted by a volunteer writer with the Friends of the Chicago River, Ed Zotti, working with city planning staff. When presented for adoption, they were actually strengthened by the Chicago Plan Commission. What had been "recommendations" in the draft became "musts."[3] The entire document leads off with a list of 14 minimum standards that have to be met. Exceptions are allowed for industrial projects; others have to demonstrate the impossibility of complying. Initial reaction in the real estate development community was generally positive.

Key guidelines among the "musts" include building setback widths, openings to the river, uses to be encouraged, a longer list of uses to be discouraged, and tree-planting standards. In the "recommended" category are such provisions as building massing along the river; avoidance of reflective glass facades at street level and lower; the desired treatments of the river edge, natural to bulkhead; landscaping suggestions; how to handle runoff; how to handle intermediate levels between the street above and the river below, when 20 feet of elevation is involved; paving suggestions; and design compatibility of fixtures.

The required guidelines have as their core two sets of minimums for riverfront setbacks, providing the space for walkways. The minimum is 30 feet in width, the optimum is 50 feet. Where there's an elevation, the river or dock level is to be 15 feet and the street setback another 15 feet at least. Optimum is 25 feet each.

The other key provision is that where a building mass fronts the river for over 400 feet, an opening of at least 50 feet is to be provided. This access is to be open to the sky, not require entering a building, and should provide a view corridor to the river.

Beyond a list of desired uses, including retail and restaurants along the riverfront level, which are "strongly encouraged," the guidelines break a bit of ground by spelling out the types of uses that are not desired along the river. There are 13 such, starting with chain-link fencing and including truck docks and storage space, as well as concrete road barriers and billboards. The guidelines include an entire subsection devoted to strong discouragement of riverside parking, giving reasons and then requiring that surface parking be at least 50 feet from the river, free-standing garages 100 feet away, and parking inside a building 30 feet away. The latter should have retail or other active use on its lower levels if it's within 100 feet of the river.

The guidelines in part III go on to detail suggestions for how to handle specific sections of the river. They ask that the ideas be given serious consideration, but note that they are not requirements. This section details how a continuous walkway could work, joining together existing sections, to make a stunning riverfront experience.

Design Features. Throughout, the guidelines are written in clear, declarative prose. They are accompanied by photographs of present Chicago River installations that are considered model (and one that illustrates a negative use), plus sketches to clarify certain provisions. One positive example the document cites is the privately financed Riverfront Park (see Chapter 5).

Appraisal. Years from now, the effectiveness of the Chicago River Urban Design Guidelines will be available for all to see. If there is any-thing approaching a continuous walkway along this dramatic river, affording views of some of the world's most stunning architecture, all who had a hand in forging these guidelines—from Mayor Richard Daley to Chicago Plan Commission Chairman Reuben Hedlund, to former Friends of the Chicago River Executive Director Beth White and author Ed Zotti—can take justifiable pride.

They will have assisted in creating an accessible riverfront in the core of a great city that for decades has been focused on its lakefront. As pol-lution gradually came under abatement along the Chicago River that slices dramatically through the center of the city, flowing underneath and beside a fabulous skyline, the opportunity for an amenity with scarcely a parallel was presented. The *Chicago River Urban Design Guidelines* rise to the moment.

A combination of a dedicated citizens' group teamed with city bureaucrats who share the vision can be a powerful instrument. If the pri-vate development community of Chicago joins in, the river guidelines will have become a force in the tradition established at the turn of the century in the extraordinary Plan for Chicago by Daniel Burnham. If there's a fault to the guide-line document, it's that there could be more

poetry about this extraordinary river resource.

Chicago River Urban Design Guidelines

Cost. $95,000
Source. 65 percent public financing from Urban Parks and Recreation Recovery Program (UPARR), U.S. Department of the Interior, the National Park Service, and the City of Chicago, Department of Planning and Development; pri-vate financing from Friends of the Chicago River, Chicago, IL
Dimensions. Length of river covered: 6 miles
Adopted. 1990

Sponsor. Reuben L. Hedlund, Chairman, Chicago Plan Commission
Sears Tower, Suite 7000
Chicago, IL 60606
(312) 744-4179

Sponsor. Valerie B. Jarrett, Commissioner; Mardel Acosta, Deputy Commissioner
Department of Planning and Development
City Hall, 121 N. LaSalle St.
Chicago, IL 60602
(312) 443-4297

Sponsor. Mary E. Lambert, President, Friends of the Chicago River
407 South Dearborn, Suite 1580
Chicago, IL 60605
(312) 939-0490

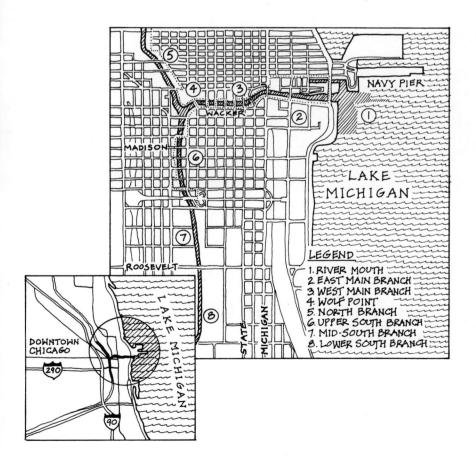

NAVY PIER

WACKER

MADISON

LAKE MICHIGAN

ROOSEVELT

STATE

MICHIGAN

LEGEND
1. RIVER MOUTH
2. EAST MAIN BRANCH
3. WEST MAIN BRANCH
4. WOLF POINT
5. NORTH BRANCH
6. UPPER SOUTH BRANCH
7. MID-SOUTH BRANCH
8. LOWER SOUTH BRANCH

DOWNTOWN CHICAGO

LAKE MICHIGAN

290

90

Part of the residential component of Battery Park City in New York.(*Battery Park City, New York, N.Y.*)

Battery Park City Master Plan
Battery Park City, Manhattan
New York, New York

Summary

A stellar piece of urban planning, knitting a new waterfront precinct indelibly into Manhattan.

South Cove at Battery Park City, a successful architect/landscape architect/artist design collaboration. (*Breen/Rigby*)

Description. The Battery Park City story is long and tortured. It began as landfill, in part for debris from the World Trade Center towers, and was completed in 1976.

A early master plan for the state-owned land was prepared in 1968 by architects Harrison and Abramovitz. Reflecting the urban thinking of that time, it would have built fortresslike superblocks on isolated "pods," with separate levels for cars and pedestrians, cut off from the nearby financial district. For *New York Times* critic Paul Goldberger, this plan "looked like Eastern European housing complexes jazzed up by Buck Rogers."[4] One project, Gateway Plaza, was executed under the earlier plan; it is a dull cluster of gray apartments begun in the mid-1970s and completed in 1982, which gives a taste of what Battery Park City could have been like.

A new administration of the public development body placed in charge in 1968, the Battery Park City Authority, took over in the mid-1970s to deal with a financial crisis that had halted development. It also set about creating a new vision for the site. In 1979 architects Alexander Cooper and Stanton Eckstut created the master plan that guides the development.

The essence of the master plan is simple: In the center is a commercial sector, to the north and south ends are residential areas. Linking the whole is a magnificent, 70-foot-wide waterfront esplanade along the Hudson River.

The Battery Park City site of 92 acres is, in the master plan, an extension of Lower Manhattan, whose east–west streets are repeated, including their slightly off-center cant. The plan provides for small lots, having the practical effect of creating parcels that have been leased to a variety of developers employing varied building styles.

The total space in the plan is broken down as 42 percent residential, ultimately for 14,000 units; 30 percent open space of parks, plazas, and esplanade; 19 percent streets, and 9 percent commercial, largely office. Battery Park City gradually filled out during the 1980s. It is now enormously popular on weekends.

Its biggest site problem is West Street, a busy six-lane roadway leading into the Brooklyn Tunnel, which severs the property from the rest of Manhattan. Two overhead walkways and three lighted at-grade crossings, plus ferry service to Hoboken, New Jersey, provide access.

The organizing principle for Battery Park City is the delineation of its streets and spaces, which together make up half the site. Existing Lower Manhattan streets such as Murray, Liberty, and Rector are extended through Battery Park City to cul de sacs at the river. At the river's edge itself is the wide, handsomely detailed esplanade, to run

The "before" of Battery Park City in the late 1970s, with landfill from the nearby World Trade Center project. (Breen/Rigby)

1.2 miles north–south along the Hudson when it is completed (Cooper, Eckstut Associates, architects; Hanna/Olin Ltd., landscape architects).

"If you can set the street-and block-plan, you've done most of the job," said Stanton Eckstut in describing the Cooper-Eckstut approach to creating the master plan.[5] Other major components of the plan were establishing building locations and mass, and a set of design guidelines for individual buildings and their architects to follow to give coherence to the whole.

The existence of the public development entity, the Battery Park City Authority, was the key, it is now agreed, in executing the plan and design guidelines. The authority, described as "brutally diligent" by Cooper, was firm in requiring developer/architect adherence. An architect who picked a deviant shade of mortar was required to take down two courses of brick; a shipment of split cobblestones was returned because whole ones were called for.[6]

Design Features. The essentials of the design guidelines at Battery Park City, apart from building size and placement, are stylistic requirements that try to interpret and apply traditional New York City detailing and form.

Thus, in the Rector Place neighborhood of 10 residential buildings, walls on the street are mandated (no recessed buildings with plazas); the first two stories of the buildings must be stone in warm earth tones; prominent cornice lines and other "expression lines" are called for, to link buildings visually with older, nearby structures; brick is the preferred material above the stone levels; roof lines are to be varied; arcades are required at certain locations, to widen sidewalks and provide weather cover, as well as to give access to retail and commercial shops.

"The premise of the Battery Park City Master Plan," authors Cooper and Eckstut have written, "is that new urban developments need not be amusement parks, but simply handsome, workable extensions of the city." Their design principles employed in the master plan are: Think small, use what exists, integrate, use streets to create place, and use design guidelines to control bulk, scale, and materials.[7]

The effect is to promote buildings of varied sizes and design, which form a cohesive whole larger than the individual components and which appear to have been present for a long time or, in other words, to fit into Lower Manhattan. This is especially true for the residential component now almost completely built in the south, but it also applies to the towers that are at the commercial core.

Appraisal. The Battery Park City master plan is contextualism incarnate and is a conscious, explicit rejection of the modernist approach to cities that features isolated enclaves. It is a major turning point in the design of cities and will likely in future years take on a larger presence in development and urban planning circles than it does already.

Battery Park City has been called by architecture critic Paul Goldberger the best urban grouping in New York since Rockefeller Center, and one of the best pieces of modern urban design.

"For this is the real significance of Battery Park City—not the specific design of its parks or its buildings, good though they are, but the message this large complex sends about the importance of the public realm. There has been nothing like Battery Park City in New York or anywhere else in our time—a 92-acre complex of housing and office buildings in which parks, waterfront promenades, streets and public art rank as important as the buildings themselves."[8]

Writing from another perspective, that of a noted preservationist and citizen's group leader, Brendan Gill wrote:

If it should turn out to be among the most profitable as well (as being the biggest) both to the city and to the developers, so much the better for all New Yorkers. Remarkable as that achievement would be, something equally remarkable might also have taken place by then: Battery Park City might have succeeded in weaving itself into the fabric of the city as inextricably, and as fruitfully, as Rockefeller Center has done.[9]

Not all, of course, are so taken. M. Christine Boyer, teacher of architecture and urbanism at Princeton University, finds Battery Park City a private preserve for the wealthy with no truly public places. "Impossible to enter from the street, it is accessible only by two elevated footbridges over West Street that tie it directly to the World Trade Center. Either bridge, if it can be found, leads the spectator into the World Financial Center's platform lobby, which links four office towers one level above the ground."[10] This seems an odd observation that ignores three at-grade walkways, and the thousands of people, many of whom do not work on Wall Street, who clearly have no trouble finding their way to Battery Park City.

And, writing in *Metropolis*, Adam Fisher finds Battery Park a "ghetto for the rich," "little more than a high-density suburb whose chief cultural advantage is a short commute," and "lacking in any sense of urban community."[11]

The more telling criticism of Battery Park City is its social stratification. In the first days it was to have a consciously mixed group of incomes, with a percentage set aside for lower-income

housing and another for moderate-income housing, but Battery Park City's financial troubles in the 1970s doomed that in favor of a straight free-market approach.

Most of the housing today is high-income. And while the same could be said of the Upper East Side of Manhattan, the key difference is that Battery Park City is a governmental creation. The defense, if that's the word, is that $1 billion in "profits" has already been generated from the project and given to the city, to help meet the city's considerable housing needs. The prospect is that in not too many years, additional billions will be generated in a like manner. But as long as there is limited housing on the site for people of modest means ($75,000 is said to be a typical condominium owner's annual income, and even the apartments are not cheap), Battery Park City is going to be vulnerable to charges that it is a state-created enclave for the upper middle class.

Already visible, however, is Battery Park City's popularity among New Yorkers of all social classes. The waterfront esplanade and the three major park spaces it links (the third park opened in 1992, to join South Cove and the World Financial Center Plaza (see Chapter 6 for a description of the plaza) are magical open spaces.

Stunning Hudson River and harbor views are the lure, and now that shops have taken root, providing snacks, groceries, and the like (some critics would have more cafes and bars on the esplanade and plaza), there's little question that this space is already being enjoyed by many New Yorkers. And when a physical link is made to nearby Battery Park at the foot of Manhattan, there is every likelihood that this place will become one of New York City's most visited.

Battery Park City Masterplan

Cost. $4 billion (estimated buildout)
Dimension. 92 acres
Completion date. 1979 (plan)

Sponsor. David Emil, President
Battery Park City Authority
1 World Financial Center, 18th Floor
New York NY 10281
(212) 416-5300

Designer. Alexander Cooper
Cooper Robertson & Partners
311 West 43 St.
New York, NY 10036
(212) 247-1717

Designer. Stanton Eckstut
Ehrenkrantz Eckstut & Whitelaw
23 East Fourth St.
New York, NY 10003
(212) 353-0400

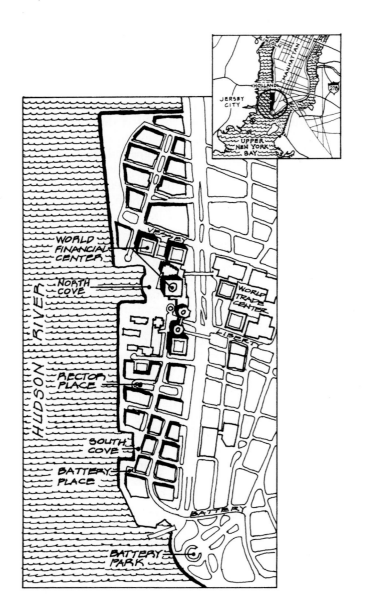

Niagara Parks: A 100-Year Vision, Niagara Region, Ontario, Canada. Moriyama &
Teshima Ltd. Partners. *(George Stockton)*

Ontario's Niagara Parks:
Planning the Second Century
Niagara Parks Commission
Niagara, Ontario, Canada
Top Honor Award 1991

Summary

A tour-de-force plan that combines long-range vision and care for the natural environment with pragmatic concerns for commercial tourism objectives.

Description. The Niagara Parks Commission was established in 1885 with the goal of preserving the natural beauty of the falls and controlling rampant commercialism in the face of the quarter-million visitors who visited annually. Today, Niagara is Canada's most important tourism destination, attracting over 11 million visitors a year. *Planning the Second Century* was built on the earlier effort with the same goals of preservation and sound development.

Ontario's Niagara Parks plan covers a 35-mile area running along the Niagara River between Lake Erie and Lake Ontario. In all, over 20 sites, including the centerpiece Niagara Falls, were identified and studied along the Niagara corridor as part of an overall system and as having potential for more active use and visitation. They include Old Fort Erie and Fort George, the towns of Fort Erie, Chippawa, and Queenston, as well as historic places, active and passive recreational areas, and wilderness.

These sites comprise the living history of 12,000 years of human heritage and 600 million years of geological evolution. The 100-year vision plan is based on an attitude toward the environment involving cooperation among jurisdictions and the public and private sectors to achieve overall health and appropriate balance between nature and technology. It is described as a "new synthesis for the twenty-first century."

In 1987–1988, at the time the plan was being developed, visitors purchased about $18 million in Ontario goods, with indirect expenditures amounting to 35 cents for every dollar. Retail sales taxes remitted by the commission to the province ran to $18 million, plus $566,000 to the local governments. While these contributions to the economy were significant, many opportunities were being lost. One major goal of the plan is to capture more of the economic potential offered by visitors by increasing lengths of stay, appealing to broader markets, and attracting visitors at all times of the year.

Several specific recommendations to achieve the goals of the plan include: provision of high-quality urban and pedestrian linkages between and among all the parks; extension of green linkages from the river into the city; extension of tourism into the region with a parkway; creation of a new canal along a hydro transmission corridor; development of major gateways to Ontario and Canada; and overall improvement of the regional transportation system, including an integrated "people mover" system and water transportation.

Specific initiatives were outlined and elaborated with respect to individual components within Queen Victoria Park and throughout the system,

from lake to lake. All of the activities and programs were designed to highlight themes unique to Niagara, including its nature and scenery, education, culture and history, adventure, and exploration and entertainment. Emphasis was also placed on detailed program and financial planning, and marketing strategies to be undertaken by the commission alone and in cooperation with other entities.

The plan closes with an outline of planning and implementation priorities and a series of specific recommendations.

Design Features. The plan document reflects the beliefs of its principal author, Raymond Moriyama:

> I believe Socrates was right when he said that life is like archery—there must be a target if a person is to succeed. If we are to continue breathing life into this project, it too must have a clear target.
>
> The target for Ontario's Niagara Parks is the preservation of nature—nurturing and enhancing not only the goose laying the proverbial golden eggs, but caring for its nesting grounds and supporting natural environment. As cities everywhere grow larger and denser and as institutions become more and more alike, there will be a shift of perception. The main attraction of Canada—and Niagara in particular—will be nature, majestic and breathtaking such as the Falls, and delicate and subtle such as wildflowers among the rocks.[12]

This caring attitude is evident throughout the plan as well as in the high quality of its presentation. The photos, the maps and illustrative drawings, are clear, informative, and well done. The layout is handsome. The prose is articulate and free of obfuscation. This is an altogether elegant planning document.

One of the most important components of the plan deals with improvements at Queen Victoria Park, on the Canadian side of the Falls. New attractions are called for, to be set among beautifully landscaped and detailed outdoor pedestrian spaces, gardens, plazas, and new viewing spots. Ontario Hydro would transform a 1903 hydroelectric power plant into a hydro museum and information center, with both indoor and outdoor exhibits, eating facilities, and shops.

A greenhouse-galleria would capitalize on the picturesque gardens Canada is noted for, and create a year-round space for displays and a concourse of shops and restaurants. A forum would take the Canadian Niagara Power Plant and turn it into a museum, park archives, performance or trade show spaces. Outdoor performance space and skating rinks would enliven the area in all seasons. One of the most exciting ideas calls for improvements of the Great Gorge

Adventure and Niagara Glen sites. Elevators will carry tourists down through the escarpment, through a tunnel to a river-level interpretative walk.

Another major idea put forward in the plan is the gateway notion. Three are proposed: at Fort Erie, at Niagara Falls (the major one), and at Niagara-on-the-Lake. Each would be an attraction in its own right, a showcase for local points of interest, and a central spot for tourist information.

Appraisal. This plan is rooted in and respects the natural and cultural history of the past, dreams of a balanced approach to economic development, is highly educational in its mission, and looks boldly toward a future that preserves a healthy environment.

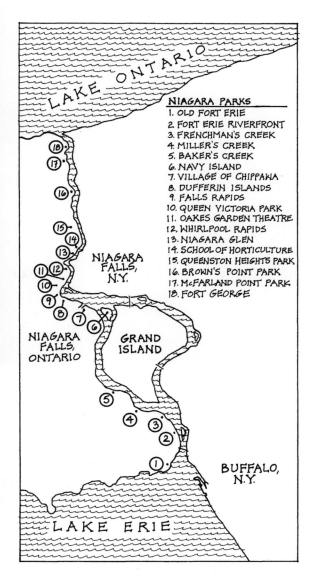

Ontario's Niagara Parks: Planning the Second Century

Cost. $350,000
Dimensions. 35 miles long
Sponsor. Dennis W. Schafer, General Manager
Niagara Parks Commission
P.O. Box 150
Niagara Falls, ON, L2E 6T2 Canada
(416) 356-2241

Architect. Raymond Moriyama
Moriyama & Teshima Planners Ltd.
32 Davenport Rd.
Toronto, ON, M5R 1H3 Canada
(416) 925-4484

Transportation consultant. Lea Associates
1240 Ellesmere Rd.
Scarborough, ON, M1P 2X4 Canada
(416) 299-9050

Marketing. Coopers & Lybrand Consulting Group
145 King St. W.
Toronto, ON M5H 1V8 Canada
(416) 869-1130

LAKE ONTARIO

NIAGARA PARKS
1. OLD FORT ERIE
2. FORT ERIE RIVERFRONT
3. FRENCHMAN'S CREEK
4. MILLER'S CREEK
5. BAKER'S CREEK
6. NAVY ISLAND
7. VILLAGE OF CHIPPAWA
8. DUFFERIN ISLANDS
9. FALLS RAPIDS
10. QUEEN VICTORIA PARK
11. OAKES GARDEN THEATRE
12. WHIRLPOOL RAPIDS
13. NIAGARA GLEN
14. SCHOOL OF HORTICULTURE
15. QUEENSTON HEIGHTS PARK
16. BROWN'S POINT PARK
17. McFARLAND POINT PARK
18. FORT GEORGE

NIAGARA FALLS, N.Y.

NIAGARA FALLS, ONTARIO

GRAND ISLAND

BUFFALO, N.Y.

LAKE ERIE

The Waterfront Plan of 1912, Toronto, Ontario. (*Breen/Rigby*)

The Waterfront Plan of 1912
Toronto Harbour
Toronto, Ontario, Canada

Summary

A far-sighted concept plan that charted the waterfront course in Toronto for 40 years.

Description/Design Features. Issuance of the plan document, *Toronto Waterfront Development, 1912–1920*, was a first product of a new agency, the Toronto Harbour Commission. Established the year before to develop a modern port, and to overcome overlapping, competing jurisdictions that had allowed the waterfront to deteriorate, the plan was a development blueprint that served into the 1950s.

The plan established major areas for port facilities and general commerce. New docks in the central waterfront were built, together with modern warehouses, in accordance with the plan. Likewise, major park areas and a new waterfront boulevard were built over time as a direct result of the plan.

The situation into which the commission stepped was described as one of disorganization, characterized by ramshackle downtown wharves, limited docking, lack of rail connections and warehouses, and only a minor amount of industrial development.

Prepared in just eight months, the 1912 plan had three principal components, including creation of new industrial lands, a 17-acre site on the western channel and a larger area from reclaimed land in Ashbridge's Bay; and replacement of deteriorating docks on the central waterfront, plus adding support facilities. The third component dealt with the public realm, contributing to significant amount of public space along Lake Ontario that citizens in Toronto enjoy today. The amusement facility known as Sunnyside, which opened in 1922 on the western shore, was one early product.

Edward L. Cousins, an engineer with the harbor commission, was said to be the key to the plan. Alfred Chapman, architect with the commission, was also instrumental. And the firm of Frederick Law Olmsted contributed the grand boulevards and the open-space links to the waterfront contained in the plan.

Much of what Torontonians know as their central waterfront today was established in the years that followed the plan, an investment that by the mid-1920s totaled $25 million (Canadian). A major amount of dredging was involved. A harbor depth of 24 feet was established; Ashbridge's Bay was dredged to establish a new, 644-acre Harbour Industrial District. A wide ship channel was also carved out of the eastern downtown waterfront, a channel that is still in place today. The hard-edge retaining wall borders of this industrial tract stand in contrast to nearby islands, with their more naturally formed shorelines.

In all, the Toronto Waterfront Plan of 1912 created about 2000 acres of waterfront land, including fill along the central waterfront where Harbourfront (see Chapter 2, Programming Facilities) is located today.

Appraisal. The Waterfront Plan of 1912 had far-reaching impact on the downtown Toronto waterfront. It precipitated massive amounts of dredging and construction that literally reshaped the area and established its essential character.

Thus today, the eastern Toronto waterfront is devoted largely to port facilities and industry. The central waterfront is emerging from the industrial/shipping land uses established by the harbor commission in 1912, while the western Toronto waterfront, where the Ontario Place amusement area and beaches exist, were designated for public enjoyment 80 years ago. In this latter aspect we see the reach of the "city beautiful" movement of the turn of the century.

What's striking is not only that this planning document actively set the course for Toronto's waterfront for four decades, but that it established principles of openness and an accessible public realm that are central to the current planning work of the Royal Commission on the Future of the Toronto Waterfront. This aspect is the more remarkable given that the 1912 Waterfront plan was prepared by engineers working for a harbor development entity.

The Waterfront Plan of 1912

Cost. $25 million (Can.) in development by 1920
Dimensions. Approximately 2000 acres
Completion date. Mostly completed by 1920; however, small sections were completed in the 1920s, 1930s, and 1950s.

Sponsor. John Jung, Director of Planning and Development
Toronto Harbour Commissioners
60 Harbour St.
Toronto, ON, M5J 1B7 Canada
(416) 863-2000

Notes for Chapter 8

1. John McCarron "Daley backing guidelines to dress up Chicago River," *The Chicago Tribune*, Mar. 13, 1990, p. 1.

2. City of Chicago, *Chicago River Urban Design Guidelines/Downtown Corridor*, 1990, Introduction.

3. Ed Zotti "A Primer for Writing Design Guidelines," *Planning*, May 1991, p. 12.

4. Paul Goldberger, "Battery Park City Is a Triumph of Urban Design," *The New York Times*, Aug. 31, 1986, Arts p. 1.

5. Carter Wiseman, "The Next Great Place: The Triumph of Battery Park City," *New York*, June 16, 1986.

6. Ibid.

7. Statement from Ehrenkrantz Ekstut & Whitelaw, reprinted in The Waterfront Center, *Waterfront Reference Book II*, Washington, DC, 1991.

8. Paul Goldberger, "Public Space Gets a New Cachet in New York," *The New York Times*, May 22, 1988, p. H-35.

9. Brendan Gill, "The Sky Line—Battery Park City," *The New Yorker*, Aug. 20, 1990.

10. M. Christine Boyer, "The City of Illusion: Or Flexible New York," *Design Book Review 23*, Winter 1992.

11. Adam Fisher, *Metropolis*, June 1992, p. 11.

12. Moriyama & Teshima Planners, Ltd., for Niagara Parks Commission, "Ontario's Niagara Parks: Planning for the Second Century: A 100-year Vision, a 20-year Plan, and a 5-year Action Plan," Toronto, 1988, pp. 20–21.

≈9≈

THE WORKING WATERFRONT

Waterfront work uses, which are often interesting, should not be blocked off from ordinary view for interminable stretches, and the water itself thereby blocked off from city view too at the ground level....Near where I live is an old open dock, the only one for miles, next to a huge Department of Sanitation incinerator and scow storage. The dock is used for eel fishing, sunbathing, kite flying, car tinkering, picnicking, bicycle riding, ice cream and hot dog vending, waving at passing boats, and general kibitzing....You could not find a happier place on a hot summer evening or a lazy summer Sunday....Penetrations into working waterfronts need to be right where the work (loading, unloading, docking) goes on to either side, rather than segregated where there is nothing much to see.

JANE JACOBS,
Death and Life of Great American Cities*

---

*Random House, New York, 1961.

Maryland Watermen's Cooperative, Annapolis, Md. (*Jane Davis*)

Maryland Watermen's Cooperative
723 Second Street
Annapolis Maryland

Summary

Revival of a maritime city's last oyster processing plant.

Description. Annapolis once was home to 18 oyster processing plants; seven were reported operating as late as 1925. In 1987, the last of these, McNasby Oyster Co., in the working waterfront section called Eastport, shut its doors. Oyster plants had moved elsewhere on Chesapeake Bay, where land prices were lower, and the oyster crop was diminishing.

The City of Annapolis, also home of a major recreational boating industry, was at the time feeling the development pressures on its relatively small waterfront, particularly from condominiums and offices. In a conscious attempt to control this development pressure, it enacted a maritime zone designed to protect the working waterfront. Flaws in the original approach were evident, and further study was commissioned to see how the stated objective of protecting the boating, fishing, and related industries could be carried out equitably and effectively. The study was completed in November 1986.

In this atmosphere, the closing of the 81-year-old McNasby plant, employing 30, had a greater symbolic impact than otherwise might have been the case. The result was a City of Annapolis decision to buy the plant, restore it to working order, and to help set up a fisherman's cooperative to run it under a lease with the city.

Acquisition for $1.2 million came in September 1989, aided by state, county, and private sources. A cooperative with 56 initial investors (at $1000 each) was set up within two months. By the next spring a full-time manager was hired, as renovation work continued. As of March 1992, the cooperative was to employ as many as 30 persons and the renovation work was all but completed.

The Maryland Cooperative contains 7,000 square feet of space, complete with conveyor belts, shucking tables, freezers, and crab-shelling space. A retail operation as well as wholesale is provided.

The transition has not been easy. Almost as soon as it reopened in 1989, the plant was shut by the state health department. Renovation was complicated by such discoveries as dry rot in the walls. The cooperative's occasional difficulty in meeting rent payments has been offset, in part, by sweat equity in the facility.[1] In late 1992, financial problems were continuing.

Design Features. On Spa Creek, behind the Maryland Cooperative structure, are two piers, one for unloading fish, oysters, and crabs from Chesapeake Bay, the other a public pier for fishing or relaxing. Both in fact are open to the public, along with a tiny street-end park at the foot of Second Street.

Appraisal. How to retain the character—and blue-collar jobs—of the working waterfront in the face of development pressures that will obviously return more for a dollar invested, is a major urban waterfront issue today. Parallels are drawn with the small farmer. Annapolis has been grap-

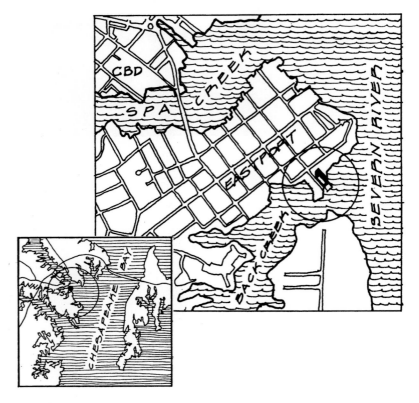

pling as long and effectively as any city with the working waterfront issue, and can point to some successes, along with some troublesome installations, on its waterfront.

One of its boldest initiatives is the acquisition of McNasby's Oyster Co. and the establishment of a cooperative, something new in Maryland. It faces squarely the fact that market forces, left to themselves, will in time remake areas like Eastport. Annapolis has acted, and the Maryland Cooperative initiative symbolizes its determination to try to restrain growth, to retain its traditional maritime character, and to take positive steps to determine the kind of place Annapolis will be.

The initiative at McNasby's has not been without opposition, as unjustified subsidy, competition with existing retail outlets, and a questionable investment in a shaky industry. Proponents look to a healthy crab crop, and crab picking, as the near-term hope to make the cooperative viable.

Maryland Watermen's Cooperative

Cost. Purchase, $1.2 million
Source. 80 percent public financing, including City of Annapolis, Maryland Department of Natural Resources, Economic and Employment Development, Housing and Community Development, and Anne Arundel County; First National Bank
Dimensions. Building, 10,000 square feet; site, 0.5 acre; pier length, 40 feet
Completion date. 1989 (acquisition)

Sponsor. Eileen P. Fogarty, Director
Annapolis Department of Planning and Zoning
160 Duke of Gloucester St.
Annapolis, MD 21401
(301) 263-7961

Sponsor. Maryland Watermen's Cooperative
723 Second St.
Annapolis, MD 21403
(410) 263-2766

Designer. Robert G. Hammond
Hammond Associates, Architects
209 West St.
Annapolis, MD 21401
(410) 267-6041

The Boston Fish Pier, Boston, Mass. (*Massachusetts Port Authority*)

Boston Fish Pier
212 Northern Avenue
Boston, Massachusetts

Summary

Handsome, brick fish-processing pier restored on a prime downtown water-front site.

(Massachusetts Port Authority)

Description. The Boston Fish Pier, opened in 1915, occupies a prominent piece of the downtown Boston waterfront. It is located immediately south of the central business district, near flourishing restaurants, in an area undergoing development speculation.

A key decision was made in 1972, when the deteriorating structures were on the verge of condemnation, to restore the facility for the fishing fleet remaining in the harbor. At the time, many portions were boarded up and a number of fishing vessels had left for other ports, or quit altogether.

The decision to restore the pier to its original purpose is a bolder step than it may sound, given the gradual decline of fisheries in general and of the Boston-based fleet in particular, plus the potential of the pier for other uses (the next-door facility is a high-tech market showroom), and the escalating Boston waterfront real estate market nearby.

The Boston Fish Pier is actually three structures (four originally, but the ice house at the front was torn down in 1968). Its dimensions are impressive: The twin structures are on 1200-foot-long piers, 300 feet wide. Originally, the pier could unload 80 boats at a time.

Armed with a feasibility study detailing what needed to be done, the new owner, the Massachusetts Port Authority (Massport) took the plunge. Over the seven years of restoration, 1976 to 1983, Massport says it spent about $17

million; the Federal Economic Development Administration contributed another $8.5 million.

The feasibility study noted that the fishing industry of the time didn't need all the space in the pier buildings; the suggestion, since carried out, was that the third floor of the twin structures become market-rate office space. The rental income, it was noted, would help subsidize industry users.

Today the striking, three-story waterfront pier structures serve an active fish-processing operation, home to a number of fishing vessels, and accommodate restaurant and office uses. The renovation provided a total of 120,000 feet of space used by the fishing industry. At the head of the pier is the nicely detailed Administration Building.

Although operating at a far cry from its peak, when 339 million pounds of fish were handled, a total of 32 million pounds were processed in 1989, half from boats using the pier (the rest were trucked in). The pier is base for 30 or so vessels.

Design Features. The rehabilitation included a new heating system, rebuilt fish-processing areas, revamped utilities, a new roof, new windows and doors, plus a totally remade third floor. Docks were replaced, the roadway and parking repaired, and new lighting provided.

The style of restoration brings back to their original appearance and enhances the sturdy, handsome industrial buildings. A dignified entrance gate faces Northern Avenue, and colorful banners add a lively touch.

The No Name Restaurant, a Boston favorite that originally served the fleet, remains at the pier. There's also a coffee shop.

Appraisal. In an era when derelict waterfront structures are often converted to new commercial uses, it's refreshing to have a building restored primarily to its original function.

A key here is the willingness of Massport to mix the pier's uses. Thus, separate elevators and lobbies service the third-floor offices, while fish processors go about their business below.

For well-meaning regulators who insist that waterfronts be occupied only by what are termed "water-dependent uses," the No Name Restaurant provides the answer. It fits and is a cherished Boston institution, whether it is "water-dependent" or not. Likewise, the third-floor offices, with their magnificent harbor views and near-downtown location, contribute to the viability of the overall project, "water dependency" notwithstanding.

The Boston Fish Pier

Cost. $25 million
Source. U.S. Economic Development Administration, $8.5 million; Massachusetts Port Authority, $16.5 million
Dimensions. Pier, 1200 feet long, 300 feet wide
Completion date. 1983

Sponsor. The Massachusetts Port Authority
10 Park Plaza
Boston, MA 02116
(617) 973-5377

Designer. Mintz Associates
16 North St.
Boston, MA 02109
(617) 523-3705

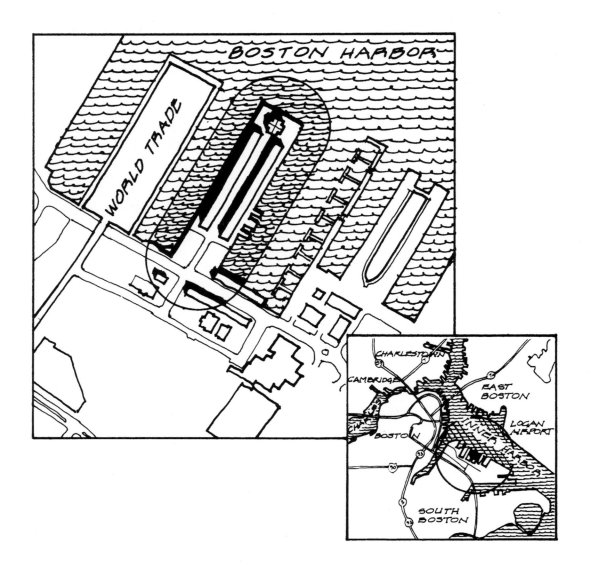

Coastal Cement Corporation Terminal and Office, Boston, Mass.(*John Cowey*)

Coastal Cement Corporation Terminal and Office
36 Drydock Avenue
Boston, Massachusetts
1988 Top Honor Award

Summary

A gritty industrial waterfront installation of exemplary design, bordering on sculptural.

(John Cowey)

Description. Situated within the sprawling port of Boston, toward the end of a huge pier, the Coastal Cement Corporation terminal and office is a standout in several ways. Its prominent, 120-foot-high silos with vibrant red accents makes it a visible landmark.

Coastal Cement is a thoroughly modern installation. One operator can monitor the unloading of cement freighters and the transfer to loading trucks and rail cars. Material is conveyed in pneumatic pipes, avoiding the cement dust usually associated with such facilities. Each silo is 60 feet in diameter and has a capacity of 10,000 metric tons.

Working with the city's Economic Development and Industrial Corporation, Coastal Cement's site includes a street-end park of 18,000 square feet, providing views of Boston Harbor to the airport, as well as floating docks for boaters. This project demonstrates the compati-

bility of heavy industry with public waterfront access where appropriate.

Coastal Cement's location as part of the South Boston Marine Industrial Park was determined by its access to one of the few remaining deepwater docks available in the harbor. The site at the end of Drydock Avenue contained a power plant serving a former Army base and Naval Annex.

Design Features. The clean lines of the gray, concrete silos, topped with bold red cornices, have a wonderful sculptural appearance. Red piping and red accents are a design element repeated throughout the terminal and office.

The small office, 14,000 square feet, is painted a delicate shade of pink, unusual for a rugged industrial facility, which immediately sets off the complex from its traditional port neighbors. The lines of the office are at once bold and functional looking.

The overall appearance is cleanly efficient

(John Cowey)

(Breen/Rigby)

looking, and dramatic enough to maintain its presence with large vessels to one side and a giant warehouse (now the Boston Design Center) on the other.

Care was taken in siting the silos to preserve the view corridor down Drydock Avenue. This long access road terminates in a vest-pocket park with shade trees. A nice attribute is a viewing platform provided at the end of the dock, also in red.

As noted by *Boston Globe* architectural writer Robert Campbell, the terminal and office "has much of the drama and sculptural power of the great industrial buildings of America's past. Coastal Cement manifests raw power, but also surprising delicacy."[2]

Appraisal. Industrial waterfront installations, given care and commitment by the sponsors, can be both attractive and readily accessible to the public. This project reflects a public/private collaboration between the Coastal Cement Corporation, the city's industrial development office, and project architects in a work that appears to serve well the interests of all parties and that also provides an installation of beauty.

Coastal Cement Corporation Terminal and Office

Cost. $8 million
Dimensions. Silos, 10,000 metric tons capacity; park, 18,000 square feet; office, 14,000 square feet
Completion date. 1988

Sponsor. Robert B. Peckham
    Coastal Cement Corporation
    Boston Marine Industrial Park
    36 Drydock Ave.
    Boston, MA 02210
    (617) 635-3342

Sponsor. Donald A. Gillis, Executive Director
    Economic Development & Industrial Corporation
    43 Hawkins St.
    Boston, MA 02214
    (617) 635-3342

Designer. John F. Miller
    HMFH Architects, Inc.
    130 Bishop Allen Dr., 3rd Floor
    Cambridge, MA 02139
    (617) 492-2200

Structural engineer. Souza, True & Partners, Inc.
    653 Mount Auburn St.
    Watertown, MA 02172
    (617) 926-6100

Designer. The Halvorson Company, Inc.
    161 Mass Ave.
    Boston, MA 02115
    (617) 536-0380

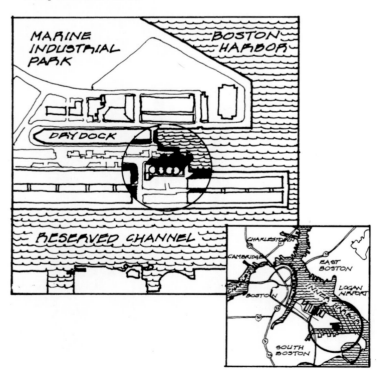

Restauracion del Antiguo Dique del Astillero, Puerto Real, Cadiz, Andalucia, Spain.
(*Leon/Arazola*)

Restauracion del Antiguo Dique del Astillero de Puerto Real y Su Enterno Poligono Rio San Pedro Puerto Real, Cadiz, Spain

Summary

A shipbuilding museum, library, and park beside a historic drydock in one of the world's largest shipbuilding yards.

Description. Cadiz has been a maritime city since its founding, beginning with the Phoenicians and, later, the Carthaginians and the Romans. Its port today is one of the most important in Spain, but the focus of its maritime business is on construction of new ships. The Puerto Real yard in Cadiz, 1 million square meters in size, is operated by Astilleros Españoles Group.

With a tradition dating from 1878, the shipyard is part of the heritage of a workforce that still lives nearby and whose parents or grandparents worked here. Establishment of a museum and library recording the traditions of the yard, beside a restored early drydock in the center of today's modern facility, is a very fitting project.

The historic and educational center is near a huge modern drydock, capable of holding two large freighters at once. The museum is not so much set off in an isolated corner as located in the middle of today's working scene.

A total of 9.5 acres is the precinct for the shipyard heritage center. The major components are: an early drydock, 1.75 acres in size, repaired and illuminated; a new museum/library facility, built on the foundation of a former pump station, with pumps restored to working condition and visible to visitors; and a new clock tower at the foot of the drydock that serves as a focal point for the entire installation.

The museum/library is a low, handsome, decidedly modern construction, situated beside the drydock at harbor's edge and containing 7600 square feet of space. There are views from here of the harbor, next-door shipbuilding operations, the restored drydock walls, and the tower. The clock tower is 100 feet tall, and sits at the foot of the drydock. The entire area is landscaped and equipped with walkways.

Included among the museum's features is a collection of tools of the shipbuilding trade, including many from the past; a collection of stunning older photographs of the yard, dating back to the turn of the century and numbering 8000 plates; a room for temporary exhibits; and a facility for showing films. There's an archives, library, and reading room as well.

There are plans to exhibit various artifacts in the open spaces. Cranes remain nearby, from the days when the drydock was active.

Design Features. Dominating the museum/library is a vivid blue cone, resembling a classic water tower. It allows natural light into the museum. The other major punctuation is a bright red pole at the entrance; otherwise the museum/library is white.

The other major intervention is the clock tower. Built of multicolored stone, its style picks up the rugged construction of the old drydock walls. A viewing platform is available at the fourth level of the five-plus-story tower.

Appraisal. The shipbuilding museum, located in the midst of a huge, working shipyard, is loaded with symbolism. It is in part a tribute to the workers who have labored here for decades, in part a reflection of the tradition of Spanish shipbuilding and seafaring, and also a showcase for a major state-owned company. The investment here is put at $4 million, almost all from the company; a small grant from the European Economic Community ($130,000) will be used to restore a nearby building.

The working waterfront in general, and shipyards in particular, are seldom celebrated. A shipyard museum and library, together with a restored, historic drydock, make a compelling and unusual installation, one that ports and shipyards elsewhere could emulate to advantage.

Restauracion del Antiguo Dique del Astillero de Puerto Real

Cost. $4 million
Source. 3 percent public financing; $130,000 award from the EEC (European Economic Community) for restoration of building at the shipyard
Dimensions. Overall site, 9.5 acres; museum, 7600 square feet; tower, 172 by 100 feet; 1.75-acre drydock; 2 acres for open-air museum and exhibits
Completion date. 1991

Sponsor. Antonio Sarabia Alvarez-Ude
Astilleros Espanoles, SA
Padilla, 17
28006 Madrid, Spain
(011-34-1) 435-7840

Designer. Juan M. Hernandez de Leon
A. Lopera Arazola, Architects
Claudio Coello, 41, 2° izda.
28001 Madrid, Spain
(011-34-1) 435-8145

Historical investigation. Rosario Martinez V. DeParga,
Civil Engineer
Santa Engracia 147
2800 Madrid, Spain

Historical investigation. Rafael Martin Campuzano,
Naval Engineer
Palma 67
11510 Puerto Real (Cadiz), Spain

Technical advisor. Jose M. Molina Martinez
Avda Andalucia, 51, 4-C
11007 Cadiz, Spain

Technical advisor. Juan Robert Rogla
Plaza Esquivel,1, 6-E
11010 Cadiz, Spain

Historical research. Mercedes Valverde Granados,
Bachelor A. History & Geography
Avda Manuel De Falla 18, 3-C
11100 San Fernando (Cadiz), Spain

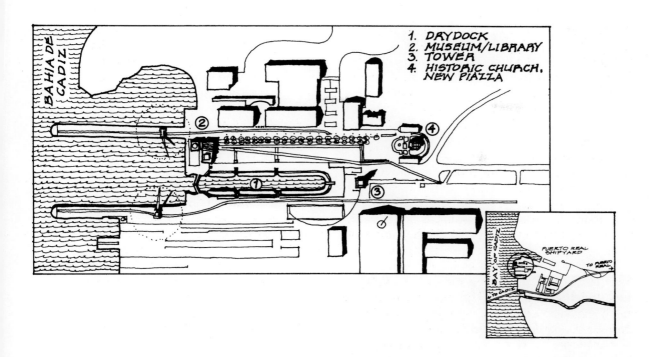

1. DRYDOCK
2. MUSEUM/LIBRARY
3. TOWER
4. HISTORIC CHURCH,
   NEW PIAZZA

S/S William A. Irvin Ore Boat Museum, Duluth, Minn. *(Breen/Rigby)*

S/S William A. Irwin Ore Boat Museum
Harbor Drive
Duluth, Minnesota

Summary

Restored ore vessel marks rejuvenated harborside waterfront.

(Duluth Dept. of Planning and Development)

Description. The S/S *William A. Irwin*, built in 1938 and retired 40 years later, was once the "queen of the lakes." At 610 feet in length and multiple stories tall, the steam-powered vessel is an imposing presence docked on the Duluth waterfront, near a channel where other "lakers" still carry their cargoes.

Its hull a dark red, bow pointed to shore, the *William Irwin* is very visible beside Interstate 35, which cuts through downtown Duluth, separating the waterfront from downtown. It helps to overcome that barrier by calling attention to the varied features nearby, including a major convention center, shops in a restored warehouse, park space and a walkway, excursion boats, a classic lift bridge, two interpretive centers, and restaurants.

After retirement in 1978, the *William Irwin* was slated to join many obsolete boats as scrap. Action by the Duluth State Convention Center Board, which operates a facility nearby, saved it. In the previous year, a record number of Great Lakes ships—43—were scrapped. At a cost of $360,000, the vessel was acquired and cleaned up for visitors.

The *William Irwin* performed a classic task—carrying hematite (iron ore) from the mines of Minnesota to mills in the lower Great Lakes. A typical journey would take 61/2 days with a crew of 32.

During its first year as a museum, the *William Irwin* recorded a "profit" of $86,000 and has been going strong since. In fact, the waterfront redevelopment in the area received a big boost in 1992 with the installation of attractive sidewalks, curbs, light fixtures, parking, and a signature light fixture at the entrance to Canal Park, on the waterfront parcel next to the *William Irwin*.

Design Features. Tours run from May to October for $5.00, with free parking. Volunteer guides, including a few who sailed on the *William Irwin*, take visitors into the vast engine room, into the lavish quarters where guests of the parent U.S. Steel Corp. were wined and dined in mahogany-paneled rooms, to the pilothouse, and through the crew's mess.

Attention to detail is excellent, There's even a misspelling left in place on a bulletin board ("personel service"), menus are on chalk boards, as they would have appeared in its sailing days, and the dining table in the guest quarters is laid out ready to serve.

Appraisal. Duluth is a gritty industrial port city. As its downtown waterfront is recast to include more public and commercial uses, in keeping with trends everywhere, it is a brilliant stroke to install a restored specimen of the vessels that helped the city prosper.

The days of steam cargo vessels such as the

William Irwin are numbered, but the shape remains classic. As author David Plowden, writing about steam freighters on the lakes, described them: "They look like the workaday carriers they are—mostly hull, huge and plain—yet they have a magisterial bearing few other vessels possess."[3]

S/S *William A. Irvin* Ore Boat Museum

Cost. $320,000
Source. 100 percent public financing
Dimensions. 610 feet long
Completion date. June 28, 1986

Sponsor. Robert Heimbach
Duluth State Convention Center Administrative
Board
350 Harbor Dr.
Duluth, MN 55802
(218) 723-2985

Sponsor. Robert Bruce
Bayfront Park Development Assoc., Inc.
353 Harbor Drive
Duluth, MN 55802
(218) 525-2016

Sponsor. Gerald M. Kimball
City of Duluth, Dept. of Planning and
Development
City Hall, Room 409
Duluth, MN 55802
(218) 723-3328

Sponsor. Friends of the William A. Irvin
350 Harbor Drive
Duluth, MN 55802
(218) 722-5573

Designer. Paul Buckhurst
Buckhurst Fish Hutton Katz & Jaquemart, Inc.
72 Fifth Ave.
New York, NY 10011
(212) 620-0050

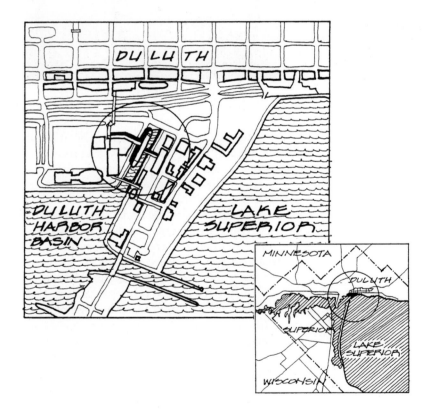

Fisherman's Terminal, Seattle, Wash. (*Port of Seattle*)

Fishermen's Terminal
1735 West Emerson
Seattle, Washington

Summary

A beautifully executed, working commercial fishing facility that simultaneously welcomes neighboring communities.

Description.   A Port of Seattle's Fishermen's Terminal has been home base to the North Pacific fishing fleet since 1913. In the early 1980s a clear need for redevelopment surfaced, because of the change in the fleet's vessel sizes and outmoded facilities.

The port began plans to redesign the area. A Fishermen's Terminal Advisory Committee, which included representatives of fishing and processing associations, marine businesses, and local neighborhood people, was distrustful of the redevelopment. They feared it would become too much of a tourist attraction, that the small, independent fishermen would be forced off, or that the port would mark up the rents too much. Throughout the design process, interested parties voiced their opinions.

The new $9.4 million new facility provides moorage, repair, and storage services for more than 700 vessels. It was completed in 1988, replacing and reconfiguring the earlier terminal.

Today the facility includes 50 acres of water and 25 acres of land. The main building—a new, 63,700-square-foot Fishermen's Center—houses retail businesses and offices serving the fishing industry. It contains a restaurant, an informal cafe, a tavern, a retail seafood market, a travel agency, a nautical supply store, a bank, a marine electronics store, as well as a few other shops.

More than 12 other sheds and structures on the site—some preexisting—house storage facilities and a repair area, as well as a 10,000-square-foot net shed. There are 880 parking spaces.

One of the key elements of the new terminal is the Seattle Fishermen's Memorial. The local commercial fishing community raised the funds and sponsored a design competition that attracted 90 entries. They gathered the names of over 400 Seattle fishermen who have been lost a sea since 1900. These names have been placed on plaques as part of the memorial. A 30-foot bronze statue depicting a fisherman hooking a halibut, by local artist Ronald Petty, is the focal point of the memorial, and in a way, of the entire terminal. Ample room has been provided around the memorial plaza for public gatherings such as the blessing of the fleet.

Design Features.   The sense of place was uppermost in the minds of many locals, who feared the renovation of the old terminal would "transform the fishermen's worn and familiar hangout, one last authentic artifact of Puget Sound's marine heritage, into a flashy tourist attraction."[4] Project designer Robert Schneider said he chose the colors and materials to be in keeping with the industrial nature of the area.

While the new installation no longer has a well-worn appearance, the strong overall impression is that of a working fishing port. The sheer number of boats here makes a strong visual statement. The memorial plaza and walkway in front of the terminal building provide access for the

Fisherman's Memorial statue overlooks harbor. (*Port of Seattle*)

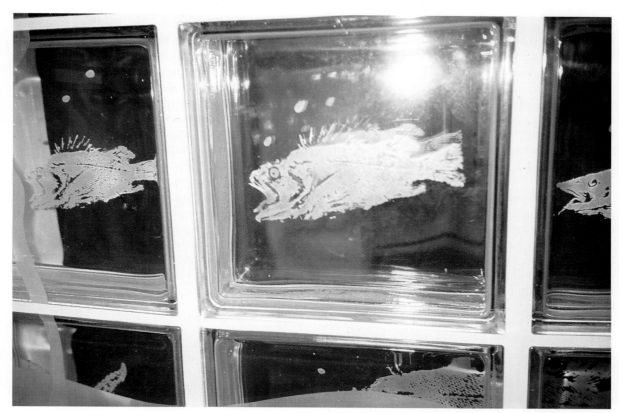

Details from the Fisherman's Terminal building both in this photo and the one below attest to the quality of design. *(Breen/Rigby)*

(Breen/Rigby)

public to view the fleet close up. Heavy wooden benches, clean-lined iron railings, and simple, light bollards complement the straightforward, industrial design of Fishermen's Terminal itself.

The main building obviously drew inspiration for its shape and color from the preexisting structures. The gray and primary colors are bold, the lines are simple. Water, fish, and industrial motifs are carried through in the detailing of the exterior entrances and interior spaces of several of the retail outlets.

Good-sized, well-conceived interpretive display plaques have been placed along the railings on the walkway/plaza, which describe various aspects of the history and lore of the fishing industry. The site signage was completely redesigned to follow industrial themes. The glass block facade that surrounds the main stair and two secondary entrances to the second-floor offices of the Fishermen's Terminal is decorated with the work of a local artist (who placed second in the design competition for the memorial). Five species of Northwest fish are etched into the glass. Inside the fish retail outlet, white ceramic walls are accented with blue tiles spread in a pattern around the room. The attention to good design carries over to the brochure on the terminal that the Port of Seattle has published.

Appraisal. As a redevelopment of a well-established working waterfront facility, the Fishermen's Terminal seems to have successfully handled the difficult design challenge such a change presents. It is no easy task to refurbish and rebuild an area without destroying its "character," particularly when dealing with traditional fishermen's dock areas. One would have to canvas old-timers to see how they react to the transformation—how it functions for the working fleet, its economics, how they react to the design, and how sociable it is.

To the outsider, Fishermen's Terminal appears to satisfy the fleet requirements both in water and on land. At the same time, the terminal offers ample physical and visual access to the waterfront and is a lively scene for the neighboring communities and other Seattle residents. The educational experience offered through the interpretive plaques and the memorial is among the best to be found.

Fishermen's Terminal

Cost. $9.4 million
Dimensions. 25 acres land, 50 acres water; Fishermen's Center, 63,700 square feet; Nordy Building, 21,000 square feet; 600 slips; 880 parking spaces
Completion date. 1988

Sponsor. Duncan Kelso
Port of Seattle
P.O. Box 1209
Seattle, WA 98111
(206) 728-3266

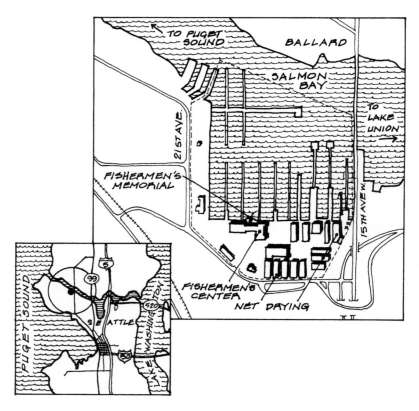

Sponsor. Seattle Fishermen's Memorial Foundation
    P.O. Box 17356
    Seattle, WA 98107
    (206) 728-3266

Designer. Robert Schneider
    The Bumgardner Architects
    101 Stewart St., Suite 200
    Seattle, WA 98101
    (206) 223-1361

Designer. Gerald Hansmire
    MAKERS architecture
    2112 Smith Tower, Second Ave.
    Seattle, WA 98104
    (206) 728-3266

Traffic/parking consultant. TDA, Inc.
    615 Second Ave., Suite 200
    Seattle, WA 98104
    (206) 682-4750

Sculptor. Ronald Petty
    3720 Sunnyside Ave. North
    Seattle, WA 98103
    (206) 545-1312

Metropolitan Toronto Police Marine Headquarters, Toronto, Ontario. (*Crang & Boake*)

Metropolitan Toronto Police Marine Unit
259 Queens Quay West
Toronto, Ontario, Canada

Summary

An accessible and stylish working waterfront installation alert to its place on the waterfront.

Description. The 23,850-square-foot marine unit installation of the Toronto Police cost $3.5 million (Canadian). Built in 1986, it is in the middle of the Harbourfront redevelopment project. A pedestrian bridge connects York and John Quays, where the police building and its boat basin are located. The nearby York Quay is the site of Queen's Quay Terminal (see Chapter 4), and of many of the venues for the extensive programming that take place there (see Programming Facilities, Chapter 2).

The marine unit houses 18 boats and life-saving dories. A public walkway surrounds the boat basin and affords views of the boat activity.

Design Features. The architecture succeeds in blending a high-tech, clean-line approach with a traditional waterfront look. Soft greens and blues accent the grayish-white building. Garage-type doors protecting nine boat bays are made of transparent glass panels, enabling people to see inside. A window on the sidewalk side of the building also allows for observation.

From every angle, the structure is interesting and attractive. The life-saving dory storage racks fit under the roof and are visible from outside, a functional design detail. The lobby occasionally houses educational exhibits.

Appraisal. Industrial waterfront buildings have a way of being nondescript, if not eyesores. The Metropolitan Toronto Police Department is to be commended for taking what is basically a garage for boats and turning it into an open, airy asset on the shoreline. This installation is a model for others building public working waterfront facilities.

Metropolitan Toronto Police Marine Unit

Cost. $3.5 million (Can.)
Dimensions. 23,850 square feet
Completion date. 1986

Sponsor. Bill Boyle, General Manager
   Harbourfront Centre
   410 Queens Quay West
   Toronto, ON, Canada M5V 2Z3
   (416) 973-4955

Sponsor. Metropolitan Toronto Police Department
   40 College St.
   Toronto, ON, Canada M5G 2J3
   (416) 324-2222

Designer. Janos Szabo
   Architects Crang and Boake, Inc.
   85 Moatfield Drive
   Don Mills, ON, Canada M3B 3L6
   (416) 449-1203

Structural engineer. Kazmar Consultants Ltd.
   1020 Denison St., Unit 101
   Markham, ON, Canada L3R 3W5
   (416) 475-8486

Mechanical/electrical engineer. MCW Consultants Ltd.
   156 Front St. West
   Toronto, ON, Canada M5J 2L6
   (416) 598-2920

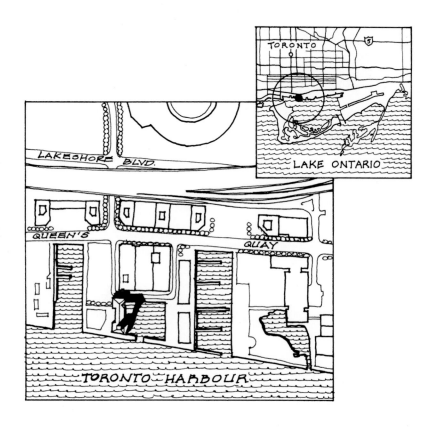

Designer. Johnson Sustronk Weinstein & Associates
290 Merton St.
Toronto, ON, Canada M4S 1B2
(416) 512-9422

Notes for Chapter 9

1. Barry Jansen, "Seafood Plant still waiting to find pearls," *The* (Annapolis) *Sunday Capital*, May 10, 1992, p. B1.

2. Robert Campbell, "Industrial, but dramatic," *The Boston Globe*, Feb. 7, 1989, p. 25.

3. David Plowden, "The last of the old lakers are steaming off into history, *Smithsonian*.

4. Sylvia Nogaki, "Fishermen's terminal," *The Seattle Times*, June 5, 1988, p.c1.

Appendix A: Friends of the Waterfront Center

Ron Alpern; William Anderson, Westrec Properties; City of Annapolis; Antonio Lopera Arazola, Architect; Margaret Barclay, Bargemusic Ltd.; Richard Bartholomew, Wallace Roberts & Todd; Frank Benson; Beyer Blinder Belle; Mrs. Barry Bingham, Sr.; Patricia Blackman, Davenport Levee Improvement Commission; Brent Blackwelder; Gerald Blessey; Olga Bloom, Bargemusic Ltd.; Bennett Blum, Mid Atlantic Company; Peter Brink; Sterling Brockwell, Jr., Moffatt & Nichol; Judy Broussard, Point Cadet Development Corp.; W. J. Burke, W. J. Burke & Associates; Ann Buttenwieser; August Ceradini, Jr., Circle Line Sightseeing Yachts, Inc.; Lisa Cheng, Hong Kong Planning Dept.; Peter Chermayeff, Cambridge Seven Associates, Inc.; Cho, Wilks & Benn Architects, Inc.; Doug Clark, Mediacom; C. Douglas Coolman, Edward D. Stone Jr. & Assoc., Inc.; Cooper's Ferry Development Association, Inc.; Coulter-Delaney; Stuart Dawson, Sasaki Associates; Neil Dean, Sasaki Associates; Charlotte DeWitt, Waterfront Festivals Ltd.; Lawrence DiVietro, Jr., Land Dimensions Engineering; The Downtown Organization; Stanton Eckstut, Ehrenkrantz & Eckstut; Ilona Ellinger; Allen Eskew, Eskew-Filson Architects; Fall River Office of Economic Development; Stefan Fediuk; John Ferland, Clean Casco Bay; James Frye, Westrec Properties; Yutaka Fukushima, TOA Corporation; Margaret Gates, Peter Gisolfi, Peter Gisolfi Associates; Alan Grainger, AIA, GGLO Architecture & Interior Design; Kenneth Greenberg, Berridge Lewinberg Greenberg Ltd.; Henry Hammond; Stanley Hara, WRAF Corporation; Michael Hargett, City of Wilmington, N.C.; Dana Hepler, Hepler Associates; Gregory Hodkinson, Ove Arup & Partners; Don Hunter, Hunter Interests, Inc.; Jones & Jones; Richard Jones, Milville Engineering Dept.; John Jung, Toronto Harbour Commission; Dale Karp, Westbank Development; Barbara Kauffman; Don Kingerski, Winnipeg Rivers and Streams Authority; Susan Kirk; Tom & Mary Kitsos; L. Michael Krieger; Florence Kurdle, Constellation Real Estate; Phyllis Lambert, Centre Canadien d'Architecture; Bob Landry, Southern Mississippi Planning & Development District; Andrew Leicester; Louisville Waterfront Development Corporation; Martha Luneau; Helen Manogue; Prof. Dorn McGarth, Institute for Urban Development Research, George Washington University; Malcolm Mead; Roy Merrens; Martin Millspaugh, Enterprise Development Company; Moriyama & Teshima Planners Ltd.; Robert Murase, Murase Associates; Ginny Murphy; Mary Ellen Murphy; Nan Nalder; Greg Neal, City of Oswego; Clive Nicholson, Clive Nicholson Associates Ltd.; Charles and Diane Norris; Budi Norwono, PT Metropolitan Kencana; Marc Older; John Olivieri, Olivieri Architects; Steve Ortner, Garfield Electric; Yoshiki Osada, Kanagawa Prefectural Government; Priscilla Parkhurst; Willem Polak, Potomac Riverboat Company; Nestor Ramos, Enartec; Mrs. R. N. Rigby; Dick & Pat Roth; Ted Rouse, Streuver Bros. Eccles & Rouse; Meme Sweets Runyon, River Fields; Harriet Saperstein; Joe Schachter, Concrete Flotation Systems; Mark Schatz, ShoreMaster; Dr. Michael Skelly, Lawler, Matusky & Skelly Engineers; Carol Sondheimer; Len Strijack, City of Winnipeg; Marvin Suer; Sharon Swanson, City of Shreveport; Athena Tacha; Mayor Totani, City of Himeji, Japan; Rodman Townsend, Knoxville Glove Co.; Walter Trace, Trace and Assoc., Inc.; Turner/Geneslaw, Inc.; Don Vaughn, Don Vaughn Ltd.; Richard Vesely, Chincoteague Island Waterfront Trust; Tom von Stein; Gerald Walker, Centruminvest AB; Ann Wells; Pat Wells; David Werren, W. F. Baird & Associates Ltd.; Paul Willen, Daniel Pang & Associates; Kathy Wine, River Action, Inc.; Hadi Wiradarma, PT Mandara Permai; Barry Young, Keys Young; Eberhard H. Zeidler, Zeidler Roberts Partnership/Architects.

Appendix B: Excellence on the Waterfront Juries, 1987–1991

(Note: Affiliations as of date of jury membership)

1987

David Wallace, Partner, Wallace, Roberts & Todd, Philadelphia, Penn., Chairman

Hon. Gerald Blessey, Mayor, Biloxi, Miss.

Ann Buttenwieser, Founder and Member, The Parks Council, New York, N.Y.

Norm Hotson, Principal, Hotson Bakker Architects, Vancouver, B.C., Canada

Michael Krieger, Manager, Hoboken Waterfront Development, Port Authority of New York & New Jersey, Hoboken, N.J.

Laurie D. Olin, Adjunct Professor, Graduate School of Design, Harvard University, Cambridge, Mass.

Wolf Von Eckardt, Author and Design Critic, Washington, D.C.

1988

Stuart O. Dawson, Principal, Sasaki Associates, Inc., Watertown, Mass., chairman

Charles M. Davis, Principal and President, Esherick Homsey Dodge and Davis, San Francisco, Calif.

Hon. David Karem, Executive Director and President, Waterfront Development Corp., Louisville, Ky.; Member, Kentucky State Senate

Roy Merrens, Professor of Geography and Environmental Studies, York University, Toronto, Ont., Canada

Ned Smyth, Artist, New York, N.Y.

1989

Charles M. Davis, Principal and President, Esherick Homsey Dodge and Davis, San Francisco, Calif., chairman

Ronald Fleming, President, the Townscape Institute, Cambridge, Mass.

Anthony Giardino, General Manager for New Jersey Projects, Port Authority of New York & New Jersey, New York, N.Y.

Ken Greenberg, Principal, Berridge, Lewinberg, Greenberg Ltd., Toronto, Ont., Canada

Sylvia Lewis, Director of Publications, American Planning Association, Chicago, Ill.

Pamela Plumb, City Council Member and Immediate Past President, National League of Cities, Portland, Me.

Clarence Roy, Senior Principal and Director, Johnson, Johnson and Roy, inc., Dallas, Tex.

1990

Ken Greenberg, Principal, Berridge, Lewinberg and Greenberg Ltd., Toronto, Ont., Canada, chairman

David Carroll, Special Assistant to the Governor of Maryland for the Chesapeake Bay, Baltimore, Md.

Don Hunter, President, Hunter Interests, Inc., Annapolis, Md.

Grant Jones, Senior Principal, Jones & Jones, Architects & Landscape Architects, Seattle, Wash.

Phyllis Lambert, Director, Canadian Centre for Architecture, Montreal, Que., Canada

Athena Tacha, Professor of Sculpture, Oberlin College, Oberlin, Ohio

William Thompson, Senior Editor, *Landscape Architecture*, Washington, D.C.

1991

Grant Jones, Senior Principal, Jones & Jones, Architects & Landscape Architects, Seattle, Wash., chairman

Donald Canty, Columnist with the *Seattle Post-Intelligencer* and Former Editor of *Architecture* magazine

Allen Eskew, Principal, Eskew-Filson Architects, New Orleans, La.

Barbara Kauffman, Project Director, Renaissance Newark, Inc., Newark, N.J.

Florence Beck Kurdle, Vice President, Constellation Real Estate Group, Inc., Baltimore, Md.

Dorn McGarth, Director, Institute for Urban Development Research, George Washington University, Washington, D.C.

bibliography

Barnett, Jonathan: *The Elusive City. Five Centuries of Design, Ambition and Miscalculation,* Harper & Row, New York, 1986 (urban planning—general).

——— *An Introduction to Urban Design,* Harper & Row, New York, 1982 (urban planning—general).

Barry, Patrick: "The Last Urban Frontier," *Environmental Action,* vol. 15, no. 9, May 1984 (urban waterfronts—general).

Barton Meyers Associates, Prepared for the Norfolk Redevelopment and Housing Authority: *Freemason Harbor/Harbour Square Master Development Plan for the Downtown West Waterfront,* Norfolk, Va., 1978 (plans).

Baumback, Richard O., and William E. Borah: The Second Battle of New Orleans. A History of the Vieux Carre Riverfront-Expressway Controversy, University of Alabama Press, University, Alabama, 1981 (urban planning—general).

Beardsley, John: *Earthworks and Beyond. Contemporary Art in the Landscape,* Abbeville Press, New York, 1984 (artistic/cultural/educational).

——— edited by Andy Leon Harney: *Art in Public Places,* Partners for Livable Places, Washington, D.C., 1981 (artistic/cultural/educational).

Behnke, Dickson Tkach: *Cleveland Lakefront State Park,* Department of Natural Resources, Office of Outdoor Recreation, Columbus, Ohio, 1979 (plans).

Bell, Frederick W.: *Economic Impact of Bluebelting Incentives on the Marina Industry in Florida,* Florida Sea Grant College Program Report No. 99, Dept. of Economics, Florida State University, Tallahassee, Fla., July 1990 (industrial/working waterfront).

Bennett, Edward H., and Andrew Cranford: *Plan of Minneapolis. The Civic Community,* 1917 (urban planning—general).

Berger, John J., Foreword by Congressman Morris K. Udall: *Restoring the Earth: How Americans Are Working to renew Our Damaged Environment,* Anchor Press Doubleday, New York, 1987 (environmental protection/enhancement).

Biloxi Port Commission, City of Biloxi and Greater Biloxi Economic Development Foundation, *Biloxi Waterfront: Facts and Opportunities,* Biloxi, Miss., 1984 (plans).

Blackman, Patricia, and Kathy Wine (eds.), *Midwest Urban Waterfronts. Conference Proceedings,* Davenport, Iowa, 1985 (urban waterfronts—general).

Boston Redevelopment Authority: *Harborpark. A Framework for Planning Discussion,* Boston, October 1984 (urban waterfronts—general).

——— *Harborpark. Interim Design Standards for the Inner Harbor,* November, 1984 (plans).

———, prepared for the Charlestown Neighborhood Council: *Charlestown Navy Yard. Master Plan Executive Summary,* Boston, May 10, 1988 (plans).

——— Sasaki Associates: *Boston Harbor: Challenges and Opportunities for the 1980's,* Boston, undated (plans).

Boyer, M. Christine: "Cities for Sale: Merchandising History at South Street Seaport," in *Variations on a Theme Park,* Noonday Press, New York, 1992 (urban planning—general)

Boyle, Paul J.: "A New Aquarium Agenda," *Museum News,* March–April 1989 (artistic/cultural/educational).

Breen, Ann, and Dick Rigby: *Caution: Working Waterfront/The Impact of Change on Marine Enterprises,* The Waterfront Press, Washington, D.C., 1985 (industrial/working waterfront; four case studies addressing the clash between growing commercial appreciation for waterfront sites and traditional marine business; also gives examples of cases where industrial waterfronts have been opened to the public as a result of growing pressures for access).

——— *Designing Your Waterfronts,* National League of Cities, Washington, D.C., 1981 (urban waterfronts—general).

——— "Festival Markets—Show Stealers of the Waterfront," *Harbor Portraits,* Journal of the New England Aquarium, Fall 1988; and *EPA Journal,* vol. 14, no. 4, May 1988 (urban waterfronts—general).

——— *Fishing Piers: What Cities Can Do,* The Waterfront Press, Washington, D.C., 1986 (parks/recreation/marinas).

——— "On the Waterfront. Revitalization from Coast to Coast," *Planning,* vol. 45, no. 11, November 1979 (urban waterfronts—general).

——— "Prospect—New Directions in Waterfronts, Here and Abroad," *Landscape Architecture,* vol. 81, no. 2, February 1991 (urban waterfronts—general).

——— "Sons of Riverwalk. How a masterpiece of Design Has Inspired Communities across the Nation," *Planning,* vol. 54, no. 3, March 1988 (parks/recreation/marinas).

——— "SOS for the Working Waterfront," *Planning,* vol. 51, no. 6, 1985 (industrial/working waterfront).

——— "Waterfronts in the 1980's: An Overview," *Journal of Housing,* vol. 41, May/June 1984, pp. 78–79, 82 (two articles) (urban waterfronts—general).

——— "Whose Waterfront Is It, Anyway?," *Planning,* vol. 56, no. 2, February 1990 (urban waterfronts—general).

——— (eds.): *Urban Waterfronts '83: Balancing Public/Private Interests,* The Waterfront Press, Washington, D.C., 1984 (urban waterfronts—general). Out of print.

——— *Urban Waterfronts '84: Toward New Horizons,* The Waterfront Press, Washington, D.C., 1985 (urban waterfronts—general; includes case studies of small cities, economic realities on today's waterfronts, civic art and water transport; the London docklands, Sheboygan, Wisc., Cambridge, Md., Biloxi, Miss., and Minneapolis are among the case studies presented).

——— *Urban Waterfronts '85: Water Makes a Difference*, The Waterfront Press, Washington, D.C., 1986 (urban waterfronts—general; waterfront subjects include citizen initiatives, waterfront wilds, water sports activities, port-initiated redevelopments, tourism, and the role of celebrations; case cities include Detroit, San Francisco, Norfolk, Annapolis, Miami, Boston, Hoboken, Cleveland, Quad Cities, and the Bronx).

——— *Urban Waterfronts '86: Developing Diversity*, The Waterfront Press, Washington, D.C., 1987 (urban waterfronts—general; Boston is the featured waterfront city, Vancouver's Granville Island project is highlighted, and other cities include Long Beach, San Antonio, Denver, South Norwalk, and Montreal; the summary document features a subtheme on urban rivers).

——— *Urban Waterfronts '87: Water/The Ultimate Amenity*, The Waterfront Press, Washington, D.C., 1988 (urban waterfronts—general; Portland, Ore., is the featured city; case studies include Austin, Daytona Beach, Buffalo, and Lake Forest, Ill.; festival organization, dock system alternatives, design details, and regulatory developments are also covered).

——— *Urban Waterfronts '88: Accent on Access*, The Waterfront Press, Washington, D.C., 1989 (urban waterfronts—general).

Breen, Ann Cowey: "The Urban Coastal Zone: Its Definition and a Suggested Role for the Office of Coastal Zone Management," master's thesis, George Washington University, 1976 (urban waterfronts—general).

Breen, Ann Cowey, Robert Kaye, Richard O'Connor, and Dick Rigby; U.S. Department of Commerce, Office of Coastal Zone: *Improving Your Waterfront: A Practical Guide*, Washington, D.C., 1980 (urban waterfronts—general; information about specific techniques that communities have used in successful waterfront redevelopment projects; case studies include Toledo, Seattle, Boston, and Wilmington, N.C.; photos, maps, and bibliography).

Bronx River Restoration: *Bronx River Restoration Master Plan*, Bronx, N.Y., 1989 (plans).

——— *Bronx River Restoration Preliminary Master Plan*, New York, 1978 (plans).

BRW, Inc.; Wallace Roberts & Todd; and Hammer, Siler, George Associates: *St. Paul Riverfront Pre-Development Plan and Summary Document*, Saint Paul, Minn., 1986 (plans).

Buckhurst Fish Hutton Katz, Planning and Development Consultants: *Bronx River Corridor: Land Use and Zoning Study*, New York, November 1985 (plans).

Buckhurst Fish Hutton Katz; prepared for Brooklyn Heights Association, Inc.: *The Future of the Piers. Planning and Design Criteria for Brooklyn Piers 1–6*, Brooklyn, N.Y., May 1987 (plans).

Buckhurst Fish Hutton Katz with Zuchelli, Hunter & Associates, Inc., for the Department of Planning and Zoning, City of Annapolis: *Maritime Zoning and Economic Strategy*, Annapolis, Md., November 1986 (industrial/working waterfront).

Buckley, Raymond M., and James M. Walton: *Fishing Piers: Their Design, Operation and Use*, Washington Sea Grant Technical Report WSG-81-1, Washington Sea Grant Communications, Seattle, Wash., February 1981 (parks/recreation/marinas).

Bureau of Planning, Portland, Oregon: *Willamette River Greenway Plan*, 1987 (parks/recreation/marinas).

Buttenwieser, Ann L.: *Manhattan Water-Bound. Planning and Developing Manhattan's Waterfront from the Seventeenth Century to the Present*, New York University Press, New York, 1987 (urban waterfronts—general).

——— *Waterfronts Alive. Tips for New York from Revitalized Shorelines across North America*, New York City Dept. of Planning, Waterfront Revitalization Program, August 1986 (urban waterfronts—general; topics covered include waterborne transportation, floating structures, marinas, marina services, public access, parks esplanades, piers design, promotion, and the "working waterfront"; an extensive bibliography is also provided).

California Waterfront Age, California State Coastal Conservancy Magazine, Oceanic Society—San Francisco Chapter, 1987 (urban waterfronts—general).

Carlo, Miguel A., Berridge Lewinburg Greenberg, and Emilio Martinez; prepared for Puerto Rico's Land Administration: *Frente Portuario. Master Plan for the Isleta De San Juan*, Hato Rey, P.R., May 1988 (plans).

Center for Municipal Studies and Services, Stevens Institute of Technology: *Waterfront Redevelopment Project Report No. 1 Existing Conditions*, Hoboken, N.J., 1976 (urban waterfronts—general).

Chamberlain, Clinton J.: *Marinas: Recommendations for Design, Construction and Management*, Vol. 1, National Marine Manufacturers Assoc., Chicago, 1984 (parks/recreation/marinas).

Chicago City Planning Commission: *The Lakefront Plan of Chicago*, Chicago, 1974 (plans).

City of Cambridge, Cambridge Community Development Department: *East Cambridge Riverfront Plan*, Cambridge, Mass., May 1978 (plans).

City of Cambridge, Planning Board and Community Development Department: *East Cambridge Development. Review Process and Guidelines*, Cambridge, Mass., June 1985 (plans).

City of Camden, Department of Community Development, Housing Authority of the City of Camden: *Camden Waterfront. A Prospectus for an Offering of Land*, Camden, N.J., undated (plans).

City of Charleston; Sasaki Associates: *Charleston Waterfront Park. Master Plan*. Charleston, S.C., 1980 (plans).

City of Chicago, Chicago Plan Commission and Chicago Park District: *The Lakefront Plan of Chicago*, Chicago, December 1972 (plans).

City of Detroit, Dept. of Recreation; Schervish Vogel Merz: *Linked Riverfront Parks Project*, Detroit, 1979 (parks/recreation/marinas).

City of Grand Junction, *Implementation Strategy for the Grand Junction Riverfront Project*, Grand Junction, Colo., 1988 (urban waterfronts—general; a multidisciplinary approach to waterfront redevelopment and design; a case study of the Colorado riverfront).

City of Hartford, Town of East Hartford, and Riverfront Recapture, Inc.: *Recapture: A Plan for Greater Hartford's Riverfront*, Riverfront Recapture, Inc., Hartford, Conn., December 1982 (plans).

City of New York, Office of Economic Development: *Lower Manhattan Waterfront*, New York, 1975 (plans).

City of Portland Development Commission: *Completing the 2nd Decade—A Progress Report from the City of Portland Development Commission*, City of Portland Development Corporation, Portland, Ore., 1979 (urban waterfronts—general).

———— *Downtown Waterfront Urban Renewal Plan*, Portland, Ore., 1978 (plans).

City of Salem Planning Department: *History of Pickering Wharf*, Salem, Mass., 1979 (urban waterfronts—general).

———— *Nathaniel Bowditch Park Plan*, Salem, Mass., 1976 (plans).

City of San Diego Planning Department: *Mission Bay Park Master Plan*, San Diego, Calif., 1978 (plans).

City of Seattle Department of Community Development: *Pike Place Renewal Plan*, Seattle, Wash., 1974 (plans).

City of Seattle Parks and Recreation Department: *Forward Thrust at the Halfway Mark*, Seattle, Wash., 1975 (plans).

City of Toledo, Department of Natural Resources: *Toledo Looks to the River*, Toledo, Ohio, 1975 (urban waterfronts—general).

Cleveland Center for Contemporary Art: *Artists & Architects. Challenges in Collaboration*, Cleveland, Ohio, 1985 (artistic/cultural/educational).

Collins, Richard C., Elizabeth B. Waters, and A. Bruce Dotson: *America's Downtowns. Growth, Politics & Preservation*, The Preservation Press, Washington, D.C., 1991 (urban planning—general).

Conservation Foundation: *Small Seaports*, Washington, D.C., 1979 (historic/maritime preservation).

Conserve Neighborhoods. Special Issue on Working Waterfronts: How Neighborhoods Are Getting Involved, Conserve Neighborhoods. National Trust for Historic Preservation, Washington, D.C., September 1985 (industrial/working waterfronts)

Consultative Committee on the Old Port of Montreal: *The Old Port of Montreal Public Consultation. Background Information Summary*, Montreal, June 1985 (plans).

Coombes/Kirkland/Berridge: *Hamilton Waterfront Master Plan*, Hamilton, Ont., September 1985 (plans).

Couch, Robert E., Clare A. Gunn, and David J. Reen: *San Antonio's River Walk: Cultural Benefits from Metropolitan River Recreation—San Antonio Prototype*, Technical Report No. 43, Texas Water Resources Institute, Texas A&M University, College Station, Tex., 1972 (parks/recreation/marinas).

Cruikshank, Jeffery L., and Pam Korza: *Going Public. A Field Guide to Developments in Art in Public Places*, Art Extension Service with the Visual Arts Program of the National Endowment for the Arts, Amherst, Mass., 1988 (artistic/cultural/educational).

Cullen, Gordon: *The Concise Townscape*, Van Nostrand Reinhold, New York, 1961 (urban planning—general).

DeWitt, Charlotte: *So, You Want to Put on A Festival. Urban Waterfronts '87*, The Waterfront Press, Washington, D.C., 1988 (urban waterfronts—general).

Diamant, R., C. Duerksen, and J. G. Eugster: *A Guide to River Conservation*, The Conservation Foundation, Washington, D.C., 1984 (environmental protection/enhancement).

Diamonstein, Barbaralee: *Remaking America. New Uses, Old Places*, Crown Publishers, New York, 1986 (historic/maritime preservation).

———— Preface by Congressman John Brademas: *Buildings Reborn. New Uses, Old Places*, Harper & Row, New York, 1978 (historic/maritime preservation).

Duany, Andres, and Elizabeth Plater-Zyberk, edited by Alex Krieger with William Lennertz: *Towns and Town-Making Principles*, Harvard Graduate School of Design, Rizzoli International Publications, New York, 1991 (urban planning—general).

Ducharme, Robert G., and Illinois Dept. of Conservation: *Urban Waterfront Renewal: The Illinois Experience*, Open Lands Project, Illinois Dept. of Conservation, Division of Planning, Springfield, Ill., 1983 (urban waterfronts—general).

Dunham, James W., and Arnold A. Finn: *Small Craft Harbors: Design, Construction, and Operation*, Special Report No. 2, U.S. Army Corps of Engineers, Coastal Engineering Research Center, Fort Belvoir, Va., December 1974 (parks/recreation/marinas).

Edward D. Stone, Jr., and Associates, and Timbes, Wilund, Usry and Carter, Architects: *Waccamaw Riverfront District Design Guidelines*, Preservation Consultants, Inc., Charleston, S.C., undated (plans).

Fairbrother, Nan: *New Lives, New Landscapes*, Penguin Books, Middlesex, England, 1972 (urban planning—general).

Fischer, Richard, photographer; introduction by John Walton: *British Piers*, Thames and Hudson, London, 1987 (urban waterfronts—general).

Fishman, Robert: *Bourgeois Utopias. The Rise and Fall of Suburbia*, Basic Books, New York: 1987 (urban planning—general).

Fitch, James Marston: *Historic Preservation. Curatorial Management of the Built World*, University of Virginia Press, Charlottesville, Va., 1990 (historic/maritime preservation).

Fleming, Ronald Lee, and Renata Von Tscharner: *Placemakers. Creating Public Art that Tells You Where You Are*, Harcourt Brace Jovanovich, New York, 1987 (artistic/cultural/educational).

Florida Department of Community Affairs: *Back to the Water: Discovering Florida's Urban Waterfronts*, Bureau of State Resource Planning, Tallahassee, Fla., April 1986 (urban waterfronts—general).

Ford, Powell & Carson, for the Galveston Historical Foundation: *Action Plan for The Strand II*, San Antonio, Tex., October 1983 (historic/maritime preservation).

Fried, Lewis F.: *Makers of the City*, The University of Massachusetts Press, Amherst, Mass., 1990 (urban planning—general).

Frieden, Bernard J., and Lynne B. Sagalyn: *Downtown, Inc. How America Rebuilds Cities*, The MIT Press, Cambridge, Mass., and London, 1990 (urban planning—general).

Friends of the Chicago River: *Chicago River Trail. A Walking Tour, North Branch Section*, Chicago, 1986 (parks/recreation/marinas).

———— and Friends of Downtown: *Chicago River Trail. A Walking Tour, Downtown Section*, Chicago, 1984 (parks/recreation/marinas).

GAI Consultants, Inc.: *Low Cost Shore Protection*, U.S. Army Corps of Engineers, Washington, D.C., 1981 (environmental protection/enhancement).

Gale, Richard P.: *America's Coastal Communities: A Survey of Characteristics and Accomplishments*, National Coastal Resource Research & Development Institute, Newport, Ore., 1990 (urban waterfronts—general; a profile of 102 coastal communities with populations ranging from 1145 (Saugatuck, Mich.) to 34,388 (Port Huron, Mich.) on the Atlantic, Pacific, and Gulf Coasts and the Great Lakes; note that the information based on Chamber of Commerce data is uncritical and may have aspects of boosterism.

Gehl, Jan: *Life Between Buildings—Using Public Space*, Van Nostrand Reinhold Company, New York, 1987 (urban planning—general).

Girouard, Mark: *Cities & People*, Yale University Press, New Haven, Conn., 1985 (urban planning—general).

Glazer, Nathan, and Mark Lilla (eds.): *The Public Face of Architecture. Civic Culture and Public Spaces*, The Free Press, New York, 1987 (urban planning—general).

Gobster, Paul, and Carol Sondheimer: *Assessing the Impact of Development of Scenic Resources of the Hudson River. A Handbook for Local Officials*, Scenic Hudson, Inc., Poughkeepsie, N.Y., June 1986 (urban waterfronts—general).

Good, J. W., and R. F. Goodwin: *Waterfront Revitalization for Small Cities*, Oregon State University Extension Service, Corvallis, Ore., 1991 (urban waterfronts—general; Resource not only for small communities, but for others interested in the subject more generally).

Goode, David, and Michael Joseph: *Wild in London*, Shell Books, London, 1986 (environmental protection/enhancement; the closing chapter, "A Green Renaissance," tells of the growing movement to incorporate nature into the city).

Goodman, Paul, and Percival: *Communitas. Means of Livelihood and Ways of Life*, Vintage Books, Random House, New York, 1947, 1960 (urban planning—general).

Goodman, Robert: *After the Planners*, Simon and Schuster, New York, 1971 (urban planning—general).

Goodwin, Robert (ed.): *Waterfront Revitalization for Small Communities, Proceedings of a Conference*, University of Washington Sea Grant Marine Advisory Services, Seattle, Wash., April 23–24, 1987 (urban waterfronts—general; Topics include financing, waterfront parks, public small craft harbors, tourism, the working waterfront, interpretation, and recreational boating; Case studies include South Bend, Port Angles, Langley, Campbell River, British Columbia, Poulsbo, Ilwaco, and Kirkland).

Gourley, Catherine: *Island in the Creek—The Granville Island Story*, Harbour Publishing, Madeira Park, B.C., 1988 (urban waterfronts—general).

Gratz, Roberta Brandes: *The Living City. How Urban Residents Are Revitalizing America's Neighborhoods*, Touchstone, Simon & Schuster, New York, 1989 (urban planning—general).

Greater Cincinnati Bicentennial Commission, Inc.; Rogow + Bernstein, Los Angeles: *Design Plan for the Ohio Riverwalk*, Cincinnati, Ohio, August 1986 (plans).

Grenell, Peter, and Joseph Petrillo (eds.): *The Urban Edge/Where the City Meets the Sea*, California State Coastal Conservancy and William Kaufmann, Inc., Los Altos, Calif., 1985 (urban waterfronts—general; dated 1985, but clearly put together years earlier;

mainly a discussion of the activities of the California Coastal Commission and the Coastal Conservancy since their creation in 1976).

Gunn, Clare A., David J. Reed, and Robert E. Couch: *Cultural Benefits from Metropolitan River Recreation—San Antonio Prototype*, Technical Report No. 43, Texas A&M University, College Station, Tex., June 1972 (parks/recreation/marinas).

Hackney, Rod: *The Good, the Bad & the Ugly. Crisis in Cities*, Frederick Muller, London, Sydney, Auckland, 1990 (urban planning—general).

Halprin, Lawrence: *Cities*, The MIT Press, Cambridge, Mass., 1972 (urban planning—general).

Harney, Andy Leon (ed.): *Reviving the Urban Waterfront*, Partners for Livable Places; National Endowment for the Arts; and the Office of Coastal Zone Management, Washington, D.C., 1979 (urban waterfronts—general).

Harris, S. P.: *Insights/On Sites. Perspectives on Art in Public Places*, Publishing Center for Cultural Resources, New York 1984 (artistic/cultural/educational).

Haroland Bartholomew & Assoc., Inc.: *Bayou Vermillion Master Plan. Lafayette, La.*, Bayou Vermillion Restoration Foundation, Inc., Lafayette, La., 1985 (plans).

Hedley, Eugene: *Boating for the Handicapped. Guidelines for the Physically Disabled*, Research and Utilization Institute, Human Resources Center, Albertson, N.Y., 1979 (parks/recreation/marinas).

Hellman, Peter: "On the Waterfront," *New York*, May 27, 1985 (urban waterfronts—general).

Herbkersman, C. Neil, for the Institute of Environmental Sciences, Miami University: *A Guide to the George Palmiter River Restoration Techniques*, Oxford, Ohio, undated (environmental protection/enhancement).

Hershman, Marc J. (ed.): *Urban Ports and Harbor Management: Responding to Change Along U.S. Waterfronts*, Taylor & Francis, New York, 1988 (industrial/working waterfronts).

Hiss, Tony: *The Experience of Place*, Alfred A. Knopf, New York, 1990 (urban planning—general).

Holland, Francis Ross, Jr.: *America's Lighthouses*, The Stephen Greene Press, Brattleboro, Vt., 1972 (urban waterfronts—general).

Hough, Michael: *Out of Place. Restoring Identity to the Regional Landscape*, Yale University Press, New Haven, Conn., and London, 1990 (urban planning—general).

Hoving, Thomas: "Museum of the Sea" (Monterey Bay Aquarium), *Connoisseur*, March 1985.

Howard Needles Tammen and Bergendoff; Cesar Pelli and Assoc.; and Urban Innovations Group (Charles Moore, Edgardo Contini): *White River Park, Indiana. HNTB Master Plan Team Report,* Indianapolis, Indiana, August 1981 (plans).

Hoyle, B. S., D. A. Pinder, and M. S. Husein (eds.): *Revitalizing the Waterfront: International Dimensions of Dockland Redevelopment*, Belhaven Press, London, 1988 (urban waterfronts—general; collection of academic essays with bibliographic sources; cases include Toronto, Hong Kong, and London).

Hoyt, Charles K. (ed.): *More Places for People*, McGraw-Hill, New York, 1983 (urban planning—general).

HRH The Prince of Wales: *A Vision of Britain. A Personal View of Architecture*, Doubleday, London, New York, Toronto, 1989 (urban planning—general).

Hudson River Valley Greenway Council, Prepared for Governor Cuomo and the New York State Legislature: *A Hudson River Valley Greenway*, New York State Office of General Services, New York, February 1991 (parks/recreation/marinas).

Hudspeth, Thomas Richard: *Citizen Participation in Revitalization of the Burlington, Vermont Waterfront*, T. R. Hudspeth, Environmental Program, University of Vermont, Burlington, Vt., 1983 (urban waterfronts—general).

Hugill, Stan: *Sailortown*, Dalton, New York, 1967 (historic/maritime preservation).

Huxtable, Ada Louise: *Architecture, Anyone? Cautionary Tales of the Building Art*, Random House, New York, 1986 (urban planning—general).

———— *Kicked a Building Lately?* Quadrangle/The New York Times Book Co., New York, 1976 (urban planning—general).

———— Preface by Danial P. Moynihan: *Will They Ever Finish Bruckner Boulevard?* A New York Times Book, The Macmillan Company, New York, 1963 (urban planning—general).

Illich, Ivan: *H2O and the Waters of Forgetfulness. Reflections on the Historicity of "Stuff,"* The Dallas Institute of Humanities and Culture, Dallas, Tex., 1985 (urban waterfronts—general).

Jackson, Kenneth T.: *Crabgrass Frontier. The Suburbanization of the United States*, Oxford University Press, New York and Oxford, 1985 (urban planning—general).

Jacobs, Allan B.: *Looking at Cities*, Harvard University Press, Cambridge, Mass., and London, 1985 (urban planning—general).

Jacobs, David, and Anthony E. Neville: *Bridges, Canals & Tunnels. The Engineering Conquest of America*, American Heritage Publishing Co., New York, 1968 (urban waterfronts—general).

Jacobs, Jane: *The Death and Life of Great American Cities*, Random House, New York, 1961 (urban planning—general).

Japan Port and Harbour Association: *Urban Waterfront Redevelopment in Japan*, Japan Technology transfer Institute, Tokyo, 1979 (urban waterfronts—general).

John S. Bolles Associates; prepared for the City and County of San Francisco, *Northern Waterfront Plan*, San Francisco, 1968 (plans).

Kashdan, Sandra: "The Age of Aquariums," *Waterfront World*, September/October 1986, pp. 1, 4—5, 14 (artistic/cultural/educational).

Kaufman, Les: *The Aquarium Explosion*, The New England Aquarium, Boston, 1989 (artistic/cultural/educational).

Kidney, Walter C.: *Working Places. The Adaptive Use of Industrial Buildings*, Ober Park Associates, Pittsburgh, 1976 (historic/maritime preservation).

Knoxville-Knox County Metropolitan Planning Commission for the Waterfront Task Force, *Knoxville Waterfront Planning Data Base*, Knoxville, Tenn., March 1988 (plans).

Konvitz, Josef. W.: *Cities and the Sea: Port City Planning in Early Modern Europe*, Johns Hopkins University Press, Baltimore and London, 1978 (urban waterfronts—general).

Kozlowski, James C., and the National Recreation and Park Association: *Videotape Series of the National Workshop on Recreational Injury Liability*, George Mason University, Center for Recreation Resources Policy, Fairfax, Va., 1987 (parks/recreation/marinas).

Krieger, Michael L.; The Port Authority of New York and New Jersey: *Waterfront Redevelopment Strategy: Phased Redevelopment of The Inner Harbor Waterfront*, New York, November 1979 (urban waterfronts—general).

Krier, Rob; Foreward by Colin Rowe: *Urban Space*, Rizzoli, New York; 1979 (urban planning—general).

Laclede's Landing Redevelopment Corporation: *Development Plan of Laclede's Landing Redevelopment Corporation*, St. Louis, Miss., 1976 (plans).

Lawson Associates Professional Engineers and John R. Snell Engineers, Inc., for the Departments of Redevelopment and Community Development *St. Joseph River Corridor*, South Bend, Ind., 1973 (plans).

Leedy, D. L., T. M. Franklin, and R. M. Maestro: *Planning for Urban Fishing and Waterfront Recreation*, FWS/OBS-8035 Fish and Wildlife Service, U.S. Department of the Interior, Urban Wildlife Research Center, Columbia, Md., July 1981 (parks/recreation/marinas).

Leicester, Andrew: *Sketchbook: "Cincinnati Gateway" Main Entrance to Bicentennial Commons Park, Sawyer Point, Cincinnati*, Andrew Leicester, Minneapolis, Minn., 1988 (artistic/cultural/educational).

Listokin, David: *Living Cities*, Priority Press Publications, New York, 1985 (urban planning—general).

Little, Charles E.: *Greenways for America*, The Johns Hopkins University Press, Baltimore, 1990 (parks/recreation/marinas).

Lowell National Historical Park and U.S. Department of the Interior, National Park Service: *Lowell—General Management Plan. The Canalway—A Proposal*, U.S. Government Printing Office, Washington, D.C., 1981 (plans).

Lozano, Eduardo: *Community Design and the Culture of Cities*, Cambridge University Press, Cambridge, England, 1990 (urban planning—general).

Lucy, Jon, and Eleanor Bochenek: *Norfolk Harborfest '86 Anniversary Analysis. Special Report in Applied Marine and Ocean Engineering No. 282*, Virginia Institute of Marine Science, Gloucester Point, Va., 1986 (urban waterfronts—general).

Lucy, Jon, Ann Breen, and Dick Rigby: "Urban Waterfronts: Positive Directions, New Problems," reprinted from *Proceedings of the National Outdoor Recreation Trends Symposium II, Vol. II*, February 1985, pp. 66–80, Virginia Institute of Marine Science Contribution No. 1223, Myrtle Beach, S.C.,1985 (urban waterfronts—general).

Lynch, Kevin: *The Image of the City*, The MIT Press, Cambridge, Mass., and London, 1960 (urban planning—general).

Machalaba, Daniel: "On the Waterfront: Tugs, Barges, Battling Quiche and Fern Bars," *The Wall Street Journal*, June 6, 1985, p.B1 (urban waterfronts—general)

Marx, Wesley: *The Frail Ocean*, Ballantine Books, New York, 1967 (environmental protection/enhancement).

McHarg, Ian L.: *Design with Nature*, The Natural History Press, Garden City, N.Y., 1969 (urban planning—general).

Merrens, Roy: *Urban Waterfront Redevelopment in North America: An Annotated Bibliography*, Transportation Research Report No. 66, University of Toronto/York University, Downsview, Ont., 1980 (urban waterfronts—general).

Merriman, Kristin: "Greenways: A New Face," *Outdoor America*, Summer 1989, pp. 22—30 (parks/recreation/marinas).

Middleton, Michael: *Man Made the Town*, St. Martin's Press, New York, 1987 (urban planning—general).

Moore, Arthur Cotton, et al.; Prepared for Office of Water Resources Research, Department of the Interior: *Bright Breathing Edges of City Life. Planning for Amenity Benefits of Urban Water Resources*, PB 202 880, National Technical Information Services, Springfield, Va., 1971 (urban waterfronts—general; early study of waterfronts includes case studies on Washington, D.C., Boston, Buffalo, New Orleans, Louisville, and Oakland).

Morgan, Murray, and Alice Shorett: *The Pike Place Market. People, Politics and Produce*, Pacific Search Press, Seattle, Wash., 1982 (urban planning—general).

Moriyama & Teshima Planners, Ltd.; ·for the Niagara

Parks Commission: *Ontario's Niagara Parks—Planning the Second Century. A 100-Year Vision, a 20-Year Plan and a 5-Year Action Plan*, Toronto, 1988 (plans).

Moudon, Anne Vernez (ed.); Foreword by Donald Appleyard: *Public Streets for Public Use*, Van Nostrand Reinhold, New York, 1987 (urban planning—general).

Municipality of Anchorage Capital Projects Office (Kramer, Chin & Mayo, Inc.): *The Coastal Trail Route Study*, October 1983 (parks/recreation/marinas).

Muntz, Geoffrey L., and Alan S. Wuth: *A Path through Time—A Guide to the Platte River Greenway*, Platte 'N Press, Jende-Hagan Bookcorp, Frederick, Colo., 1983 (parks/recreation/marinas).

Muretta, Peri, Marc J. Hershman, and Robert F. Goodwin: *Waterfront Revitalization. Plans and Projects In Six Washington Cities*, Technical Report WSG 81-4, Washington Sea Grant, University of Washington, Seattle, Wash., June 1981 (urban waterfronts—general).

Naim, Ian: *The American Landscape, A Critical View*, Random House, New York, 1965 (urban planning—general).

National Capital Commission: *A Future for Our Rivers. A Synopsis of the Conference Held in Canada's Capital by the National Capital Commission*, June 8–11, 1987 (urban waterfronts—general).

National Endowment for the Arts, Design Arts Program: *Design Competition Manual*, Vision, The Center for Environmental Design and Education, Cambridge, Mass., 1980 (artistic/cultural/educational).

——— *Design Competition Manual II: On-Site Charrette*, Vision, The Center for Environmental Design and Education, Cambridge, Mass., 1982 (artistic/cultural/educational).

——— *Design Competition Manual III: A Guide for Sponsors*, Vision, The Center for Environmental Design and Education, Cambridge, Mass., May 1984 (artistic/cultural/educational).

National Growth Management Leadership Project, Friends of Oregon, "Growth Management in the 1980's," *Developments*, vol. 1, no. 1, Winter 1990 (urban planning—general).

National Parks & Conservation Association, edited by Marjorie R. Corbett: *Greenline Parks. Land Conservation Trends for the Eighties and Beyond*, U.S. Government Printing Office, Washington, D.C., 1983 (environmental protection/enhancement).

National Research Council: *Managing Coastal Erosion*. National Academy Press, Washington, D.C., 1990 (environmental protection/enhancement).

National Research Council, Committee on Urban Waterfront Lands: *Urban Waterfront Lands*, National Academy of Sciences, Washington, D.C., 1980 (urban waterfronts—general; includes papers on the ports of Boston, Baltimore, New York City, San Francisco, Jacksonville, and Pensacola).

National Technical Information Service: *Prospects and Strategies for the New England Ports*, Vol. 1, NTIS PB 82114448, Springfield, Va., 1981 (urban waterfronts—general).

——— *Harbor Management Strategies for New England*, Vol. 2, NTIS PB 82114455, Springfield, Va., 1981 (urban waterfronts—general).

New England River Basins Commission: *People and the Sound. Shoreline Appearance and Design: A Planning Handbook*, National Technical Information Service, Springfield, Va., 1975 (urban waterfronts—general).

New Jersey Committee of the Regional Plan Association: *River City*, Newark, N.J., 1986 (urban waterfronts—general).

New York City Planning Commission: *The New York City Waterfront*, New York Department of City Planning, 74-05, June 1974 (urban waterfronts—general).

New Urban Waterfronts, theme issue, *Landscape Architecture*, February 1991 (urban waterfronts—general).

Notter Finegold + Alexander, Inc., of Washington, D.C.; prepared for Charles Center-Inner Harbor Management, Inc.: *Baltimore Waterfront Study—Fells Point and Canton Urban Design Plan*. Department of Planning, Baltimore, November 1988 (plans).

Office of Maritime Preservation: *Historic Maritime Resources: Planning for Preservation*, The National Trust for Historic Preservation, Washington, D.C., 1990 (historic/maritime preservation).

Office of the City Manager, City of Wilmington, North Carolina: *Wilmington Looks to the River, A Plan for the Redevelopment of the City's Waterfront*, Wilmington, N.C., July 1982 (plans).

Oldenburg, Ray: *The Great Good Place*, Paragon House, New York, 1989 (urban planning—general).

Outerbridge, Graeme, photographs; David Outerbridge, text: *Bridges*, Harry N. Abrams, New York, 1989 (urban waterfronts—general).

Parks Council, with Buckhurst Fish Hutton Katz and Quennell Rothschild Associates: *Creating Public Access to the Brooklyn Waterfront*, The Parks Council, New York, February 1990 (plans).

Pei Property Development Corp. and Buckhurst Fish Hutton Katz: *Duluth. A Plan for the Duluth Downtown Waterfront*, Duluth, Minn., December 1985 (plans).

Peine, John D., and Debora A. Neurohr: *Illinois and Michigan Canal Corridor. A Concept Plan*, Chicago, November 1981 (plans).

Perkins & Partners and Design Consortium: *Jacksonville's Southbank Riverwalk: A Master Plan for Southbank Riverwalk Jacksonville*, Downtown Development Authority, Jacksonville, Fla., 1985 (parks/recreation/marinas).

Plowden, David: *Bridges. The Spans of North America*, W. W. Norton, New York and London, 1974 (urban waterfronts—general).

Proctor, Mary, and Bill Matuszeski: *Gritty Cities. A Second Look at Allentown, Bethlehem, Bridgeport, Hoboken, Lancaster, Norwich, Paterson, Reading, Trenton, Troy, Waterbury, Wilmington*, Temple University Press, Philadelphia, 1978 (urban planning—general).

Project for Public Spaces, Inc.: *Managing Downtown Public Spaces*, Planners Press, Washington, D.C., 1984 (urban planning—general).

Quennell Rothschild Associates for City of New York Dept. of General Services, Office of Community Development: *Bronx River Hike & Bike Trail*, New York, (parks/recreation/marinas).

Ray, Daniel K.: *Water Warks 1991*, The Center for Great Lakes, Harbor House, Boyne City, Mich., 1991 (urban waterfronts—general)

Redstone, Louis G.: *New Dimensions in Shopping Centers and Stores*, McGraw-Hill, New York, 1973 (urban planning—general).

Reed, Richard Ernie: *Return to the City. How to Restore Old Buildings and Ourselves in America's Historic Urban Neighborhoods*, Doubleday, Garden City, N.Y., 1979 (historic/maritime preservation).

Regional Plan Association: *The Lower Hudson*, A Report of the Second Regional Plan, New York, December 1966 (urban waterfronts—general).

Relph, Edward: *The Modern Urban Landscape*, Johns Hopkins University Press, Baltimore, 1987 (urban planning—general).

River Corridor Committee, Dayton Area Chamber of Commerce, with The Miami Conservancy District; Moore Grover Harper architects, *Riverdesign Dayton. A Pioneering Design Process Results in the Catalogue of Opportunities for a Great American River*, Dayton, Ohio, 1977 (plans).

Riverfront Recapture, Inc.; City of Hartford: *Riverfront Guide*, Riverfront Recapture, Inc., Hartford, Conn., July 1982 (urban waterfronts—general).

Roma, Architecture and Urban Design; prepared for Portland Development Commission, Portland Design Committee, and City of Portland: *South Downtown Waterfront—Portland, Oregon: Design Manual*, Portland, Ore., Spring 1981 (plans).

Roper, Laura Wood: *FLO: A Biography of Frederick Law Olmsted*, The Johns Hopkins University Press, Baltimore, Md., 1973 (urban planning—general).

Rossi, Aldo; Introduction by Peter Eisenman: *The Architecture of the City*, The MIT Press, Cambridge, Mass., and London, 1982 (urban planning—general).

Royal Architectural Institute of Canada: *Metropolitan Mutations. The Architecture of Emerging Public Spaces*, Little, Brown and Company (Canada), Boston, London, and Toronto, 1989 (urban planning—general).

Royal Commission on the Future of the Toronto Waterfront: *Interim Report*, Toronto, Ont., August 1989 (urban waterfronts—general).

———— *Watershed*, Toronto, Ont., August 1990 (urban waterfronts—general; a product of the Royal Commission's ambitious publishing program, which includes 10 book-length reports, five working papers, five technical papers, the first interim report, and eight newsletters; underlying this report is a deep concern for the environment).

Rudofsky, Bernard: *Streets for People*, Van Nostrand Reinhold, New York, 1969 (urban planning—general).

Rybka, Walter P.: "The Ship Is Now Real and Beautiful: A Report on What Transpired between the Return of the Bark *Elissa* to Galveston as a Hulk in July 1979 and Her Sailing out Rigged through to the Royals in September 1982," *Sea History*, Winter 1982/1983 (historic/maritime preservation).

Salvesen, David: *Wetlands. Mitigating and Regulating Development Impacts*, The Urban Land Institute, Washington, D.C., 1990 (environmental protection/enhancement).

San Francisco Bay Conservation and Development Commission: *Public Access Design Guidelines*, San Francisco, 1985 (urban waterfronts—general).

Sande, Theodore Anton: *Industrial Archaeology. A New Look at the American Heritage*, Penguin Books, Middlesex, England, and New York, 1976 (industrial/working waterfronts).

Santa Monica Pier Corporation: *Santa Monica Pier...A New Era*, Santa Monica Pier Restoration Corporation, Santa Monica, Calif., 1988 (plans).

Sasaki Associates, Inc., Carlton Abbott and Partners, Inc., and Anderson Associates; for the York County Board of Supervisors, *Yorktown Master Plan*, Yorktown, Va., Apr. 3, 1992 (plans).

Satterthwaite, Ann: *Fishmongers in a Concrete Jungle: A Case against Sterilizing the Urban Waterfront*, Unpublished, 1974 (industrial/working waterfronts).

Schervish Vogel Merz PC, Architects/Landscape Architects; for the City of Detroit, Recreation Department: *Linked Riverfront Parks Project*, Detroit, Mich., October 1979 (parks/recreation/marinas).

Schwab, Jim: "Riverfront Gamblers," *Planning*, September 1989, pp. 15–18 (urban waterfronts—general).

Scully, Vincent: *American Architecture and Urbanism*, Henry Holt, New York, 1969 (urban planning—general).

Sennett, Richard: *The Conscience of the Eye. The Design and Social Life of Cities*, Alfred A. Knopf, New York, 1990 (urban planning—general).

Shoemaker, Joe, and Leonard A. Stevens: *Returning the Platte to the People*, The Platte River Greenway Foundation, Denver, Colo., 1981 (parks/recreation/marinas).

Shore Erosion Control, A Guide for Waterfront Property

Owners in the Chesapeake Bay Area, U.S. Army Corps of Engineers, Baltimore, Md., undated (environmental protection/enhancement).

Sidney M. Johnson & Associates; for the City of New York Parks and Recreation Department: Waterfront Management Plan, New York, 1990 (plans).

Sorkin, Michail (ed.): Variations on a Theme Park: The New American City and the End of Public Space, The Noonday Press, New York, 1992 (urban planning—general).

Spirn, Anne Whiston: The Granite Garden, Basic Books, New York, 1984 (environmental protection/enhancement).

Stallings, Constance: "On the Waterfront," Open Space Action, August 1969, pp. 5–16 (urban waterfronts—general).

Stanford, Joseph M. (compiler and ed.): Sea History's Guide to American and Canadian Maritime Museums, Sea History Press, Croton-on-Hudson, N.Y., 1990 (historic/maritime preservation).

Stilgoe, John R.: Borderland. Origins of the American Suburb, 1820–1939, Yale University Press, New Haven, Conn., and London, 1988 (urban planning—general).

"Theme: Docklands Challenge," The Architectural Review, vol. 181, no. 1080, February 1987 (urban waterfronts—general; an excellent critical overview of docklands development around the world).

Thirteenth Street Architects, Inc., and the Pier Restoration Corporation Staff: Santa Monica Pier Design Guidelines, American Institute of Architects, Washington, D.C., 1987 (urban waterfronts—general).

Thompson, J. William: "Waterfront Park—Charleston Park Reflects Its Historic Context," Landscape Architecture, vol. 81, no. 2, February 1991 (parks/recreation/marinas).

Tobiasson, Bruce O., and Ronald C. Kollmeyer: Marinas and Small Craft Harbors, Van Nostrand Reinhold, New York, 1991 (parks/recreation/marinas).

Torre, L. Azeo: Waterfront Development, Van Nostrand Reinhold, New York, 1988 (urban waterfronts—general).

Tunnard, Christopher, and Henry Hope Reed: American Skyline, Mentor Books, The New American Library, New York, 1956 (urban planning—general).

U.S. Commission of Fine Arts and Office of Archeology and Historic Preservation; National Park Service, Department of the Interior, Georgetown Historic Waterfront, U.S. Government Printing Office, Washington, D.C., 1968 (plans).

U.S. Department of the Interior, Heritage Conservation and Recreation Service (now National Park Service): Urban Waterfront Revitalization—The Role of Recreation and Heritage, U.S. Government Printing Office, Washington, D.C., 1979 (parks/recreation/marinas).

——— Urban Waterfront Revitalization. The Role of Recreation and Heritage. Vol. 2. Eighteen Case Studies, U.S. Government Printing Office, Washington, D.C., 1980 (parks/recreation/marinas).

U.S. Dept. of the Interior, National Park Service: Chicago's Navy Pier. Executive Summary Study of Alternatives, U.S. Government Printing Office, Washington, D.C., 1986 (plans).

——— General Management Plan. Lowell National Historic Park, Lowell, Mass., September 1981 (parks/recreation/marinas).

U.S. Environmental Protection Agency; U.S. Dept. of the Interior, Heritage Conservation Recreation Service: Recreation and Land Use: The Public Benefits of Clean Waters, U.S. Government Printing Office, Washington, D.C., February 1980 (environmental protection/enhancement).

ULI—the Urban Land Institute: Adaptive Use. Development Economics, Process, and Profiles, Urban Land Institute, Washington, D.C., 1978 (historic/maritime preservation).

Untermann, Richard K.: Accommodating the Pedestrian: Adapting Towns and Neighborhoods for Walking and Bicycling, Van Nostrand Reinhold, New York, 1984 (urban planning—general).

Urban Waterfronts, theme issue, Progressive Architecture, June 1975 (urban waterfronts—general).

Urban Wildlife Research Center, Inc., for the U.S. Department of the Interior, Fish and Wildlife Service: Planning for Urban Fishing and Waterfront Recreation, Biological Services Program, FWS/OBS-80/35, U.S. Government Printing Office, Washington, D.C., July 1981 (parks/recreation/marinas).

Wallace, David: "An Insider's Story of the Inner Harbor," Planning, September 1979, p.20 (urban waterfronts—general).

——— "Many Ingredients Key to Festival Market Success," Center City Report, International Downtown Association, Washington, D.C., February 1984 (urban planning—general).

Wallace Roberts & Todd; and Morrissey-Johnson, Inc.: Downtown Waterfront Master Development Plan: Norfolk, Virginia, Norfolk Redevelopment and Housing Authority, Norfolk, Va., April 1981 (plans).

Wallace Roberts & Todd; Louis Berger & Associates, Inc.; and Ralph B. Hirsch; prepared for The State of New Jersey, Dept. of Environmental Protection, Hudson Waterfront Walkway Plan and Design Guidelines, Trenton, New Jersey, March 1984 (plans).

Waterfront, theme issue, Process: Architecture, no. 82, Tokyo, November 1984 (urban waterfronts—general; a publication full of photos of waterfront projects from all over the globe and accompanying text on each of the cases).

Waterfront: una nuova frontiera urbana 1991. Citta' D'Acqua, Venice, Italy, 1991 (urban waterfronts—

general; catalog for an exhibition of waterfront projects around the world that was mounted in conjunction with the conference of the same title held in Venice in January 1991).

Webber, Peter (ed.): *The Design of Sydney. Three Decades of Change in the City Centre*, The Law Book Company, North Ryde, N.S.W., The Carswell Co., Agincourt, Ont., 1988 (urban planning—general).

West Side Waterfront Panel; A Report to Governor Mario Cuomo and Mayor David N. Dinkins: *A Vision for the Hudson River Waterfront Park*, West Side Waterfront Panel, New York, September 1990 (plans).

White, Morton, and Lucia White: *The Intellectual Versus the City*, Mentor Books, The New American Library, New York and Toronto, 1962 (urban planning—general).

Whitney, Charles S.: *Bridges. Their Art, Science & Evolution*, Greenwich House, New York, 1983 (urban waterfronts—general).

Whyte, William H.: *City: Rediscovering the Center*, Doubleday, New York, 1988 (urban planning—general).

——— *The Last Landscape*. Anchor Books—Doubleday, Garden City, N.Y., 1968 (urban planning—general).

——— *The Social Life of Small Urban Spaces*, The Conservation Foundation, Washington, D.C., 1980 (urban planning—general).

Wille, Lois: *Forever Open, Clear and Free—The Struggle for Chicago's Lakefront*, 2d ed., University of Chicago Press, Chicago, 1991 (urban waterfronts—general).

Wilson, William H.: *The City Beautiful Movement*, The Johns Hopkins University Press, Baltimore, 1989 (urban planning—general).

Wisconsin Department of Resource Development: *Waterfront Renewal*, Madison, Wisc., 1966 (urban waterfronts—general).

Witzling, Lawrence, and Jeffrey Ollswang: *The Planning and Administration of Design Competitions*, Midwest Institute for Design Research, Milwaukee, Wisc., 1986 (artistic/cultural/educational).

Woods, Sonja: *Racine Lakefront Development Corp.*, Downtown Racine Development Corp., Racine, Wisc., 1984 (parks/recreation/marinas).

Woolpert Consultants and The Governor's Task Force on the Waterfront: *Cleveland Waterfront Masterplan Update*, Report of the Governor's Task Force on the Waterfront, State of Ohio, Dept. of Natural Resources, Ohio, 1987 (plans).

Wrenn, Douglas: *Urban Waterfront Development*, Urban Land Institute, Washington, D.C., 1983 (urban waterfronts—general

Wylson, Anthony: *Aquatecture: Architecture and Water*, The Architectural Press, London, and Van Nostrand Reinhold, New York, 1986 (urban waterfronts—general; comprehensive coverage of "waterfront" in all aspects: context, maritime cities, river corridors, resorts, piers, marina communities, water features, and water spaces; many historical references; no bibliography).

Zeidler, Eberhard H.: *Multi-Use Architecture in the Urban Context*, Van Nostrand Reinhold, New York, 1983 (urban planning—general).

ZHA, Inc.: *Yorktown Market Study*, County of York, Va., January 31, 1992 (plans).

Zunker, Vernon G.: *A Dream Come True: Robert Hugman and San Antonio River Walk*, San Antonio, Tex., 1983 (urban waterfronts—general).

Index

About the Authors

Ann Breen is cofounder and president of The Waterfront Center. She was previously Waterfront Coordinator of the U.S. Department of Commerce, National Oceanic and Atmospheric Administration. **Dick Rigby** is cofounder and codirector of The Waterfront Center and was previously editor at the Marine Technology Society. They helped prepare *Improving Your Waterfront: A Practical Guide* and have written numerous articles on urban waterfront issues.

Founded in 1981, **The Waterfront Center**, Washington D.C., is an independent, nonprofit organization dedicated to the careful planning and diverse development of America's waterfront neighborhoods and communities. Offering a variety of educational and advisory services, publications, annual conferences, specialty workshops, and community consulting, the center is a unique information resource for those planning and designing new urban waterfront projects.